RAVEN'S EYE

a quest story

PHILIP THATCHER

CORONA
PRESS

For performance rights to *Raven's Eye III*, please contact the author at
Corona Press
1605 Kilmer Road
North Vancouver, B.C.
V7K 1R6
Canada

Canadian Cataloguing in Publication Data
Thatcher, Philip, 1939-
  Raven's eye

ISBN 0-9686687-0-4

  I. Title.
PS8589.H356R38   2000   C813'.54   C00-910187-X
PR9199.3.T442R38   2000

Cover painting: "Raven's Eye" (2000), by Aiona Anderson

Corona Press logo by Daniel Koppersmith
Author photograph by Frank Doll
Layout and Design by The Vancouver Desktop Publishing Centre
Printed in Canada by Printcrafters

For my students and colleagues
at the Vancouver Waldorf High School
and in memory of
Yataltanault (Carole Anne Newman)
and Yah-Xath-anees (Ernie Willie)
who gave me Raven

I

ONE

Inside
the sun
eagle circles
shining
still

Glance back
the last
  within

Then soar
    down
  down
 into
the green crown
of the cedar
people
  down
    down
      to the branch
    laden with copper
    leaves and dreams
    down
  down
through the moon's
radiant back and into
the gleaming curve
of her

to wait
as he cloaks his self
with himself
            until
her light can hold
the weight of him
            no more

        Now plunge
        down
                down down

        Now follow
        the shining seed
        down
                down down

Now
beating of
black wings
    Auxw!
            down down

        Smoke rises
        from the hole
            Hauw!
                    down down

        Fire rises
        to enfold him
            down
                    down—

        Ghe-la-kasla!
        You who come to us,
        welcome—
        child of the Wanookqway,
        People of the River

        Listen!
        Our story
                yours

begins
> *on the first day*
high upon our mountain
when the great waters
had passed

> *The first light*
was very high about us and
Eagle said to our ancestor
Duxdzas,
> *He-whose-eye*
sees-every-river,
> *Go down*
that one way, until you
come to your River,
to that place where
you can be

> *Down went*
our People, not knowing
that place, but Mountain Goat
met us the second day
and said,

> *First light is*
getting tired and weak,
yet I see from here
your River
and a way down
> *to where mist*
will rise about you

The third day light got lost
in the mist and the Wanookqway felt
cold, so cold the heart wanted
to stop—

> *Then*
Grizzly grew out of the dark, grew
big beside us
> *Take my skin,*
said Grizzly, for I will sleep now

and give it back to me
when your River sees through
to the sun

      So the Wanookqway walked
that long day into its long night
and when the mist grew deep
beyond any seeing,
our River spoke:
          Follow me
          down

             down
into the dawn of the fourth day,
to where your little brother
Candlefish
will greet you. Take him for your
first food. Light him and he will
burn for you until Raven brings you
             the sun

       Auxw!
          Out—

Ha! And here comes Raven
sailing down the mountain,
streaking through that mist—

      Look what I have!
Raven says,
        And it's all
yours, here at your River's
mouth, where I am going to
throw it
        out over
        the big water—

    Hauw!
         Out—

So, welcome
among us. Ghe-la-kasla,
Gwawinastoo—

Blaze Watson takes the basin that holds her new grandson's afterbirth and goes outside. "Has Weesa come, Adha?" her granddaughter asks.

"Weesa has come. Margaret, please tell your dad and your Uncle Sam, Weesa has come. David, find Uncle Charlie, and tell him.

"Yes, Adha."

"Now, please."

"Yes, Adha."

Margaret looks into the basin. "Adha, what are you doing with Weesa's blood bag?"

"Ahh! I'm going to give Raven a good feed."

Adha, to her grandchildren, and Axilaogua (She-who-holds-Names), to those within the big house, Blaze Watson empties the basin onto the beach at the river's mouth. She looks long at the new crescent moon hovering above the setting of the sun. "Ghe-la-kasla, Gwawinastoo! See through."

Quo-k . . .?

His hands reach for the voice. Sun-drenched air touches down upon his fingers, his cheeks. The smell of salmon and smoke hang thick about him, tease at each nostril. He sneezes!

Gwaau . . .?

He turns his head toward the sun, the sound, and would lift himself upright if he could—

Something above him
hovers
then carves down
gently,
relentlessly
and he shrinks back into
the blanket—

Qua! Qua!

But the shining edge
cuts at the shielding skin
without mercy—

Qua! Qua!

As the last tissues
split apart, he cries out
once
twice,
but his cries do not reach

into the smoke house—

Qua! Qua!

And then beams of light
strike through and daylight
stakes its claim.

Quo-k . . .!

Now he lays hold of each light beam,
lies long in the silence as the beams swing
wildly past one another again and again
until they strike together
and he can hold them fast.

Quo-k!

And there's Raven
sitting on the smoke-house roof, beak
busily cleaning his talons
his every
feather black-blue
and shining.

Gwaau . . .?

Gwaau . . .?

Wide-eyed, he watches Raven do a little dance
along the edge of the roof. Raven laughs
as the child laughs and laughs.

"Name this child."

"Nathan Solomon."

"Nathan Solomon, I baptize thee in the name of the Father, and of
the Son, and of the Holy Ghost."

Light bounces off a pair of glasses as a drop of water runs to the
end of Nathan's nose. He sneezes .". . . and do sign him with the sign
of the cross . . ."

Nathan watches the hand descend, the thumb moving up and
down, back and forth along his forehead. The hand lifts .". . . and to
continue Christ's faithful soldier and servant until his life's end.
Amen."

Taking hold of Aunt Minnie's necklace with one hand as the other reaches for Uncle Slim's string necktie, Nathan laughs as Aunt Minnie wheezes. Then he becomes very still and watches as his Adha gives over Harvey and Hazel's baby.

"Name this child."

"Naomi Gloria."

"Naomi Gloria, I baptize thee . . ."

After the baptism, the certificates await the signatures of Slim and Minnie Simon, godparents of Nathan, and Blaze Watson and Isaac Jacob, godparents of Naomi. Blaze looks down at the names and dates as she signs.

Name: Nathan Solomon Jacob
Date of Birth: March 20, 1969

Name: Naomi Gloria Silas
Date of Birth: July 17, 1969

Date of Baptism: September 29, 1969
Place of Baptism: Doxology Landing, B.C.

Then everyone gathers at the house of Edith and Isaac, Nathan's parents. Harvey Silas and Nathan's Uncle Charlie sit on the newly covered couch; his Uncle Slim plays the guitar and sings "Amazing Grace." Mr. Blaisdell, the priest, chats with Blaze and Sadie Moon, eats a sandwich, drinks his tea and waits for the plane to take him back to Port Hardy. Hazel stands at the stove, holding Naomi. Minnie holds Nathan while her sister, Lila, stirs the soup. "It was good, your asking Isaac to be godfather," Minnie says to Hazel.

"Yes, well, Blaze almost made it a condition, if she was going to be godmother. By the way, what is she up to?"

Minnie strokes Nathan's cheek and does not answer.

"You know what I'm meaning. Putting the afterbirth on the beach for the ravens to peck at. I didn't know we still did that kind of thing."

"Ooh! So a Weesa will see as Raven sees. I remember hearing about that," says Lila, and goes on stirring.

Minnie considers a moment. "I think Axilaogua is holding names for these two, big names."

"Ooh!" says Hazel, and says no more.

Out in the carving shed, between the house and the river, its front open to the beach so he can see through the gap between the islands, Isaac works on the snout of a grizzly mask. Mr. Blaisdell approaches, followed by Edith, carrying Nathan. "I'll be going back on the afternoon plane," Mr. Blaisdell says.

Isaac glances up at the sun. "It should be here any time now."

"I hear you were at Masset for that pole raising. Quite an occasion, so I was told."

"Yes. It was a good day."

"It's been quite a summer. A man on the moon, and the first pole raised up there this century, though you can hardly talk about the two events in the same breath. Do you know the carver?"

"Up there everyone pretty much knows everyone."

"Do you yourself come from a family of carvers?"

Isaac's knife hovers at the tip of the grizzly's snout. "Only my father."

"I'd better gather my things together. Thank you for the lunch, Edith. You have a fine-looking son."

Edith sits on the log beside her husband. Isaac raises his eyebrows and studies the teeth of Grizzly that grin up at him. "Sometimes there's not much there, to get your teeth into."

His wife frowns at him, then the frown becomes a little smile. Isaac picks up his knife. "He's a good enough man. He just needs to learn a few things."

Nathan stares along his mother's shoulder and sees his father, knife in hand, sitting in a shaft of sun. Isaac looks over and laughs with Nathan.

Sadie Moon is the bosom of Duxsowlas. Children come to Sadie's, where every jam jar stands on her table, open always. Women bring gifts of smoked sockeye, half-smoked humps, only to receive twofold again from Sadie's store. Men look for their women at Sadie's, and mothers for their children. Sadie lives alone, yet all of Duxsowlas comes to Sadie.

The grease pit is beyond Sadie's house, by the river on the way to Bone Spit. The spring-young oolichan are dropped into the burning water, come apart from skin to bone, until the warm, sun-tinted oil floats at the top, precious as gold and awaiting the scoop.

Sadie brings a pot of tea and bread down to Edith and Hazel, Minnie and Slim, who sit outside the smoke house, not far from the grease pit. "That batch should be cooling down," says Slim.

"That's the batch Slim is giving away at his potlatch," Minnie announces.

Nathan walks over to the smoke house, then back, over, then back.

"If that Weesa talks like he walks, we're in for it. Damn! You make the tea too hot, Sadie," says Hazel.

Quo-k . . .

Nathan listens.

"Quo-k," Uncle Slim repeats. Then he chuckles.

"Quo-k," Nathan ventures. Hazel snorts.

"That's Raven, Weesa, hanging around the grease pit, figuring out his next move. Go play, Weesa, with Raven."

"Play," says Nathan, as he disappears around the back of the smoke house. Naomi slips out of Hazel's lap and follows. Raven waits at the grease pit, balancing at its edge.

Quo-k . . .?
Play, Nathan

Raven cocks his head toward Nathan, then toward the grease pit and dances his little dance.

Dance, Nathan
Quo-k!

Nathan's feet lead him along the edge of the pit toward the hop and bob of Raven, whose eye is ever on Nathan. Naomi stops, her eyes very wide as they see Raven bow to the grease pit then come upright, still dancing. Laughing, Nathan bows to the grease pit but does not come upright. Naomi cries out.

Edith, Sadie, Minnie, Slim, and Hazel come running. Raven spreads his wings leisurely and glides into the nearest cedar tree while Nathan sinks down into a warm bath of golden light and remembers. The light wraps around Nathan, draws his knees up against his stomach, his arms against his sides, covers his nostrils. Remembering, Nathan's eyes close as the light warms, becomes brighter, stronger.

Edith's arm crashes through the skin of oil, finds her son, and yanks him free. She slaps at his back and grease flies from his nose and his mouth until he wails, and only then does she hold him to her.

Naomi sobs and reaches for Nathan as Hazel tries to calm her, and Raven observes it all from his cedar branch. Then Nathan stops crying. His tongue licks along his grease-covered mouth, and he smacks his lips. He licks again and smiles.

Relieved, Edith, Minnie, Slim, Sadie, and Hazel smile at one another. "Well, Weesa, I guess that's one way to become a good, grease-loving Wanookqway," laughs Sadie.

"Some initiation," Hazel says, "and what a way to die."

Slim licks at his lips. "Yeah. I'll remember that, when my time comes."

November pours down upon Duxsowlas, the day of Uncle Slim's potlatch. Nathan sits beside his sister and his mother, his gaze lost in the blazing fire, his ears full of rain sounding upon the big house roof until the whistle pierces through and Hamatsa plunges past the guardian curtain, the Tlaamelas, out onto the big house floor—

> *Haau—!*
>
>   *thromthromthromthrom*
> *thromthromthromthrom*
>
>   *Haau—!*

Nathan slips away from Margaret's hand, past the sharp eye of Edith, and makes his way, bum first, down to the big house floor.

> *thromthromthromthromthrom*

Now Hamatsa crouches down amid the circle of four who stand by him, then rises into his dance around the big house.

> *Haau—!*
>
> *throm*
>   *throm throm*
> *throm*
>   *throm throm*
>
> *Haau—!*

Nathan stands at the edge of the big house floor. His feet begin to rise and fall with the beating of the long log drum. Again, Hamatsa crouches down within his guardian ring, rises, circles the big house, countering the movement of the sun—

>   *Haau—!*
>
> *throm throm*
>   *throm*

throm throm
     throm

Haau—!

thromthromthromthrom
thromthromthromthrom

Hamatsa cries out, circles frantically, then vanishes behind the Tlaamelas.

Nathan stands at one end of the log drum, as the drummers sit silently for a long moment, and watches his father, Uncle Charlie, Uncle Sam, Harvey Silas, and others he has never seen. Uncle Slim glances up at Nathan from his end of the drum and winks.

throm throm throm throm throm

And now the Humsumth masks appear, first Huxwhuxw, then Crooked Beak, each making in turn its circle of the big house, as Adha's voice rises, strong and clear, above the male voices sounding from the drum.

Ha ma myy
    Ha myy Ha myy

The mask of Raven enters from behind the Tlaamelas. Cedar hangs in strips from the head of Raven and moves as Raven moves, with deliberate, searching steps, the whole length of the big house.

Ha myy Ha myy

Nathan stares at the cedar-ringed ankles that rise and fall, as Raven looms above then moves past Nathan, and Nathan falls in step behind Raven, footfall for footfall, until Margaret's hand clamps down on Nathan's arm and, with her head high and face red, she scoops her brother from the big house floor.

Now three years old, Nathan stands at the bank of the river. The newly risen sun splashes down the western slope of Duxdzas, the mountain up the valley, and arrows its light toward the gap between Sand Island and Log Island.

Isaac has pulled his small boat up onto the beach. He tinkers with the outboard motor while Nathan heads off toward a dead seal. Raven

18

has just arrived and is busy pecking out the seal's eye. Hands in his pockets, Nathan stares at Raven's beak as Raven swallows, gazes back at Nathan, and does not flinch. Nathan turns away to see his father observing him. He walks over to the boat, climbs in, and studies his father's hands upon the motor. "Dad, he ate seal's eye."

Isaac turns a screw, then nods. "The eyes are the first thing Raven eats."

Considering his father's words, Nathan looks again at the seal's carcass. But Raven is gone.

THREE

The totem pole stands between the big house and the river. Crowned with morning light, the eagle gazes over his beak, as from a great distance, down to the river's mouth. Beneath the spread of Eagle's wings, Mountain Goat's eyes also survey the beach, his horns sweeping like beacons up from his forehead, while below him Grizzly's paws probe forward, as if the paws and eyes of Grizzly want to feel their way through what surrounds him, as if Grizzly is about to shed his skin.

Raven stands at the bottom of the pole, his legs and feet almost human on the ground, wings pinned to his sides, with one eye focused forward, right through the gap between Sand Island and Log Island, while the other strains along an upward slant as if the weight upon his head is just too much, or as if he is looking for something he has lost.

Nathan, Naomi, Hector Dawson, and Peter Dick, Nathan's cousin, stand before the pole. "I bet my Uncle John carved that pole," Peter says.

"I bet that's older than your uncle," Hector retorts.

"I'm going to look at Sisiutl," announces Nathan.

Sisiutl is painted on the front of the big house, an enormous double-headed sea serpent, one head reaching up to swallow the north corner of the house, the other reaching for the south corner. But it is the great head above the centre door at which the children gaze. Two necks stretch forth from the cheeks of Sisiutl, two horns jut up from his forehead, the two eyes of Sisiutl stare out as he bares his teeth.

"Let's go see Teacher," Naomi says and takes Nathan by the hand.

Nathan's face breaks into a laugh. "Ashes, ashes, all go bump!"

"On your bum!" roars Peter Dick.

Howling, the children race from the big house over to the school, which stands beside the soccer field. Teacher has the classroom with grades one to four. Margaret, in grade four, and David, in grade six, are out on the soccer field for recess, while the grade ones and twos circle with Teacher:

> *Water, water, wallflower*
> *growing up so high.*
> *We are all God's children*
> *and we all must die . . .*

Nathan, Naomi, Hector, and Peter stand just outside the circle. Naomi turns round in place as the circle moves to the left. Nathan gazes at Teacher, as he has gazed for many mornings all fall long. Teacher came to Duxsowlas when the chum salmon were being tucked into their winter cans.

> *Except for little Vera,*
> *the fairest of us all.*
> *She can dance,*
> > *she can sing,*
> *she can wear a wedding ring.*

Nathan soaks in the voice of Teacher, the sweep and swish of her long skirt. Teacher's voice sings like no other he has heard, not the singing of his mother's voice, or his father's, or the voices of Adha and Sadie, not the deep rich pounding of the waves through the gap between the islands and onto the beach of Duxsowlas, but the lilt and sadness of another sea washing up on another shore far away.

> *Fie fie fie for shame*
> *turn your back to the*
> *wall again . . .*

Vera Dawson turns until her back is to the centre of the circle and then the circle moves again as the song repeats. One by one, Teacher points to Robbie Williams, Angie Dick, and Steve Silas. Nathan reaches for Naomi's hand as Naomi turns round and round in place. Then the circle opens and she pulls Nathan in with her. Teacher starts, smiles, and begins once more.

> *Water, water, wallflower*

growing up so high.
We are all God's children
and we all must die

Except for little Naomi,
the fairest of us all.
She can dance,
              she can sing,
        she can wear a wedding ring.

Teacher points to Naomi.

Fie fie fie for shame
turn your back to the
wall again . . .

Nathan's hand tightens around Naomi's, but she wrests it free and turns to face the outside as the circle moves. Nathan, however, does not move with the circle. He stares up at Teacher, wants to cry, and then turns away. He sees Margaret standing at the classroom steps, watching him intently.

Children, children,
turn around!

Teacher sings, and now everyone in the circle faces its centre.

Recess ends. The children return to their classrooms. As Teacher bends down to him, Nathan can still feel his sister watching them.

"Perhaps that one was too old for you, Nathan," Teacher says. She straightens and Nathan sees his father walking across the field toward them. Teacher smiles a special smile, while Margaret climbs the steps but goes on watching as her father, also smiling, speaks with Teacher, one hand upon Nathan, the other upon Naomi.

After Teacher has followed Margaret up the steps and waved at them one last time, Naomi looks up at her godfather.

"I like Teacher," she says.

"Her name is Emer," Isaac answers. He smiles, and Nathan knows his father likes Emer, too.

Christmas holidays bring the closing of school and the coming home of Don Williams, Pam Silas, and Jane Dawson from high school in Port Hardy, as well as the arrival of Slim and Minnie with a planeload of presents, one for each child of Duxsowlas. The teacher of grades five to eight flies out, but Emer stays. Naomi and Nathan follow the crunch of her boots across the thin cover of snow as she visits from house to house—that is, unless Nathan is stalking Old Man Williams on his afternoon walk down to the river. Nathan picks up a stick, like Old Man's cane, and limps in imitation behind Old Man's limp, until Old Man suddenly whirls half-around and waves his cane over Nathan's head: "You watch out! I hit you between the eyes, like I hit Sisiutl, and poof! No more Weesa!"

Nathan is startled, as always, then he runs off laughing when he spys the twinkle between the lines of Old Man's frown.

Most often, Emer comes to visit Isaac and Edith, and sometimes Adha, next door. Or Nathan sees his father somewhere in the village, standing with Emer, speaking with her, or just walking with her. Once Emer walks out to the carving shed and spends a long time watching Isaac's knife bite deep into the yellow cedar wood. At the corner of the house, Nathan stands quietly and watches the two of them.

Then Nathan dreams, one long night before the end of Christmas time, dreams as snow drifts down silently upon Duxsowlas. Within his dream another silence whitens about the figures of Emer and Isaac, and Edith. The whiteness deepens to violet, then darkens about the three—Emer, Isaac, and Edith—until only the darkened circle itself is left with Nathan standing before it, holding a candle Adha has given him and peering into the darkness.

On a March Monday, the younger children arrive at the school to discover their teacher is not there.

"Where's Teacher?" Vera Dawson asks.

"I saw her get on your uncle's seine boat yesterday," Robbie Williams says to Margaret.

"Where did Charlie take her?" Steve Silas presses, a funny glimmer in his eye.

"I don't know," Margaret answers, curtly, and says nothing more.

Emer does not return to Duxsowlas. Another teacher comes, as teachers often come and go, and the children, most of them, forget about the teacher with the strange singing in her voice.

Nathan sits beside Isaac and watches his father carve. "Naomi misses Emer-Teacher," Nathan says after a time.

Isaac's reply does not come at once, but only after he finishes a long running cut along Sea-Eagle's beak. "Emer has gone home."

"Where does Emer stay?"

Isaac moves the knife carefully along the cheek line of the mask. "A long way away."

The following summer, Nathan watches his mother's stomach grow bigger and bigger. His brother Frank is born in December, just after the darkest day of winter. Edith's head lies on the pillow, her face white within the white hiss of the gas lamp as her baby moves about in her arms.

"I think this one had better be your last," Sadie Moon says, and then she becomes busy with cleaning up the after-effects of birth.

Margaret helps Adha bake at the stove while Nathan stands close to the bed and looks long at his new brother. "Ghe-la-kasla, Weesa," he murmurs, then walks outside, down the porch steps to the dark rain-drenched earth. The clouds overhead begin to break apart and a few stars flash back at him as he feels Adha coming down the steps. Adha stands beside Nathan, straight and strong in the darkness. Nathan shivers.

"It's cold," he says. Adha's arm drops around her grandson's shoulders.

FOUR

The river of the Wanookqway comes to light far up the valley to the east, where stands Duxdzas, the mountain that sees every river everywhere, and winds its way down to the village at its mouth, Duxsowlas, where the river sees through. Near the south bank of the river stands Nathan's house, then Adha's, then Uncle Charlie's, behind Adha at the north end of the soccer field. The big house and the totem pole are upriver from Uncle Charlie.

The school extends along the east side of the field; Peter's house and Hector's are south of it. Farther south stands Naomi's house, then Sadie Moon's. Beyond Sadie's, the beach curves out to the southwest, across a narrow neck of land washed over at high tide, to end at Bone Spit, the graveyard of Duxsowlas.

Two islands lie between Duxsowlas and the open Pacific. Sand Island, to the south, rises from its crescent beach to a line of Sitka spruce and Sitka alder that hangs over the island's rocky spine, to brush against the landing at its east side. Harvey Silas's seine boat is tied at the landing, along with his shiny speedboat with the big, twin outboard motors. Uncle Charlie's seine boat, older than Harvey's, is also tied up at the landing. Nathan's father often fishes with Uncle Charlie.

Log Island lies to the north. There is no sand on Log Island, only rock and salal and Sitka, and logs piled up, log upon log, all along its Pacific reach. Every loose log that drifts down that stretch of coast seems destined for Log Island.

Between Sand Island and Log Island lies the gap through which Raven released the sun, through which the setting sun shines directly into the river's mouth and along its bank to where the totem pole stands, at the times of the spring and fall equinoxes.

The Giant stands at the north end of Log Island, a cedar so massive and so old that the people of Duxsowlas cannot remember a time when the Giant was not. Perhaps, Adha tells Nathan, perhaps it was from the Giant that the Wanookqway first gathered bark for the T'seka, the Red Cedar Bark Ceremony.

Port Hardy lies southwest of Duxsowlas, near the northern end of Vancouver Island, and Thumb Harbour to the south along the mainland coast, where the loggers cut patches from the side and down the back of the mountain, and where Rick Smith maintains his store and pub. On an April day early in Nathan's ninth year, Uncle Charlie's seine boat heads south to Thumb Harbour.

Uncle Charlie stands in the wheel-house of his seine boat, watching closely as David, now sixteen and home for the Easter holidays, holds the wheel. Nathan sits on a high stool and his father stands beside his uncle.

"We should pick up some groceries, too," Isaac says.

Uncle Charlie grunts. "Maybe. If we can get Rick's big-time prices down to our size. Tell him to make it up by charging more for his drinks, and his under-the-counter liquor. That might discourage a few long distance travellers I know."

David's face goes blank, even though Uncle Charlie's eyes look straight ahead. Isaac rubs Nathan's cap against his hair and Nathan grins. Thumb Harbour, he muses, looks as if the Creator had leaned his thumb into that stretch of coastline while thinking about something else. As David steers through the base of the thumb, Nathan looks up at the bare patches of mountain where trees once stood.

"I'd better take it now," Uncle Charlie says.

"Whatever you say, Uncle." David steps back from the wheel, then goes out on deck.

"What's eating him?" Uncle Charlie asks Isaac.

Isaac lifts Nathan from the stool. "It could be he's feeling the weight of all those names you're about to place on his head."

Rick Smith has come down to the landing. "How's it going, Charlie? Ike? Hey, look at this little guy! Is he getting big, or am I shrinking?"

Nathan smiles shyly. David stands, hands in his pockets, and says nothing. Nathan goes with Uncle Charlie and his father into Rick's store where Uncle Charlie looks his shipment over.

"I've got something else for you, Ike," Rick says. He reaches under the counter, pulls out a large canvas bag, then grins and shrugs as Isaac and Uncle Charlie stare at it. "Yeah, I know, the mailplane should have brought it right to Doxology, but I told him you were coming down, and he was in a hurry to get back. Maybe he thought the world was going to end and wanted a long, last night with a lady friend. You know how these things are."

Isaac smiles, but not with his eyes, as his hand closes around the top of the bag.

Uncle Charlie takes the wheel on the trip back to Duxsowlas. Nathan sits on his stool, going through the mailbag, while David stands out on deck.

"They slapped our hands into the desk top whenever our language slipped out and now that we've learned theirs, the mailplane forgets where we are. Maybe they think we've forgotten how to read," muses Uncle Charlie, after a long hour out of Thumb Harbour. The wheel-house door flies open and David sticks his head inside.

"Dad! Uncle! Look, porpoises!" Three black-and-white forms streak past the bow of the seine boat, catching the sun along their sides as they leap then plunge down into the swells of blue-green water.

"Ghe-la-kasla!" Isaac breathes and lifts Nathan from the stool so he can see. Uncle Charlie's face relaxes. "David, you go tell those guys to keep this boat on course. No side trips and no funny business!"

His face come alight, David grins at Uncle Charlie. "Okay, Uncle. Whatever you say."

"That's good," Isaac says, as David makes his way to the bow.

"Dad, where's Doxology, and why is this letter to you going there?" Nathan holds the envelope in his hand, with the address that reads:

> Isaac Jacob,
> Doxology Landing, B.C.

Isaac chuckles as he hands the envelope back to Nathan. "That's where we live, Son. At least, that's where the government thinks we live."

"The missionaries gave our village that name," says Uncle Charlie, "when they first came to us on their boat and asked our people the name of our village. 'Duxsowlas,' people said. 'That sounds like Doxology,' said the missionaries, after tying their tongues into a knot. 'Duxsowlas,' our people said. 'Yes, that sounds like Doxology,' the missionaries said. So Doxology Landing is what they called Duxsowlas, and that's where the government has been sending our mail ever since."

"Somehow it reaches us, one way or another, so I guess we've been lucky that way," Nathan's father says.

In June, the bishop comes to Duxsowlas, to confirm Margaret, Mary Silas, and Billy Dick. The service is held in the school and Mr. Blaisdell presents Margaret, Mary, and Billy to the bishop. The girls are dressed all in white, while Billy Boy wears a white shirt and a pair of pants a size too big, and does all he can to keep his feet fixed in one place.

Edith sits with Adha and Nathan in the front row of chairs beside the Silas and Dick families. Frank, now three, stands in the makeshift aisle and gazes solemnly at the bishop's robes and ring. David and the older boys stand against the back wall, while Isaac, as always, sits on a bench next to the classroom door, beside Old Man Williams. Uncle Charlie never comes to services, not even today.

When the bishop has finished his questions, one by one Margaret and Mary and Billy kneel, and he places his hands upon Margaret's head. "Defend, O Lord, this Thy Servant with Thy heavenly grace, that she may continue Thine forever . . ."

Mary and Billy Boy have bowed their heads, but Margaret's head stays upright, her eyes fixed upon the space before her, her face strong and clear. When she finally stands, Nathan releases the breath he has been holding.

After the service, the congregation heads over to the house of Nathan's Uncle Sam and Aunt Lila for a feast. Halfway across the soccer field, Edith notices that Frank is missing his cap.

"Lost it," Frank says, and beams at his mother.

"Maybe it fell off when we came down the steps," Nathan suggests.

"Then it's probably somewhere around there. Would you please go and find it," Edith says.

Nathan races back to the school and finds Frank's cap under the steps, where it had slipped through. He is about to crawl out when he hears footfalls above him, then the voices of the bishop and Mr. Blaisdell.

"I see what you mean about that old woman, Blaze. She is quite a powerhouse," the bishop remarks.

"Full of stories and a good soul, though a bit of a pagan, I think, from some things her granddaughter let slip," says Mr. Blaisdell.

Standing beside the steps, Nathan watches the two men cross the soccer field. He wipes Frank's cap clean on his pants, wonders what being a bit of a pagan is all about, and goes on wondering late into the summer, as he sits with the other children, watching Adha's fingers weave cedar bark together into one of the neckrings David will wear this coming winter when he becomes Hamatsa. "What was my last word, yesterday?" Adha asks the children.

"Flood!" Peter proclaims.

"That's pretty close. What did I tell you, about the Flood?"

"Everyone went up the mountain," says Naomi.

"Our people went up Duxdzas, at the head of our river," Nathan says.

"And they took their canoes," Hector ventures.

"Some people came down from their mountain in canoes as the water fell," Adha says, "but the Wanookqway waited until the water had gone right down and our ancestor, Duxdzas, could see on every side to find the best way down for us while the light, still young, was shining high and clear—clear enough for Eagle to see a way down to our river. Then our people began their long journey."

"Did Eagle come down with them?" Hector asks.

"Eagle never comes down, not right down," Naomi says.

"Too many questions. Just listen!" Adha insists. The children fall silent and Adha waits for the silence to take command. "When the Wanookqway had journeyed down for a long day, the light became tired. That's when they met Mountain Goat. He had enough seeing left to show them where they could enter the forest. Then the great mist fell upon the Wanookqway until they could see nothing more, not even each other or themselves."

"And that's when Grizzly came," Nathan interjects, listening closely to Adha's words and watching her face just as closely.

Adha nods. "Grizzly came and said, 'I, too, am sleepy, and I have no light for you, but my skin will warm you. Take it and give it back to me when you can see through.' The mist hugged the forest and the Wanookqway felt the dark would never end. And then the first oolichan, that we call Candlefish, came up the river, swimming very hard, and then another, and the Wanookqway burned the first for light and ate the other for first food as the mist began to come apart and Raven brought the sun."

When the story is done, Nathan stays with Adha and Naomi. He watches as Naomi, her hands already seeing how the cedar wants to be woven, works alongside Adha. Strips of cedar bark from the trunk of the Giant lie across the railing of Adha's porch, drying in the summer sun, until Frank happily pulls them down.

"Where did Raven find the sun?" Nathan asks, and then is amazed at his question. Adha goes on weaving.

"Maybe he just brought it down the mountain," she suggests and watches Nathan's face. "And then, maybe not. Ask your father what he knows about it."

FIVE

Late in September, Isaac and Nathan go up the river to check and set Isaac's trapline. Their boat parts the current, first due east, then curves to the south, past the snags jutting up from the slate-grey water, until at Snag Point the river bends sharply eastward once again.

Farther upriver, under the long morning shadow of Duxdzas, Isaac collects a few pelts, among them a dark glossy fisher whose eyes have long gone to glass. "Sorry you had to come this way, little brother. But we're happy you stayed," Isaac says as he frees the body from the trap.

On their way downriver late into the afternoon, Isaac turns the boat toward the sand and pebble-strewn beachhead of Snag Point. Trunks of great trees, long uprooted and moved by the river's relentless thrust, lie about the point at the water's edge. Isaac ties the boat to a bone-dry root, then takes out the fillets of half-smoked salmon. "Let's crisp it up here, for an early supper. See what you can find for firewood, Son."

By the time Nathan returns with a second armload, Isaac has lit the fire and the salmon is cooking. Nathan looks about at the gnarled cottonwoods that half circle Snag Point and hold it apart from the forest. The open ground has been washed over and worn down by the river's many springtime rages. The first whiff of crisping salmon draws Nathan back to the fire. He is about to sit when a dark shape streaking along the river catches his eye. Raven glistens with the afternoon sun. His wings spread right to the tips of each feather, then contract suddenly to two wedges tight against his body, as Nathan's eye follows him just above the treeline along the opposite bank. Raven's shadow drops down behind him into the trees. Raven's beak opens into the sun as his wings spread wide.

Auxw!

    Auxw!

And then Raven is gone.

Nathan looks back to the fire and sees Isaac's gaze on him. He sits beside his father, and before he even knows they are coming, the words are out.

"Dad, where did Raven find the sun?"

Isaac places another stick into the fire. His eyes search for something out on the river, before he begins. "The world had gone dark for some time, though the people got by as best they could, feeling their way around things and even trying to fish some.

    But Raven, he figures enough is enough. Then he hears there's something called daylight, locked up in a box and tucked away in the house of a man who lives at the head of a river—some say it was the Nass, way north of here—maybe where the river would come out to greet the sun, if the sun were there.

    Raven makes his way to that place without bumping into too many mountains and trees, and looks that man's house over while the man is out fishing. Some say that man was a fisherman, or maybe a great chief, or someone with an even bigger name. The man was a good builder, and Raven sees he's not going to break into that house so he does some thinking. While he's doing that, out comes the man's daughter. Raven keeps a thoughtful eye on her as she goes to the river, and then he knows how he's going to get into that house.

    When that girl kneels down at the river for her drink, into her hand floats the needle of a hemlock, so small she doesn't feel it go down when she swallows. But after a time she knows something's going on, when her belly starts to grow, and her father knows too, though he can't figure out any more than she how that growing belly got started. Never mind, that baby is soon born and makes himself right at home in his grandfather's house, while that old man acts like any other grandfather. He thinks his grandson is the best-looking boy ever born, though that boy has quick eyes that are into everything.

    Pretty soon the boy starts to crawl around, until he finds three boxes tucked away in a corner. He starts to cry, right in the middle of supper, and points to one of the boxes.

And that grandfather . . . At first he won't let his grandson near those boxes, but all of a sudden, he gives in and lets him play with one. The boy waits until no one is thinking much about him, then off comes the lid and up through the smokehole go the stars. The old man doesn't like that, but the boy makes up to his grandfather and waits a while, until someone visits and starts telling a good story. Then the boy throws another fit, and the old man says to his daughter, 'Give him another of the boxes, and keep an eye on him.'

But that mother has other things on her mind, and the boy just waits until he can open the box up, and up the smokehole goes the moon. The old man feels his heart is going to break when he finds his moon gone, but he loves his grandson."

"Though he doesn't know his grandson is Raven," Nathan says.

Isaac falls silent and inspects the salmon. "Funny thing about that man, because his mind seems to be going two ways. One way, it sounds as if he means to keep all that light tucked away forever, but another way, it sounds as if he knows what's going on all the while, knows one day he has to let that light go. It's hard to know what was going on inside that old man. Anyway, the old man soon forgave his grandson. Then the boy, who is packing away a lot of food every day, grows big enough to make one hell of a noise, one day when his grandfather is trying to sleep. His mother tries hard to calm him down, but he keeps on pointing to that last box and howls.

The old man sighs as if his heart really will break, and says, 'Give him that last box, the box with my daylight in it.' As soon as he hears that, the boy knows this is what he came looking for. The box is barely in his hands, when off comes the lid and the sun throws daylight into every corner of the house, just as the boy becomes Raven. He snatches up the sun in his beak, then shoots up through the smokehole, his feathers turning black as night."

"Wasn't he already black?" Nathan asks.

"Some say Raven was white, once, every feather of him. When Raven is through the smokehole and out into the world, he flies with the sun to the bank of a river, maybe the Nass . . ."

33

"Or maybe our river," Nathan ventures.

"Maybe. Anyway, there are people along the river bank, fishing for oolichans. Raven tucks the sun under his wing and says, I'm going to give you daylight. Those people don't know what to make of that. Some think it sounds too good to be true, while others get mad at Raven and call him a dirty thief. Then Raven lets the sun go and there was nothing but daylight."

Isaac takes the salmon from the fire while Nathan lets the story seep in.

"Weren't the people happy when daylight came?" asks Nathan.

"Not everyone, it seems. Some people were wearing animal skins and skins of birds, and couldn't get free of them soon enough. So they're in those skins even though they're our relatives, and they have places where they can take the skins off and dance and be human, like us. And maybe some people felt they were going blind and looked for a place to hide from all that daylight. My mother's people, up in Haida Gwaii, told of a time Raven was walking along a beach, the one they now call Rose Spit, and he came upon a big clam shell. He cocked an ear and listened hard, and sure enough, voices were moving about in that shell, and Raven thought to himself, 'I've heard those voices before.' So he talked to them in a soft easy way and said, 'It's all right. The daylight won't hurt you.' So one by one, the voices come out, maybe people who hid in that shell when daylight first came. Here's your salmon, but watch your tongue when you bite."

Nathan, however, sinks his teeth eagerly into the crisped salmon, and Isaac's voice falls silent as shadows from the cottonwoods lengthen across Snag Point. When he has finished eating, Nathan listens to the river as it washes against the snags, and then releases his next words. "Steve told me another story about Raven. One his dad told him."

Isaac goes on eating, and Nathan continues. "Steve said Raven was out fishing, for halibut, with Bear, and Bear didn't know how to fish for halibut. So Raven said he needed something from Bear, for bait . . ."

Nathan stops, reluctant to continue. Isaac places another stick into the fire. "A bit of Bear's foreskin, maybe."

"Yes, that's what Steve said."

"It's the sheath that goes around your penis." Isaac chuckles as Nathan's eyes widen. "We didn't need halibut bait when you were born, so your Adha left yours on you. Go on with the story."

"Well, Bear didn't like that idea much, though Raven said he'd cut only a little bit of . . . of Bear's foreskin away. But then Raven cuts Bear right through the . . ."

Isaac looks up at the first stars, twinkling out into the azure twilight. "Testicles. The balls right under your penis."

"That's right." And now Nathan's words tumble forth. "Then Raven cuts Bear open, right to the throat and kills him. Steve laughed, and thought it was a funny story."

Nathan stares into the fire. Isaac continues to watch the stars grow stronger. "Well, it can be a funny story, depending on who tells it, and how. But I guess you think Raven was pretty mean to do a thing like that."

"Why did he do it, Dad? Why did he kill that bear?" Nathan whispers.

"Could be Raven decided he just didn't like him. Some think that's reason enough for one person to cut into another. Go on with the story."

"That's all Steve told me."

"Ahh! Then I'd better finish it. There's also a cormorant in the boat who has seen everything, so Raven cuts out his tongue, then fills the canoe full of halibut and takes the fish to Bear's wife, saying he can't figure out what's happened to Bear, but she'd better cook up the fish, for a feast when Bear does get home. While she's doing that, Raven puts hot rocks in the halibut stomachs and invites Bear-woman to swallow the stomachs down. When she does, she starts feeling funny. So Raven gives her a big drink of water until her stomach steams up and she's as dead as her husband. Then Raven cuts up both bears and eats them, along with all that halibut."

Nathan waits out the silence until his father speaks again.

"There's all kinds of stories about Raven that go up and down the coast, like Raven himself does. Some make you laugh, some make you cry, and some make you feel good, about Raven, and about yourself. Sometimes Raven does things for others, sometimes things that help only him, things that are smart, but mean, or things that are stupid and bring him nothing but shame. Yet all the time he's searching that daylight, for something . . ."

Isaac stands and stamps the last of the fire into ashes. "Untie that boat and let's head down the river, because daylight is what we've just run out of."

Nathan sits on the bottom bench along the left side of the big house, near the drum, and finishes eating his apple. That afternoon his Uncle Sam, the speaker for Uncle Charlie's potlatch, welcomed the guests. The mourning songs have now been sung, supper served, and everyone waits for the T'seka, the Red Cedar Bark Ceremony, to begin, when David will become Hamatsa and receive a name from Uncle Charlie.

Nathan's cousin, Peter, sits beside him, wearing his new baseball hat. Hector joins them.

"That was a good stew," Hector sighs. Nathan and Peter glance at one another and smile as Nathan inspects a broken fingernail.

"Can I borrow your knife, Peter? This cracked nail hurts."

Peter hands the knife to Nathan. "You're lucky I've got it on me. Angie borrowed it from me last week and wouldn't give it back until today. It's hard to argue with your sister when she's bigger than you."

Nathan cuts the nail away and returns the knife to Peter, just as the drummers return to their places and take up their drumming sticks. Silence falls upon the big house. The drummers sit poised, and then the whistle sounds . . .

Haau—!

thromthromthromthromthrom
thromthromthromthromthrom

Haau—!

From the world behind the Tlaamelas, Hamatsa appears, clothed about the neck, waist, ankles with hemlock branches, because David dances for the first time, after his four days alone in the forest and his meeting with the being of Bakbakwalanooksiwae . . .

Haau—!

thromthromthromthromthrom

Sam Dick and Bert Dawson, Hamatsa's glawemth, attend David, capture him, then place the cedar rings along either side of his neck until they cross over at David's chest . . .

Haau—!

Haau—!

Now Hamatsa struggles more intensely within himself, against himself, toward himself, as he circles wildly around the floor, then plunges past the Tlaamelas and disappears. The big house breathes out, and then Hamatsa reappears . . .

Haau—!

throm

throm throm

Haau—!

throm

throm throm

Remembering what Adha has told him, Nathan observes the reaching of David's hands into the space before and above him, first one, then the other, hands that tremble from what the eyes of Hamatsa have seen, hands that have learned how to grasp both evil and good, as the voice from the drum sings of Hamatsa's struggle to wrest into humanness the grip of Bakbakwalanooksiwae upon him . . .

throm throm

throm

throm throm

throm

Haau—!

thromthromthromthromthrom

thromthromthromthromthrom

Haau—!

Again, David breaks his step, rushes in frenzied circles about the big house, then vanishes behind the Tlamelas . . .

throm throm throm throm

Now the Humsumth masks appear, first that of Huxwhuxw. The mask begins its circle of the big house. Adha raises her rattle and her singing reaches out to Huxwhuxw, an arrow sounding through the men's voices that throb in chorus from the drum. Naomi stands beside Adha, also holding a rattle, her button blanket with the crescent moon on its back the exact image of the crest upon Adha's blanket, the horns rising up on either side of the moon's curve . . .

37

Ha ma myy

Ha myy Ha myy

Nathan watches Naomi's rattle move in time with Adha's. Naomi's lips move with Adha's, as Huxwhuxw's feet dance in a half- circle before the drum, his eyes and beak sweeping the big house, searching . . .

thromthromthromthromthrom

"He eats out people's brains," whispers Hector.
"What?" Nathan stares, half-angrily, at Hector.
"That's what Steve said. He bites open people's heads and eats out . . ." Nathan brushes aside the last of Hector's words and watches closely as Huxwhuxw begins his second circle of the big house, and Crooked Beak enters from behind the Tlaamelas to re-enact the pattern of Huxwhuxw . . .

throm throm throm throm

Raven is the last of the Humsumth masks to enter, as Huxwhuxw and Crooked Beak circle the big house yet again . . .

Ha ma myy

throm throm throm throm

Ha myy Ha myy—

throm throm throm throm
throm throm
thromthromthromthromthrom

Now Raven moves his half-moon before the drum. Raven's eyes search every corner of the big house as he crouches, sits, searches . . .

Ha myy Ha myy

For what? Nathan asks himself as he watches and wonders. What is Raven searching for?

Ha ma myy

He lee kila yus
Bakbakwalanooksiwae

Raven's beak snaps open, shut, open, shut, searching . . .

Haa-p!   Haa-p!
Haa-p!   Haa-p!

Raven rises to his feet, and one by one the Humsumth masks exit into the world behind the Tlaamelas. Edith's hand tugs at Nathan's sleeve, and he follows her behind the screen.

Hamatsa dashes out onto the big house floor . . .

Haau—!

Hamatsa makes a last frenzy of circles about the big house . . .

Haau—!   Haau—!

Then he vanishes once again.

throm

    throm throm

throm

    throm throm

The confident beating on the log drum brings the long silence to an end. Aunt Lila, David's Hiligaxstay, dances past the Tlaamelas, turns once, against the clockwise turning of the sun. The conscience of Hamatsa, she leads her nephew, now clothed with his button blanket, back into the circle of his people. Carved wooden skulls dangle from David's blanket, and Aunt Lila wears the figure of an eagle upon her cedar headdress.

All about the big house, the women stand. Their hands rise, fall, weave back and forth—glugwala, a treasuring of Hamatsa, as if their hands would welcome David and cradle what has been born in him.

David's family dances behind him: Uncle Charlie, Edith, Aunt Minnie, Isaac, Uncle Slim, Uncle Sam, Margaret, Nathan, Billy Boy, Angie, Peter, and Adha, with Frank in tow.

throm

    throm throm

Frank dances with the blissful freedom of a child too young to know he is dancing, while Nathan struggles with the steps Adha's hand drum has beaten into his feet.

throm

    throm throm

As his family turns one by one to go past the Tlaamelas, Nathan suddenly catches a glimpse of Margaret and cannot puzzle out the riddle upon her face.

The big house falls silent after the dancers leave the floor. Then Uncle Charlie appears, with David, and the rest of David's family, and the speaker announces that David is now to receive his name from Uncle Charlie. David stands, expressionless, as his new name is spoken:

> Kisoowaci Xwagwana,
> His-Canoe-Holds-a-Treasure.

Then David's eyes widen in astonishment when Uncle Charlie presents a gift David did not expect, a canoe of cedar, almost like the ones of old, with a Sisiutl painted along each of its sides. The big house gasps with David upon seeing the craft that itself is a treasure.

Adha steps forward and beckons to Naomi. Naomi comes onto the floor and stands with Adha as she begins to speak, first in Kwakwala, then in English.

"My goddaughter, here beside me, was born the day after those Americans left for the moon. I guess she decided to stay up there until she knew what they had on their minds. I don't know what those moon travellers found, or thought they were looking for, but this goddaughter of mine brought the first light of the new moon with her, when she came to be with our people. And tonight, I, Axilaogua, am giving her one of the names I hold: Makwalaga, Moon Woman."

Naomi stands with quiet dignity as her new name is spoken.

The dances of the T'seka continue until those to be shown that night have been shown, and then with a roll of the drum, the speaker rolls Uncle Charlie's potlatch over from its dark side to the lighter side of the Tla'sala, which starts with another feast.

"One feast at a time, you guys," Grace Dawson smiles, as Hector, with Nathan and Peter close behind, wedges his way up to the tables laden with food. Nathan turns away from the table and finds Naomi beside him. Suddenly, he feels shy in her presence, as if the Naomi he had known no longer stands in that body. Then her eyes tell him she, too, is feeling strange and shy of herself.

"You're a good singer," Nathan says.

Naomi looks down at the floor, then up at Nathan. "Your Adha is the really good singer, but she is going to teach me all the songs."

"That's some name she gave you," Hector interjects.

Peter looks aslant at Hector, then laughs. "Time to get yourself another feast, Hector."

"Bring a feast for me, Hector, please," Naomi says, also laughing.

The Tla'sala begins with the sounding of rattles and the first of the peace dances. Uncle Charlie, Adha, and Isaac appear before the drum and begin to dance, facing the fire that blazes up from the centre of the big house.

throm throm

throm throm

Adha wears her button blanket with the moon crest while Uncle Charlie wears a Sisiutl crest, and Isaac, a Raven, yet Raven looks as if he is about to split in two, his beak coming apart from the tip and curving away with the two halves of him to either side of the blanket.

throm throm

throm throm throm

A rattle in hand, each dancer wears a headdress rimmed with high, white spines; ermine skins hang down from its back and sides. White eagle down, nestled into the crown of each headdress, rises into the air, then falls to the big house floor.

throm throm

throm throm

Nathan gazes at the frontal piece upon his father's headdress, carved from black argillite. A crescent moon curves along the left side, its face searching out the dark, encircled space before it. Isaac's raven rattle holds the sun in its beak.

throm throm

throm throm throm

Uncle Slim and Bert Dawson clown their way through the front door of the big house.

"Yo!" shouts Uncle Slim.

"Yo!" Bert answers.

"Yo-yo, yourself!" shouts Uncle Slim. He points at Bert as voices about the big house start to chuckle and laugh. Uncle Slim wears gum boots and carries a mop head. "Time to clean this place up!"

The laughter grows as Bert and Uncle Slim waltz up to the peace dancers and look them over. Uncle Slim drapes the mop down from the back of his head, like the headdresses of the dancers, and dances in front of Isaac, swinging his hips as he mimicks Isaac's steps. The big house erupts in fits of laughter as Uncle Slim plays out his parody.

throm throm

throm throm throm

Suddenly, Isaac strides past Uncle Slim, across the floor and out the front door of the big house. Uncle Slim looks amazed and gestures to Bert; they follow Isaac out as the dance ends, and the chuckles and laughter subside. Bert and Uncle Slim reappear at the front door. Uncle Slim displays Isaac's blanket and headdress, then Bert and he go out again.

Naomi stirs beside Nathan. He steals a glance at her, to find her glancing at him.

throm

throm

The Tlaamelas is drawn aside. A figure robed all in black passes through into the big house. Uncle Slim and Bert follow, sounding their rattles.

A single eye of the Raven mask peers out from the folds of the blanket held draped across its beak. The eye alone is visible. All else is shrouded by the black expanse of the blanket.

throm

throm

The Raven mask circles the big house, turning, ever turning, as the arm beneath the blanket draws back to reveal the cheekline about the eye, then the beak, but only one half of the mask. The other half stays hidden by the drape of the blanket along the Raven's beak.

Like the blanket, the face of the Raven is also black, save for the thin red line that closes the upper and lower halves of the beak together, as if holding fast a secret that cannot yet be shown or is not yet known, and the slivers of white that curve away on either side from the black circle of the eye.

throm

    throm

        throm

Nathan leans forward as the Raven turns past the last corner of the big house and comes toward him, returning to the world behind the Tlaamelas. He knows this dance is his father's glugwe, the treasure Isaac can show at this moment in the potlatch, knows his father is the figure beneath the dark folds of the blanket, behind the black eye of the Raven mask—

throm

    throm

        throm

The Raven passes in front of the drum, turns before passing through the Tlaamelas, and pauses, his one eye fixed upon Nathan.

Three weeks after Uncle Charlie's potlatch, the plane from Port Hardy, with Minnie and Slim, brings David and Margaret home for the Christmas holidays. When Margaret climbs out of the plane, everyone notices her glasses.

"She couldn't read a word on the blackboard, no matter where she sat," says Aunt Minnie.

Margaret, however, seems oblivious to the fact of her glasses, even though her hair, now shoulder length, spills down over them as she stands at the kitchen counter and works spruce branches into an Advent wreath.

Nathan plays cribbage with Uncle Slim at the kitchen table, while Frank looks on and makes up his own rules. Isaac is outside, carving, and Aunt Minnie sleeps on the couch, while David visits with Billy Boy and others at the far end of Duxsowlas. Edith and Adha stand at the counter next to Margaret, preparing bread to go into the oven. Margaret fixes candles to the wreath. "We can light all four, tomorrow."

"How many times have I told you not to lead a face card in this game?" Uncle Slim says to Nathan. Nathan scowls and changes his lead.

"Don't lead with an eight, either."

Nathan glowers at his uncle, then changes his lead again, to an ace of clubs.

"Now that's a good lead. A pair for two," Uncle Slim says.

Nathan's annoyance at his uncle's trickery is muted by a startling observation. He notices for the first time that his Uncle Slim is not slim at all. As he plays out his hand, Nathan glances furtively at the way Uncle Slim's belly overreaches his belt and presses against the edge of the table.

"You've got good hands, but why are they working with spruce, when there's cedar about?" Adha says to Margaret. Margaret's hands freeze above the candles; she brushes back her hair again.

"Because they use spruce at the church in Port Hardy."

Aunt Minnie starts to snore. "Why is Auntie making noise?" Frank asks.

"She's just saying her prayers, Weesa. Slim, turn your wife over before the volume increases," Edith says, with the straightest of faces.

Uncle Slim chuckles as he counts his hand, his crib, then pegs. Adha stops at the table on her way out the door. "When you've finished beating your Uncle, come over and help me with those baskets," she says to Nathan.

Nathan does not beat Uncle Slim, but at least he is not skunked and can leave with his dignity intact. Snow falls lightly as he walks over to Adha's house. The living room and kitchen are at the back, where her window looks out at Uncle Charlie's and the big house, and into the surrounding forest. Adha sits at a table that holds several cedar baskets in the making.

"You can work on that one, for Naomi. And don't worry if some voices tease your hands for making a basket. Working with the cedar will open up your fingers, so they'll listen better when your dad teaches you to carve."

Taking the basket, Nathan tries to remember what Adha has already taught him. The strands are big, the weave of the basket generous, and his confidence steadies as his hands find their way. The scent of the cedar begins to fill him as his thoughts go, first, to becoming a good carver like his father, then, inexplicably, to his brother, moved by the throb of the log drum, to David ringed about with cedar and crying the cry of Hamatsa.

"Steve says Bakbakwalanooksiwae wants Hamatsa to eat human flesh, and Huxwhuxw eats out people's brains."

"Does he? Steve seems to have a lot to say, these days. Though the way some people are tied to their brains, Huxwhuxw might be doing them a favour, if eating out brains is what he does."

"Why does Hamatsa keep crying out?"

"Well, he's been out in the forest a few days without eating, and he's become one with the being of Bakbakwalanooksiwae."

Nathan wonders who or what Bakbakwalanooksiwae is, but the name daunts him and he holds his tongue about that. Adha takes up Nathan's basket. "Now figure out a handle for it. Naomi will like that gift."

"Huxwhuxw, Crooked Beak and Raven also cry out."

"They're looking for Hamatsa."

"Why are they looking for Hamatsa?"

"You are full of questions, aren't you?"

"Is it bad to ask questions?" Nathan meets his grandmother's gaze.

"That depends, on how well you listen and look before you ask. That's a good handle. Just make it a couple of strands thicker."

"What are you singing, when you sing to Huxwhuxw and Crooked Beak, and to Raven?"

Adha considers a moment. "There may be different ideas about that, even different songs. But we want to heal Hamatsa and give him courage, and we want Raven, Huxwhuxw, and Crooked Beak to help Hamatsa and not to hurt him. And in the end, when Hamatsa has met Bakbakwalanooksiwae and himself, we want him to stand with his people and say,

Nu gwa am, I am. Take that basket to Naomi and tell her Santa came early this year."

The winter night has gathered about Nathan's house by the time he returns, to find the wreath placed on the coffee table with three of the four candles lit. Frank sits on the floor, the glow of candle light soft upon his face. Nathan sits down beside him, as Edith washes her hands at the sink, then sits on the couch. Coming in from a bedroom, Margaret sits beside Edith, as Isaac opens the door, takes off his boots, then joins Nathan and Frank on the floor. Slim and Minnie appear, fill up the couch space, and no one speaks.

David walks in. He stands a moment, hands in his jeans pockets, then pulls a kitchen chair forward. Nathan looks up at his brother and feels his own heart turn as the candle light relieves and deepens the shadows upon David's face. David's eyes are the eyes of one still haunted, hungry, and not yet healed.

Nathan's gaze follows Frank's back to the candle light, falling upon the cedar leaves someone has woven in among the spruce.

SIX

Nathan's ninth birthday, an early Easter, and the first run of oolichan have come to Duxsowlas.

Upriver, trying to net some fish, Nathan comes upon fresh bear droppings and then some very fresh tracks, going farther upriver. "Grizzly is awake and wants his skin back," Nathan thinks to himself, "and I haven't got it. So I'm going home with my fish."

Downriver, almost to the big house, a sound in the cedars overhead brings Nathan to a stop. The dark shape of Raven glides down onto a stump. Nathan stands very still.

"Ghe-la-kasla! Haven't seen you for a while," Nathan murmurs. Raven flicks his wings as Nathan crosses a patch of sunlight and stops within the shadows, amazed that Raven is still there. Raven's eye peers at Nathan, as the eye of the Raven mask had peered at him from the dark folds of the blanket. Fascinated, Nathan takes another step, looks right into the eye of Raven and gasps at the image of his own face gazing back.

Raven drops his head, hops casually from the stump onto a deadfall, and glances back, once . . .

Gwaau . . .?

before lifting himself out into the light and across the river.

Shaken, Nathan goes into the big house, where he can sit alone beside one of the four house posts and stop shaking. He looks up at the four human figures that tower about him, one pair facing east, the other pair west, as the beams of the big house press down upon their heads. Their arms reach out in gestures of welcome, their mouths open as if to speak, their eyes gaze into distances beyond his seeing—two pairs of eyes gazing up the valley toward Duxdzas from

46

which the Wanookqway once came, the other four eyes searching the sea to the west.

Voices approach the big house and become clear as Harvey Silas and Bert Dawson sit down on the bench outside. "One of these days, Charlie's going to stand up at a potlatch and claim his family built this big house," Harvey growls.

"I've never heard of them claiming that," Bert answers.

"It'll come. That's why they're all bunched up at this end, because they think they own whatever goes on in here." Bert does not reply, and Harvey continues his monologue. "Puclalas. That was Henry Watson's potlatch name."

"It was a good name," Bert says.

"Place-where-People-are-never-Hungry. Yeah, well, I remember summers that boat of his would come in half-empty, and winters when he hardly had two fish to rub together. Charlie, Lila, Edith, and Minnie ran from one table to another just to keep the skin on their bones."

Bert chuckles. "They were good eaters, all right. And so was I, when they fed me, and when Henry Watson was keeping the potlatch alive, in this village."

"Yeah, and look at the one Charlie just gave. Big names, big canoes, and just enough stew to fool your tongue into thinking your belly's been fed. Slim's the only one in that family who can put on a feast."

"My stomach wasn't complaining," Bert says.

"And that glugwe of Isaac's. What was that about? Nothing said about his family or where he got the right to show that dance, as if marrying into the Watson clan gives him all the right he needs."

"He carves good masks. I'd like to be able to carve as good as that."

"He's after big names, that's all. Big names from Axilaogua, for those kids of his."   .

"That was a big name Axilaogua gave to your Naomi," Bert observes, but Harvey rants on.

"That's the reason he's married Edith and carves their masks. But I can put him and Charlie and all of them in their place. There are ways of putting them in their place."

Bert waits the silence out, then says, "That's a good seine boat you have, Harvey. A good, new boat."

"It's a good boat, all right. I put a lot of money into that boat."

"And that speedboat of yours is good, too."

"Nobody around here can touch it," Harvey says.

"You know, Harvey, if I had a seine boat like yours, and that speed boat, too, I guess I'd be happy with what I had, and not be wanting things that belong to someone else."

Nathan finds a hole in the planking of the big house and peers out, just as Bert stands and stretches. "Think I'll head down and see what Grace has done about lunch."

Naomi's father sits and watches Bert make his way across the soccer field, then he suddenly spits something out and stalks off.

When Nathan leaves the big house, he walks down to the river's mouth, where he can sit upon the big log on the beach and not think about what he has just heard, but listen instead to the river speaking to the incoming tide.

The Sunday after Easter, Edith gathers up Nathan and Frank and walks along the beach toward Bone Spit. The day is young and most of Duxsowlas still sleeps, except for the seagulls that cry *Tseque!* as they scout the beach where the tide has withdrawn for traces of seafood, and for Sadie Moon who is hammering at a loose plank on her porch.

"You're going to wake the dead," Edith calls. Sadie comes down the steps, hammer in hand.

"The dead where you're going are too far gone from here to mind what I'm about, and for that matter, so are the dead back that way."

"Yes, we heard the party. Who was there?"

"A few people we know, including Ed Williams and our friends next door," Sadie says, tilting her head toward the Silas house. Edith sighs. "I'm glad I stopped when I did."

"Yes. You were getting close to the edge." Sadie glances at Nathan and Frank. "You guys going to pay your respects to your granddad? That's good. Nineteen years ago today."

"You have a good memory," smiles Edith.

"I always remember, even things I wish I could forget. Easter came early that year, too. At least he made it through to then."

Edith nods. "Come on, you two, let's go while the tide's out. Otherwise, we'll have to swim back."

That thought excites Frank. "Can we stay, until we can swim?"

"No way! That water would freeze the ass on a duck."

"I beg your pardon! When did that kind of talk start tripping across your tongue?"

Nathan winces from his mother's words and hangs his head.

"There are some older kids around here with sooty tongues. But you better get a leg on, Edith, or that tide will catch you out," Sadie says.

The sandy neck of land that lets Duxsowlas people cross over to Bone Spit at low tide is never truly dry, but the sand holds firm enough to leave footprints that do not fill with water as soon as the feet of Edith, Nathan, and Frank are clear of them. Frank makes his footprints with great care, so he can walk in them the other way when he returns. Bone Spit itself widens out into tall grass, Sitka, and cedar rising up about the graves and a few gravestones. Edith places the daffodils she has grown and some wild blossoms at the foot of her father's gravestone and remains with one knee to the ground, her head bowed.

Nathan reads the words on the gravestone:

Henry Watson
1908-1959
Puclalas
Even strangers were fed
from his hand

Edith sits beside her father's grave and looks about the graveyard. "We used to put our dead in boxes in the trees, when there were more trees here. Then we started putting their bodies in the ground, keeping families together. Behind your granddad's grave lies his family, and Adha's. Let's just stay a while. The tide will wait."

Nathan wanders from gravestone to gravestone, looking at names he can barely read, while Edith sits beside her father's grave. His inspection completed, Nathan leaves Frank to carry on and sits beside his mother. "Where did granddad get his name, Puclalas?"

"It was a big name in his family. His granddad gave it to him, many years ago."

"Does it mean anything, very much?"

Edith looks hard at her son, until Nathan begins to squirm under her gaze. "I think some one has been stuffing your ears. Am I right?"

Nathan studies the ground, picks up a stone and balances it in his hand. Edith turns away, a long way away, before she speaks again.

"Some people see with their eyes only. Do you understand? Sometimes your granddad would go out in his boat and come back with half a load of fish to everyone else's boatload. That's what some saw and remembered, and still talk about. What they didn't see were the stops he made along the coast on the way home, dropping off fish into the laps of people who couldn't feed themselves.

I'll tell you a story about your granddad. One year nobody was catching fish, anywhere. All the springs, sockeye, coho, humps, and even chums decided they'd go holiday that year, anywhere but where the fishing boats were. Your granddad couldn't fill a net either, until he went far out, beyond the north end of Vancouver Island, to a place he remembered hearing about years before from an old, old man, and that day he didn't have nets enough to pull in all the fish he found. Your granddad started for home with a boatload of happy fishermen, and then they met a seine boat flying a flag they'd never seen, although they knew where it was from.

It was a Russian flag on a Russian seine boat, in Canadian waters where it had no right to be. Your granddad came alongside and started giving those Russians hell for taking our fish, only to hear from one of them who could speak some English that they didn't have a single fish on their boat. That's why they had risked coming into our waters, because they were scared of going back with nothing. Your granddad knew what was going on in the world, and he could picture those fishermen on their way to prison just for being down on their luck. So he turned to the men on his boat and said, 'Unload our fish into that boat, every one of them.'

That set everybody's head spinning, but your granddad meant it, and they knew he meant it because he was Puclalas, so they did what he said, and that was the happiest boatload of Russians on the Pacific Ocean. Your granddad came home with an empty boat, and he and his crew just smiled when people said how sorry they were for him.

It looks like the tide is getting tired of waiting for us. Besides, Mr. Blaisdell is coming in this afternoon, and I have to set up the school for service this evening."

"Is the bishop coming this year?" Nathan asks, still thinking of his granddad.

"No. There's no one to be confirmed."

"Why did the bishop say those words, when he put his hands on Margaret, and Mary, and Billy Boy?"

"Laid his hands. What words?"

"Defend . . .?"

"'Defend, O Lord, this Thy Servant with Thy heavenly grace.' What about them?"

"What does it mean, asking God to defend us? What does He defend us from?"

Edith laughs and puts her arm around Nathan. "From many things, I guess, though not from everything. But mainly, from ourselves."

Frank stands before them, holding the white tailfeather of an eagle. "Look!"

Edith takes it, turns it over once, and returns it to Frank. "That's a very special gift Eagle left for you. Come on, let's beat the tide!"

Nathan brushes the sand from his jeans as he stands and takes a last look about the graveyard. Then what he has not seen dawns fully upon him. "Mom, where is Dad's family? There aren't any Jacobs here."

"Your dad's family isn't from here," Edith answers. She takes Frank by the hand and starts to walk.

On the last weekend in April, Isaac takes Nathan upriver to shut the trapline for the season. Nathan listens to what his father tells him about taking care of himself out in the open, because, Isaac says, he will need that knowing one day. Nathan also observes the greying hair in his father's beard and on his head, and realizes Isaac is older than Edith, even older than Uncle Charlie, though not as old as Adha, and walks with a slight limp—a limp Nathan had not noticed until now, not even when the Raven mask made its long circle of the big house.

Coming downriver, Isaac suddenly guns the motor and swings the boat about, nosing the bow into the current and right against the last of the snags below Snag Point. "Tie us up to it," he tells Nathan. Nathan clambers forward and knots the rope around the snag as Isaac cuts the motor. Now only the rush and sighing of the river reaches their ears.

"It's good to stop in the middle of something that's moving you along," Isaac says.

Nathan listens to the river speak, yet also remembers what he felt during last Sunday's church service. "Why do you always sit at the back during the services, by the door?"

Isaac swats at an early mosquito. "Well, for one thing, the air is better back there with the door open, even when it turns cold, and sitting there I can listen both ways, to what Mr. Blaisdell says and to what our sister Hummingbird is saying just outside, going from flower to flower. And often, Old Man can't understand Mr. Blaisdell's words, so I help him make them out."

Nathan frowns. "I can't understand many things Mr. Blaisdell says."

"Then don't listen to all of it, but the man he talks about, listen to him. Look! Just above the point. Look high."

Nathan's eyes follow Isaac's gesture. He cranes his neck and then he sees the eagle, floating high above Snag Point, its outspread wings commanding the currents of air that carry it.

"Look, Son! There's another, and another."

As if born of the sky itself, a second eagle forms from out of the blue, then a third, and then a fourth, appearing at the edge of the sun.

"And another, Dad! Three others, over toward Duxdzas!" Nathan cries, almost standing as he points.

"Sit down, or this trip is going to have a wet ending!" Isaac barks. Then his voice changes as he searches out each of the eagles once again. "My father used to say that Eagle was the nearest of all living things to the Creator, because he could fly closest to the sun."

The lines drop away from Isaac's face, and he suddenly is young. Nathan, too, follows the eagles in their flight as all seven now circle above Snag Point, and he remembers Naomi's words: *Eagle never comes down, not right down.*

Why should Eagle ever come down, Nathan wonders, when he can stay up there close to the sun, as Isaac's father had said? But who was Isaac's father? The question rises up within Nathan, but the presence of the eagles and the way his father has spoken about them stops the words from coming forth.

"You're wondering about your grandfather, and who he was." Isaac chuckles at the astonishment on Nathan's face. "Sometimes you can feel when a question is stuck. Now, how about unsticking us from that snag?"

SEVEN

Early on the first Saturday in May, a week before the Christian feast called Pentecost, Isaac wakens Nathan. "There's a new moon tonight. Get dressed and bring a warm jacket."

Above the beach at Duxsowlas, banks of cloud rolling in from the west meet the grey blankets that drape down upon the valley from Duxdzas. Nathan shivers as he climbs into the boat. Isaac heads across the water toward Log Island, and Nathan pulls his hat down tight upon his head. They climb the rock-lined east bank, then walk through the salal to the fire Isaac has laid in a clearing just shy of the log-jammed shoreline to the west. Nathan rubs his hands together and sniffs the scent of burnt cedar and something else, then sits, his back to Duxsowlas.

Isaac sits facing Nathan, beside some boughs of hemlock, his hand drum, and a small bag. With a stick, he draws a line in the earth from east to west and a crossing line from south to north. After rolling a burning ember from the fire to the crossing of the two lines, Isaac opens the bag and places its contents upon the ember. "Cedar, and sweetgrass, from the prairies to the east."

The rich scent of the cedar joins with the sharp sweetness of the grass to grace Nathan's nostrils, as Isaac begins to pray in a tongue Nathan has never heard. Eyes closed, his father speaks the rhythms of the prayer that move within Nathan beneath his understanding, except for the sounding of what must be a name, *Wakan Tanka*. When the prayer ends, Isaac passes the face of his drum through the cedar and sweetgrass smoke, then the drumming stick. Setting the drum aside, he scoops the smoke with his hands, first along his head, then his shoulders, one arm then the other, up and along his chest, down his thighs, and across his loins.

"You do the same," Isaac says. Nathan imitates the movements of his father and finds that his hands want to take the smoke right down to his feet. "Go ahead. Take it right down."

As he wafts the smoke to his feet, Nathan realizes his runners have taken on a scent of their own and wonders if doing this prayer will clean the scent out, only to feel he shouldn't be thinking such a thought. Isaac takes up the drum and begins to chant, the words rising softly from his lips as the stick touches the drumskin with a steady throb. Now, the chant throbs within Nathan, calling forth the picture of a parting of the ways long ago, a parting filled with pain.

Isaac's voice rises into one last note, then dies away with the last throb of the drum. When the chant has been taken up by the clouds overhead, Nathan's father begins to speak.

"Your grandfather and his people called the creator, *Wakan Tanka*. Your grandfather should be speaking to you now, but he could not be here, so I must speak both as father and grandfather. Your brother is now Hamatsa, which means that you will not be, not in that way. Some families nowadays have more than one Hamatsa, but that is not the way of your Adha and your uncle. So you must find another way, your way, of knowing what Hamatsa knows and becoming what he becomes. Today is a good day to start."

Isaac takes the stick with which he had made the cross and places it in the fire. "Stay here, without any food, until I come for you. Go where you wish on this island, but if you go south, then go as far north and stay as long. The same if you walk east. Balance it by walking west, and walk the island in a circle, too. See those hemlock branches? Once a day, go into the water up near the Giant and rub yourself with hemlock needles until your skin feels clean and new. Yes, I know. The water's cold enough to freeze the ass on every duck around, but it won't kill you."

Nathan scowls again as Isaac chuckles; he looks up at the thickening clouds and shivers as his father finishes speaking.

"And you may be rained on, so find yourself a shelter if you want to stay dry. Here's a bottle of water. That stick I put in the fire will be the last. When it's gone, the only fire you'll have will be whatever is in you. Keep your eyes and ears open, and remember that everything that comes to you is related to you, even if it's been pushed away. Ha-la-kasla!"

Isaac takes the drum and the bag in hand, walks through the salal and Sitkas, and is gone.

Hands stuffed in his pockets, Nathan tries to calculate how long the fire will burn. He glances skeptically at the hemlock branches, as the clouds above continue to thicken. "Maybe I should go into the water now, while the fire's still burning."

He undresses and picks his way toward the Giant, hemlock branch in hand. "I should have kept my clothes on until I got there." he thinks, as the salal pokes and prods his skin. Looking through a break in the chain of logs into cold, black water, Nathan tries the hemlock branch on his arm. His arm protests and seeks refuge and warmth against his side. Lowering himself into the water as far as his bum, Nathan yelps as his lower limbs scream, then die away into a numb silence. On the verge of crying, he frees his body from the water. Of its own will, his right hand takes hold of the hemlock branch and brings it down across his legs, to beat the life back into them.

Back at the fire and feeling miserable, Nathan fumbles at his clothes and wants to go home, but he realizes he would have to swim. So he puts on his jacket and walks to the south, the distance from the fire to the Giant, then west where he sits on a log. The sky above him is on the move as more clouds march in from the west, a relentless wind at their back. Along the horizon, the first curtain of rain appears. Nathan watches, fascinated, for the curtain is alive, flashing light then darkening again, as it closes in upon the log where he sits.

The wind strikes first, driving the water before it up and over until the first wave crashes apart against the log reef of Log Island. Nathan jumps up, too late, and then the rain hits him. Already drenched, Nathan is now soaked to and beneath the skin. The fire has died with a last, sodden hiss by the time he reaches it, and he turns to the Giant for refuge. At the trunk, the salal parts for him and lets him slide beneath its branches. But drops of rain follow after him, drip their way past the leaves, down to the ends of the branches to gather there before dropping into Nathan's ear, on his nose, lip, neck, and into the folds of his socks, pants, shirt, and jacket. Nathan closes his eyes and wishes himself into another world where the rain could never find him. When he opens them, he sees an ant following a raindrop down the bridge of his nose. He sneezes, but the ant continues on to the tip of Nathan's nose then onto a leaf, a branch, and down to the wet ground where it meets another ant, and the two set to work pushing a dead fly toward a hole at the base of the Giant. Nathan observes the way the ants move the fly along and wonders if they are related to one another and maybe to him.

"Ghe-la-kasla," he says to the first ant. "Is that your uncle, or my auntie?" And then he laughs and goes on laughing until his eyes close and he sleeps.

Nathan awakens into a darkness so close he can barely breathe. His eyes open wide, but he cannot even see his hand when he lifts it to push the salal aside. He tries to make out the trunk of the Giant, to trace the line of it upward to the crown gripped by a black mist, but his eyes give up as his other senses awaken, the dry rasp of his tongue against the roof of his mouth, the ache in his hip flattened upon the wet earth, the wetness of his clothes and skin, the musty green odour of salal, and the rot of last season's leaves, still decaying to earth, and sounds—the steady drop, drop of water down from the Giant, the soft, yet restless, lapping of the ocean against the logs, the slap of wave against this log, that log, then suddenly something above him, its wings brushing against the night. Frightened, Nathan sucks in his breath then releases it, as if to feel out the dark about him, to feel past his fear and learn what the dark wants with him, and finds that the darkness is warm about him, like a blanket lost once upon a time or shrugged aside and forgotten, finds that he is wet, but not cold and not lost. Unafraid now, Nathan relaxes into the darkness and thinks that it too might be related to him. He closes his eyes and listens with care to each drop of water, each wave lapping, and to the darkness itself, then sleeps again.

At dawn, Nathan awakens to hear his bladder screaming at him. He coaxes then prods his confused body to its feet, up through the ceiling of salal and a spray of raindrops, then into the wool-grey mist that holds Log Island fast. Out of respect for the Giant, he holds his urine in check until he stumbles through the salal to a nearby Sitka. Releasing his water into the earth, he wonders if the Sitka too might be one of his relatives.

As soon as his bladder is at ease, Nathan's stomach comes alive and wants breakfast. He retraces his steps to the Giant, sits, and tells his stomach to be quiet. His stomach pays no attention and continues to growl and grumble and rage with sounds Nathan has never heard it make. In desperation, he talks to his stomach, pleads with it, promising a fabulous feed when this ordeal is over, but his stomach goes on whining and howling. "Just like Raven; yeah, you're just like Raven, acting as if yours is the only mouth open in the whole world."

Nathan's stomach calms down. He wonders if it might be listening now, waiting for him to go on. So he begins to tell stories to his stomach, about Raven, nothing that has anything to do with food, until he decides his stomach really is listening. Then he socks it to his stomach, tells it every food story he knows, how Raven went about tricking food away from other creatures, and how they, in turn, took pity on him when he was hungry and miserable. But whenever Raven tried to catch food their way, he made a mess of things because he was trying to do it their way and not his own.

"Are you listening?" Nathan says to his stomach, then finishes by telling how the Wanookqway came down, long ago, from Duxdzas, from light into mist, and had to wait for oolichan to bring them their first meal. "So you have to wait, too," Nathan says, and calms his stomach right down.

The mist lightens about him. Nathan's clothes are damp but no longer soaked through. He takes them off, lays them out on a log, and reaches for a hemlock branch. This time, he goes into the water up to his neck. The water grabs but does not bite right through his skin. Nathan's limbs dull down to a lovely numbness as he moves them about. When he climbs out, he takes the hemlock and rubs the numbness until it sparkles.

Naked, Nathan sits at the foot of the Giant and watches as rays, then planes of light, thrust the mist apart until the ball of the sun sucks the last grey wisps into itself, leaving only the clear blue of the sky as it climbs through the day and sinks into the afternoon. Nathan thanks the log for looking after his clothes, and dresses except for his socks, which refuse to dry completely. So he tosses them aside, slips his bare feet into his runners, then walks southward to some logs piled up well above the high-water line. He settles himself upon them, stretches his legs out, and watches the sun set with quiet dignity.

Only the immense blue of the sky remains. Nathan gazes into the blue as it deepens to indigo and the first stars begin to shine. High above the horizon to the west, he can make out two bright stars Adha had called the Twins: "The Creator put them there to remind us that nothing is ever alone, that every being has a twin somewhere."

Near the Twins, another star beams steadily, only Nathan's teacher this year had said it was not a star, but a big planet named Jupiter after the chief god of the people called the Romans. Below the big planet, Nathan's eye spots the Hunter, with the Dog at his heel. "They've been at it a long time. I wonder if they ever catch anything?"

Night seeps in from the east until the sky is soaked through with a darkness that shines from somewhere deep within itself, beyond the shimmering of the stars. Nathan lifts the brim of his hat and sees another planet almost overhead, a red flare insisting upon recognition. "The teacher called that one Mars. That one likes to fight."

As the night moves on in its great arc, one by one the Twins, the Hunter, the Dog, and the two planets journey toward the dark line in the west. "Are they my relatives, too?" Nathan wonders, as he watches them disappear. "If so, they should tell me where they are going."

The teacher had told the grade four class about the stars and planets when he was supposed to be talking about something else, only the stars and planets had made him more excited. A few nights later, Nathan, Peter, Hector, and Naomi had stayed outside long enough to look at the sky for themselves.

"The stars don't move around the sky and they shine by themselves, while the planets move around and don't shine," said Peter, his arms folded.

"Then how do the planets shine?" Hector asked, because he didn't always listen to what was said in class.

"They reflect the sun's light, like the moon," Peter answered.

"That big one looks to me like it's shining good enough," Hector said.

After a long time, Nathan spoke out: "The stars do move. Look, the Hunter has gone over there since we first came out."

"It's the earth that moves," Peter said.

"That's not how I see it," Nathan insisted. "The stars shine and the planets shine. The planets move and the stars move. I don't see any difference."

"But there is," Naomi said. "The stars shine and move by staying at home, and the planets don't."

On into the night, Nathan watches the Great Bear circle the Star-that-never-moves, its tail sweeping down to the west in the same pattern as his people circling the floor of the big house. At the edge of dawn, the indigo sky takes a deep breath and Nathan suddenly sees a great button blanket shimmering high above him, like the shimmering of button crests in the warm light of the big house fire, and feels as if a blanket wants to enfold him. His head comes to rest upon a log and he falls asleep.

Hauw!

Nathan's head jerks upright and swings around to see the sun rise from behind Duxdzas. Groggily, he lets himself down from the log pile and walks into the sun to his friend, the Sitka spruce. He rubs the glare of the sun from his eyes as his stomach stirs in hope of food, then gives up and stops growling.

Having longed for the sun the whole of yesterday, Nathan blinks in surprise at finding he cannot look it directly in the eye and that its gaze presses too closely upon him, even when its rays only glance back from the ridges of water rolling toward Log Island, the green of the salal leaves, the whitened skin of the logs, and the tiny crystals ground to earth at his feet. Even his own skin, like rich bronze armour, repels the light that strikes it.

As the sun strengthens its hold on the day, Nathan explores Log Island, keeping his movements in balance and following the ever-shifting drama of light and shadow from one end of the island to the other. By noon, the light has won out at the south end and has driven the shadows right back to the trunks of the Sitka, right under the branches and leaves of salal. At the north end, the spread of the Giant becomes a refuge where the shadow world can gather and hold its own. Nathan joins the shadows beneath the Giant to keep them company, because, he decides, "They're my relatives, too, and I'm going to look after them."

"What would it be like," Nathan wonders, "to live in a world in which light drove out every last shadow? Light needs something dark like me to bounce from," he thinks, and sees the light is doing just that, bouncing itself off of every dark thing it can get at, as if it would turn the world about him into one big mirror.

"It is not good for light to have its own way, all the time," Nathan concludes. He closes his eyes and listens past the light to the slap of a wave upon a log, the whirr of a swallow's wing as it darts back and forth, and the buzz of a fly figuring out where to land next.

By afternoon, the light begins to ease off and the shadows lengthen from where they have been hiding. Nathan returns to his pile of logs and feels the warm wind upon his face. Sitting upon the log pile, he follows the sun on its way to the horizon, discovering as it sinks that he can almost look it in the eye. The sun's light is softer now and kinder, as if the sun is tired from all that climbing up and down the sky and would like a good, long rest. Then Nathan notices the disc that hovers before his eyes, that moves as his eyes move, slipping between his eyes and the sun, and darkening the sun down just enough for him to look at it. He tries to blink the disc away, even crossing his eyes, but it slips back into focus, letting him hold his gaze on the sun as it touches the horizon.

Suddenly, the sun explodes into feathers of light that float up and out from it—red, pink, and orange as the sun sinks, then vanishes. Releasing his breath, Nathan lifts his gaze from the horizon to see if the big planet has come out, then catches his breath again. A thin, gleaming crescent hangs above the sun's setting. The sky darkens, and now a thin shining line appears, reaching from the tips of the crescent and encircling the dark space within.

His eyes widened to their brows, Nathan concentrates on nothing but that dark encircled space cradled by the new crescent moon. The stars flash out and the moon sinks ever lower until it touches the dark rim of the ocean. At that moment, Nathan sees a shining within the dark circle, a light breaking through from behind or breathing in on the darkness, or both, and then the shining suggests itself into a figure as the moon slips past Nathan's gaze and is gone. Exhausted, Nathan's eyes want to close, but he rubs them to expel the weariness and stares at the horizon.

He sees nothing. Maybe he is trying too hard. Closing his eyes, he waits until he can settle down within himself, then looks again at the horizon. His heart jumps as his eyes find the shining crescent once more, even though he knows the moon itself is no longer there. Yet the shining crescent presents itself to him, cradling the encircled darkness and whatever is trying to make itself known within that.

Nathan settles himself within and will not let the image go. As the stars and planets travel overhead, he sits on his log with a wind from the west pressing against him, holds the crescent at the horizon and waits, with a patience he would never have thought possible. Then, at the first reach of dawn from the east, Nathan sees the barely shining figure within the dark circle form itself into the wings, then beak, of a white bird, the shimmering light bringing the bird alive, right into its tail feathers as the dark orb itself becomes Raven's eye.

Nathan's eyes close and his chin drops until it touches his chest.

"Ghe-la-kasla."

Lifting his head from the log, Nathan sees his father sitting beside him. "Ghe-la-kasla, Dad," he replies, suddenly faint from hunger.

Isaac puts one arm around his son and hands him a piece of barbecued salmon.

"Your Mom cooked this up, on the beach, early this morning."

Nathan eats in silence, sipping now and then from the water bottle Isaac has brought. Then, when he has given his stomach the feed he had promised, he begins to speak, hesitantly at first, as Isaac listens to every word—about the rain, the ants, the thick darkness filled with sounds, and all his other relatives including the stars and the shadows, and, at the last, about the crescent moon, the dark circle and the gleaming figure he thought he saw, before the dawn overtook his eyes.

"Just before I fell asleep. It looked like Raven, but it was white and trying to fly." Nathan falters and falls silent, as he feels the silence within Isaac move. Never has he felt or seen his father be so moved. Isaac rubs at the watery film that swims across his eyes, before he speaks.

"A hundred some years ago, just below the Medicine Line, there was a big fight between the people called the Sioux and Cheyenne, and the American cavalry. The Cheyenne and Sioux—Lakota, they named themselves—were camped by a river they called the Greasy Grass when the soldiers hit them on a Sunday afternoon late in June. A Lakota warrior, Spreading Eagle, took his gun and crossed the Greasy Grass to fight the soldiers. His oldest son went with him because he was sixteen and a warrior. By day's end, the soldiers who had come along the bluffs above the river as far as Spreading Eagle's lodge had been wiped out, including one of their leaders with a big name, Custer. But Spreading Eagle was also killed, coming out of the river right when the fighting started, and he died in the arms of his son. That warrior was your great-grandfather. He had two other sons, a boy of twelve, called Wounded Drum, and a boy of seven. That youngest boy was your grandfather.

Four nights before the fight, the moon made itself new, where the Twins live. Two nights later, your grandfather saw the first thin curve of it, as you did last night. That night he dreamed a dream of many pictures, at first a white raven flying above the sun, flying higher even than the spotted eagle, Wanbli Galeshka, who circles close to the sun but not above it. So strong was the dream, your grandfather felt he was awake in it right to the last pictures, the sun falling apart into many feathers in the west, then the crescent moon above the sun and the dark circle within the crescent's shining. Within that circle, a white raven tried to spread its wings and fly free."

Isaac's hand trembles upon Nathan's arm, and Nathan realizes his arm, too, is shaking, as his father speaks again.

"Your grandfather awoke and told the dream to his father. Spreading Eagle took him that day to the lodge of a holy man, Tatanka Yotanka, the one the whites called Sitting Bull. He had just come from a sun dance east of the Wolf Mountains and had seen many soldiers falling from their horses, soldiers who had no ears. Yet Tatanka Yotanka was ready to hear your grandfather's dream.

When your grandfather had spoken his dream, the holy man waited until the last of the fire was gone from the pipe they had smoked. Then he spoke. 'Young men go forth in search of a vision and the spirit of Elk, Bear, Wolf or Eagle answers as he chooses and chooses the power he will give. But White Raven has hunted for you and for your help, that he may spread his wings and fly again. What he asks of you is what he will give you. If you will take what he gives, you must find those who know Raven, what he knows and what he cries, and who cry and laugh with him for what he knows. Then your eyes may see through your dream, to that place where White Raven would spread his wings.'

Isaac smiles. "Remember, your grandfather was only seven and knew of no other people than the Lakota, their Cheyenne brothers and friends, and those who were their enemies, and the whites, but what would they know? So he asked, 'Where will I find a people who know Raven?' Tatanka Yotanka lifted the pipe until the stem pointed north, west, then northwest. He lowered the pipe and spoke nothing more.

After sundown that day the crescent moon came out again and stayed until the night on the Greasy Grass misted over. Your grandfather could barely see the dark circle and nothing of his dream in it, so he let it go, went visiting up and down the camps of the Lakota and Cheyenne, and watched the young men and women dance away the night because nobody saw in the night anything of what was coming with the day."

Once again, Isaac falls silent. Nathan relaxes in the curve of his father's arm and waits.

"When the fight was over, the people went many ways the next day, leaving soldiers still alive along the bluffs farther back from where Custer and his soldiers died. The oldest brother, One Eagle, took your great-grandmother, Drum Woman, and his two brothers and wandered about with some others for the summer and a winter, and into another summer and winter, but the buffalo were hard to find, and the soldiers kept coming after them, like wolves after a wounded bull.

Tatanka Yotanka and those with him had crossed the Medicine Line into this country. So Wounded Drum said, 'Let us go into the Grandmother's country and find them.' Then, a few years later, Tatanka Yotanka went back across the Medicine Line, and One Eagle and Drum Woman went with him. But Wounded Drum and your grandfather headed north, to be with Poundmaker of the Cree, and were with his people at Cutknife Hill when they fought the Canadian soldiers. After that fight, Poundmaker knew the prairie would drink the blood of his people if they kept fighting, so he went to Fort Battleford to surrender, but sent your grandfather and his brother south to the Nakoda, near the place called Morely, in Alberta, because the Nakoda were the people of Poundmaker's father.

Wounded Drum stayed with the Nakoda, but your grandfather went north again, then west until he came to this ocean, and to Haida Gwaii where he met and married your grandmother. The song I sang the morning we came here was the song Wounded Drum sang to his brother as your grandfather rode away."

Nathan's head swims with all Isaac has told him, and with exhaustion. But now there are things he wants to know. "How did Grandfather know to come to Haida Gwaii?"

"He met a Haida in Montana working on a white man's ranch before he went north of the Medicine Line. The Haida told him where to look for the people of the Raven."

Nathan sits and considers the things he has seen and heard. "What do I do, now?" he asks, when he is able to form a question.

Isaac looks out into the clear sky to the west. "Some things are bigger than one person's life. Your grandfather did not see through, all the way through, to where White Raven's wings want to spread. But what he dreamed is now what you have seen, and you alone can decide what you will do with what you have seen."

"It was Raven's eye. The whole picture looked like Raven's eye," Nathan says.

"Then become Raven's Eye, so you can see through Raven's eye, because that is your name, Gwawinastoo, Raven's Eye, the name Axilaogua is holding for you and will give you, when she knows you are ready to take it."

"I was upriver, past the big house, and met Raven. When I looked into his eye, I saw . . . I saw nothing but me, looking back at me . . ."

"Then see through that. Begin by seeing through that," Isaac says. He takes his drum in hand, gathers in the silence and the day's light and begins to sing the song he had sung the first morning, the song Wounded Drum had sung long ago to the brother beginning his search for the People of the Raven, to the grandfather Nathan must now see through.

EIGHT

A few days before Nathan's twelfth birthday, the teacher of the grade six class walks out in tears and threatens to resign.

"Well?" Edith says, folding her hands together and looking across the table at Nathan.

"Well, what?"

"Don't you play dumb with me. She said you were right in the thick of it. One of the ringleaders, she said."

Nathan shrugs and says nothing.

"What's she done to you and the others that you treat her like dirt?"

"She didn't do anything," Nathan says, at last, aware that Adha is listening in as she cooks soup at the stove.

"Well, then?" Edith asks.

Nathan shrugs again. "I don't know why we started picking on her. It's just . . ."

"Just what?"

"Just the way she teaches."

"What about the way she teaches?"

"It doesn't . . . it doesn't have anything to do with us. With me."

Adha turns away from her soup. "Give a for instance."

"Well, she's been teaching us science, and she said that we're all just animals, nothing more than smart animals."

"Well, the animals are our relatives," Adha says.

"I know, but it didn't feel like she was saying that." Confused, Nathan hesitates. "Is that what it means when we say the animals are our relatives? That we're just animals?"

Adha sighs. "No, it doesn't mean that. It means that our animal brothers and sisters are more than just animals, and we are who we are."

Adha returns to her soup, as Edith says, "All right. She may have said something that doesn't fit with the way we see things, but next time walk by it and don't treat her like dirt. No person deserves to be treated like that. Do you understand?"

The quiet force of his mother's words puts Nathan firmly in his place. "Yes," he nods.

"Go on, then, and make sure a few others get the same message."

Outside, on the bottom porch step, Nathan gathers himself together then walks over to his father's carving shed. Isaac is somewhere else, maybe with Uncle Sam or Bert. Nathan sits on the stump and picks up the eagle mask his father is making for Bert's potlatch next fall, when Hector will become Hamatsa. He wonders if Hector's mother is giving Hector hell, but then Hector had held back some, also Peter and Naomi. Not so Nathan. He had been one of the instigators and for what reason? Nathan doesn't dislike the teacher, though he and everyone else knows she won't stay beyond this year.

As Nathan turns the mask over, the thought occurs that, maybe, he wants to be thrown out of school, or held back so he won't have to go to Port Hardy at the end of grade eight. Port Hardy didn't do much for David who had graduated in June and stayed there trying to find work, even though Uncle Charlie had offered to take him on as a fisherman. Troubled, Nathan remembers the last time he saw David, David's mask drawn down the whole length of himself to make himself as invisible as possible.

Margaret is different, because she is smart, studies, and gets top grades. She will graduate in June and go to college in Vancouver, she says, and then to one of the universities, and stay with a white friend, a girl in her school whose family is moving to Vancouver. The thought of going as far away as Vancouver is more than Nathan can think. He doesn't want to leave Duxsowlas even for high school, but wants to stay with his father and mother, and Adha, even Uncle Charlie, and with Frank.

Nathan chuckles as he thinks of Frank, with his own little room now at the back of the house filled with eagle feathers that Frank finds wherever he turns, ever since he found that first feather at Bone Spit three years ago.

Last summer Uncle Charlie had taken Edith, Nathan, and Frank out in his new boat, not a speedboat like Harvey's but still with a big outboard engine. Coming around the north end of Log Island, Uncle Charlie had slowed the boat so they could look up at the Giant, then beneath the Sitka alder that grew out from the rocky east bench of the island. "Uncle, look!" Frank had said, from the bow. Uncle Charlie nosed the boat closer to the island.

"What's he found?"

"Don't know. What are you looking at, Frank?" Edith had replied.

"Over there, on the water!"

Nathan moved forward, beside Frank. "It's an eagle feather, Mom."

"Ooh, God, another one!" Edith groaned.

Uncle Charlie laughed. "It was you that told him Eagle was leaving them just for him."

"I know. Believe me, I know. Nathan, help him reel it in, please."

"I can get it," Frank insisted. Uncle Charlie slowed the boat to a crawl, and Frank leaned out over the water with Nathan's hand gripping at his belt. When his bum was back on the bow seat, Frank held up his prize—a long wing feather.

"Well, that one is a beauty, I must admit," Edith had said.

She looked the feather over as Uncle Charlie laughed again and said, "We should give you a name, Frank, to go with all those feathers: Dzulhdzulas."

Frank liked the sound of the name. "What does it mean?"

"'Where you go?' . . . Then something about feathers," Nathan had ventured.

Edith smiled. "That's pretty close. 'Where you go for feathers,' that's what it means."

"So when anybody in Duxsowlas wants a feather, he knows where to go," Uncle Charlie said, laughing yet again. Nathan remembers that laugh because Uncle Charlie has never laughed that much and now carries a sadness about him.

The sun peeps out at Nathan from behind a layer of cloud. He heads along to the soccer field where Peter and Hector will be kicking a ball around. He wants to know what their mothers said to them.

Easter comes late that year, after the spring salmon have started to run. Home for a few days, Margaret stands in the kitchen with Edith cutting the salmon into fillets, while Nathan and Frank lounge in the living room. Nathan studies an old newspaper and Frank rereads a well-worn comic book. Troubled beneath her usual reserve, Margaret wipes her glasses with a towel, then goes again at the salmon with silent intensity.

"Don't butcher them," Edith warns.

"I'm not," Margaret shoots back, keeping the knife in motion. Then she stops, knife poised above the fish. "Has Minnie told you?"

"About what?"

Margaret brushes back a lock of her hair and stares forward into the cupboard door. "That figures." She starts to cut again, but slowly now, as she feels her mother looking at her.

"It's about David."

"What about David?" Edith sets her knife down and wipes her hands on her apron. Although Nathan keeps his eyes fixed upon the newspaper, he feels Margaret's quick glance at Frank and at him.

"He's suspected of molesting a young boy."

"Ooh! My God," Edith whispers.

Margaret watches her mother's reaction, then drops her knife onto the counter. "Does that really surprise you, Mom? Those who are abused become abusers. Or haven't you figured that one out? I need a break; see you in a while."

Then she is out the door. Edith sits at the kitchen table, her knife still in her hand, then sets the knife down and goes into her bedroom.

"Nathan?" Frank says, after a moment.

"Yes?"

"What's an abuser?"

"Something I don't think you want to know about," Nathan says. He puts the paper down and walks outside. Margaret is nowhere in sight. Nathan goes over to the carving shed where Isaac's tools lie idle because Uncle Charlie and Isaac are out fishing. He picks up a D-shaped adze from the stump and turns it about in his hand as he turns Margaret's words about in his head, only they are not in his head he finds but stuck somewhere in his chest, stuck so tight he can barely breathe.

The adze is carved in the shape of a raven, the tailfeathers sweeping in from the tip of the handle to become wings pressed tightly against the body that curves around the handle, then flattens across the top into the raven head from which the sharp, beak-shaped blade protrudes.

Nathan touches at the blade with his thumb, and then the sound of angry voices draws him back to his house. As he climbs the porch steps, the voices pierce him through.

"For Christ's sake, Mom! Can't you see what's happened to Pam, and Mary? And to David?"

"Don't you tell me what I can see or can't see!"

"Deny, deny, deny! That's how you live, that's how everyone here lives. Go to the potlatches, go to church, go through the motions, and always look the other way. Well, I'm tired of looking the other way, and my life is too short to waste on people too stiff in their necks to turn their heads and look things in the eye."

Nathan peers through the doorway as Margaret disappears into one of the bedrooms. Edith stands at the counter, her face white. Frank gets up from the couch where he has cowered the past few moments and goes to the bedroom door. His voice is shaking as he speaks. "What are you doing, Maggie?"

"Packing up my life, little brother, so I can get on with it." Her voice rises above the sound of drawers opening, closing, then the snapping shut of a suitcase. She emerges from the bedroom, a canvas bag slung over her shoulder and the suitcase in her hand. "This is all I need. Give the rest away. I'm going out on tomorrow's plane. I'll spend the night with Sadie."

Margaret walks to the door, and Frank starts to cry. Edith stares at her daughter and does not move, does not speak. Margaret turns to her once more. "You know, Mom, the only reason no one pushed his way into me is because I stayed away, right away. I wish David could have done that." She walks past Nathan, down the steps.

Dazed, Nathan follows her. At the bottom step, Margaret drops her bags, swings about, and holds him close. He clutches her and feels her tears against his cheek. "Goodbye, Nathan. Look out for yourself."

He stands and watches his sister cross the soccer field with quick, determined steps, her canvas bag swinging back and forth from her shoulder.

Edith does not speak to Nathan or Frank the rest of the day, nor the next morning. At the first sound of the plane, she goes out on the porch, sits, and watches the plane touch down, then gun its way over to the landing. Nathan stands behind her and sees the figure at the landing climb into the plane. Then, the whirling propeller blowing the water around it to a fine spray, the plane taxis along Log Island, turns, and with a roar takes off past Bone Spit, leaving only its echo resounding up the valley as it climbs the sky southward.

Sadie crosses the soccer field taking her time. She climbs the steps and sits beside Edith. "I've got a pile of salmon that need to be filleted.

How about coming down and giving me a hand, Edith?" Sadie says, at last. Edith leans against Sadie and sobs. Sadie puts her arm around Nathan's mother and holds her fast, while Edith rocks herself against the warmth of Sadie. "Come on, Edith. Come and help me with that salmon."

Late in the summer, most of Duxsowlas decides to boat over to Sand Island for a salmon barbecue and a day of lying in the sun. Nathan, Peter, and Hector sit on the sand, eating salmon and passing the dish of oolichan grease back and forth. "Good grease. Go get some more, Nathan. My mom has cut me off," Hector says.

"Forget it, Nathan! If Hector is going to be out in the forest without food for four days, he'd better start training now," Peter insists.

"What's it like, being alone for four days?" Hector asks Nathan. Nathan looks down at his foot, which is drawing circles in the sand. He doesn't want to talk about his time on Log Island.

"It was okay. It would be different for each person, I guess."

"Were you scared at all?"

"Yes, once or twice."

"I'm going to come down through the smoke hole. That's how the Hamatsa used to come into the big house, in the old days. They're going to catch me with a blanket."

Nathan and Peter laugh. "They'd better have a lot of guys on that blanket," Peter says.

"I hope your sister comes home for the potlatch. Vera, Angie and the others look up to her," Hector says to Nathan.

"Do you think she will come?" Peter asks, when Nathan does not answer Hector.

"No, I don't think so," Nathan says. Then he goes away, into himself.

Two weeks ago, when everyone else was asleep and the summer night suddenly turned cold, Nathan had gotten out of bed, gone to the closet where the blankets were kept and pulled one out. The half-empty bottle was tucked away at the back of the closet, into the folds of the blanket beneath the one he had just taken. He held the bottle in his hand and knew at once what it was. But whose? Isaac or Edith? He put the bottle back. The next day when no one was around, he went into the closet again. But the bottle was gone.

Nathan began to look for other hiding places and found a bottle nearly full at the back of the top cupboard in the kitchen, and then another tucked down inside the water tank of the toilet when he had lifted the tank lid to find out why the toilet bowl wasn't filling as it should. Isaac? No, Nathan knew, as he stood with the dripping bottle in his hand; no, it did not belong to his father.

Fall mist wanders in from the Pacific and down from Duxdzas, as Duxsowlas makes ready for the Dawson potlatch. Bert and his family have prepared several years for this gathering when Hector will become Hamatsa, and Duxsowlas will remember Old Man Williams who died two weeks earlier. Isaac has carved several masks for the dances, the women have been gathering food for the feasts, and Hector is about to go out into the forest, to meet the being of Bakbakwalanooksiwae.

Hector, Peter, and Nathan stand at the carving shed as Isaac puts the finishing touches on a salmon mask. Isaac looks about him for the paint he will need soon, finding it is not there. He thinks a moment, then remembers. "Your uncle took that can to touch up some of his masks. Go and see if he still has it."

Nathan leads the way up to Uncle Charlie's, but Uncle Charlie is not home. Nathan calls out again.

"Maybe he's at my house, with my dad," Hector suggests.

Nathan is about to close the door, when he glimpses the chest in the corner of the room, partly open with a painted beak exposed to view. He has seen the chest many times, always closed, and knows it is where his uncle keeps his masks. Nathan pushes the door wide open and walks into the room.

"What are you doing?" Hector asks.

"Taking a closer look," Nathan replies, his fingers upon the chest.

"A look at what?"

Nathan does not answer. He lifts the lid back to the wall and gazes down at the Raven Humsumth mask.

"Wow!" breathes Hector, looking wide-eyed at Raven, then at the Huxwhuxw and Crooked Beak masks beneath it.

Nathan lifts the Raven mask from the chest and turns it until the beak stretches out before him and he is looking down at Raven's eyes. He turns the mask to the left, then the right, and studies each of Raven's eyes as the beak swings from side to side. Hector and Peter watch. Hector shifts uneasily from foot to foot. Peter looks on fascinated as Nathan lifts the mask and places it down upon his head until the strips of cedar along the sides and back close around his head and shoulders.

"We shouldn't be here, doing this," Hector says.

"Try on the Huxwhuxw, Hector," Nathan says from beneath the Raven mask as he feels around for the string that moves the beak.

"No way!" Hector replies.

"I think we should go, Nathan," Peter decides.

Nathan finds the string and pulls it. Raven's beak snaps open. Nathan laughs and snaps the beak again as he begins to dance Raven's dance about the room. He swings the beak right around almost hitting both Peter and Hector, but Peter ducks and Hector jumps back. Peering through the cedar strips, Nathan sees another Raven mask looking at his from the mirror on the wall beside the chest.

What are
you looking at, Raven?

I'm looking at you, Raven.

Why are you looking at me,
Raven?

What else is there to look at,
Raven?

So, what can you say for yourself,
Raven?

Only this,
Raven.
as Nathan pulls the string:
Haa-p!

Nathan turns away from the mirror into the silence that has suddenly gripped the room. He lifts the mask from his head and sees Uncle Charlie standing in the doorway. Nathan stares at his uncle as Peter and Hector back themselves against the wall. Never has Nathan seen his uncle this angry, his Uncle's face almost white and his eyes ablaze with rage. Nathan looks down at the mask in his hands.

"Go! Go now!" Uncle Charlie says, seizing the mask from Nathan.

The three boys do not stop walking until they are in the middle of the soccer field. Hector and Peter avert their eyes from Nathan's.

"No point in us standing here," Peter says, and he and Hector set off for home. Nathan walks back to the carving shed, as if in a dream.

"What about that paint?" his father asks.

"I didn't see it," Nathan says, and walks away.

In the days that follow, Nathan waits with held breath for someone to speak to him, but no one does. Hector disappears into the forest upriver, the food goes into the ovens, and the Dawson potlatch begins late one afternoon with the mourning songs, especially those in memory of Old Man Williams. The Wanookqway gather in the big house and listen to the songs and speeches, and to Ed Williams telling who his father had been. Another song ends and then Uncle Charlie rises from his seat at the drum; he comes forward wearing his button vest and holding his talking stick. A hush falls upon the big house as if everyone there, Nathan included, had known such a moment had to come.

Uncle Charlie begins in Kwakwala, reminding the Wanookqway of who they are and how they have come to be at the mouth of their river. Then the English words start to come: "That Old Man was one of our elders, one of those who taught me to love and respect our stories, our dances, our masks. When I think of that Old Man, here, today, I am ashamed that I did not listen more or care more about what he was trying to tell me. And I am ashamed of those in this village and in my own family who do not respect our stories, our songs, our masks.

Our masks are not toys. We do not play with them when we show them, for they show who we are. They are as sacred to us as the things in a church are to those who go there. Years ago, people in villages along this coast stood at the water and saw our masks being taken away because a law other than our own tried to tell us we could not go on being who we are. Residential schools tried to tell us we could not be who we are, that we were a vanishing race and would end up in museums with our masks. That's what they tried to tell us—the Indian agents, the priests, teachers, and anthropologists, and we, even we, began to tell ourselves we didn't need those stories or dances, those masks anymore."

Nathan cannot look at his uncle or bear the sound of his uncle's voice.

"We are not toys or museum pieces, to be played with. We have not vanished; the dances and masks to be shown tonight are our witnesses to my words. The Wanookqway kept their masks, maybe because we were too small a people for the police boats to find, or because there were elders, Henry Watson, my father, along with Amos Dick, Lucy Dick, Simon Dawson, and this Old Man, who never let us forget what our dances and our masks were telling us. It's time we learned to respect what our elders knew and show respect for what we do when we come here and for everything sacred to us, because I am tired of being ashamed."

Nathan's shame burns red in the silence that gathers in the last of his uncle's words. He cannot lift his head to look about him, as Uncle Charlie returns to the drum and his Uncle Sam says some more gentle words before the time of mourning ends and supper begins. All through supper, Nathan sits at the far end of the big house, his eyes staring down into the plank of wood beneath his feet. Frank hands him a plate of food, but he sets it aside after one or two bites. He barely hears the first throbbing of the log drum or Hector's cry from the big house roof.

Haau—!

Hector drops down through the smoke hole into the waiting blanket, is caught without mishap, and begins his circling of the big house as the changing rhythms of the drum mark the stages of Hamatsa's return to the waiting circle of his people.

Haau—!

throm

       throm throm

throm

       throm throm

Haau—!

Hector circles, whirls about and about, then is led from the floor.

throm   throm   throm   throm

Mask by mask, Huxwhuxw, Crooked Beak, and at last, Raven, enter, coming from the world beyond the Tlaamelas, that other world Hamatsa has seen, that will not let Hamatsa go.

74

Ha ma myy

Ha myy Ha myy

Nathan lifts his head, stares across the big house; the voice of Naomi rises strong and clear above the beating of the drum. Naomi wears her cedar headband and her button blanket with its crescent moon crest. She moves her rattle as her voice falls, rises, and reaches out to the presence that dances the mask of Raven about the big house. Adha stands beside Naomi, but it is Naomi's singing that questions Raven and brings the healing words.

Ha ma myy

He lee kila yus
Bakbakwalanooksiwae

Naomi is beautiful and strong in her singing, in who she is, and Nathan can feel nothing but shame as he gazes at her.

At last, Hector reappears, his sister Vera leading him onto the big house floor. Hector's button blanket with its dangling skulls and his strong step show that he has returned to the circle of the Wanookqway, at peace with all who have witnessed his returning. But Nathan is not at peace with anyone in the big house, least of all himself. He does not hear the name Hector is given or anything that is sung or said the rest of the evening.

The potlatch ends with the distribution of gifts. In the relaxed movement of people back and forth, Nathan looks for a chance to slip away.

"This is for you, Nathan." Hector hands him a baseball hat. "It's for you, and so is this. Our family made it." Hector's other hand holds a canoe paddle. The two necks of Sisiutl run up the paddle's neck from either side of the blade to become two heads where the neck widens into the handle. The central face of Sisiutl fills out the blade, the two sides of it meeting at the tip.

Nathan takes the hat, then the paddle, but can find no words as he looks them over. The hat, too, is well-made with a Raven crest above the letters that spell out Dawson Potlatch, 1981. Hands in his pockets and wearing a button vest that comes down over the top of his jeans, Hector watches Nathan a moment.

"Well, I guess I'll see you soon," Hector says and walks away.

Nathan puts the hat on and pulls the brim of it down low on his forehead. He wants to cry but cannot make the tears come.

Glad that Christmas is over, Nathan pulls the candles from the wreath he had made, wishing he had watched Margaret more closely when she made wreaths. Margaret did not come home, nor David, nor Slim and Minnie, maybe because the fishing had been bad that year and maybe because Nathan's mother is now drinking openly.

One night at dinner, Frank had asked where the ketchup was.

"There isn't any," Edith snapped.

"Yes, there is. I saw you put it away, yesterday."

"Then it's put away. Stop whining and eat."

"But why can't I have some?"

Edith slapped her fork against the table and glared at Frank. "You really want the ketchup, do you?"

She kicked the chair out from under her, went to the cupboard next to the sink, and threw the door open. Her hand took the ketchup bottle by the neck, turned it about, then she smashed the bottle against the edge of the sink. Glass and ketchup splattered into the sink and across the room. Edith dumped what was left in the bottle into a dish, along with fragments of glass, and set the dish in front of Frank. "You wanted it. Now eat it!"

Frank looked up in disbelief and started to cry. Nathan stared into his plate, without moving, while his father sat quietly, looking at something beyond the wall of the house.

"Maybe you want to cut your inside to pieces, but don't cut up his, or Nathan's," Isaac said, his eyes now fixed on Edith.

Her gaze riveted upon her husband, Edith leaned against the sink and folded her arms. "Don't you preach to me, Isaac. You have no ground on which to preach to me." Crying, she walked outside, into the rain.

Having stripped the wreath of its candles, Nathan walks out onto the porch and heaves the wreath into the rain, toward the river and the forest beyond, to whatever is out there, Bakbakwalanooksiwae, maybe. "Just when you think the world has ended, you look about you and find it's still there," Adha had said. But Nathan's shaming at the big house stays with him, and he feels something in his world has ended, or changed for good, even though his life goes on. Peter and Hector are still his friends, though the hat Hector gave him is buried beneath a pile of clothes in a corner of Nathan's room and the paddle stands in another corner, gathering dust.

"Are we still friends?" Naomi had asked, a week before Christmas.

"Yeah, sure, we're friends," Nathan had replied. But Naomi, too, is changing, in the body she clothes with her button blanket or her jeans and leather jacket with the long fringes that sway down from the sleeves, and in the person that looks out from her body.

Hauw—

A raven lands near the river, looks around for something worth looking at, then spreads its wings. Nathan watches it go until it vanishes into the treeline upriver. Even the ravens have distanced themselves from him lately. As he walks back into the house, Nathan's eye is caught by a grey shaft of light that slides through the living room window. He follows the light, then holds his breath. The rifle has always been there, on the rack above the chest of drawers in the corner, but he has never truly seen it until now. He crosses the room. The rifle is old, a Winchester from the last century, yet for all the tarnish on it, the breech gleams out at him in the rain-filtered light.

Nathan takes the rifle from the rack. His hands close about the barrel, the stock, then explore the lever with a sureness that startles him, as if they know, of themselves, what they are about. He throws the lever, easily, and squeezes the trigger, taking aim at the coffee pot on the stove. As soon as the click sounds, he realizes the sound could have been different, that the gun might have been loaded and the coffee pot torn wide open, or that someone might have come through the doorway as he pulled the trigger.

He returns the gun to the rack, one hand coming to rest upon the stock. The other, shaking, drops down to the top of the chest, beside a photograph. It, too, has been there, leaning unseen against the wall. Nathan reaches for it and lifts it into the light.

Isaac wears the uniform of a soldier and stands beside a white man with laughing eyes and hair falling down over his forehead. The white man also wears a uniform, though it is different from his father's. He and Isaac stand with their arms around each other's shoulders. Both men are very young.

Even younger, maybe fourteen or fifteen, is the girl who stands in front of them, holding a small dog, her eyes also full of laughter, as though she wants nothing more from life than to be standing there with the two men. Nathan studies the girl's face. Although the photograph has faded with the years, he knows he has seen her face somewhere else, but not as the face of a girl.

Nathan stands a long time before the chest of drawers, one hand still on the stock of the rifle, the other holding the photograph, yet another riddle in his life.

NINE

David comes back to Duxsowlas in July, defeated and angry. He drinks too often to hold a job yet can find no reason to stop drinking. Rumours of his having molested a child remain only that. He moves in with his cousin, Billy Boy, until Sam tells him to go. He then moves into the empty house behind Harvey and Hazel's and throws parties throughout the summer, borrowing Harvey's speedboat whenever he wishes for trips to Thumb Harbour. Rarely does David appear at the other end of Duxsowlas, only now and then to grin knowingly at Edith or to see what he can borrow from Isaac, and he never goes near the house of his uncle. Uncle Charlie, in turn, spends days at a time away from Duxsowlas, fishing alone, and never speaks of David.

On a clear August day, Isaac sits at the kitchen table playing solitaire, while Edith bakes and is sober enough to guide the dough into the pan, then to the oven. Nathan and Frank sit on the couch. With Hector's walkman wrapped about his ears, Nathan drifts away for a time, from the uncertainty without and within.

David throws the door open. It crashes shut behind him as he drops down into the chair opposite Isaac. A grin slants across his mouth as he breathes alcohol fumes out into the room. Nathan draws the earphones away and observes while David's gaze wanders from Edith to Isaac, then back. "So where the hell is Uncle? I drop by to visit my favorite uncle, and what do you know, no Uncle."

No one answers David. David slaps the table and laughs. "That's what I love about my family. Always keeping track of one another. I bet Uncle is out in his boat, riding the waves. Uncle should have been a cowboy, bumping and humping horses across the wide prairie, like John Wayne, and shooting Indians out of the saddle, only they didn't wear saddles, those old-time Indians. They just dropped off, bareback, and played dead. But what the hell? We're all playing dead."

David falls silent. Edith pounds another lump of dough into a tin, her hands moving furiously. Isaac considers the seven of hearts and where to lay it down. Apprehensive, Nathan and Frank eye David closely.

"You got a spare bottle, Mom? I'll bring one back for you from Thumb Harbour, tonight."

Edith's hands stop, her fingers embedded in dough. She closes her eyes.

"Come on, Mom! From one drunk to another, because that's all that's left, getting drunk, and getting fucked, and there's not much of that going on around here."

Edith turns on him, her voice a hiss and a whisper: "If you ever, ever again walk into this house and talk to me like that, I will take one of those bottles you know so much about and ram it so far down your throat you'll have to start breathing somewhere else!"

David stares into the ceiling awhile after the door slams shut behind Edith. "Whoo-ee! Granddad should have called her Blaze, too. Well, so much for that little family visit."

"When are you going to Thumb Harbour?" Isaac asks.

"As soon as I can get my ass into that boat." David stands, steadies his hand against the chairback.

"Don't," Isaac says.

"Give me a reason."

"There's a storm on the way."

"Bullshit! The weather report said nothing about a storm."

Isaac glances out the window. "Maybe not, but it's coming anyway, and it will be there waiting for you when you leave Thumb Harbour."

David shakes his head, but Isaac's words won't be shaken away. "Then who's bullshitting me? You, or the guy on the radio?"

"The guy on the radio won't be in the boat with you or with anyone else along for the ride." And now Isaac looks directly at David. David stares back.

"I'll think about it," David says. Isaac watches the door close behind him, then plays another card.

By morning the storm that had swept along the coast is well out at sea. Nathan awakens early to the sound of something scraping at the side of the house. He dresses and goes outside to find David trying to pull his canoe from beneath the house where it had been left, barely used. Nathan rubs the sleep from his eyes and realizes David is sober.

"Give me a hand with this, Nathan, please."

"Sure. Where are you taking it?"

"To the soccer field. Where else?" Then David smiles at Nathan's confusion. "Maybe we could put it in at the river mouth." Sheepishly, Nathan smiles back.

"I guess it's been awhile since I've teased you," David says when they have set the canoe into the water and he has finished examining it. "Don't know why I'm looking so closely for trouble spots when I can count on one hand the times I've taken it out. Tell Uncle I used it. That may make him happy."

"Where are you going?" Nathan asks, puzzled by the way David speaks.

"Out to Log Island. To think about things. That's far enough away for me to think about things without torching others with my thinking." David brings his gaze back from Log Island, to fix it upon Nathan.

"What are you looking at?" Nathan asks.

"At my little brother, only you're not so little anymore. You know, you almost split Mom in two when you were born. But Maggie and I were really excited when you came, even though you were the funniest looking Weesa we had ever seen."

As he listens, Nathan is nearly overwhelmed by the warmth and longing he suddenly feels toward the brother who has moved along the edge of Nathan's life and along an edge of his own. David comes around the end of the canoe and hugs Nathan. "Give a hug to my little, little brother, too, after you push me off the beach."

David climbs into the canoe and takes hold of the paddle as Nathan pushes him free of the land. He strokes the canoe about for a last glance at Duxsowlas. "Ha-la-kasla, Nathan," he says, and begins to paddle in the direction of Log Island.

In the dead of night, Nathan awakens with a start. The cry echoes at his ear as he goes from his bed to the front door. His mother stands on the porch. As her face turns to meet his, he sees the light flickering from her cheek and then the flames rising from Log Island.

"David?" Edith whispers.

Nathan leaps from the porch and races for the beach, the pebbles stabbing at his feet as they scatter aside. He can see figures gathering at the water's edge. Two shapes heave Uncle Charlie's boat into the water. He cries out as he leaves the land behind and the water rises up about him, his arms stroking for the boat until his body also screams out for want of air to keep it going.

Isaac sees Nathan coming and calls to Uncle Charlie. The boat slows enough for Isaac to grip Nathan by the shoulder and pull him in. Uncle Charlie opens the throttle wide, and the boat leaps forward toward the gap between Sand Island and Log Island. But the fire has out-manoeuvred them and blanketed the gap over with red heat that hisses down into the water, as the flames try to leap across to Sand Island.

"Outside!" Isaac bellows, and Uncle Charlie spins the boat about to speed north along the wall of flame that devours the treeline right to Log Island's north end. The boat ploughs out into the first swelling of the ocean rolling in from the darkness to the west. Uncle Charlie turns toward the shoreline, but the fire repels them, again and again, thrusting the boat back against the incoming swell until the whole of Log Island is wrapped in flame.

The boat slows to a crawl. Uncle Charlie's hand goes slack on the throttle. His eyes search the shoreline helplessly like those of Isaac and Nathan. Having secured the island to itself, the fire now turns all its force on the north end where the Giant stands. Flame upon flame gathers at the foot of the Giant and leaps upward to take hold of the lower branches. Once dark against the night, the crown of the Giant begins to glow. As if to absorb the heat of the fire and release Log Island from its grip, the Giant draws the frenzy of flame into itself. With a roar, the crown of the Giant explodes into the night, showering sparks in all four directions, sparks that fall into the swelling of the ocean about Uncle Charlie's boat. Log Island groans and sighs as the fire drops away from the Giant and folds back into itself, flame upon flame about Log Island, to burn out into the night.

Uncle Charlie's face is stricken in the afterlight, his hand on the throttle. Isaac bows his head a long moment, then takes the throttle from Uncle Charlie. Nathan reaches out and leads his uncle forward, as if he is leading a child whose world has been violated beyond any healing. Slowly Isaac rounds the north end of Log Island. Above them the crown of the Giant presses its light against the layers of cloud. The swelling of the water dies down to a glassy expanse that laps quietly onto the beach of Duxsowlas. Isaac slows, then cuts, the motor.

Within the light that dances up from the water, Nathan can see the two heads of Sisiutl dancing. Gently the water rises then falls as the nose of David's canoe washes softly up onto the sand and comes to rest.

The voice at the drum lifts the mourning song high above the drum's slow, steady throb. But for the tears gathered at the corners of the eyes, the faces about the big house contain grief and do not wear it as an open, contorted wound.

> We have known this time before,
> many times,
>> known a life can come
> to such an end. We have witnessed
> this ending too many times before,
> to pretend we do not know this is
>> the way a life can end.

So the masks of grief would speak, given any inclination to speak. Only Mr. Blaisdell tries to place words into that silence as he stands before the open hole at Bone Spit.

"Blaze has told me David's name was Kisoowaci Xwagwana, His-Canoe-Holds-a-Treasure. David's canoe was fashioned to hold David, but he could not, did not see his life as a treasure to be held. What then does it take for someone to treasure the life he is given, as much as Christ treasures it, enough to die for each one of us? That we might treasure ourselves? What does it take to believe in that treasure?"

The questions hang in the grey stillness above Bone Spit as Mr. Blaisdell commits David's bones and ashes to the earth. Then the shovels and spades lift the earth from the mound beside the grave, let it fall through the light rain until the wound in the earth is closed and Duxsowlas leaves Bone Spit to its own silence.

Mr. Blaisdell stays the night at Adha's, drinks tea with Edith and Isaac, and tries to visit with Uncle Charlie. The next morning Nathan and Frank stand on the beach and watch Mr. Blaisdell's plane dodge the clouds until it is no more. Nathan looks over at Log Island, now only a scar scorched into the skin of sky and water, and at the black trunk of the Giant, its crown stripped of any pretense to life.

"Are you going away, too, Nathan?"

"What are you talking about?"

"Maggie went away. Now David's gone away. Are you going to stay, Nathan?"

Shaken by the tears he sees in his brother's eyes, Nathan turns away and cannot find nor make an answer.

TEN

On the morning of Nathan's fourteenth birthday, a Sunday, Isaac, Edith, Adha, Uncle Charlie, and Frank are seated at the table when Nathan walks into the kitchen.

"You don't look quite ready for this new day in your life. What can I cook up for you to help you get here?" Edith asks. She is sober and has stayed sober since the day of David's death.

"A strong cup of coffee."

"Are you drinking that stuff already?"

Nathan nods, still rubbing the sleep from his eyes. His mother sighs and puts the water on for a fresh pot. "Well, it's your birthday, I guess. Sit down and I'll cook up some hot cakes to go with it."

"Here," Frank says, as Nathan sits in the chair beside his. Nathan takes the parcel wrapped in a page from the comic section of a newspaper. Nathan grins at the cartoon figures and unwinds a length of string that secures the parcel many times over. The paper unfolds to reveal one of Frank's feathers from the wing of an eagle, wrapped around at its base with a strip of blue cloth into which Frank has stuffed eagle down. A leather thong hangs down from the cloth.

"Adha helped me with the stitching," Frank says shyly. A twinge of pain rises into Nathan's eyes as he looks at his brother.

"It's a nice present, Frank."

Uncle Charlie shifts his weight forward and feels for his words. "Your Adha and I are giving a memorial potlatch in the fall, for David. It's good that grade nine will be in Duxsowlas this year, because it will be very important that you are here for that potlatch."

Nathan swallows as he begins to understand what his uncle might be saying and realizes this is the first time his uncle has ever spoken to him in this way. He glimpses the touch of sorrow in his uncle's gaze and is almost moved to ask, "What's wrong, Uncle? What has happened to you? What has hurt you?" Instead Nathan simply nods, to show he understands.

"There's another present, a piece of hard work," his father says. "Your Adha and your uncle have asked me to carve a memorial pole for David to be raised at the head of Bone Spit. I need someone to carve with me, and I want you to be that person. I hope that sounds like a birthday present."

Nathan takes a deep breath and looks around at his family. "It sounds good."

Edith sets hot cakes and coffee down in front of Nathan. "I think I'll stock up on band-aids," she says.

"My present is waiting for you where I stay, when your stomach is tired of hot cakes and coffee," says Adha.

Nathan takes his time eating, savouring the hot cakes, the coffee, and the gifts he has been given or promised. He savours another gift as well. The band council of Duxsowlas has decided to take the education of its children more firmly in hand. Starting next fall, the grade nine students will stay in Duxsowlas instead of going to Port Hardy.

Later in the morning, Nathan walks through Adha's house to her sitting room and waits for her to finish crocheting a few last stitches. He notices her fingers do not move as easily as they once did.

"The present I'm giving you is not one you can hold in your hand, but maybe your ears will make a place for it and your heart. You know David's canoe?" Adha lays down her hook and takes off her glasses.

"Yes."

"What's on the side of it?"

"Sisiutl."

Adha gazes past her grandson, into the forest upriver. Then she continues. "David could not look Sisiutl in the face, even though Sisiutl was there on both sides of his canoe. Not many people can look Sisiutl in the face, and you might end up being one of them unless you can find a way of facing up to Sisiutl. How many faces does Sisiutl have?"

"Three, I think?"

"Why do you say, I think?"

"Because maybe the faces are all the same?"

Adha studies him. "Maybe, in the end. But along the way you'll have to decide where you are going to begin. Some people can look at that face in the centre all their lives long, look at it so strongly and cleanly that they never have to worry about those two faces at either end—as if those necks and heads looking opposite ways don't exist for such people. But there are others who can't meet that face in the centre without first meeting those faces at either end of Sisiutl and bringing them together, even if they're split in two trying to do that. I think you are going to be one of those others, and that's my gift to you this birthday, telling you what I think. If I'm right, don't spend much time with that centre face or pretend you can meet it until you've learned what each of those end faces is about."

Unable now to bear Adha's gaze, Nathan looks away from her into the forest and upriver. When he feels the chairback creasing the flesh beneath his shoulder blades, he brings his eyes back to hers. "Thanks. I'll try to remember that."

"That's good. Damn! Where did I put that crocheting hook? And my glasses?"

By early April, the right log of cedar stretches the length of Isaac's carving shed. Isaac and Nathan strip the bark from the log with elbow adzes and a chainsaw, then round it down until it becomes a pole-to-be. Nathan brings blistered hands and aching joints to school throughout April until his muscles and blisters become callouses.

Once the pole is rounded, Isaac sketches in the first of the main figures, starting with Raven at the bottom. Raven's beak will extend down from the point between his eyes to his human-shaped feet. The eyes themselves will be big and round, painted solid black, with their sockets raying out on either side—unlike the eyes of the Raven on the village pole that gaze starkly outward and upward as though, thinks Nathan, Raven would ask himself a question, if he knew what his question was.

Above the sweep of Raven's eyebrows, Isaac draws the face of Sisiutl, whose piercing gaze is anything but inward. The pupils of Sisiutl's eyes pull together in their sockets and seem to search for the one able to meet whatever he sees of himself in the eyes of Sisiutl.

Reaching upward, the two necks bend back toward one another and form two heads, back to back, that look up to the last length of pole, where Isaac's pencil lifts away from the wood.

"We'll let the pole tell us what it wants to go there, when it's ready to speak."

By May the lines, curves, and crevices of Raven have declared themselves, and those of Sisiutl are close behind. One day, Nathan looks up from Raven's beak to see a figure coming toward them from the house. His father straightens up and his face breaks into a broad smile. "Yo, John!"

"Yo, Isaac. Ghe-la-kasla."

"I was beginning to think you had died and not told anyone."

Sam Dick's brother, and Peter's uncle, grins back at Isaac, and at Nathan. "I know. It's taken me a long time to make it here. And who is this person? He was falling into grease pits the last I heard."

Isaac laughs at the question on Nathan's face. "I guess you don't remember. We'll remind you in a few minutes, when we break for tea."

John Dick walks around the pole, his eyes touching along the length of it then returning to the open stretch above Sisiutl. He strokes his chin and smiles quizzically, as Isaac chuckles. "I know, it's not an orthodox way of starting out, but I want the pole to tell me what it wants there."

"Has it spoken anything yet?"

"Maybe. But I'm going to listen and look some more before I start cutting. We can't wait too much longer, though. That Raven wants to keep us moving."

Now John Dick chuckles. "He looks like he's thinking about running for chief councillor."

"Peter thinks you carved the Raven on the pole by the big house and the rest of it, too. At least, that's what he thought when we were little," Nathan says.

John Dick's eyes widen, but he looks pleased.

"That pole was done well before my time, but I'd like to think I'm that good with a knife."

"Whoever did it sure carved Raven's eyes in a funny way. One of them looking out to sea, the other at the sky."

John Dick thinks about that. "It could be he wanted to give you two ways of seeing the same thing. Isaac, did you say something about tea?"

Edith points to the bearskin draped across the couch as the three of them walk in. "Something John brought us, from his trapline. I wonder how Grizzly will feel about us keeping his skin on our couch."

"I'd forgotten you were a hunter," Isaac says quietly.

"Only when my gun works. And speaking of guns . . ." John Dick's eyes light up at the sight of the rifle on the far wall. He turns to Isaac. "May I have a look?"

Isaac nods. John Dick brings the rifle to the table, sits and begins to inspect it, leaving his tea untouched. "I suspect there are museums that would want this as much as they wanted our masks."

"It was my grandfather's," Isaac says.

John Dick sips at his tea and inspects the rifle even more closely. "Has Peter worked on the pole with you?"

Nathan laughs. "He came one day, but decided playing rock and roll was more to his liking."

John Dick works the lever and looks at the breech. "It seems I'm going to be the only carver in our family. I warned Sam about letting him buy that guitar. Isaac, has this gun ever been fired?"

Startled, Nathan's father leans back in his chair. "I can't think that it hasn't been. My grandfather took it into a fight, and so did my father."

"Did either of them fire it?"

"They must have," Isaac insists.

"Have you ever fired it?"

"No, though there are cartridges for it in the top drawer. I've fired other guns, many times, but never that one." A shadow crosses Isaac's face as he speaks, while John Dick looks again at the rifle in his hands.

"I wonder," he says.

Light plays across Nathan's hands as he works with his knife to deepen the shadow cast by Raven's wing across his human knee. As he works, Nathan thinks about things, things that have a way of hiding themselves behind themselves.

He was standing at the school drinking fountain on Thursday, about to turn the handle, when Naomi bumped him to one side.

"I was here first," she said, staring at him and waiting for him to do something.

"Okay, you were here first," Nathan said, looking at her strangely before he walked away.

Friday noon, he was sitting on the top step of the porch to his classroom, eating lunch, when Naomi sat down beside him.

"You're sitting in my place." She slapped her bum against his and started to push.

"Since when is this your place?" Nathan returned, aware that his own bum was confused and awaiting instructions.

"Since always. You're an insensitive pig, Nathan. So smarten up!"

Naomi kept pushing with her bum, relentlessly, until the edge of the step was nearly under Nathan's bum. "The hell with this!" he decided and started to push back, hard enough to move Naomi along the step until he was sitting back where he had been sitting. Naomi took a deep breath, then went at him again. Back and forth the two of them went, bum to bum, while their schoolmates gaped from the bottom of the steps until they stopped, suddenly, and moved apart.

In the last hour of that school day, Nathan sat at his desk, a box of pencils open before him. He looked up. Naomi stood at his desk, her arms folded across her breast, her head cocked to one side, looking down at him. Then she picked up the pencil box, turned it upside down, and the pencils fell with a clatter on Nathan's desk, bounced and rattled all about and rolled off, one by one.

Naomi replaced the pencil box and returned to her desk. Everyone in the classroom left off writing or drawing and watched Nathan walk down the aisle to Naomi's desk. Naomi looked up from her binder, set her pencil down, and folded her arms. Nathan took the binder, opened the snaps, turned it upside down, and shook the paper loose. Sheets of paper rained down on Naomi, the last one lighting on her hair then sliding along her nose. Nathan placed the binder down amid the paper and went back to his desk.

The teacher sat and watched it all, a knowing look playing on his face, picked up his pencil, and returned to whatever he had been doing.

A shadow falls on Nathan's hands. Naomi stands beside the pole. "You'll go blind, working in the dark."

"It's not dark yet."

"No, but it's on its way," Naomi says, as the sun sets and the pole sinks into shadow.

Nathan puts the adze down. "Maybe you're right. Let's go sit on the log by the river and look at the sunset we've just missed."

Log Island darkens to a charred line against the horizon as they sit, not too close to one another, and each waits for the other to speak.

"What are you trying to prove?" Nathan asks.

"For a long time I just thought the cat had your tongue and wouldn't give it back. But then it got mine, too, and I was becoming desperate."

Nathan takes a deep breath. "Are you going to shove me first or am I going to shove you? To loosen up our tongues."

"Do we still need to do that?"

"No, I guess not," Nathan replies. He slips his arm about her and draws her to him.

Naomi closes the door of her house behind her. From Peter's house, the first phrases of a song reach out to Nathan as he heads home.

> The first time
> ever I saw your face
> I thought the sun
> rose in your eyes . . .

Looking out into the darkness to the west, he sees the crescent moon above the horizon.

> And the moon and the stars
> were the kiss you gave
> to the dark
> and the endless skies
> my love . . .

Nathan walks toward the song.

> And the first time
> ever I kissed your mouth,
> I felt the earth
> move in my hand . . .

Peter sits on his porch, his transistor radio beside him. Light from a gas lamp pours out through the open doorway. Nathan climbs the steps and sits beside Peter. After the song plays itself out and the last strokes of the guitar lift away into the night, Peter turns the radio off. Only the hiss of the lamp touches into the darkness.

"That's Roberta Flack. She's a good singer," Peter says.

"It's a good song," says Nathan.

Peter smiles. "I know. I have eyes. I'm going to learn that song, on my guitar. I'm learning the traditional songs, too. My dad is teaching me so I can sing in the big house. I'm going to sing both ways. I might even know a song in time for your uncle's potlatch."

"That would be good," Nathan says, as his Aunt Lila appears in the doorway. "You two look as if you could do with some freshly baked bread, and jam, and a cup of tea. It's ready right now."

As he stands, Nathan looks again where the moon had been, but it has dropped below the horizon.

ELEVEN

On the longest day of summer, the sun splits the clouds open as Peter steers his new boat upriver.

"It's a good boat, Pete," Nathan says, his T-shirt flapping against his skin.

"It's been used, but I don't mind."

"Your dad's pretty good, to let you take it upriver the first day you have it," says Hector.

"He's given me some lessons and advice, and anyway, he said it's yours now. If you crack it up the first time out, you can spend the day swimming home."

Curving into the big bend at Snag Point, Peter suddenly slows right down. "Holy man! Look at that! One, two, three . . ."

The trees about Snag Point are filled with eagles, eagles on the dead branches of cottonwoods, on the naked crowns of spruce and cedar.

"Watch that snag, Pete!" Hector calls out.

"I see it. Six, seven, eight . . ."

"Pete!"

"I see it! Twelve. Twelve of them. But what are they doing here?"

"Hanging out, I guess," Hector says, even though Peter has directed his question to Nathan. Strangely troubled by the question and by the presence of the eagles, Nathan watches Peter's hand as Peter dodges another snag and begins to count again.

Just after midnight Nathan leaves Peter's house. At the edge of the soccer field, the figure waiting beside the goal post comes toward him. Naomi's eyes are big in the darkness as they search out his. Suddenly, she takes him by the hand and draws him after her, skirting the tree line at the back of Duxsowlas until they are clear of Sadie's. She leads him out onto the sand and across the neck of Bone Spit. When they reach the graveyard, Naomi sinks to the ground and pulls Nathan down beside her. Her arms close about his neck and the rest of her presses against him. Then she becomes very still, but for the beating of her heart as she trembles within the circle of his arms. Nathan's head spins. The warmth of her stirs into him and he feels his body awakening to her.

"Don't, please don't!" she whispers, yet her arms tighten about him.

"What is it, Naomi?" Nathan pleads, his hand stroking her hair back from her cheek. Her eyes search him out again, full of a knowing she does not want but can no longer evade.

"My father came into my room last night, sat on my bed, and started to touch me . . . O God, Nathan, I knew something was wrong when Pam left, and then Mary, and when Mary started to drink and throw herself like a bone to anybody who wanted her. But I didn't want to believe it could be my father, my father screwing their lives around, until last night . . ."

She sobs and Nathan holds her. "What did he do to you?" he chokes out, a rage greater than any he has known, ever, pounding through his blood.

"Nothing, yet. He just sat and touched me, and said things to me. But he's going to try; I know he's going to try to put himself inside me." Naomi grips Nathan's shoulder as she speaks, her eyes terrified, yet becoming hard with the resolve in her voice. "But he's not going to do that, Nathan. I'll take myself where he can never touch me, ever, before I'll let him do to me what he did to my sisters."

Nathan pulls her to him and holds her fast, his eyes staring up at a moon filling itself out as it slips between the clouds and passes over their heads into the night. Then Naomi draws herself away from his embrace and sits up. Brushing her hair back, she gives him a resigned smile. "I'd better make for home. I'll get hell as it is, for being out this late."

"What can I do?" Nathan asks, his hand on hers.

"Not much. I don't know what anyone here can do." Her hand parts from his. The moon casts her shadow across the sand as she goes; then a cloud closes over the moon's face.

The rain pelts down on Bone Spit until just before dawn. Nathan wades through the rising tide and into the first light of day, his rage plunging him into the forest upriver until, exhausted, it dissolves into tears and impotence. Going home he avoids the carving shed where Isaac works and waits for him. Instead, he crosses the threshold of his house and goes straight to the rifle on the wall. He opens the top chest drawer and lays his hand on the box of cartridges. At the sound of a footstep behind him, he closes the drawer.

"What's wrong with you?" his mother asks.

"Everything."

From the porch he looks across the water to the landing where Uncle Charlie's seine boat is tied, and Harvey's. Both boats are out of commission, waiting for parts to arrive. Down on the beach below the soccer field, Harvey Silas has taken the engine of his speedboat apart. Nathan watches Harvey straighten up, inspect something in his hand, then take up a screwdriver, and crouch down over the engine. When Harvey stands, Nathan sees he is wearing a T-shirt and swim trunks that tighten about the bulge of his testicles. From the way Harvey moves, Nathan knows he was drinking last night.

Nathan realizes that if he took the rifle from the wall and loaded it, a single squeeze on the trigger would blow Harvey's penis out from under his crotch and drop him face forward into his boat. Nathan closes his eyes and sees Harvey falling. When he opens them, he is no longer on the porch but at the corner of the house. Nathan looks long at his father, bending down beside the pole, his knife in hand. His father, and Naomi's godfather.

Isaac glances up as Nathan places his hand upon Raven's beak. Isaac's knife has deepened the cheek line about one eye, now clearly formed, while the other is only a hint of what it will be.

"I thought you had gotten lost last night. Then I heard you crashing around in the woods this morning."

"I was with Naomi," Nathan says.

Isaac lifts the knife and waits. Suddenly, Sam Dick is beside them. "Yo, Isaac! We need you. There's been an accident."

Isaac and Nathan trot down the beach alongside Sam. Harvey Silas lies beside his boat, his swim trunks and the sand about him soaked with blood. Hazel and Sadie try to stem the flow of blood with Harvey's T-shirt. Sam picks up the screwdriver that has fallen on the sand and looks at the blood on its shank and tip.

"Right into his penis, testicles, and the groin," he says to Isaac, both astonishment and disgust playing upon his face.

"He's bleeding badly. We'd better take him to Port Hardy," Isaac says, after looking at the wound.

Sam's eyes gauge the wind-whipped water. "There's not a working boat here that will make it."

"Charlie's might. Nathan, go and find your uncle."

But Uncle Charlie and the rest of Duxsowlas are already coming toward Harvey's boat. Everyone stares at Harvey and no one says very much. Naomi gazes down at her father, a clash of feeling rocking her to and fro. Nathan cannot read the look on his uncle's face, or his mother's, or Sadie's, or even Hazel's—nor on any of the faces gathered about the boat.

"Your boat could make it to Port Hardy," Isaac says to Uncle Charlie.

Uncle Charlie looks long at Harvey Silas, then runs a hand through his beard. "I don't think so. It's too rough for me to take that boat out."

Isaac straightens up, looks around at each of the faces, then looks somewhere within himself, before he nods and says, "Then I think I'd better take him, if you can do without your boat for a few hours."

Uncle Charlie's eyes widen at Isaac's words. "I guess I can get by without my boat."

"Isaac, don't! Please!" Edith grips him by the shoulder.

"A plane might come in, Isaac, if we radio," Sam says, but without conviction.

"No. It's too rough for a plane." Isaac turns to Edith and places his hand on her shoulder. "You told me once I had no ground on which to judge anyone. That hasn't changed."

He holds her by the shoulder and by the eyes until Nathan can see there is something she understands. Then he turns to Nathan. "Go get Uncle's boat, Son, and bring it along to here." But Nathan does not understand. Looking out at the waves beaten about by the wind, he knows only that his father is about to risk his life for the man who intended to abuse Naomi. Nathan shakes his head and doesn't move.

"Go for that boat, Nathan!"

By the time Nathan noses the boat up on the beach, Edith and Adha have padded strips of sheeting against Harvey's groin and bound them together as best they can. Harvey shivers as Sam, Isaac, and Bert put him in Charlie's boat. Suddenly, Frank appears, running from his house and dragging John Dick's bearskin behind him. Without words, Frank gives the skin to his father and Isaac wraps it about Harvey's back and shoulders before pushing the boat out and climbing in.

Crying and dazed, Nathan locks one hand about the rope leading to the prow of the boat. Then he grasps the boat with the other hand and starts to climb in.

"Get out, Nathan, now!" Isaac commands, and the command breaks Nathan's grip. Stunned, Nathan backs away, unable to comprehend what his father is about to do. Isaac starts the motor and the line that connects Nathan with him begins to slip past Nathan's fingers to the last knot, then to its end. Isaac brings the boat about so that he can meet the face of his son. "Ha-la-kasla, Gwawinastoo. See through."

Isaac opens the throttle and the boat beats back the waves, along Sand Island, past Bone Spit and out into the churning water beyond.

Nathan sits out the day at Bone Spit, his back against David's headstone, his eyes on the open water and the fury of wind and rain upon it, until Duxsowlas darkens into night.

"You'd better go, Peter. Your family will wonder where you are."

"My family is with your family, probably. We're one family, remember? And they'll know I'm with you."

"Tell them I'll be home soon."

"All right. I'll go," Peter says. He stands and looks down at his cousin. "Are you mad at me? Because my dad didn't stop your dad from going?"

Nathan pulls his shoulders against himself and doesn't answer.

"Do you want me to go, too?" Naomi asks, after Peter has gone.

"I don't know what I want."

"Are you mad at me?"

"I don't know that, either."

"There's supper on the stove," Edith says tonelessly, as Nathan comes through the door.

"Isaac might have turned in at Thumb Harbour," Aunt Lila suggests.

Edith closes her eyes and shakes her head. "No. No, he didn't do that. Where's Frank?"

"You sent him to Charlie's, some time ago, for that spare lamp," Uncle Sam says.

"So I did." Edith rubs at her eyes.

"Nathan, please find Frank and tell him it's bedtime," Adha says.

Nathan forgets about the supper he didn't want anyway and walks through the rain up to Uncle Charlie's. The front door is ajar and a sliver of lamplight shines out. His feet make no sound as they climb the sodden steps. He pushes the door open.

Frank sits on the couch, beside their uncle. Uncle Charlie has his arm about Frank and is talking to him. But that is not what Nathan sees. Instead he sees the way Frank draws back from Uncle Charlie, curling himself into the couch, the look of a trapped animal on his face. Startled, Nathan's gaze rivets upon his uncle. Uncle Charlie's arm falls away from Frank as Nathan continues to stare, struggling to read his uncle's eyes. What? Confusion? Pain? Panic? Something more? What? What's bothering you, Uncle? What's going on, Uncle? What are you doing, Uncle?

The questions rise up as far as Nathan's throat but no farther. In anger, he throttles them, swallows them back down, and continues to stare. "Let's go home, Frank," he says.

Frank gets up from the couch without looking at his uncle or his brother, slips his gumboots on at the door, and steps outside. Nathan stays a moment longer, the rain dripping from his hair, his jacket, and his gumboots, pelting down upon the roof overhead. "Goodnight, Uncle."

Outside, Frank is waiting for him.

"Go home, Frank."

Frank doesn't move.

"Go home, Frank. Tell Mom I'm going somewhere."

"Where?"

"Somewhere. Go home, now."

Nathan watches until Frank is almost at their house. Then he walks off, into the rain.

Nathan sits on the stump beside his father's carving shed. Adha stands before him, the crescent moon blanket draped about her, her drum in hand. Her face searches his and pleads with him.

"Your uncle is going to sing the mourning songs for Harvey, and for your father."

"I'm sure Uncle will do everything the way it should be done," he replies, his voice like stone.

Then he is left alone, while the rest of Duxsowlas gathers in the big house.

throm

throm

throm

Nathan stares through the gap between Sand and Log Island, the drone of yesterday's plane still in his ears, far off at first, then becoming clear and sharp as the plane emerged from the clouds and banked down toward the stretch of water between Sand Island and Duxsowlas. Edith, then Adha, came out to the porch and stood alongside Nathan. The plane bounced down onto, then through, the tossing water to the landing. One policeman climbed out, then the other, and their hands lifted the first of the two bodies from the plane.

throm

throm

throm

His eyes still fixed on the gap, Nathan sees the date on the death certificate: June 22, 1983. Sees his mother's face, white with silence, and his brother's, not yet believing that their father is dead. Adha's face, like granite as the world about her falls apart . . . Naomi's eyes seeking his, and Uncle Charlie's hands upon Isaac's body, his eyes veiled and giving nothing back to anyone.

throm   throm   throm

Nathan climbs the porch steps, takes the rifle from the wall and the box of cartridges from the drawer. He unties Isaac's boat and pushes it out until the river licks at his gumboots. The motor catches hold and he heads upriver, putting the big house behind him.

Easing the boat onto Snag Point, Nathan secures it, takes the rifle and steps past the snags into the open space half-circled by trees and by eagles. Nathan counts them, slipping cartridges, one by one, into the rifle. He throws the lever, looks again at the twelve eagles.

He wants to shoot something. What?
What does he want to shoot? Then he knows.
The light. He wants to shoot the light right out of the sky,
today, and forever. Nathan aims the rifle at the sun and
squeezes the trigger, squeezes again, and again,
the eagles about him rising up in panic, into a
widening circle. Squeezes again, again, squeezes
his fury into the eye of the sun, the sound of his fury
spiralling up from Snag Point.
                         He reloads, fires yet again,
and again, fires the eagles into a screaming frenzy,

the eagles who never come right down, squeezes, fires,
shoots the eye of the sun back into itself, as one by one
the circling eagles dive into the orb of it,
and the sun explodes with the last crash of the rifle.
Feathers pour forth from the sun, falling down,

                                                down,

all about Nathan and about Snag Point all that long afternoon,
and then the sun drops, naked and red
into the dark, swallowing water at the horizon.

Quo-k . . .?

Nathan looks at the rifle in his hand, then listens again. Pushing the
branch aside, he steps into the darkness of cedar. Perched on a dead
branch, Raven waits for him. Nathan smiles at Raven, steps forward,
knowing what he will see when he gazes into the eye of Raven, not
caring any longer what Raven or he will see when their eyes meet.

Gwaau . . .?

Raven turns from the shadow of the cedar and opens his eye to
Nathan, but no eye is there to be seen. Instead, Nathan gazes in shock
into a red, gaping socket, empty and dead like the unseeing eye of the
full moon that stares down upon him the whole night long. Adrift in
his boat until the current whips the line around a snag in midriver,
Nathan stares back at the moon. Then the mist closes in and the moon
is gone.

The rattle of the motor cut through the mist. Nathan's footsteps
crunched up from the beach, up the steps. Ignoring the faces turned toward him from the kitchen table—Edith, Adha, Uncle Charlie,
Frank—he crossed the room and returned the rifle to the rack.

"Sorry, Uncle, but I won't be around for your potlatch."

Putting his house and his family behind him, Nathan walked down
to the river and watched the sun tear the mist apart. But he could hear
nothing. The river did not speak, the birds withheld their cries, the trees
stood dumbly in the silence. Lost in the silence, Nathan stood the whole
of that long morning: the silence and the light and that was all.

II

ONE

"Which name do you use?"

The counsellor peered at him over the top of her glasses, but he said nothing. With a glance at his aunt, the counsellor's eyes asked the question again. His aunt's puzzled look passed the question back to him, but he shrugged it aside.

"Well, you have only two choices, unless you want to be called Jacob. Which name were you called by at home?"

He sat, his eyes hooded over, and pretended she didn't exist.

"What about your first name, then?"

His silence stiffened. She rebalanced the pencil between her fingers and tried again. "Then your second name?"

He shrugged, and perhaps he nodded. With a nod of her own, the counsellor underlined the second name on his application form.

Outside the flat-roofed building, his Aunt Minnie studied him. "You're really going to be called by that name? Solomon?"

"I don't care. One name's as good as another."

Now Solomon stood on the street they called Granville, his jean jacket soaked through, along with the knapsack slung over his shoulder, and still the rain drizzled down—not a rain stabbing at the skin, but washing over it, again and again, until the skin threatened to dissolve.

That night, after he had registered at the high school in Port Hardy, he lay on the bed in the room Aunt Minnie and Uncle Slim had given him, the same room in which David, then Margaret, had stayed, and stared into the ceiling. When he had left Duxsowlas in the summer and moved in with his aunt and uncle, he could still pretend that when the summer ended he would go home and start grade nine there with Peter and Hector and Naomi. Now he could no longer pretend. Tomorrow he would be going to school here in Port Hardy. He was not going home.

Solomon observed the beggars along the end of Granville near the Sea Bus terminal—men who had long ago staked out their respective territories and who, without the flutter of an eyelid, begged their way confidently through the day. Solomon started to beg near one of them, too near he soon realized, then began to work his way up the street as the day's rain started to work its way down upon him.

He had tried to make school work, had tried to make living in Port Hardy work, but was soon bored with most of his teachers and his classes. English had been all right at first, but the teacher got onto him about his spelling, so he gave up on English. At nights he watched TV with Uncle Slim and Aunt Minnie but soon tired of that and began to excuse himself earlier in the evening to go to his room and do nothing.

Then the kid everyone called Rambo started picking on him, a native kid with some tough native and white friends. Solomon had been sitting in the mall drinking a Coke when an arm from out of nowhere knocked the cup from his hand. The drink splashed across his jacket and into his face. Startled, he looked up and saw Rambo's sullen face inches away from his own.

"That was clumsy of me, wasn't it, Weesa?"

Later in the week, Solomon had come back to his table in the library to find his books scattered across the floor. A day into the following week, a shoulder against his back sent him sprawling into his open locker. Then that Friday, Solomon walked out the main door of the school, and the next thing he knew, he was face down in the dirt. Rambo withdrew his foot, his back to the wall against which he leaned, his eyes big and innocent.

"Looks like you skinned your knee, Weesa. Maybe your dad will kiss it and make it better."

Without thinking what his next move would be, Solomon charged Rambo, took him by the shoulders, and threw him against the wall. Rambo rebounded, gripped Solomon about the middle, and hurtled the two of them across the pavement and against the opposite wall. Rambo's knee forced itself between Solomon's legs and wrenched upward. Solomon tightened his arms about Rambo's head, but Rambo's knee moved toward Solomon's crotch.

Solomon drew his arm back and drove his fist full force into Rambo's face. Rambo groaned and his knee fell away. Solomon released his grip and hit Rambo again. Rambo slumped against the wall, his face rolling upward as he collapsed to the ground. Solomon whipped about, ready to take on Rambo's friends, but they backed off, their eyes hard upon him as they lifted Rambo to his feet.

That night a girl in his class knocked on the window of his room, and he went outside to see what she wanted.

"To save your ass, if I can. The word is out. They're coming for you, tonight, tomorrow, or whenever, even if they have to break that window and pull you from your bed."

"So?"

"Look at me! Look at me and listen! The last time they talked about anyone the way they're talking about you, they took a kid out on the tidal flats and rearranged his body and his life. Some woman may marry him, one day, but she's going to be a sad woman whenever she puts out the bedroom light. Am I getting through to you?"

"Yes. But what can I do?"

"Take yourself out of here. Go home."

"I can't go home."

"Then go somewhere else."

"Where?"

"Wherever you know someone. Where do you know someone?"

"I have a sister in Vancouver."

"Then go to her."

On Saturday night, Solomon found a hotel near the bus depot with a telephone in the room and spent Sunday phoning his way through the white pages of the Vancouver telephone directory. Starting with the listings under Jacob, one column of them, he had gone on to Jacobs, then the Jacobsens and Jacobsons, in the event Margaret had played about with her name, but gave up when he had called the last Jacoby.

Monday morning he went downstairs to the lobby to pay for another night with the last of the money he had stolen from Aunt Minnie's handbag, only to be handed a bill for his phone calls. He discovered that the cash in his pocket fell short of the bill. The desk clerk started to berate him, then with a flip of the hand, dismissed him. Solomon went hungry until that evening, Halloween, then begged a meal from a cafe and spent the night curled up behind a garbage container in an alleyway. Firecrackers exploded in nearby streets, and fireworks flared out in the sky overhead. That night he dreamed of Raven.

Raven perched on the edge of the garbage container eating french fries. His feathers, several of them broken, were wet, ragged, and covered with bits of garbage; two tail feathers had been torn away. Raven looked disdainfully at Solomon, then flew off, the last of the french fries in his beak.

The next morning Solomon gravitated toward Granville Street. By the afternoon, he had worked his way past the Bay and Eaton's, past the buskers with their guitars, saxophones, harmonicas, drums, and other musical sounds strange to his ears. He begged less than five dollars into his pocket, yet he walked along the blocks with the movie theatres and kept his hand out. Midway along the second of those blocks, he leaned against a post and gave his hand a rest. A voice whispered at his ear: "I've got a nice warm place, and another way of making some money, when you get sick of this shit. I'm in the arcade, across the street. Ask for Diamond." The voice faded away into the rain. Solomon moved on and wondered what the voice was offering him. It didn't feel very good.

When the rain grew dark, he went into a cafe, ordered a cup of coffee and a bowl of soup, and stayed as long as he could. Then he left, having counted the last of his change and knowing what he had left would take him nowhere. At last he came to the street called Davie. He stopped at the corner, his begging hand in his pocket, his clothing drenched, and knew he did not know where he was going to go next. He closed his eyes against the rain and heard the bare hint of a whisper at his ear, the words broken, yet pulling at him: "Warm room . . . arcade . . . Diamond . . ."

Then, as Solomon went on listening, another sound wove its way into his ear. The stroking of the strings, gentle yet strong, drew him across Davie Street. There he found a man sitting on a folding stool tucked underneath a narrow, green awning. The instrument the man played looked like a wing, and the sound of its strings were sinews touched by the wind as the wing flew.

The man played on until the melody had run its course. Solomon listened as the winged thing sang to him and did not feel the rain. "Hello," he said, as the man looked up at him. "What is that?"

"A Celtic harp," the man replied. He was wearing a thick, woollen overcoat and a tweed cap. "I play along the other end most of the day, but come this way last thing at night. People are always surprised to see me here. And I like that, surprising people."

"It has a good sound," said Solomon, feeling out the lift and lilt of the man's voice and knowing he had heard the like of it once before in his life, somewhere else, long ago. Impulsively he reached into his pocket, pulled out the change he had left, and dropped it into the opened box in front of harp. The harp player watched him, stunned.

"Wait, wait just a minute! I can't take that from you."

"Why not, if I want to give it to you?"

"Because that's every last cent you have. Am I right?"

"But I want to give it to you. It's just the way I am. And I'll do better tomorrow."

The harp player cocked his head. "No, I don't think you will," he said, and pointed farther up Granville Street. "Go to the next corner, Drake Street, the one before the bridge, and turn left. Go down that block and cross over. The building on the corner is Emergency Services. They'll find you a bed for the night."

Solomon peered up the street, through the dark and the rain.

"Emergency Services is my gift to you," the harp player said quietly. "I'll take your gift, if you'll take mine. That's just the way I am."

"Thanks," Solomon murmured. "You make good music. I'm glad I met you."

The young man at the desk set his pen down. "That's all you want to tell me?"

"Yes." Solomon was shivering now that he was indoors, and his wet clothing was becoming dank and almost unbearable from his own stench.

"Okay, Solomon. Sit out there a moment while I make a phone call."

Solomon walked around to the other side of the glass partition, sat and listened to the man's voice through the glass. "Hello, Deborah? I'm Tim, from E.S. I have an intake for you . . . Yes, I know, but I don't want to send him there . . . I understand, a heavy house . . . well, she's heavy enough. But I don't think this one is, except for his size. He's just wet, and very scared . . . Your couch for tonight? That's okay . . . Good, Deborah; thanks again. Good night."

Well after midnight, Solomon walked up the steps of a big, double-storied house. Tim's knocking brought a grey-haired woman to the door. "You must be Tim, and Solomon. I'm Sue, the nightworker. Come in." The entrance hallway led past a flight of stairs into a darkened living room. "It's the couch for tonight, Solomon; one of our girls is leaving tomorrow, and the day staff will sort things out then."

"Tell Russ to phone us when he does the intake," Tim said, "and we'll give him what we have, which isn't much. We'll also find a social worker for him. Good night, Solomon. Sleep well." Tim put out his hand. Solomon returned the handshake, then watched Sue as she spread sheets on the couch.

"I'll be working around the house," she said, "but I'll try not to disturb you. The toilet is downstairs."

But he was too tired to go to the toilet, too exhausted to do anything except crawl between the sheets and let the world fall away.

TWO

Solomon awoke into a pale blue light that filtered in from the window beside the couch. Across the room from him, a set of glass doors opened into a dining room where a tall, lanky man was setting spoons and bowls on the table. Solomon sat up and blinked. A girl with long, blond hair stood by the couch at a right angle to his; she wore a short night-dress and was tearing through a pile of laundry. Feeling Solomon's eyes upon her, she whirled about.

"What the fuck are you looking at?" She stared him back into the sheets, then returned to the laundry pile. "Where are my socks? Ray, where are my goddamn socks?"

"If you put them out last night, Shannon, they're there, somewhere," the tall man answered.

"Somewhere, my ass! That sleazebag can't wash anything without losing it."

Ray appeared at the dining room doorway. "Abusing Sue is not going to find your socks, Shannon."

"Screw you, you goof!" She stomped, barefooted, out into the hall-way. A door slammed, shaking the panes in the dining room doors. Ray shook his head then grinned at Solomon. "Good morning. You must be Solomon."

"Yes."

"Welcome to Fireweed. You'd better get dressed. Breakfast will be on the table in fifteen minutes."

Solomon found the toilet downstairs and washed. But the clothes he put on still smelled, and looking at himself in the mirror didn't make him feel any better. When he had finished looking, he went upstairs into the dining room.

"Take a seat, Solomon, next to Joey." Solomon sat down, as Joey slid along the bench and grunted into his oatmeal. A girl sat opposite them. "This is Denise," Ray said. "Solomon is moving in today."

Denise looked up from her bowl, throwing back the hair from the side of her face. "Into Kim's bed?"

"Not quite," Ray laughed.

"That means we have to change rooms, again."

"I'm afraid so."

"Great!" Denise snapped. "That's just great!" She took her bowl into the kitchen and tossed it into a sink full of dishwater. Another girl walked in as Denise walked out.

"This is Kimberly. She's moving into a foster home this morning." Kimberly didn't look at Solomon or anyone else. She sat near Ray and touched her spoon into the bowl of oatmeal Ray had set before her.

"All packed, Kim?" She nodded. "It looks like a good placement, Kim. You can make it work, this time," Ray said.

"Sure," Kimberly said. "Like last time." She pushed the bowl away and left the room.

"She's been kicked out of three foster homes," Joey volunteered, to no one in particular. He dropped his spoon into the empty bowl. "Congratulations, Ray. You've learned how to cook oatmeal. Now you can go and find a real job."

"Joey, your bowl," Ray said, when Joey was almost through the doorway. Joey walked back to the table, took his bowl into the kitchen, then made a sweeping bow. "At your command, Sire."

"Russ is the program supervisor," Ray said to Solomon when they were alone. "He'll meet with you this morning. In the meantime, look around and settle in. You needn't worry about school today."

At that moment a young woman walked in. "Judy, this is Solomon."

"Hello, Solomon. I can't pry J.D. out of bed," she said to Ray, "and we have to leave now."

"Leave J.D. to me," Ray said.

After Judy left, driving a van full of residents to school, Solomon lounged on one of the living room couches until well into the morning. A man came in, greeted Solomon, then walked into the office at the back of the house. A social worker came for Kimberly and took her away, then Ray dragged the vacuum from the hall closet and took it upstairs. Finally, the man called him into the office. "Take that chair, Solomon; my name is Russ. I've just talked with E.S. Diane Jamison will be your social worker. She'll come over this afternoon. For now, let's go over what you told Tim last night. Solomon is your first name?"

"Yes." He had hesitated, and felt Russ watching him.

"And your birthdate is March 20, 1969?"

"Yes."

"Where does your family live?"

"I have a sister, here in Vancouver somewhere."

"And she is your only family?" Russ asked.

"Yes."

"What is her name?"

"Margaret."

"The same last name as yours?"

"Yes . . . yes, I guess so."

"When did you last see her?"

"Two, maybe three years ago."

"Would you want to live with her, if we can find her?"

"Yes." Solomon felt the veil slip aside as pain flooded up into his eyes.

"Then I hope we can find her," Russ said. He took a sheet of paper from the desk drawer and handed it to Solomon. "This is a contract, for the time you stay with us. We ask every resident to sign it."

Solomon looked the contract over. "It's a list of ground rules for living here," Russ continued. "We expect you to go to school, keep the curfews, and respect the house and not trash it whenever you become angry with the world, or us, or yourself. We also ask you not to abuse staff or other residents, physically or verbally."

Solomon raised his eyebrows. "So I noticed," he said, wondering if Shannon had signed this contract. Then he read the words through, and with a shrug signed on the bottom line.

"One more thing," Russ said. "We assign one of our staff to each resident as an individual counsellor. Judy will be your counsellor. You probably met her this morning."

Solomon shrugged again as he wondered why he needed an individual counsellor. "Judy will meet with you when she returns from school," said Russ, "after you've met with Diane. For now, you can move into the three-bed room upstairs. We'll move Joey and J.D. in with you."

"There was a girl at breakfast who didn't like the idea of changing rooms," Solomon observed.

"No one does," Russ returned, "and you won't either, when you have to do it. But it goes with living here."

South of city hall and not far from the Vancouver General Hospital, the Fireweed Crisis Shelter sat midway along a tree-lined block of Yukon Street. Large, rambling steps led into the entrance hallway, then into the living room and to the office behind the living room. A staircase ran from the hallway up to the TV room and bedrooms on the second floor.

The house van made frequent trips to the emergency ward of the Vancouver General Hospital. On the night of Solomon's first day, Chandra, a girl who had stayed invisible most of the afternoon, announced at dinner that she was thinking about slashing her wrists, then went downstairs, making certain she left the washroom door open, and started cutting into her skin with the dull kitchen knife she had stolen and hidden away. Dazed, Solomon stood on the sidewalk with Joey and watched the van speed away with Chandra inside.

J.D. and Joey became Solomon's roommates, and Solomon learned as much about the working of Fireweed from Joey during his first weeks in residence as from the staff—where he could hide a joint or a bottle or a sharp knife, where each member of the staff could be a soft touch, how to wheedle more bus money than you needed out of staff, and other ways of beating the Fireweed system. Solomon filed Joey's words away and added his own observations to them.

Russ was the big boss who worked weekdays from nine to five and met with residents who had screwed up, to make sure they knew they had screwed up. Margo cooked for the residents and gave them hell if they were late for meals or didn't show up. Solomon quickly came to respect her. Sue was an older woman who worked night shifts. Solomon decided she liked staying up all night and had found a job at which she could be paid for doing that.

The rest of the Fireweed staff worked day and evening shifts through the week. Solomon liked Ray especially because Ray was easygoing, fun to be with, and had a way of saying things so that you didn't forget what he had said. One morning, as Ray drove them to the Crossroads Alternative School, Denise asked, "Where did the name Fireweed come from?"

"Have you ever been in a forest after a fire has swept through it?"

"I don't know," Denise answered. "Yes, once."

"Did you see the tall pink flowers growing up through the burn?"

"Maybe."

"That's fireweed. The back petals are shaped like a pink cross. It's the first living thing to grow back, from the wreck of everything else around. It says there is nothing that can't grow back, no matter how much of it has been burnt to the ground."

Then there was Judy. Solomon had to take note of her because she was his counsellor, but he didn't know what to make of her the first time she asked him if he wanted to go for a walk in Stanley Park, wherever that was. A week later she took him bowling. Solomon liked the ice cream she bought him, but thought throwing a ball into a row of wooden stumps was about the dumbest thing he had ever done, and told her so. That was the last time she took him bowling. Then Judy discovered that Solomon could play cribbage and tried to interest him in doing that. But playing cribbage with Judy wasn't much fun for Solomon because Uncle Slim had taught him too well, and he beat her almost every game they played. "I could cheat when I play you, and you wouldn't even know," Solomon told her, "but I don't need to."

Judy did not give up, however. She tried to interest him in someone called Emily Carr, who painted totem poles and trees, only the trees didn't look like trees he had ever seen. She also wanted to take him out to the Museum of Anthropology. "What's out there?" he asked.

"Totem poles and northwest coast masks. Would you like to see them?"

He drew back into himself. "No, I wouldn't."

"She's trying to relate to you," Joey said later.

"What does that mean?"

"You know, get next to you, inside that thick head of yours and under your skin. Find out what makes you tick so she can advise your social worker on the planning of your future." Joey laughed. "It's a lot of bullshit, man."

Two weeks after his intake, Solomon met a second time with his social worker at Fireweed. Diane Jamison was a short, busy person who had spent their first interview writing things down in her little notebook. What kind of a placement did he want to go to next? she asked him. Solomon glanced at Russ, then Judy, because he hadn't a clue what his social worker was talking about. "Diane's asking you where you want to live, when you leave here," Judy interpreted.

"I want to live with my sister," Solomon stated.

"Your sister . . . the one named Margaret?" Diane scanned a page of her notebook.

"Yes. She lives here in Vancouver."

"Where does she live?"

"I don't know."

Diane glanced at Judy then Russ. "Well, it could take us a while to find her," she said to Solomon. "We could place you in a foster home while we look."

"I don't want to live in a foster home," Solomon said, becoming restless in his chair. There was something about this person, the way she looked at Russ and Judy, then at him, that he didn't like.

"When did you last see your sister?" Diane asked.

"When I was twelve. She came here to go to school."

"Have you considered the possibility, Solomon, that even if we do find her, she might not be . . . in a position to take care of you?"

"Or she might be in school, or working, or married, and able enough to care for Solomon," Judy interjected, her eyes firm upon Diane. Solomon looked over at Judy and his feeling about her began to change.

"I think it's worth a try, Diane," Russ added. "Solomon's doing well with us. Finding his sister seems like a good bet."

"All right, we'll try to find her," said Diane, though Solomon heard no conviction in her voice. "You can stay here in the meantime, Solomon, so long as you keep your life together."

Solomon's feeling about Judy changed even more when she took him to Joe's on Commercial Drive and taught him to shoot pool. Solomon quickly added a taste for cappuccinos to his liking for ice cream and developed a new respect for Judy whenever she had a cue in her hand. She beat him consistently for weeks on end, never throwing a game to him like a bone to make him feel good about himself. He began to concentrate on beating Judy, not just now and then, but as consistently as she was beating him.

Solomon found it hard to feel much for the other residents at Fireweed. Shannon told staff and her peers they were all fucked in the head. Joey snatched at any opportunity to set someone up against someone else, and J.D. spent more of the day in his bed or being coaxed from it than on his feet. Denise was more interesting; she was often abrasive, yet truthful and vulnerable, especially when she told him of the day she had come home after school, discovered her house was empty, and found her things in a box in the carport along with a note: "We have moved to Ontario. Enjoy the rest of your life."

But Denise was the first to move on, when her social worker placed her in a foster home. Christmas came and went, and in January, a long-term group home agreed to take Shannon. She made two preplacement visits, announced that the staff and residents were also fucked in the head, but then agreed to move. A week later, Joey's social worker pulled off a minor miracle in persuading Joey's parents to let him return home. Joey protested, but not convincingly, and was happy to leave Fireweed. Solomon and J.D. moved into the room with two beds. Then one morning, easygoing Ray came into the room and told J.D. to get his ass out of bed. J.D. took a swing at Ray, which Ray deflected as he spun J.D. about and put him in a hold. Ray locked J.D.'s arms across his chest, and crossed his legs over J.D.'s. J.D. could do nothing but thrash about in Ray's grip until he collapsed. Then Ray let him go. That night J.D. stalked out of Fireweed into the rain and did not come back.

New residents came and went while Solomon stayed. Arnie taught Solomon to shoplift, first at a few 7-11s, then at department stores downtown. Solomon was amazed to discover how easily he could take something in hand and walk out the door. Arnie encouraged him in that conviction, up to the afternoon the two of them were in Eaton's looking at a display of belt buckles.

"Get one for me," Arnie hissed. Solomon ran his hand across one buckle, then another, then back to the first and was about to close his hand around it when something like a light touch upon his shoulder stopped him. He drew his hand away from the buckle and started toward the Granville Street doorway. A man wearing a dark suit stepped in front of him.

"Would you empty your pockets, please." It was not a request, and Solomon knew he had no choice. He emptied out his jacket, then jeans, pockets, including a wad of toilet tissue. The man looked the items over, then looked him over, taking his time. "All right," he said. "You may leave."

His hands shaking, Solomon stepped out onto the street. Arnie was nowhere to be seen, and Solomon did not go shoplifting with him again.

Solomon celebrated his fifteenth birthday at Fireweed. Then spring touched down into the bare trees along Yukon Street, and the trees blossomed. The pink and sweetness of the blossoms pained Solomon, a relentless pain that opened wounds within him, as the blossom-lined streets prepared the city for Easter.

Solomon and Mike, a new resident, stepped off the bus and crossed Cambie Street. "At least I don't have to go to Mass this year and hear about some loser being killed on a cross."

Solomon stopped short, in the middle of Cambie Street. "Who was killed?"

Mike swore at him and dodged a passing car. "You, you goof, if you don't get your ass off the street."

"Who was killed?" Solomon asked again when they had reached the sidewalk.

"Jesus. Who else?"

Solomon stared at him. "Jesus was killed?"

"Man, you are from somewhere else. Killed, crucified for our sins, and all that bullshit."

That night Solomon lay awake while Mike snored in the other bed and tried to digest what he had heard. He remembered Mr. Blaisdell's words at David's burial: ". . . as much as Christ treasures it, enough to die for each of us . . ."

He knew that Jesus had died, but not that Jesus had been killed. That had never dawned upon him, not in all the years he had sat through the services at Duxsowlas. Words came back to him, circled one another: ". . . crucified also for us . . . suffered and was buried." Or the words of the other creed they had said: "Was crucified, dead, and buried . . ." Dead, yes. He knew that. But crucified? What was that all about?

Sue looked up from the office desk.

"Where's a dictionary?" he asked.

"At this time of night?"

"Yes. And a Bible, please."

Solomon took both books into the dining room, turned on the light and sat down at the table. He opened the dictionary first and looked up *crucify*, then *crucifixion*. He found both words. At least he was learning to spell at Crossroads School. After reading the definitions, he closed the cover and started to think.

So that's what *crucified* meant. Jesus had not simply died; he had been killed. But who had killed Jesus? And why? Solomon opened the Bible to the Gospels in the New Testament and started to read. He soon bogged down in the first of the Gospels and flipped through to the second, the one called Mark. This one was more direct, and Solomon read it right through.

Then he sat back and closed his eyes. There were some things he couldn't puzzle out, but one thing was clear. Some people hadn't liked Jesus. Then his father's voice came back to him: "Could be Raven decided he just didn't like him. Some think that's reason enough for one person to cut into another."

But how could that be reason enough? He had never liked Naomi's father, long before he had overheard Harvey badmouthing his family. But would that in itself have been reason enough for him to kill Harvey?

Even more, Jesus had let them kill him. That was what struck Solomon most forcibly and was the hardest thing for him to figure out. Was it because Jesus didn't think much of himself? David hadn't thought much of himself and had taken his own life by setting fire to Log Island. But that didn't seem to be the case as far as Jesus was concerned. No, it had to do with something Jesus thought was important . . . *enough to die for each of us . . .*

What about his father, then? Why had he killed himself trying to save Harvey Silas? Solomon sat into the night trying to see through. When Deborah came on shift the next morning, she found him asleep at the table, slumped over the opened Bible.

On the last Sunday in April, Shannon was kicked out of her group home, and Emergency Services brought her back to Fireweed. The Fireweed staff gritted their teeth, put on their armour, and waited for the abuse to begin. But no abuse came. Shannon was a model resident from the moment she walked through the doorway. Solomon observed her closely all that week. Shannon said please and thank you, always took her bowl or plate to the sink, kept the curfews and her side of the room neat and clean. Solomon also saw that she did not unpack her belongings.

One warm evening, Ray took several residents to a nearby park for a softball game. Shannon stayed behind and vanished into her room soon after dinner. Solomon also stayed because Judy wanted to play cribbage with him and he couldn't be bothered with saying no. As he waited for her to finish some paperwork in the office, he suddenly had a feeling about Shannon. He walked into the hallway and opened the door to her bedroom. Shannon stood before a wall mirror putting on makeup. "Didn't anyone teach you to knock before you come into someone's room?"

Solomon sat on one of the beds and shook his head. "We didn't knock much where I lived."

"It takes all kinds, I guess. What do you want?"

"Oh, I thought I'd see what a clean room looks like."

"Fuck you. You've been watching me all week." She uncapped her lipstick and worked its redness into her upper lip. Solomon looked her over, the tight leather jacket, tight white pants, and white shoes with very high heels. A small clothes bag was sitting on her bed.

"Where are you going?"

"To stay with a friend. He's going to look after me; his name is Diamond." Her hand paused at her lower lip as she glimpsed Solomon's face in the mirror. "You know him?"

"Sort of. I ran into him when I first came here. I think he wanted to be my friend, too."

"Too bad you didn't take him up on it. I'm going to get stoned with him, then laid. Because that's what it's all about, getting stoned, and getting laid."

"My brother once said something like that."

"Then you have a smart brother."

"He's dead."

She looked back at his face in the mirror. "How did he die?"

Solomon gazed into the mirror at her and did not answer. "Solomon, you are one weird person," Shannon said. She capped her lipstick, took another look at herself, then put the lipstick into her purse. "Have you got your allowance?"

"Yes."

"Give it to me, please."

Solomon reached into his pocket and handed the money to Shannon. "Why don't you ask Judy for yours?"

"Because she'll see I'm going and try to stop me. And because she's a loser. They're all losers. Do you think they'd waste their time with us if they were anything but losers?"

"So you think we're losers, too?"

Shannon gazed at him as if she pitied him. "You figure that out when you're ready to stop dreaming about going anywhere from here but down."

On the Saturday following Shannon's disappearance, Judy found Solomon in the TV room. "How about a cappuccino and three lightning games?"

Solomon considered. "There's a *Rocky* movie on at four."

Judy glanced at her watch. "We'll be back by then."

As he chalked the tip of his cue, Solomon wondered what he felt like telling her this time. Whenever they played, she would drop questions on the table between them, as if she didn't really care what he might say in response. So he answered just as casually, telling her one time about going out on his father's trapline and crisping up a salmon for supper. Another time he had told her about going to Sadie Moon's and stuffing himself full of bread and jam whenever he wanted to do that. He'd even talked a little about Frank one time, and about Frank's passion for feathers, though he clammed up suddenly when he realized more had slipped past his mouth than he had intended.

"We had a meeting with Diane yesterday," Judy said, sinking the two ball in a side pocket just before she spoke.

"Oh, yeah. And what did Diane have to say?"

"She's found a foster home for you. She plans to move you into it early next week."

His cue slipped on the cue ball as he jerked himself upright. "I thought she was looking for my sister?"

"She has been, she told us. But with no success, and she has to move you, Solomon." Judy's eyes searched his, asking him to understand. Solomon felt his fingertips becoming cool and calculating as they played up and down his cue. He understood. "Up her ass, then. I don't care where she puts me. It's your shot."

"Take your shot again. Your cue slipped."

"It's your shot."

"Okay," she said and bent over the table. Her cue slipped, and the cue ball wobbled past the ball she had aimed for. Solomon smiled to himself, stepped into the breach, and thrashed her.

"How about another?" she asked. He shook his head. Now that he had broken her game, he was no longer interested in playing with her.

Once back at Fireweed Solomon returned to the TV room in time for his *Rocky* movie. He rolled the TV set, attached to a long extension cord, over to the doorway and turned it to face the wall where he would be sitting, because the reception was better that way.

Then he lost himself in the movie, right into its closing frames. Rocky was in the ring with a black fighter called Clubber, trying to regain his title. Clubber was punching the hell out of Rocky, then Rocky came back and punched the hell out of Clubber, and now the two of them were punching the hell out of one another.

Someone called upstairs to him. A moment later, a relief worker named Derek appeared in the doorway. "Dinner, Solomon," Derek said.

If it had been Judy, Solomon might have shut the TV off and gone downstairs to eat, even though he was pissed off at what she had told him. But Derek was only a relief worker, and Solomon didn't see any reason for listening to him. "When this is finished," he said.

"Dinner won't wait, nor will Margo."

"Then tell her to eat it if she's that worried."

"Solomon, dinner is now, please."

"Fuck off!" said Solomon. Derek reached around the TV and went to turn it off. Solomon jumped to his feet and thrust Derek away, intending to make his point then go back to Clubber and Rocky. But Derek closed in from behind, locked Solomon's arms together across his chest, then locked Solomon's legs tightly between his own as the two of them dropped to the floor. Shocked, Solomon's body went limp for a second or two, then exploded. His legs shot forward, nearly breaking Derek's grip on them, and his feet struck the TV.

Solomon rolled and bucked, trying to crush Derek's head against the wall as the TV rolled from the room and across the hallway to the top of the stairs. The stand fell away and the TV flipped up and over to the extent of the cord. Rocky and Clubber each got in one last punch before the cord snapped away from the wall and whipped past Derek's head as Solomon banged him hard against the floor. The TV struck the wall at the foot of the stairs with a shattering of wallboard, plastic, and glass.

Solomon clamped his teeth into Derek's hand and bit as hard as he could. Derek gasped and wrenched his hand away before Solomon could bite again. Solomon struggled to free his arms, to elbow a path through Derek's ribcage, but Derek's lock on him held. Screaming, then cursing, Solomon thrashed Derek about the room, but Derek would not let him go. He rolled, rolled again, and then he saw Judy crouching down before him, her heels against the wall. "Solomon . . ." He rolled again as far as his side.

"Solomon." Her voice was quiet, firm. He stayed on his side, still fighting Derek's hold, but listening. "Solomon, Derek will let you up and let you leave when he knows you won't hurt him, or me."

He tested Derek's hold again, but Derek was not going to give way. Solomon started to cry.

"Derek will let you go when he knows you won't hurt him or me," Judy repeated. Suddenly, Solomon went limp in Derek's arms. Derek released him at once and rolled clear of him.

Solomon came to his feet and ran down the stairs. He didn't slam the door, but left it open behind him, swaying in a soft May wind.

It was well after midnight before he walked back into the house, then into the office. Judy sat at the desk, and Sue sat on the couch reading the log. Sue glanced at Judy. "I'll start the laundry," she said.

Solomon sat on a chair and waited.

"You're grounded for the weekend," Judy said. "You may go with the house on rec and that's all. I'm going home now to have the longest, hottest bath of my life and sleep all weekend, and I don't want anybody phoning me to tell me you've gone to the moon or anywhere. If that happens and if I ever catch up with you, I'll break your neck. Do you understand me?"

"Yes."

"One thing more before I leave. I doubt the TV will be repaired this weekend, maybe not in your lifetime, so you'll have a lot of time in which to think about your life. Please find a way to meet Derek before you move on from this house."

Solomon lowered his gaze. "No way. There's no way I will do that."

"There is a way. There's always a way. Wipe the snot from your nose, do some thinking, and find it. And if you don't own a handkerchief, take your allowance instead of giving it away, and go buy one."

Judy held his gaze. Then he felt a smile creep across his face. "You sound like my mom. She used to talk to me like that, kick me in the ass whenever I was messing things up. She was good at that until she started drinking." He looked away and fell silent.

"When did she start drinking?" Judy asked.

"When my sister left home." Tears started to gather at the corners of his eyes. "My sister heard that my brother had abused someone, and tried to tell my mom that he had been abused. But no one listened to her, not even my mom. So she left."

"Abused by someone in your family?"

He hesitated, then nodded. "I think so."

"Has anyone ever abused you?" He shook his head; then he peered through the open window beside the desk seeing something flare up somewhere . . .

"David, my brother, killed himself. He set an island on fire, a whole island. It was the island my father took me to, when I was nine."

"That was a special time with your father?"

"Yes." Then he ran out of words but remained in his chair, still thinking things over. "My mom used to go to church a lot and so did my sister," he said, after a while, wondering why he was saying that.

But his words seemed to wake Judy up. "Did your sister go to church often?" she asked.

"As often as my mom did. My mom always went to services whenever the priest came, and my aunt and uncle also went. But I bet Maggie never missed even when she went away to school."

Now Judy seemed to be watching a moth drift in from the dark beyond the window, circle the desk lamp, then veer back toward the darkness. "Which church did your sister go to?"

"Anglican."

Then Solomon left the room to go to bed, as the night air wafting through the window brought the scent of flowers from the garden bed beside the house, and as Judy remained at the desk, her fingers playing upon the telephone directory.

Solomon walked into Fireweed after school on Wednesday. Judy met him at the stairs. "Would you come into the office, please?" She had a funny light in her eye. Why was there a funny light in her eye? He followed Judy into the office, then stopped.

Her hair was much shorter than he remembered it, close to her neck, and she was older. Still young, but older. Judy pointed him toward a chair, but he could neither see it nor move toward it. Russ and his social worker were also in the room, but he did not see them, either.

"Hello," she said.

He stared back.

"I had to do some fast thinking when the phone call came, to figure out who Solomon could be." She paused. "You're my brother, all right, but you're not little anymore."

His hand found the chair. He sat and went on staring. She smiled at him through the tears that had welled up in her eyes. "I changed to contact lenses three years ago. I decided I was too young always to be losing my glasses, the way Adha was losing hers." Margaret looked over at Judy then at Diane. "Your counsellor found me; she called every Anglican church in the city until she found the one my husband and I go to. Since then your social worker and I have had a long talk. You can live with us if you want to do that."

The room rocked back and forth as he rocked back and forth in his chair, suddenly sobbing, and he could not stop, stop the room from rocking or himself from sobbing.

That night Fireweed celebrated Solomon's leaving. Margo cooked up every chicken she could find in the freezer and baked an enormous cake which everyone ate and no one could finish. Solomon sat at the head of the table like a king about to go forth and do some fine and wonderful thing, wearing a hat no one had seen until that night, with the words Dawson Potlatch, 1981 written across the front of it, under the Raven design.

He was showered with gifts. Russ gave him a Swiss Army knife on behalf of Fireweed, and his fellow residents had prepared a survival package for "life out there," including several rolls of toilet paper and instructions for home-growing a certain useful plant.

After dinner Solomon walked up to Derek and shook his hand. Then as a grand finale, Ray took all the residents on a special movie outing, with a long detour for ice cream afterward, and they arrived back at Fireweed well after the curfew that everyone had agreed to ignore.

The next morning a little Honda zipped along Yukon Street and pulled up in front of Fireweed. Margaret and her husband came up the walk to the front steps where Solomon and Judy waited for them.

"This is Cameron, your brother-in-law," Margaret said, then to Cameron, "and this brother of mine is your brother-in-law."

Cameron McLean was a little taller than Margaret, with sand-coloured hair. His sea blue eyes, with secrets of their own, flashed up then away. "Hello, Solomon," he smiled, as they shook hands. "Welcome to our family."

Judy went with them to the car. "He's a neat kid," she said, with a last look at Solomon, who had stuffed himself into the back seat.

"I know," Margaret said. "I grew up with him." Then she smiled. "But thank you for reminding me."

THREE

Solomon half-dreamed on his way from Fireweed to his new home, while discovering that there wasn't much room between the back of the front seats and the front of the back seat in a little Honda. Margaret laughed as he shifted his legs and the rest of him yet again. "We'll have to knock the back end out and push that seat right to the bumper if you're going to spend much time in it."

Cameron also laughed as he crossed Hastings and continued north on Nanaimo Street. "Hold on, Solomon; we're nearly home."

Home was a compact two-storey house on Trinity Street. The window in Solomon's room upstairs looked out over several rows of rooftops down to Burrard Inlet with its grain elevators, docks, and the large ships unloading or taking on cargo. The mountains rose steeply along the north shore of the inlet.

Margaret left him to settle into his room, and Solomon realized that he could now truly unpack the few belongings he had. He had lived almost as a stranger at Slim and Minnie's house, and had kept everything locked away at Fireweed, except when he had to change rooms.

Solomon put his jacket upon a hanger and placed the hat Hector had given him upon the hook attached to the closet door. The rest of his clothes he placed in the top drawer of the chest; then he took the feather Frank had given him for his fourteenth birthday and looked about the room for somewhere to hang it. He spotted a nail protruding from the wall above the head of his bed and tied the leather thong dangling from the cloth sewn about the base of the feather to it so that the feather hung down from the nail. Then he stood for a while at the window and watched a ship sail past. Going into the bathroom, he looked at his face in the mirror. Had he changed as much as Margaret had? The face looking out at him, however, seemed to be that of his usual self.

Over the next couple of days, he told Margaret and Cameron about staying with his Aunt and Uncle and why he had to leave Port Hardy, though he said nothing as to why he had left Duxsowlas, and neither of them questioned him about that. Life at Fireweed was the easiest place to begin speaking freely, and Solomon went to town characterizing the antics of his fellow residents, and his own, and the responses of some of the staff. More than once Cameron and Margeret doubled up with laughter, and that encouraged Solomon to think of yet another story.

"You've got Dad's storytelling tongue, with Mom's wit at the end of it," said Margaret. "A fearsome combination."

Then Margaret and Cameron told him something of themselves. Cameron taught history at Simon Fraser University, and Margaret had been one of his students. They had married last summer about the time Solomon had left Duxsowlas. Solomon reflected later that Margaret now sounded very much like their mother. He also realized he didn't know if she knew David and Isaac were dead. On his way to bed one night, he said, tentatively, "David burned himself up in a fire two years ago, and Dad drowned in a boat accident."

"I know," Margaret replied, giving him the space to say more if he wished, yet not pushing him to do so. There was nothing more Solomon wanted to say, and he went upstairs.

He also spent those first days looking about the house itself, including the bedroom where Cameron and Margaret slept and the little room next to it where they shared a desk because Margaret still had a year of university to complete. But his attention was primarily claimed by the prints and carvings that covered the walls in every room, even the bathrooms—prints and carvings by native artists with names strange to Solomon, though Cameron seemed surprised that Solomon had not heard of them: Bill Reid, Robert Davidson, Art Thompson, Norval Morrisseau, and others. Solomon wandered from room to room looking at the creatures that stared back at him, some of them familiar from the big house at Duxsowlas, the village pole, and other poles he had seen: Eagle, Sisiutl, Grizzly, Frog, among others, and of course, Raven. He came back, several times, to a print called *Transformation #3* by someone called Eric Gray. Inside the form of Raven's body—it had to be Raven though nothing written on the print said so—a human figure was preparing to unfold itself, to step lightly, toe outstretched, through the space in the formline between the base of Raven's wing and his tailfeathers. Only the head, where the outer form and inner figure joined together, was drawn unambiguously in the form of Raven.

On the adjacent living room wall, another Raven perched on something, a clamshell maybe, that was lined about the inside of its rim with little human figures, each squatting with hands upraised to the height of the head. A face peered out at the world from the inside of Raven's eye. *Children of the Raven* the print was called, by Bill Reid.

The Sisiutl print hung on the wall above the desk in the little room. Solomon assumed that it and the other prints all belonged to Margaret, but when he said something to her about them, she shook her head and smiled a funny smile. "They're Cameron's. When we moved in together, they came with him, every one of them, and I had to move enough of myself aside to let them in." In that instant, Solomon saw in his sister's eyes the same riddle he remembered seeing there the night of Uncle Charlie's potlatch and David's Hamatsa dance, as their family was turning to go past the Tlaamelas.

"We're going to church," she said the following morning as they were finishing breakfast. As Margaret spoke, Solomon realized she was assuming he would go with them. He set his fork down. "I'm not going to church these days."

"Since when?" Margaret asked.

"Since Port Hardy," he replied. He had tried going to church with Aunt Minnie and Uncle Slim, but Mr. Blaisdell had left by then. Although Solomon hadn't understood or listened to all the words Mr. Blaisdell had said, at least he had some feeling for the man. The new priest didn't awaken any feeling in Solomon, and one Sunday morning he had told Aunt Minnie he wasn't going with them. Aunt Minnie had sighed, but then said, "I'm not going to tell you what to do with your life, on any day of the week. You're too big for me to be doing that, and besides it's not our way."

Margaret heard him out, then said, "Maybe it's time you started going again."

Solomon folded his napkin while Cameron sat and watched them both. "Or maybe it isn't time, just yet," Cameron said.

"No, I don't think so," Solomon agreed, and decided he liked his new brother-in-law.

"Okay, you win this one," Margaret said after a moment. "If Auntie wasn't going to tell you what to do about that part of your life, I guess I'm not going to do that either. So you can do the breakfast dishes while we're gone, in case you've forgotten what a sink looks like."

After lunch, Solomon washed the dishes again, then went into the living room. "Have a seat, Solomon," Cameron said, "and let's talk about school."

"School?" Solomon slumped down in his chair.

"Sorry to shatter your Sunday with such a painful thought," Margaret said, "but we'd better get down to it, before the thought becomes strange as well as painful."

Solomon grinned and shrugged. "All right. Show me where the school is, and I'll go."

"Were you going to school when you were at Fireweed?" Cameron asked.

"Yes, one called Crossroads. But I don't want to go back there."

Cameron paused, thinking about something. "Are you interested in, open to a school that's a bit different?"

"How do you mean, different?" Solomon asked.

"There's an independent school not far from Commercial Drive, across the street from Chinook Park, with a high school that's started up this year. I've made an appointment for an interview tomorrow afternoon, if you'd like to take a look at it."

Solomon looked at Margaret, but Margaret simply said, "This is Cameron's idea. He's talked with the teachers and thinks it might be a school worth considering. But it's up to you."

Solomon tried to think in what way a school could be different from school. "I guess so," he said.

"Good," said Cameron. "I'll phone tomorrow and confirm that we're coming. In the meantime, this may tell you something about the school." He handed a brochure to Solomon.

In his room, Solomon undressed, got into bed, then looked at the brochure. Black lines swept across the white at the top of the paper, each line distinct yet strangely at one with all the other lines, and took the white of the paper with them as, like a wind knotting into itself, they flowed together into a human form just down from the left corner of the page. He read the words below the logo: Chinook Park Waldorf School.

Then he put the light out and slept.

Cameron nudged the car up against the curb beside Chinook Park, and the three of them crossed the street. A flat-roofed, concrete building set back from the street snuggled down alongside a small playing field. "This is the elementary school," Cameron said. "It used to be a public school. The high school is a little farther."

Two blocks along, Solomon crossed a street and found himself standing in front of a firehall. "This is it," Cameron said.

"This is what?" said Margaret.

"The high school."

Margaret stared at the firehall, then glanced sideways at her husband. "Cameron, is this a joke?"

"No," Cameron laughed. "The Fire Department moved somewhere else, where there are more fires I suppose, and the school has leased the building."

"A high school in a firehall? I don't know about this, Cameron."

"Let's meet these people, and then we can decide. Is that all right with you, Solomon?"

"Why not?" Solomon said, intrigued with the idea of going to school in a firehall.

A tall man with red curly hair met them as they walked in the doorway. "Mr. and Mrs. McLean?"

"Cameron. And this is Margaret," said Cameron.

"And you are Solomon. Hello," the tall man said. "I'm Paul Kane, and I teach science and math. We're just putting the finishing touches on a meeting, if you'll give us a few minutes of grace. Please come upstairs and look around while you wait." At the top of the steps, Paul Kane pointed to his right. "There's the grade nine classroom. We'll be with you soon."

The grade nine classroom had not begun its life as such, though two blackboards had been attached to the wall facing the doorway and some desks faced the blackboards. To the right of the desks, a firepole disappeared through a hole in the floor. Solomon left Cameron and Margaret looking at the paintings and drawings tacked to the side walls and wandered through a doorway near the firepole that opened into an even larger room. The walls were lined with lockers and a girl stood at one of them, wrestling with the handle. She wore her hair in a pony-tail that jiggled as she tugged at the locker handle. When she saw Solomon, she stopped tugging. "Hello. Who are you?"

"I'm Solomon."

"I'm Sandra, and my locker is stuck. Would you kick it for me, please? Right there." She pointed to the corner below the handle. "Don't bash it in. Just hit it dead on."

Solomon walked up to the locker and kicked it as she had asked. The locker door popped open. "Thanks. I'd have done it, but I wrecked my toe this afternoon chasing a volleyball into a post downstairs. You kick well." Sandra took her day pack from the locker and closed the door. "Are you going to join our class?"

"Maybe."

"I see you're a person who's definite about things," Sandra said as they walked into the classroom. "But you'll have to come tomorrow, so you can kick my locker open."

"This is my sister and her husband," Solomon said, introducing Sandra to Margaret and Cameron because it seemed like the right thing to do.

"Hi," Sandra said, "and goodbye." She reached for the firepole, wrapped her legs about it and vanished down through the hole.

"Thank you for waiting," said Paul Kane from the other doorway. "Please come into our faculty room."

Once they were inside the faculty room, Paul Kane introduced them to two more teachers. "This is Candace Waverly. She teaches English and history. And Rebecca Edwards who teaches art and crafts. Our French and German teachers are based at the elementary school, and Darryl Storm, our eurythmy and P.E. teacher, had to be elsewhere today."

Then they all sat around the faculty room table, and Solomon waited for whatever was coming next. "Let's begin with you, Solomon," Paul Kane said. "Why do you want to come to our school?"

Solomon let the question wash over him at first, like one of the big waves that he remembered rolling onto the beach at Sand Island and didn't feel it tug at him until it was on its way out to sea again. Then its undertow pulled him awake. "I don't have a school to go to," he said.

"That's a good reason," said Paul Kane, "for a start. Where did you last go to school?"

"Crossroads. I was staying in a group home."

"Solomon came to live with us last Thursday," Margaret said.

"What subjects in school do you like?" Paul Kane asked. "And what don't you like?"

Solomon considered. He had never thought much about what he liked or didn't like in school because school had always been something he had had to do, whether he liked it or not. "My spelling is pretty good, now," he said.

"Well, that would be an addition to the class!" said Candace Waverly.

Solomon thought some more and remembered the teacher who had given him a mixed-up picture about the relationship between animals and human beings. "I don't like teachers who confuse things."

"Confuse things in what way?" asked Paul Kane.

"They don't think enough about what they teach. And they think things are less than what they really are."

Rebecca Edwards raised her eyebrows and nodded. "Well, this might be a good place for us to tell you and your family what our school tries to be about," Paul Kane said.

Solomon listened as the teachers spoke. From what he could make out, some things in this school were much like any other school, except there was a long lesson first thing in the morning which they called the main lesson, and they taught just about everything, including a lot of art. There would be plenty of homework they said, and he wouldn't have a choice about which subjects he took because each student did everything, if possible. They also said they taught their subjects in a way that had to do with him.

"And you're saying you lead everything back to the human being?" Cameron asked Candace Waverly.

"We try to do that," she replied, "to help the students see that everything in the world out there corresponds to the world within themselves, and that there is a place out there for human beings, something our modern world seems to have forgotten."

"I see," Cameron said and seemed to be impressed.

"And what's a eurythmy teacher?" Margaret asked. "The one who had to be somewhere else."

All the teachers laughed. "Where are you, Darryl, when we really need you?" said Rebecca Edwards. She stood and loosened her arms. "Imagine that every sound in our speech, and every tone in our music, has a gesture, a movement through which it can become visible. And then imagine that the human form can make that gesture visible and move it in space. That's what eurythmy is, making those gestures visible and moving them in space. Like so—"

She spoke the sound "Ah" as her arms lifted up from her shoulders and stretched out above her head in the form of a V, then "Eh" as she brought her arms down and crossed them together, sharply, near the wrists, in front of her breast. "You can also gesture consonants, and diphthongs." She stretched one arm outward until her hand was level with her ear, and brought the other to rest above her head in a parallel gesture, her palm facing upward as if it were resisting something bearing down upon it. She repeated the whole of the gesture and the sound she had spoken with it. As Solomon watched her intently and listened, the walls of the room melted away and the sound of her speaking transformed:

Au—

Auxw!

And now he was standing on the pebbles at Snag Point, the smell of crisping salmon in his nostrils, as the dark shape of Raven streaked downriver into the setting sun. He listened, wanting Isaac to begin the words of Raven's story. But the only sound he could hear was

Auxw!

Au—

"The sounds themselves are archetypal," Rebecca Edwards concluded, "yet they sound uniquely in each language, and so the gestures transform somewhat, to capture the sounding of a particular language." She sat down. "I hope I haven't been one of those teachers who confuse things."

"Fascinating," Cameron said, looking at Margaret for her reaction. But Solomon found that Margaret was looking at him, maybe asking herself where he had gone those couple of moments. "I take it this is your only class in the high school, so far?" she asked Paul Kane.

"Yes. We began the high school last fall and this is our lead class, all eleven of them. Here is a class photograph, from this year."

Solomon took the photograph from Paul Kane and began to study each of the eleven faces. He found Sandra, the girl he had just met, then moved to a girl who looked native, standing in the back row beside another girl who could be her twin but for the white skin beside the brown. Both girls had long brown hair and strong brown eyes.

A boy with deep blue eyes, dark hair, and very pale skin knelt in the front row. Solomon went back to his face several times and thought he saw something in those eyes that he understood. Another boy knelt beside him, with dark skin, but he was not native, and Solomon couldn't figure out where he might be from. A boy stood just behind them, not very tall, his hands in his baggy jeans pockets while the tail of his T-shirt flopped about his hands. He was grinning at the camera from beneath a mop of curly hair, as if life were a joke, probably on him, but that was all right.

At one end of the back row, a tall girl stood somewhat aloof from the others, as if she belonged to the class but not entirely. Next to her, a boy wearing a baseball cap spread his legs apart, waiting for someone to throw him a ball. Beside him a large boy, not quite fat, pondered what day of the week it might be and whether that mattered.

At the other end of the back row, a light-haired, slender girl in bare feet floated up from the ground, though a hint of something else glimmered in her eyes. In the front row, to the right of Sandra, one more girl was kneeling. Her gaze was clear and directed right at Solomon—not at the eye of the camera, but right at him.

"What's the next step from here?" Cameron was asking.

"To find out if we are the right school for Solomon," Candace Waverly replied. "He can join the class for the rest of this week. I'm finishing a main lesson in Canadian history, and he will be in time for Riel, Big Bear, and Poundmaker."

Fully present now, Solomon tried to remember where he had heard the name Poundmaker.

"Please think about what we've told you and phone me this evening if Solomon wants to come tomorrow," Paul Kane said, "since I'm the class guardian."

"We'll do that," said Cameron. "By the way, what are you people going to do about that firepole in the classroom?"

"Nothing," Paul Kane laughed, "though at first we thought we'd take it out or cover the hole over. However, we decided to call in a fireman to teach the students how to use it, and since they now know how to use it, we'll leave it just as it is."

"They're interesting people, all right, but are they teachers?" Margaret wondered on the way home.

"I wish I had had such a teacher," Cameron replied.

Solomon stood at his window that night and watched the inlet darken into a hazy blue tapestry dotted with lights, moving and still. When he decided he had stood long enough and that simply standing wasn't going to make things any clearer, he went downstairs.

"I'm going to try that school," he said.

Margaret's eyebrows lifted. "Then you had better phone Mr. Kane soon, before you have to get him out of bed to tell him that."

Solomon went to the phone and dialled the number.

"Good morning, Solomon." Mrs. Waverly met him as he walked into the classroom and shook his hand. "Take that desk, beside Izzy. Izzy, this is Solomon; he is visiting us this week."

Solomon sat down beside Izzy, the boy with his hands in his baggy pockets and the joke on his face. "Hi," Izzy grinned, and went on writing frantically in the paper-covered book spread open on his desk. "This is my main lesson book, where we write up the notes we've taken in class until our notes make sense. I'm finishing what I should have done last night but didn't."

Izzy saw Mrs. Waverly looking at him and put his book away. He stood, and Solomon saw the other members of the class standing at their desks, so he stood as well. The talking in the classroom died down to a few whispers. Then the door behind Solomon opened as a girl, the one whose bare feet had been floating up from the ground, slipped past him and took the vacant desk in front of his.

"You're late, Sigune," Mrs. Waverly said.

"The bell hasn't rung."

A few voices laughed, and then the large boy who had been figuring out what day of the week it was said in a flat voice, "There is no bell, Sigune."

"I know," she smiled.

Then everyone spoke something, together. It might have been a prayer they were speaking but not really, or a verse, but it felt like something more than other verses Solomon had heard.

"Let's review yesterday," said Mrs. Waverly, after everyone had sat down, "to wake up our memories and give Solomon a picture of what we are doing. Solomon is visiting us for a few days. Please introduce yourselves to him at break and see he doesn't get lost on the way to the store."

Solomon tried to look back at each of the faces looking at him, but it was too much, though he did return Sandra's little wave of the hand.

"1880 to 1885," Mrs. Waverly began. "What was happening in what was called the 'Northwest' during those years?"

"Everyone was mad at the government," said the native girl.

"Who was everyone, Juliet, and why were they mad?"

"The Métis, for one," Juliet answered.

"And who were the leaders of the Métis? Astrid?"

"Louis Riel and Gabriel Dumont," said Juliet's white twin, who sat at the desk beside Juliet's.

"And who else was upset?"

"The Indians," said the boy with dark blue eyes.

"Why, Alex?"

"Because the government had made treaties with them through people they trusted, like the Mounted Police and the missionaries, and now they were all starving."

"And why were they starving? Sigune, would you please practise your penmanship later."

Sigune closed her main lesson book and looked attentively at Mrs.

Waverly. "Anwar, why were the Indians starving?" Mrs. Waverly asked the dark-skinned boy.

"Because the Indian agents didn't always give out the emergency food the government had promised, and because some of the farm instructors didn't know how to farm."

Solomon listened as Mrs. Waverly reviewed with the class the events leading to the 1885 rebellion: The discontent of Métis, Indians, and even white settlers; the mass killing of the buffalo by white hunters; and the setting of fires along the border by the American cavalry so the buffalo couldn't cross into Canada.

"They were mad because Sitting Bull was here," said the girl who had seemed to be standing aloof from the others. Solomon straightened in his seat and leaned forward.

"Yes, Catherine, that was one reason. Lorne, would you please tell us who Sitting Bull was and how he came to be in Canada?"

The large boy folded his hands and thought a moment. "Well, I suppose I could, if you wish. Sitting Bull was a powerful Sioux chief and after the battle of the Little Big Horn, he and some 5,000 friends decided it would be a good idea to come to Canada for a holiday."

Everyone laughed, including Mrs. Waverly. Then she began to unfold the events of the Northwest Rebellion itself. Everyone became very quiet as she spoke of the killing of nine whites on April 2, at Frog Lake, by warriors who had followed Big Bear in refusing to settle on a reserve and had now broken with Big Bear's leadership.

"The other Cree leader who played a significant role was Poundmaker." Mrs. Waverly took a book from her desk, opened it, and held it up so the class could see the photograph.

"He's cute," Sigune said, after taking a close look.

"Cute is hardly the word," intoned Lorne, as Solomon sat very still, trying once again to remember where he had heard of Poundmaker.

"Poundmaker was a very striking man," Mrs. Waverly continued, "not only in his appearance. Like Big Bear he saw what signing the treaties could mean for his people. At the same time, he tried to find a nonviolent way of dealing with white settlers and the government. He didn't rush to join with Riel when the rebellion started, even though the Métis pressed him to do so. In the end, he had only one major run-in with the Canadian forces, and that was on May 2 . . ."

"Where was that?" interjected Sandra.

Suddenly Solomon remembered where and from whom he had heard of Poundmaker. "Cutknife Hill," he blurted out.

Everyone looked around at him, including the girl in the photograph with the clear, direct gaze. She had not spoken during the review, but there she was now looking right into him.

"That's right, Solomon. Cutknife Hill was the battle site," Mrs. Waverly said. Her eyes took Solomon in. "What else do you know about that battle?"

Solomon swallowed. "Not much. Only that my grandfather was there with Poundmaker."

All eyes in the room continued to stare at him. "My grandfather was also at the Little Bighorn," Solomon went on. "His father was killed, fighting Custer. He was seven. My grandfather, I mean."

Then everyone laughed, Solomon included.

At break several members of the class took Solomon in tow and headed for the nearby corner store. Along the way Astrid, Juliet, and Anwar split off from the group. "Where are they going?" Solomon asked.

"To their hideaway, where they can smoke in peace," Sandra said.

"Unhealthy!" said Jason, the boy with the baseball cap on his head.

"Jason is our class jock," Sigune said, "so he never does anything that's not one hundred percent pure. You even bring your own drinking water to school, don't you, Jason?"

"Tap water is just recycled shit," Jason returned. "Besides, Sigune, I have to set you a good example."

"I've never heard that name, Sigune, before," Solomon said.

"Well, it's like this," Sigune replied. "My mother is heavy duty Waldorf, and named me after this woman in the Parzival story."

"What's that story about?"

"It's a main lesson we're going to do in grade eleven, and it's supposed to be a profound experience and change all of our lives. I think I'll read the first and last pages, then throw the book away."

Outside the store, Solomon stood with the others, sipping at a can of pop. "Your grandfather was really at Cutknife Hill and the Little Bighorn?" said Alex.

"Yes."

"Far out!" Izzy said. But Sigune cocked her head skeptically. "Really? Your grandfather really was there?"

Solomon's eyes widened at her as she studied him. "Excuse me, if I presume to doubt you," Sigune went on, "but another guy visited our class, last fall, and tried to bullshit us with some far-out stories about himself. His visit didn't last long."

The anger flashed up in Solomon, then he let it die away. "I guess that's one way not to impress people. But I'm not bullshitting you, Sigune. What I told you is true, unless my father was lying to me, and he doesn't . . . he didn't ever lie."

Everyone of them caught the nuance in his words, and as one they backed off, then changed the course of the conversation.

After break Solomon was treated to his first eurythmy class in the room with all the lockers. The teacher, Darryl Storm, stomped in, pulled off his boots, and put on a pair of what looked like cloth slippers. Then he crossed the room, introduced himself to Solomon, and handed him a like pair of slippers. "I had to guess what your size might be, but I think these eurythmy shoes will fit you."

Solomon looked uncertainly at Darryl, then took off his runners, and slipped the eurythmy shoes on.

"We'll begin with 'I Think Speech,'" Darryl said, when the class had formed a large circle, "to help Solomon catch on. Solomon, just watch what we do and follow along as best you can. Remember, please, ignore the lockers and walls, and reach all the way to the horizon itself. I think speech . . ."

Solomon imitated Darryl's movement, stretching his arms out level with his shoulders.

"I speak. To the horizon, Izzy. Don't stop at the back of the locker," Darryl said, as he raised his outstretched hands level with his larynx and placed his right foot out to the right.

"I have spoken." Solomon dropped his hands to the plane of his heart, and placed his left foot out to the left. He moved with Darryl and the class through the next three lines and finished with his arms crossed, at his chest.

Then Solomon's feet fumbled through something called "threefold walking," followed by a series of short-short-long steps, long-short-short steps, and long-long steps, until Darryl said, "We'll finish with a rod exercise to keep us honest." He opened a corner locker, took some copper rods from it, and tossed one to each member of the class. Solomon nearly ducked as the rod came flying toward him, but then caught it.

"Everyone pair up, please," Darryl instructed. Solomon turned about to find the clear-eyed girl standing before him. "I'm Anika," she said.

"Start with the rod in your right hand," Darryl continued, "toss it to your left on short, then back to your right on short, and throw to your partner on long."

Anika held Solomon's eyes as Darryl began: "Short-short-long."

Anika threw her rod and suddenly Solomon was standing with a rod in each hand while she had none.

"You're supposed to throw when I do, on long."

"Okay," Solomon blinked as he tossed the rod back to her.

"Let's all do it this time," Darryl said. "Short-short-long." Solomon threw the rod awkwardly, but Anika caught it, and then they were into another, "Short-short-long." After a few more throws, their rods began to sing as they threw, caught, threw, caught, her eyes never leaving his, and his eyes not wanting to leave hers. The two of them went on throwing, catching, throwing, even after Darryl had stopped speaking, "Short-short-long."

"I think we're supposed to stop now," Anika said. Solomon made a last catch, then noticed that everyone was looking at them.

The next morning he tumbled out of bed early, spent a few moments with the bathroom mirror to reassure himself that his face was a face someone would want to look at, and was off to school before Cameron or Margaret realized he had gone. On Thursday afternoon, he sought out Paul Kane. "I like this school," Solomon said. "I want to stay."

"That's good news, Solomon. I would like you to stay, and I think my colleagues will agree. I'll phone you tonight."

Solomon was sitting at his desk reading *Huckleberry Finn*, the book the class was doing for English, when Margaret called him downstairs. He took the phone receiver from her.

"Welcome to the class of 1987, Solomon," Paul Kane said. "Tomorrow we'll teach you how to use the firepole."

"Thanks," Solomon replied. "I already know."

FOUR

"My socks stink, my feet stink, and I stink," Astrid said. She shifted the angle of the stick from which her socks dangled to catch a fresh patch of heat from the ever-shifting fire. The smoke also changed direction, and Solomon moved yet again to avoid its path.

A short distance away water tossed and frothed as it dashed itself down the bed of Cottonwood Creek's south fork toward its meeting with the Stein River. The little world about the campfire was heavily treed, dark, and damp from the day's rain that still fell in intermittent drizzles, and stuffed full of tents, their peg lines by now well entangled with one another. Almost everyone, grade nines and tens, had gone to bed in the hope that their sleeping bags would be dry or dry enough when they crawled into them. The teachers had also turned in for the night and only Anwar, Juliet, Astrid, and Solomon remained hunkered down about the campfire along with Barry White, Juliet's cousin. Earlier in the evening the rocks around the campfire had been covered with wet socks trying to dry, but only a few were left. The rest, dry or not, had gone into the tents with their owners. Astrid, however, vowed she would not go to bed until her socks were dry. "What were you laughing about out there?" she asked Solomon.

He had gone out into the bushes to relieve himself, when he met Juliet and Astrid coming back to the campfire from a smoking session down by the creek. After they had talked a while and it looked as if the girls weren't in a hurry to move on, Solomon said, "Excuse me, but I came out here to take a leak and I'd better get on with it."

"Go ahead," Juliet said. "We'll turn our backs."

Solomon doubted he could go ahead with the girls standing at such close range, but he found a pine nearby and managed to start things flowing. Then he remembered standing before a Sitka spruce on Log

Island, wondering if the tree on which he was urinating might be a relative. He chuckled at the thought.

"I was thinking that the pine on which I was pissing might be related to me," Solomon said.

Astrid burst out laughing. "Shh!" Juliet giggled. "Mrs. Waverly will have a bird if we wake her up."

"All my relations," said Barry White.

"What does that mean?" Anwar asked.

"Just what Solomon was saying, though his tongue was in his cheek. All the animals and plants and people in this valley, in the world, are a big family, each one related to all the rest."

Anwar lit a cigarette. It was late, there were two other smokers at the fire, and he didn't feel like hiking out into the bushes for his smoke. "Well, if we're all related, we're not a very happy family," he said.

"Now what do you mean?" Astrid asked.

"Do you have to ask? Read the paper, watch the TV. Everyone's at war with someone else. That's all I can remember before I came here. Nothing but war."

"Where were you before you came here?" Solomon asked.

"The Middle East. My dad is from Iraq and my mother from Egypt. He's Muslim and she's a Christian. I was born in Egypt, but we got out of there after the war with Israel in 1973 and moved to Lebanon." He flicked the ash into the fire and laughed drily. "Then we got the hell out of there and came to Canada. My parents named me after the man who was the last president of Egypt, the one who made peace with Israel. At least he tried to do something before they knocked him off."

"Do you miss not being there, where you were from?" Solomon asked.

"I don't think about it that much," Anwar said. "All I do know is if I were almost anywhere in the Middle East, I'd be in some army by now. And probably dead." He tossed his cigarette into the fire. "I'm going to bed. I just hope Jason isn't snoring."

"And I'm on my way, too," said Astrid, satisfied with the state of her socks. "Goodnight, guys."

Barry White also stood. "Don't spend the night out here," he said to Juliet and Solomon. "We have a couple of stiff climbs tomorrow."

Solomon pulled his jacket collar up around his neck as the rain started to trickle down, and stared into the fire while the flames crackled and spun about what remained of the wood. Juliet took a stick and poked at the coals. "You don't mind sitting in the rain?" she said.

Solomon shook his head. "There's a lot of rain where I come from."

"And where do you come from?" She wasn't looking at him, but Solomon knew she was opening a door if he wanted a door opened.

"Duxsowlas. Across from Port Hardy and then north."

"Why did you leave?"

"I had a disagreement with my uncle. After my dad died. A guy in our village had been drinking while working on his boat and shoved a screwdriver through his balls. My dad took him out in my uncle's boat, and they both drowned on the way to Port Hardy." As he spoke, Solomon was aware that he was saying more to Juliet about his leaving Duxsowlas than he had said to anyone else. He also realized that Anika had slipped out of the darkness as he had been speaking and was sitting on the log opposite him.

"Did your dad drink?" Juliet asked, also aware of Anika but not bothered by her being there.

"No, but my mom did, for a while," Solomon replied, deciding he, too, didn't mind Anika being there.

"My dad drank," Juliet said, "a lot, for as long as I can remember. When my mom got fed up with him, she moved to Vancouver with me. That's when I came to the school."

"But you go back sometimes?" Solomon asked.

"To see my aunts and uncles. I don't know where my dad went."

Solomon picked up a stick and dropped it into the fire. "I don't know when I'll go back," he said. "If I ever go back." He let his words die into the night and the silence; then he stood. "Goodnight."

Juliet looked up at him. "Goodnight."

"Goodnight," Anika said and did not look up.

During the night a wind swept into the valley of the Cottonwood and broke the cloud cover open. At daybreak, Solomon crawled out of his sleeping bag, then over Izzy and Alex, and out of the tent into a clear September morning. The air about him was still cool and damp, and voices groaned sleepily from the tents near his as Barry White and Paul Kane began the wake-up call. Solomon looked over at the tent in which Sandra and Sigune were sleeping. The tent roof sagged, weighed down with a pool of water the rain had made during the night. Sigune stumbled out of the tent, then ducked as someone inside stood and the pool of water flew up into the air.

Solomon walked down to the creek, splashed the icy water over his face and neck, arms and shoulders, and remembered plunging into ocean water at Log Island.

"Don't worry about wet tents," Barry called out after everyone had eaten breakfast. "Pack them as best you can and let's move."

The sun rose and dispersed the last of the clouds. They hiked in single file until they came to Cattle Creek, where they took a break and filled their canteens and water bottles. Solomon filled his bottle then cupped water into his hands and drank.

Quo-k . . .

Water splattered from his face as his head jerked up. The raven was across the creek perched on a boulder, half in the sun and half in the shadow thrown by a large fir. The raven stared back at him with interest, it seemed, and both its eyes were intact. Solomon stood slowly, his eyes steady on the raven. The raven's eyes were too far away for him to see what might be in them, but the raven shrugged his wings and finished cleaning his breast with a click of his beak, seeming to be at ease with Solomon's presence.

Maybe it's all right, now . . .?

Barry White led them across the log that spanned Cattle Creek, and then the trail began to climb very sharply. Solomon had thought he was in pretty good shape but was changing his mind with every step uphill. He wasn't alone; almost everyone was puffing and panting, except for Sandra and Jason who were up front with Barry, and two energetic grade nine boys who stayed at Barry's heels with a clatter of canteens and other accessories.

Just when Solomon and those near him had decided there wasn't another uphill step left in them, the trail began to level out along a high bluff. He caught glimpses of the Stein River in the distance, its slate green coils winding back and forth through the valley to the south of them. The line of the hike undulated along the bluff, with students and teachers walking in pairs or threes, or singly as did Solomon.

Stripped down to a T-shirt and a pair of shorts, and wearing the hat Hector had given him, Solomon drank in the sharp, clean scent of pine and stretched his legs into the trail. Now and then a wind pushed against him, tugged at his hat, then died down. Solomon didn't worry much about that until a sharp gust struck the side of his head and whipped the hat away. Solomon snatched at it, missed, and watched the wind dribble the hat along the trail ahead of him, then lift it over the side of the bluff. Solomon lost sight of the hat for a moment, then saw it again hanging from the tip of a thick root that curved out from the bank a short drop below the trail. The wind tugged some more, but the hat stayed put.

Solomon had only one thought: he didn't want to lose that hat. He dropped his pack to the ground and eased himself over the edge of the bluff and down the bank toward the root. The earth seemed compact beneath his feet and hands, though he realized the root was farther down the bank than it had appeared to be from the trail.

Solomon placed his foot beside the root and reached for his hat. His foot shot out from his body and he began to slide until both his hands grabbed hold of the root and stopped him from sliding farther. Hoping that the root would hold, he looked uphill past his hat still dangling from the root tip and fixed his eyes on the edge of the trail.

The root held. Solomon drew himself up the bank until he could rest his knee on the root. He placed his hat firmly on his head, then gripped the root with his foot. The edge of the trail was just above him and just beyond his reach. He tried to grip into the bank with his free foot, but the earth that had seemed so firm on the way down crumbled as he began to shift his weight. He tried twice more, then brought his foot back to the root.

Solomon rested his forehead against the bank and didn't know what he was going to do next, feeling as he had felt that moment when he had stood on the corner of Granville and Davie. He glanced up again toward the trail and into a pair of deep blue eyes. Alex was leaning over the trail edge, his hand almost in reach of Solomon's. "Reach for me and hold on," Alex said.

Solomon nodded and drew his breath in. His hand leapt upward as his foot pushed the root away. Their hands gripped and Alex drew him up the bank and onto the trail. When Solomon stood up, he saw that Sigune and Anwar had been holding onto Alex. He looked at each face, then came back to Alex and to those eyes that knew something he knew. "Thanks," he said. "I was really stuck there."

He glanced over the bank and saw what he had not noticed moments earlier. Below the root the bank fell way more steeply, then more steeply still. If he had kept on sliding, his body would now be down at Cottonwood Creek.

Paul Kane came along the trail with Catherine, Lorne, and Anika. "What happened?" Catherine asked.

"The wind blew my hat off and I climbed down to get it," Solomon said. "I almost didn't make it back up."

"That must be a very special hat," Mr. Kane said after a long look down the bank.

"It is. But it was dumb of me, I guess, to go after it when no one else was around. Thanks again," Solomon said to Alex and the others.

The trail crossed a shoulder of the bluff, ran downhill only to arrive at a last gruelling climb up a mass of rock Barry called Unnecessary Knob, before dropping sharply down into the Stein Valley. At the bottom, they crossed Cottonwood Creek once again, then flopped down upon their packs beneath the pine trees in a spacious camping area.

After they had pitched their tents, dried them in the wind and the afternoon sun, and eaten dinner, Barry called them to the campfire. Solomon saw an open space on one of the logs and sat down beside Anika. As she shifted her body to make more room for him, he glimpsed the light of the fire touching at her face.

Barry stood at the fire and waited for everyone to stop talking. Then he spoke about the Stein Valley. It had long been a sacred place he said, both to his people and the people of Mount Currie farther west.

The valley was a place where people had come to meditate, to pray, to be alone with themselves. It was a place where young people came for vision quests as early as age eight or nine. Some would stay in the valley a few weeks, others much longer, depending on what the Elders thought their tasks in life might be. The pictographs they would see the next couple of days, painted upon granite faces of rock, might be pictures of what some had seen during their vision quests.

A logging company wanted to put a road through the valley and log parts of it, but the people for whom the valley was a sacred place, along with others who cared, would never let that happen.

Then Barry finished, saying that the Stein River was the soul of the valley and would help them become clean within themselves. So early tomorrow morning, they were going in for a swim, every one of them. Laughs and groans of disbelief greeted Barry's last words. He laughed as well, and said he was just kidding, but they'd find out tomorrow he really wasn't kidding.

A few figures wandered away from the fire, but most stayed put talking. "Did you come here, for that kind of vision quest?" Sandra asked Juliet.

"No. We moved just before I would have been old enough."

"Did you have vision quests where you're from?" Izzy asked Solomon.

"Yes, in a way," Solomon answered, and then decided to risk himself more than that. "When I was nine, my dad took me to an island near our village and left me there for three days."

"What was it like?" Sigune asked.

"It was damned cold the first day, after the fire went out and the rain started. I slept under a bush that night with the water running down my neck. Man, was I hungry the next day!"

"Your dad didn't leave you anything to eat?" said Izzy.

"No, but my stomach didn't know that."

"So what did you do?" Anika asked.

Solomon tried to remember what he had done, then started to laugh. "I told stories to my stomach."

"You're not serious!" Sigune said. "This time you can't be serious."

"It's the truth, I swear. It was the only way I figured I could shut my stomach up, by outtalking it."

"What stories did you tell?" asked Alex.

"Stories about Raven, mainly."

"Tell us one," Anika said, her eyes intent upon his.

"Well, I guess I could," Solomon said, and told the one about Raven trying to steal the bait from the hooks of halibut fishermen. Raven's beak was yanked from his face in the process, so he had to disguise himself with a blanket to go into a house and get it back. Then he started the one about the time Raven stole a salmon. Solomon had liked this story when Isaac first told it and put himself into telling it now—so much so that those who had drifted away from the fire came back and other conversations died away. Solomon realized that his story had become the centre of attention; he carried on more enthusiastically.

Those people were so mad at Raven, Solomon said, that when they found him sleeping, they tore his gizzard out of his rear end and went off with it. So Raven flew along until he saw some boys kicking his gizzard about, like it was a soccer ball, but when he tried to get it back, Raven found out he wasn't a good soccer player. When he finally did fly off with his gizzard, it was full of dirt, and try as Raven would, he couldn't wash it clean. "Even Tide didn't work," Solomon said, "and Raven's been stuck with that dirty gizzard ever since."

There was a round of applause as Solomon finished. When Barry White had stopped laughing, he said, "Boy, I'm not going to let someone from the coast outdo me when it comes to stories. But you'll have to wait until tomorrow night for mine."

"Did he mean it, about that swim?" Izzy asked Solomon as they crawled into their sleeping bags. "Maybe he really was joking."

Barry had not been joking, however. The next morning, before the sun had even risen, he shook each tent awake. Rebecca Edwards and Darryl Storm made the rounds a second time.

"Are you guys serious?" Astrid groaned.

"We're serious. Let's go," Darryl said.

Jason charged down to the river bank then stopped, plagued by second thoughts. Solomon and Izzy walked past him and climbed down the bank. "We're crazy," said Izzy.

"We sure are," Solomon agreed, and both boys fell into the water. Then everyone else plunged in. Solomon let the river take him, let it turn his body over and about, let it wash over and into and through his skin. The Stein swept Alex alongside him. Alex and Solomon laughed and rode the current one more time before swimming toward the bank.

As he rubbed himself dry, Solomon realized he had not felt so clean since his four days on Log Island. Maybe things were all right now.

The last day of the hike Barry led them up and across a slide of shale and granite called the Devil's Staircase. One more stretch of easy walking brought them to the Asking Rock, close to the trail head. "Whenever you enter or leave the valley, you can make an offering here, and ask the Spirit of the Valley for a safe journey in, or give thanks for having had a safe journey."

Solomon looked the face of rock over. Others about him were leaving pinches of tobacco on little ledges that jutted out or sticking coins into cracks. He was thinking about his offering when his eyes found a wider, deeper incision into the rock, and he knew there was nothing to think about. He lifted the hat from his head and looked at the black and red lines that formed the figure of Raven and the words beneath. He pictured Hector standing before him in the big house at Duxsowlas, hands in his pockets, knowing that Solomon, though it had been another name then, needed something special from him right at that moment.

Solomon folded the hat and tucked it tightly into the opening in the rock face. He stood, eyes closed, giving thanks and asking, an asking too deep for words, a question wanting to be put to himself or to someone. When he opened his eyes, he saw Alex looking at him. Solomon grinned in return, and the two boys started up the hill toward the trail head.

Solomon stopped short, as Izzy and he walked along Commercial Drive, and asked himself how he could have forgotten that Joe's was there. "What's wrong?" Izzy asked.

"A lapse of memory," Solomon smiled. "Let's go inside."

"I've never played this game," Izzy said, looking the cue over.

"I'll teach you, while we drink down a couple of cappuccinos." By the end of the afternoon, Izzy had connected with his cue and Solomon had cleaned away a good deal of rust from his game. They came back the next day, three days before the end of the Christmas holidays, bringing Alex, Jason, Sandra, and Sigune with them. Solomon wasn't so sure about Sigune and cappuccinos because she was off the ground enough as it was. However, she took to her cue with enthusiasm while Sandra and Jason gave him some stiff competition.

On Monday the grade ten class went back to school, and an expanded group that included Anika went down to Joe's that afternoon. Before they headed for home and their first evening of homework, Izzy said, "We should come here at lunchtime."

"I don't think so," Alex said. "It would be tight, getting here and back, and shooting a decent game in between."

"But it would be a neat way to spend lunch break," Sigune said.

Solomon and Izzy glanced around at the others, and Izzy's eyes began to twinkle. "I have an idea," he said.

The next day Solomon and Izzy sought out Darryl Storm. "We've noticed you have a hard time getting here from the grade school for P.E. on Thursdays," Izzy said. Darryl agreed. The grade school's lunch break was on a different schedule than that of the high school.

"We thought maybe we could begin P.E. later that day," Solomon suggested, "to give you more time to eat lunch."

Darryl studied the two faces before him. Solomon kept his blank and Izzy struggled to keep the imp right at the back of his eye. "And what would that give you in return?" Darryl asked, a smile tugging at his mouth.

"A longer lunchtime at Joe's," Izzy said, unable now to keep the grin away from his mouth.

"And we were thinking that we could extend the eurythmy class, last period on Monday, to balance things out," Solomon added.

Darryl's smile broadened. "Extend the last period of the day? On a Monday? And who, pray tell, are the 'we' you speak of?"

"The whole class," Solomon replied. "Almost."

"Except for Catherine and Lorne. And Juliet, Astrid, and Anwar," said Izzy.

Darryl laughed. "All right. I'll take your proposal to the other teachers, and you persuade those you have just named that they, too, would benefit from a longer Thursday lunch break in return for a longer Monday afternoon in class. Persuasion is the word I used, not coercion, bribery, or blackmail."

Seven pairs of hands swept Juliet, Anwar, and Astrid off course, as the three of them were heading for their lunchtime smoke.

"What are you guys doing?" Astrid gasped.

"Taking you to Joe's," said Jason.

"Get real! I don't shoot pool," Juliet protested.

"We'll teach you," Solomon said.

"And Joe's has ashtrays, too," Sigune said.

"And cappuccinos and ice cream," added Sandra.

"I hate coffee!" Anwar said.

"Then try an almond milk," Anika replied. "You'll like it."

"You guys are going to thank us for this," Izzy grinned. "You'll see."

Catherine and Lorne were another matter. "Why should I go home later on Mondays, just so you guys can shoot pool?" Catherine asked.

"I was asking myself that," Anwar said, "a couple of hours ago, but it's fun and Joe's is a neat place."

"You like eurythmy," Anika suggested, "and you don't like P.E., so it wouldn't be such a bad deal for you."

Solomon observed Catherine as that look of uncertainty came down upon her face. "No, it wouldn't be, I guess."

"Well," Lorne said, when their eyes turned to him, "I suppose I could study the binding on my math book, practise digesting, and commune with myself during that lunchtime."

On Wednesday, after morning break, Solomon and Izzy danced into math class. "Yes, yes, yes!" Izzy chirped.

"But, we're back on time on Thursdays," Solomon cautioned, "and no pushing Darryl to let us go earlier on Mondays."

"No problem!" their classmates chorused.

The next several Thursdays and Mondays worked wonderfully. During those lunchtimes Solomon learned much about his classmates.

Astrid played violin in the Vancouver Youth Symphony. Solomon observed her hands, her fingers long and slender, as she brought her cue up to the cue ball and her fingers became more sure with each shot she made. Alex lived with his mother, who was still angry with the husband who had left her years before, and he felt the absence of the father he had once known—something Solomon understood well. Sigune, in turn, loved her parents in spite of the funny name they had given her, but wished they would lighten up and have some fun before they died.

Anwar's family name, Al-Ansari, went back many centuries to those who had stood by Mohammed during his darkest hours, yet Anwar was uncertain about being either a Muslim or a Christian or whether that even mattered. Jason loved his baseball team, Sandra knew she could outrun Jason, and Juliet was determined to stop smoking one day.

Solomon already knew Izzy pretty well and felt he knew Anika. They didn't say much to one another, but that was okay because there was something between them on another level, beyond words.

About Catherine and Lorne he learned little because their classmates wouldn't talk about them when they weren't present—something that impressed Solomon very much.

Solomon learned some things about himself as well. First, he was doing with his classmates the very thing Judy had done with him when she had brought him to Joe's—listening to them, asking a question, then listening some more. He chuckled at himself, once he twigged to what he was about, and wondered if they were on to him as he had been on to Judy. He also discovered he no longer cared that much whether he won or lost a game. With Judy, winning had mattered, but now what mattered was just being with his friends and even helping them to play better.

Solomon also learned that shooting pool at Joe's took its toll on his time for doing homework.

"Solomon, what can you tell us about Cyclops?" Mrs. Waverly asked.

"Not much," he swallowed. "I'm a few pages behind."

Mrs. Waverly gave him that look of hers, then called upon Catherine to tell the class about Cyclops, perhaps because she could count on Catherine having done the reading.

Cyclops, said Catherine, was a gigantic creature with one eye who lived in a cave and wasn't into extending hospitality to strangers. So when Odysseus and his men dropped in for a visit, Cyclops devoured two of them for dinner and another two for breakfast, then blocked the cave entrance with a stone when he left for the day. But Odysseus sharpened a length of olive wood, and he and the remaining men went for Cyclops that night.

"Just after Cyclops gets drunk and pukes up two more men he has eaten," said Sigune. "That is so gross!"

"Yes, it is gross," agreed Mrs. Waverly, "so we won't start reading there but a little past there. Anika, please."

Anika began to read, and Solomon followed in his book. Odysseus heated up the olive beam until its sharpened tip glowed. Then he and his men seized it, plunging it deep into Cyclops's eye and twirling it until the blood boiled round the hotpoint, and the fire scorched the eye to its roots.

The class drew in its breath when Anika stopped reading. "That is also gross," Sigune said.

"Solomon, are you all right?" Mrs. Waverly asked. Solomon stared straight ahead and did not hear or see her. Above his head the ball of the sun burned and bled while the sound of the rifle whirled about his ears and the feathers began to fall about him . . .

"Solomon?" He blinked and saw her looking at him.

"I need to go to the washroom," he said.

"Can you wait until break?"

"No." Then she nodded, and he left the classroom. Inside the boys' washroom, he leaned his bum against the sink and closed his eyes. Still, the sun bled and the feathers kept on falling . . .

He forced himself to turn around and look into the mirror, into the raw, empty socket if it should be there. Instead a pair of eyes, dark and searching, found his and held his gaze. Sharp and black, he thought, like those of Raven, and both of them there, so it should be all right. But it wasn't all right. Who was he kidding, whatever the mirror told him, telling himself it was all right?

Solomon washed his face and went back to class. At lunchtime, he slipped away from the others and found a tree in Chinook Park that seemed welcoming enough. He leaned against the trunk and tried to still the panic within him. After a while, he looked up to see Alex sitting down beside him. "That's some shadow you've got," Alex said.

"What are you talking about?"

"The shadow that's on your tail."

Solomon twirled some blades of grass about his finger. "How do you know so much?"

"Maybe it takes one to know one," Alex said.

Solomon looked out into the park at the last of the yellow leaves dangling precariously from the trees about them. "What do we have next?"

"Pool. Then P.E. It's Thursday."

"That's good," Solomon said. But he still didn't feel good about what had happened and played badly that day.

"What happened to you when I was reading?" Anika asked, after he missed his shot and as she went to take hers. Suddenly, he wanted to tell her, tell her everything, to pour words into the warmth of her beside him. But he didn't. "An off day, I guess," was all he said.

"This is working out well," Sandra said after a few Thursdays had passed. "Perhaps we could squeeze out another long lunchtime."

Izzy's eyes lit up again and he started to think about how that might be done. Solomon, he, and a few others clustered in front of the school at morning break the next day to firm up their strategy.

"Forget Ms. Edwards's class on Friday," Jason advised. "There isn't a hope in hell she'll go for it."

"Then it's Mr. Kane and math," Izzy concluded. "I hope he's in an understanding mood."

"He'll understand," Solomon said, "because he's our class guardian and that's his job, to understand things."

The strategy of the grade ten class was simple. Friday morning math classes had been an ordeal. Preweekend memory lapses about homework abounded, as well as lapses in attention span during class itself. But that was going to change, Izzy and Solomon had assured Mr. Kane. The class would complete all homework assigned and would work intensively at whatever task Mr. Kane set for them in return for an extension to their lunch break. Bemused, Paul had listened then agreed. A short but engaged Friday class was a better bet than a longer, nothing class, he said.

That Thursday as Solomon drew a bead on the thirteen-ball, Juliet glanced up from watching him, and blinked. Catherine stood at the end of their table toying with a cue. "What do I do with this thing?" she asked.

Catherine joined them again the next day, the first of their Fridays, then the following Thursday. The day after, in the course of a second round of very intense games, Astrid glanced at her watch. "Oh my God!" she said.

They walked into art class fifteen minutes late. Lorne was sitting, paintbrush in hand and an inscrutable look on his face as his classmates filed through the doorway. Ms. Edwards waited until they were all in the room. "Grace is part of life and of your lives this afternoon," she said, very quietly. "But, please, do not ever be late again for this class. Is my meaning clear?"

Straight-faced and sober, the class indicated they understood her meaning very well. Straight-faced except for Catherine. Glancing at her, Solomon saw a little smile dance along her mouth as if she were glad someone had caught her out for something. "We're sorry," Solomon said to Ms. Edwards. "We got carried away, I guess."

"Thank you for your apology and please don't be carried away again. Now, let's go to work."

The following Thursday Lorne walked into Joe's, took a cue from the rack and pondered it for a moment. "Am I guaranteed to hit something with this?" he asked.

Anika and Sigune laughed, and Solomon grinned. "Sure, if you follow the instructions."

Lorne looked around at the eleven of them. "Well it gets lonely, you know, eating lunch all by yourself."

On Friday the sun made a special visit to Vancouver, cleansing the sky of rain and then any trace of cloud. It feels like spring, they all agreed as they headed for Joe's after an exemplary math class. The light overhead teased and tugged at them as their jackets came off, and they all felt wonderfully lightheaded. The pool playing, too, was exemplary as Lorne, the newcomer, made a niche for himself alongside Sandra, Jason, and Solomon. But then all their cues worked miracles that day while the hands behind the front counter put a little extra love into the cappuccinos and almond milks, and no one, not even Astrid, bothered to look at a watch.

Alex was the first one through the door of the art room at a quarter past two. The rest followed. Mr. Kane and Ms. Edwards waited until each of them had found a chair and sat. After the silence had made itself felt, Mr. Kane began: "A good idea has to work if it is to continue to be a good idea. Yours stopped working at 1:30 this afternoon. Does anyone want to offer a good reason as to why it stopped working?"

No one glanced at anyone else, and no one spoke.

"Then your lunchtime pool playing is over, and you will make up this class next Friday afternoon. To make sure there are no surprise afterschool plans on that day, I will phone your parents or"—with a glance at Solomon—"the equivalent and tell them what's happening, and why."

Downstairs and outside, the class of 1987 went into a huddle. "We have one pissed-off art teacher, guys," Juliet said. Then Astrid exploded. "And she has one pissed-off student! That is so dumb, the two of them coming down on us like heavyweight champions of the world."

"Come on," said Alex. "We blew it."

"Once! We blow it once, and they act like their world is falling apart. Screw them!" Fuming, Astrid broke from the group and stormed down the street. Wide-eyed, Juliet watched her go, then said, "See you on Monday, everyone." She jogged off after her friend.

"My, my," said Lorne, "this has been a day of revelations. I suppose I'll go home now and tell my parents what a bad boy I've been."

The tension broke and a few voices laughed. "It's the first time anyone in this school has slapped my wrist for anything," said Catherine. "But do us a favour, Solomon, please?"

"What favour?" he asked.

"Don't apologize this time. It was a good idea, whatever Mr. Kane thinks of it now."

Solomon took his time going home, however. Margaret and Cameron were waiting for him when he walked into the house. Cameron beckoned toward the couch, and Solomon sat. "Mr. Kane phoned us," Cameron said. "Perhaps you would tell us what this is all about."

So Solomon told them, observing each of them as he spoke. Cameron seemed concerned but not upset. Margaret's face, however, was dark with something Solomon could not see through. "Maybe we should send you to a school where you can screw around without costing us money," she said, when Solomon had finished speaking.

Surprised, Solomon protested. "I haven't been screwing around. Today's was the first class I've ever missed."

"Maybe. But you have a track record of instigating disruption and upsetting teachers, like the time you were in grade six."

Solomon stared at her. "How do you know about that?"

"Mom told me when I came home that Easter."

"And then you went away before that teacher did," Solomon said, the words rising up and spilling out. He checked himself, then finished what he really wanted to say. "I didn't drive her out. She got a big headache from all that stuff she was trying to teach us and went away to give her head a rest. Which is what I'm going to do now." Solomon stood up and walked out of the house.

When he returned that night, Margaret sat alone at the kitchen table. "I guess I owe you an apology," she said as he sat down across from her.

"Maybe and maybe not. But you sounded too much like Mom when you spoke and that's not good."

"Why isn't it good?" Margaret asked.

"Because you're too young to sound that much like her, and besides, you're not her. You're Maggie not Mom."

She dropped her chin to the cup of her hands. "It's been a long time since anyone's called me by that name, even you. I left it behind in Duxsowlas when I stepped into that plane."

"Mom started to drink after you left."

"I was afraid she might. She did some, a lot, before you were born."

"Did it make you feel better, leaving?"

"Yes, better and worse, but I couldn't see me staying there, knowing what I knew but not being able to do anything about it."

Solomon fell silent. Then he said, "You were right, about what was happening."

Her gaze held him fast. "How do you know?"

"Because I left for the same reason you did." Then he told her about Naomi's coming to him afraid of her father, and what Harvey had done to himself the next day, and what their father had done about that. And then about climbing the steps of Uncle Charlie's porch that night, and what he had seen when he opened the door . . .

Margaret breathed out slowly. "No wonder Uncle was glad to see the back of you. Oh, God! And away I went and left you and Frank behind—"

"And then I left Frank," Solomon said. He closed his eyes and saw Frank beside him on the beach as the plane with Mr. Blaisdell inside climbed out of sight . . . "Are you going to stay, Nathan?"

"I've asked myself how badly Uncle hurt David, if he was going to do that to Frank," Solomon said after a few moments had passed. Margaret's eyes widened as he spoke, but she kept them fixed on the calendar hanging on the kitchen wall. "Do you have any homework?" she asked.

Solomon laughed at her question. "It's Friday night. But I'm going to turn in early."

"I'm sorry," Margaret said as he stood. "Sorry I had to turn my back on you and leave you behind, Nathan . . ." Then she shook her head. "Sorry again. The name just slipped out."

"That's okay," Solomon said. "It was my name there." Upstairs, he wondered if it could still be his name. But no, it would just confuse everyone telling his classmates and teachers he wasn't Solomon but another name. Better to leave things be.

On Monday morning, the grade ten class went straight to work and by Wednesday they had made it clear they just wanted to put this week behind them. Resigned to a long afternoon on Friday, all twelve were in the art room by 1:30 sharp. "We're going on a field trip," Ms. Edwards said. "Bring your sketch books, please."

Their surprise became amazement when they found themselves outside of Joe's then inside the door. "Solomon, would you please order a cappuccino for me? Make it strong. Now then, we are going to practice sketching the human body in concentrated action. And as we have a double period, I want at least two top-notch drawings from each of you before we leave these tables at the end of the afternoon."

Well into the afternoon Rebecca, partnered with Jason, was engaged in a close match with the team of Sandra and Solomon. She glanced up from her cue to see Astrid sitting nearby, sketch book in hand and pencil poised above it. "I'm waiting for your body to act concentratedly, Ms. Edwards," Astrid said, her eyes touched with light once again.

Do not go gentle into that good night . . .

Solomon needed one more poem for his main lesson book on the art of poetry, due tomorrow. "It looks like you're about to burn both ends off another candle," Margaret said as he came downstairs for a last snack.

"I guess I am. I'll try to blow the candle out before it burns right through." Back at his desk, Solomon studied that last blank page in his main lesson book. Nothing. He turned to the front, where he had copied in the poem by Dylan Thomas, and read the poem through. As he read, he listened to the voice of the poet speaking to his dying father and thought of his own father.

Rage, rage against the dying of the light.

So now I'll write something that sounds like him. I could do worse, I guess.

He thought about doing a rough draft, but no there wasn't enough candle left in him that night for rough drafts. He'd have to do it right the first time, right onto that white naked page. He checked the ink in his pen then brought it to the paper:

Don't ask me if I love the light

He blinked in surprise then let his pen go on writing:

Blind I am, my seeing gone
What I once saw, I see no more
My seeing died, when daylight dawned

That's pretty good. Not as good as Dylan Thomas, maybe, but pretty good for last thing on a Thursday night with this book due first thing tomorrow. Solomon took a deep breath, and his pen continued on its way:

> Raven came and brought the sun
> And

Knocked? No, kicked.

> And kicked the shadows all about
> And with the sun, Old Raven brought
> the day,

And?

> and dawning of my doubt

Now finish it, somehow.

> Light is cruel, as well as kind,
> And is not gentle with the night
> So understand if I rage, rage

Solomon stared at the page and saw the words form as his pen worked to catch up with them.

> Against the coming of the light

He read the poem through, looking into the mirror of his own words and at the image they gave back. Then he closed the book and blew out the candle.

FIVE

"Who can tell me what this is?"

The grade eleven class looked at the photograph Paul Kane held up before them in the course of their main lesson on astronomy. "An eclipse of the sun," Sandra said.

"That's right. How does an eclipse of the sun come about? Lorne, please."

Lorne tapped his fingers on his desktop. "The moon's path crosses the sun's, and the moon stops in front of the sun while the two have a little talk."

"Then the moon gets bored and goes her way," Sigune added.

"Yes, so it seems," Paul said. "At what phase of the moon does this brief encounter take place?"

"The new moon," Anwar said, "when we can't see it because it's so close to the sun. Every twenty-eight days, or maybe twenty-nine, from what you said."

"Good. So, every twenty-nine days we should see the moon eclipsing the sun, but we don't. Why not?"

"Ah, okay," Alex said. "Because the two paths don't always cross at every new moon."

"That's right. The moon's path and the sun's—we called it the ecliptic—can vary by as much as five degrees, so the two don't always meet at the new moon, although every new moon is a potential eclipse of the sun, and an eclipse of the sun is the only time we ever see a new moon. Now, let's look at some more photos." Paul set photographs of solar eclipses along the ledge of the blackboard, and the class observed them.

"They're beautiful," Anika said. "In that one, it looks as if the sun has wings."

"Where do you see the wings, Anika?"

"In the light that flows out from behind the moon."

"Does anyone know the name given to that light?" Paul asked. "No? Well, it's called the sun's *corona*." He wrote the word on the blackboard. "Coming from the Latin word meaning crown as in *coronation*, or *crowning*. So, the corona is the sun's crown, visible only when we see a solar eclipse. Because an eclipse lasts only a few moments, the corona rays out only so far before, as Sigune put it, the moon becomes bored and goes on her way. Then we see the sun again as we usually see it. But some astronomers have suggested that if the moon were to engage the sun in a longer conversation, the corona would continue to ray out even farther from the sun and would embrace much, perhaps all, of our solar system."

"Does that mean that we're inside the sun, somehow?" Astrid asked. "That other part of the sun, I mean."

"Well, that could be a way of thinking about it," Paul replied. "One more question before we break. What makes it possible for us to observe the sun's corona at all?"

"The eclipse," Solomon said, quietly. "The moon shuts out the sun as we usually see it."

When the lesson ended, Solomon walked to the blackboard and stood beside Anika. "You're right," he said to her. "It is beautiful."

Izzy tugged at his sleeve. "Let's go, man. Your break and mine is slipping away." The two of them with Alex headed down to the second floor. "The firepole," said Izzy. "We've neglected the firepole."

The three of them veered away from the others into the grade nine classroom. A lone grade nine boy, Jim, sat at his desk writing furiously into a main lesson book. "You're one enthusiastic student," Solomon said.

"I don't have much choice," Jim grunted. Alex glanced at the book. "I thought that Physiology block ended a week ago."

"Tell me about it," Jim snapped.

Solomon glanced over to the tackboard where Paul Kane had left some drawings and photographs of the eye, the ear . . . The eye! Solomon stepped over to the tackboard and stared at the photograph of the human eye. It was the same picture, the same as the ones they had been looking at moments before—the black disc at the centre and a corona of light about it, raying out, raying in, on all sides. "What are you doing?" Jim asked as Solomon took the photograph from the board.

"Research," Solomon answered and followed Alex and Izzy down the pole.

Studying the photograph that night, Solomon thought about eclipsing the sun. Is that what he had tried to do once by shooting the sun in the eye? But the sun had come back the next day and cast even more of his world into daylight. Trying to eclipse the sun that way had changed nothing, other than setting him up to leave Duxsowlas.

The picture of the raw, naked socket in the head of Raven surfaced again within him, and he shuddered as he tried to make it go away. Yet as Solomon looked again at the photograph, he could see the feathers of light exploding out from the pupil into the iris. Feathers raying out from an eclipsed sun, like great cosmic wings.

He put the photograph down, rubbed his eyes, and went downstairs to see if his sister had been kind to the fridge that day. She had. Solomon made himself a sandwich then joined Margaret and Cameron in the living room. Cameron sat with students' work in his lap while Margaret read. She had graduated from SFU last June with her BSc in biology and now was continuing her training as a lab technician.

As he chewed on his sandwich, Solomon looked along the walls at Cameron's many prints. His chewing slowed, and he straightened up in his chair. What was he seeing? He stood up to look more closely at each print. What? Standing before *Transformation #3*, he looked intently at the eye of the Raven. Ovoid, not round, yet black and solid within the lines of the socket that rayed out on either side: Was the dark expanse of the ovoid an eye, Solomon asked himself, or only a black emptiness? Or an eclipsed eye . . .?

Solomon went around the room again now that he sensed what he might be looking for. It was there in other prints, too. Not in all of them but in enough of them, though each eclipsed eye was different if that was what he was seeing—the dark of the pupil shutting out the rest of the eye, eclipsed eyes peering out from heads, the joints of shoulders and hips, kneecaps, and ankles, while sockets rayed out like the corona of the sun.

He turned to Cameron who had set his marking down and was observing Solomon. "May I take a couple of these to school tomorrow, please? For my astronomy class."

"Well, yes, you can," Cameron replied, wondering what this was all about and wanting to know which prints Solomon wanted to take.

"Jason has a car," Solomon said. "I'll phone him for a ride."

"Astronomy?" Margaret asked, bemused as her brother took two of the prints from the wall. "That's right," he replied. "We're turning Raven into an astronaut."

"May I put a couple of things alongside those photographs?" Solomon asked at the start of the main lesson. Paul Kane looked at Solomon's exhibits. "Yes, you may, if you'll begin the lesson by telling us why you are doing that."

Solomon placed the photograph of the human eye between two of the eclipses and a print on either side of them. He walked to one end of the blackboard and stood while the class looked.

"Well?" Jason asked. Solomon could see Jason was thinking about having driven out of his way that morning to collect Solomon and his exhibits. But Solomon folded his arms and let the class go on looking. Then Anika glanced over at him and began to smile. Paul Kane stood at the other side of the room and waited for whatever might come.

"Wow!" Izzy exclaimed. "That really is far out!"

"They look the same," Astrid ventured. "The eclipse is like the eye, and the eye like an eclipse. But are they the same thing?"

"Let's do some research," Paul said. "Please pick a partner and face that person. Now then, look your partner in the eye for a couple of moments and just observe."

Solomon paired with Anika, and the two sat beside the pair of Sigune and Alex. "All right, what did you see?" Paul asked, bringing the exercise to a close before too many pairs dissolved into giggles.

"The pupils are dead, while the irises are alive," Anika said.

"And what does that mean, the iris is alive?"

"It's like something is raying out from the pupil," Juliet said.

"What does the pupil do in contrast to the iris?" Paul asked.

"It lets the light in," Alex said.

"So it's as if the pupil in our eye lets the light in by eclipsing, in part, something that rays out. How might that compare with what happens when the moon stands still in front of the sun?"

"It's the other way around, maybe?" Solomon suggested, trying to make his suggestion sound more casual than it felt. "The sun pours out what we call daylight, and the eclipse covers the daylight up . . ."

"To let that other light out," Sigune interjected. "Whatever it's called."

Then Solomon remembered something. "I was watching the sun set one time, and I saw a black disc, the size of the sun, between my eyes and the sun itself. I tried to blink it away, but it always came back. It almost was like an eclipse, only some of the sun's light still came through."

"It may be that we can look at the sun, even at the end of the day, only by enacting a mini-eclipse and shutting out some of its light," Paul said. "Anwar, you seem skeptical about all of this."

"Well, it all sounds pretty neat," Anwar said, "but the sun is still the sun and the eye is the eye, and they're different."

"And what about those prints?" Catherine said to Solomon. "Are you suggesting that the artists who did them had eclipses on their minds?"

"I'm not sure what I'm suggesting," Solomon replied. "All I know is what I see."

"Or think you see," Anwar said.

"Then maybe what I think is part of the way I see," said Solomon. He looked again at one of the photographs and pictured the moon beginning its journey away from the sun, rising above the sun until, with the first sliver of light, the crescent began to form.

"But we're not like that," Sigune protested, pushing her voice against the counter-pressure of heavy metal that thumped off the walls of Anika's downstairs rec room. "That's what they think, though," Sandra said.

"Who thinks what?" Jason asked as he and Solomon joined the group sitting on the floor beside the couch.

"Grade nine, and ten," Sandra replied. "They think we're stuck up."

Sigune lifted her bare feet onto the back of the couch. "I'm always up," she mused, "but I don't think I'm stuck there."

"Get real, Sigune," Sandra laughed. "The whole world is waiting for you to come down."

"Then let it wait. It's old enough to have waited before," Sigune quipped.

Anika and her mother, Nancy, came downstairs with platters of Chinese food, making their way past the dancers in the middle of the room. "That's a good way to end the Easter break," Solomon said to Anika as she set the platters down on a table.

Anika laughed and touched her knee into his back before following her mother upstairs to bring down even more food. "She likes you," Jason said to Solomon.

Solomon started, looked at Jason, and wondered what was coming next. "Get with it, man. She likes you!" Jason pressed.

"Jason—!" Sigune glared at him from the couch.

"What's bugging you? She likes him, right?"

"Yes, but you don't just put it out like that," Sigune insisted.

"Jason, you are somewhat crude at times," Sandra stated.

Alex crossed the room. "Dance?" he said, to Sigune. Sigune blinked up at him then laughed. "Hey, why not? I'm always up for a dance with a blue-eyed man."

Solomon straightened up, looked right at her, and made a wide-eyed face. Sigune laughed again. "I like brown eyes, too. Yours especially." Then, with Alex, she swayed herself out onto the floor.

Jason watched them go. "And he likes her." Solomon scrutinized him then grinned a little grin. "You're full of it tonight, aren't you?"

"The world is full of it," Jason replied. "Alex likes Sigune only he doesn't know it yet."

The Monday after the end of the Easter break, Candace Waverly began the Parzival main lesson with the grade eleven class and told them they each had to retell part of the story to the others.

"That'll be a cinch for you," Izzy whispered to Solomon. "You're an ace at telling stories."

Candace began the storytelling with the life of Parzival's father, Gahmuret.

"Let me get this straight," Anwar said the following day. "He was born in the West, then goes all the way to the East, right? Because he wants to serve the strongest man in the world."

"That's right," Candace said. "That man turns out to be the Caliph of Baghdad, called the Baruch by Wolfram the storyteller."

"And he ends up with a black wife in the East and a white one in the West after he goes back there, and gets both of them pregnant? Then he returns to the East and is killed," said Astrid. "He was one busy man."

"So Parzival, the one born in the West, has a half-brother in the East. That's cool," Izzy said. "Do they ever meet?"

"The story will tell us that," Candace said.

Then Catherine took up the story. After Parzival was born, his mother hid him away from any talk of knighthood because she didn't want him to know about that. But then these four shining knights galloped into his life, and that was it for Parzival. He was off to King Arthur's court to become a knight. On the way, he found a woman alone in her tent, kissed her, and rode off with her ring and brooch. Then he met his cousin, Sigune, whose beloved knight, Schianatulander, had just been killed and was lying dead in her lap.

"He did a lot of stupid things along the way," Juliet remarked. "That woman in the tent was sure in trouble when her husband came home."

"He was just following his mother's advice," said Catherine. "She told him to greet everyone he met, and especially women, with a kiss."

"What do you expect? His mother sent him out dressed like a fool," Sandra said.

"And he didn't even know his real name," said Alex, "until his cousin told him."

"With the dead dude in her lap," Jason said.

"And what does the name Parzival mean?" Solomon asked.

"To pierce through," Candace replied, "or see through, perhaps."

"I don't think much of the way he got his armour after he left King Arthur," Anwar said. "Putting a javelot through the Red Knight's helmet and into his eye. What a hell of a way to die, if you're a knight."

"How do those who meet Parzival see him?" Candace asked.

"They see him as someone beautiful," Catherine said, "and strong. In fact, once he puts the dead knight's armour on, Parzival jumps on the horse and looks like he's been a knight all his life."

Anika continued the story. Having taken the Red Knight's red armour, red shield, spear, sword, and red horse, Parzival rode off, looking good. Then he met Gurnemanz, a grey-haired man who taught him how to use his weapons and how to act like a knight. Gurnemanz also gave him more advice. When Parzival left Gurnemanz, he rode on alone until he came to the kingdom of Condwiramurs, a maiden queen whose castle was under siege. Condwiramurs came into Parzival's room at night, dressed as if she wanted him to make love to her, and climbed into his bed. But what she really wanted was someone who would listen to her, Anika stated, ignoring a few oh-yeah-for-sure looks that crossed some faces. Condwiramurs told Parzival she would take her own life before she would let Clamide, the man besieging the castle, take her by force. So Parzival said he would do whatever he could to help her.

Solomon gazed out the window so that no one, Anika especially, would see the pain stabbing into his eyes.

"Then she left him and went back to her own room before daybreak," Anika said.

"Right," said Jason. "And the next morning Parzival jumped out of bed, into his armour, onto his horse, and did a Rambo on all those knights attacking her city."

"But he didn't kill Clamide," Catherine said.

"No," said Anika, "though he wanted to, at first, so Condwiramurs would be free of him forever."

"Why didn't Parzival kill him?" Anwar asked. "Because I think I would have."

That night Solomon sat on his bed, book in hand, and tried not to think about Naomi or her father or anything that had to do with the life he had left behind in Duxsowlas. But this story was beginning to knock chinks out of the wall he had built up within himself to keep that world at bay, and Solomon didn't like that. He toyed with the book until his hand made its way to the page where the story continued and before he knew what was happening, Solomon was into it once again.

Sandra carried on the following morning. Parzival spent several months with Condwiramurs then left her to seek out his mother. But he didn't know where he was going and left it to his horse to figure that out. After dragging the reins over fallen trees and through marshes, the horse brought Parzival to a lake where he met a fisherman wrapped in fur and sitting in a boat. The fisherman sent him to a nearby castle for the night. When Parzival arrived there everyone welcomed him, and he learned the fisherman was really a king but not a very healthy king. The king could hardly sit up straight, had the shivers, and didn't look well at all. Parzival sat through a long procession that ended with a beautiful woman bringing in something called the Grail, which she placed on a table, and then everyone ate, taking food from the Grail, as much as each person wanted. When the meal was over, the king gave Parzival a sword, which meant Parzival was to ask the king a question. But Parzival said nothing, and then everyone went to bed, and Parzival had one miserable night. He also felt miserable when he awoke the next day and found the castle empty except for his armour and his horse. As he rode away, a squire called him a goose for not asking the question, whatever the question was. Next he met Sigune, who still had the dead knight on her lap, only now he was embalmed, and she was sitting up in a linden tree as she held him. Anyway, Sigune really gave Parzival hell when she learned he hadn't asked the question and called him a venomous wolf.

"So why didn't he ask the question, whatever it was?" wondered Izzy.

"Because Gurnemanz had advised him not to ask too many questions," Sandra said.

"Play it cool in other words. So much for advice," Alex observed.

"What do you think the question might have been?" asked Candace.

"Probably something simple or obvious," said Juliet. "I mean, he only needed to use his eyes to see something was wrong with the fisherman, or king, especially when that person brought the bleeding spear into the hall. But then Parzival doesn't seem so bright when it comes to seeing things that are obvious."

"Do you always ask someone, 'What's wrong with you?' Even if you can see something is wrong?" Anika queried.

"Perhaps Parzival just didn't care enough to ask," Lorne mused.

Or maybe he choked the question off and decided not to ask, Solomon thought, though he did not speak his thought.

"I just want to be clear about something," Sigune said out of the blue. "That lady with my name was sitting in a tree when Parzival met her the second time. In a tree, no less, holding this embalmed knight, the same dead knight she had been holding ever since Parzival first met her. Have I got the picture?"

"Yes, you do," Candace replied, a twinkle in her eye.

"And how long had she been holding that knight?"

"Fifteen months, perhaps, given the time frame of the story."

Sigune's eyes flared. "That," she said, "is gross!"

"That is so gross!" she repeated, stomping out of the classroom and down the stairs as soon as the lesson was over

"So, what's your problem?" Astrid asked, at Sigune's back with Alex and Solomon beside her.

"My problem," Sigune said, outside the school, "is a mother who has named me after a ridiculous woman who spends her life holding a dead knight in her lap. I think I'll change my name."

"Hey, look!" Astrid exclaimed as Sigune tramped down the street. "She's wearing boots. She's never worn boots before."

Alex nodded, his eyes on Sigune. "I know. I noticed this morning." He went on looking at Sigune.

"What's gotten into you?" Solomon asked.

"Sigune. She's beautiful in boots."

So on Parzival rides, alone and lost in the forest, sweating inside his armour because he suspected there was something he could have—should have?—done back there in the Grail Castle, but didn't do.

Solomon closed the book and wanted to put it down. This story was getting even closer to the bone. But he read on because tomorrow it was his turn to tell the next stretch of the story.

After a night in the forest, Parzival comes across three drops of blood in the snow that look like the cheeks and mouth of his wife. He sits on his horse not able to tear his gaze away from those drops of blood, not even when two knights, in turn, ride out of Arthur's camp to deal with this Red Knight whose erect spear presents a challenge to them. Parzival awakens from his trance, dumps both of them from their horses, and goes back to his drops of blood. Then Gawan rides out, does not challenge Parzival, but figures out instead what is going on and throws a scarf over the drops of blood. So Gawan becomes Parzival's friend and takes him to Arthur's camp, which is good because Parzival needs a friend about now.

In Arthur's camp, everybody falls all over Parzival, telling him how beautiful he is and how famous he has become, and Arthur wants to make him a knight of the Round Table. That sounds good to Parzival, and he thinks that what happened, or didn't happen, in the Grail Castle might not matter so much after all. Then right in the middle of their meal, a woman called Cundrie rides in on a mule and is so strange looking that Wolfram seems hard put to find the words to say how strange she looks. Cundrie nails Parzival in front of everybody, saying he may look beautiful but inside he is as ugly as they come because he didn't ask that question. She then finishes him off by telling him he is nothing but a snake's fang, cursed, done for, and of no further use to anyone—pretty much what Sigune had said to him.

"And then Parzival denies God? Why?" asked Sandra.

"Why not?" Anwar returned. "God didn't do much for him."

"That's what Parzival seems to think," said Solomon. "He says if God is all God is supposed to be, he would never have allowed me to be shamed." Solomon stopped, suddenly. The other members of the class waited for him to go on, then glanced at one another when he didn't.

"What was Parzival's picture of God, Solomon, when he left home?" Candace asked. Solomon looked over at her and knew she was trying to help him out, but he couldn't take up the cue.

"Didn't his mother say God was like the light?" said Anika. "Brighter than the daylight. Which is why he thought the knights were gods when he first met them because their armour shone."

Solomon gazed out the window remembering what his mother had said, once, when he had asked what God defended people from: "From many things, I guess, though not from everything. But mainly, from ourselves."

"So if Parzival left home with that idea of God, where does that leave him now?" Juliet wondered.

"In the darkness," Solomon said, bringing himself back to them. As he spoke, he decided his mother had been somewhat wiser than Parzival's.

"Is there anything good in what has happened to Parzival in the darkness he now feels?" Candace asked.

"Maybe," Solomon said. "He decides he's going to find the Grail again and ask the question he didn't ask before."

"After everyone's told him he's a hopeless case," said Jason. "Good luck, Parzival!"

On Sunday night, Margaret called upstairs. "The phone is for you."

"Solomon? It's Alex. Can you talk for a few minutes?"

"Sure," Solomon said, taking the phone from the kitchen counter into Cameron's study. Alex, however, was the one who wanted to talk. "I took Sigune out last night. And I told her I liked her."

"Ooh," said Solomon. "What did she say?"

"Well, I didn't just say I liked her. I said I was in love with her."

"Ahh," Solomon said. "And what did she say to that?"

"She became very upset and wanted to know why I thought I was in love with her."

"And?" Solomon prodded.

"And I didn't answer that question very well. I mean, I couldn't tell her it was because she looked beautiful in boots. The more I talked, the more confused my words sounded. I guess I'm not so good at telling someone how I feel."

"At least you didn't dump her pencils all over the classroom," Solomon said.

"What do you mean? Dump her pencils?"

"Never mind. What happened in the end?"

"She told me it was dumb to be in love with her, and would I please stop being in love with her. Over and out. That's what I get for opening my dumb mouth."

Moments later, Margaret called upstairs again. "It's for you," she said.

"Solomon, I have a big problem," said Sigune's voice.

"Ahh," he said. "I think I know about your problem."

"Has Alex called you?"

"Yes. Not so long ago." There was a silence at the other end of the line. Then Sigune said, "Solomon, what am I going to do about this—this thing Alex has about me? I don't want him being in love with me."

"Then you do have a problem," Solomon said.

"Solomon, you have to talk to him. About not being in love with me."

"And what do you want me to say?"

"Just tell him, that's all. Tell Alex to stop being in love with me."

Solomon thought for a moment. "I don't know about that, Sigune. I don't think being in love works that way."

"Thanks," he said to Margaret as he replaced the receiver.

"My pleasure," Margaret said. "But the next person that calls will have to take the phone up to you."

But there were no other phone calls that night. Jason had been right about Alex liking Sigune, Solomon realized as he cleared the homework, finished and unfinished, from his desk. Had Jason also been right about Anika liking him? Yet as soon as Solomon began to think about his feeling for Anika, he saw Naomi's face in the window before him.

Astrid and Juliet took up "Book Nine" the next day. After the story veers away from Parzival into the first adventures of Gawan, Parzival rides back into it, four or five years after his visit to the Grail Castle, and meets Sigune again. "This time she is living in a hermit's cell, and her dead knight is in a coffin," said Astrid. "She asks Parzival how his search for the Grail is going, so she knows something of what he's about and seems more kindly disposed toward him."

"After that," Juliet said, "Parzival meets a grey knight and his family, and the grey knight tells Parzival he shouldn't be riding around in full armour on Good Friday. To which Parzival replies, 'Good Friday? What's that all about? And anyway, I hate God, because he has doomed me to a life of shame.' The grey knight tells Parzival he should think about that some more and sends him in the direction of a hermit's cave. Parzival then decides his horse knows more than he does, drops the reins, and the horse takes him to the hermit, named Trevrizent, who, as it turns out, is Parzival's uncle."

"The two of them talk about everything under the sun," said Astrid. "Or rather Trevrizent talks, about God and creation, and the Grail, and Anfortas, the wounded king, and how he was wounded, and where, and about Parzival's family."

"And about Parzival in a way," Juliet said, "because it all comes back to him and the question he didn't ask."

"And Anfortas, the wounded king, is also Parzival's uncle?" said Anwar.

"Yes. And the knight he killed and whose armour he had taken was his cousin. Just about everyone and everything in the story is related to Parzival," Juliet said.

"But he didn't know that until now," said Astrid. "He's been riding around alone, not knowing it's all related to him."

"What a place for a king to be wounded," Izzy said. "In the testicles! That would put a crunch on your life."

"What does the story tell us about the Grail itself?" Candace asked.

"Isn't it a cup, the cup Christ is supposed to have used at the Last Supper?" asked Catherine.

"That's one tradition," Candace said. "Does this story refer to it as a cup or chalice?"

"Not really," said Astrid. "Wolfram calls it a stone, a stone fallen from heaven."

"Well whatever the Grail is, Trevrizent doesn't give Parzival much hope of seeing it again," Anwar observed. "He tells Parzival only those who are called will find it, and Parzival doesn't seem to be one of them."

"But one thing I don't understand," said Sandra. "Parzival tells Trevrizent he has two goals, to find the Grail and also his wife. Finding the Grail may not be the easiest thing to do, but why doesn't he just go back to his wife if that's so important?"

"Maybe some things aren't so easy to go back to," Solomon said. It was the only time he'd spoken during that lesson, and something in the way he spoke shut down any further discussion of the story.

He sat at his desk that night and tried to move his pen into the opening line of the essay he had to write for this main lesson: "When Parzival first comes to the Grail castle, he doesn't ask the question the wounded king needs from him. Why? Because Parzival is missing something in himself." Solomon tried to keep the pen moving and hoped it would think for him, but the pen stopped and went nowhere. He put it down, got up from the desk and went into the bathroom to brush his teeth. The face in the mirror looked out at him as if it wanted to ask him a question: "About my uncle? Forget it! He abused one of my brothers and was starting in on the other. End of story."

But the face in the mirror wouldn't let the question go.

Sigune stomped to the front of the classroom more than ready to speak. "Okay. The story of Gawan and Orgeluse. Gawan rides, like Alice, into Wonderland, meets this gorgeous woman, Orgeluse, and thinks he is in love with her. Everyone around there tells him he's funny in the head, being in love with Orgeluse, because she has wrecked the life of many a knight. But our hero proclaims, 'I do love that lovely lady,' and tells her, 'May I die if ever a woman pained me so.' Being no fool, however, she tells Gawan he's a fool and to stop slinging his eyes at her because loving her is a hopeless cause and she will prove that by putting him through the wringer until he is all wrung out and done for."

"Well, that was told with relish!" Lorne said, as Sigune sat down.

"You bet," Sigune replied, crossing her arms and her boots. "I like that part of the story."

"Are you okay?" Solomon asked Alex, on their way to a friendly tree in Chinook Park. Alex smiled a dazed smile and shook his head in disbelief. "She's still beautiful. And I don't know where I'm at."

"Forget her, man," Jason urged, at lunchtime. "She's not worth it. No woman is worth it. Tell her to go talk to herself."

"Butt out, Jason!" Alex snapped, and walked away.

Jason shrugged and shook his head. "I don't get it. I'm only trying to straighten him out."

"Yes, I guess you are, Jason," Solomon said, "and no, you don't get it, much of the time."

By the end of the week everyone was ready for the week to end. "Parzival and now Hamlet. Give me a break," Catherine said to Solomon as they walked into their Friday English class.

"Why doesn't Hamlet get on with it?" Anwar asked, toward the end of class. "He knows he has to kill his uncle, and why he has to kill his uncle, but he doesn't kill his uncle. He goes around instead asking himself whether he will be or not be. It's like he's standing in front of a mirror the whole play, looking at himself looking at himself."

"He should have put his sword through his uncle when his uncle was down on his knees," said Jason.

"But his uncle was praying," Astrid returned, "and Hamlet didn't want to send his soul to heaven. I can relate to that."

"Yeah, that works for me, too," Izzy drawled. Candace Waverly smiled with him, knowing this was not the day to press their understanding of the play toward any kind of fine tuning.

"Mrs. Waverly, you should reconsider the timing of Parzival and Hamlet, next year."

"Why so, Lorne?"

"Well, it really is too much, all at once. And it's somewhat confusing. We're supposed to want Parzival to heal his uncle, and Hamlet to kill his. It's hard to keep your sympathies straight."

In the dark of Sunday morning, Solomon dreamed:

He stands wrapped in a depth of shadow. In the distance behind him, the Giant burns. The light from its burning licks at the blood-red armour that chains him about, as the red of it drips down upon the sand at his feet. A button blanket covers his shoulders, drapes down his back, and he cannot see the crest upon it. His right hand is heavy with the red sword it holds as his left shakes the rattle, very softly, the raven's beak extended toward the sand.

His heart at the back of his throat, he steps from the shadow out onto the moonlit beach. His uncle kneels before him, a button blanket draped down his back and a crown of cedar upon his head. His uncle's body trembles as he prays, if that is what his uncle is doing. As Solomon steps closer, the crest upon the blanket stares out at him. Sisiutl—

He raises his sword into the full moon, to drive it between the eyes of Sisiutl, into his uncle's heart, and tries to swallow his own heart away from his tongue, but his heart will not move. His uncle's body stiffens, as if expecting the blow it knows must come, and then the head of Sisiutl rises up from out of the blanket, stretches up, up into the light pouring down from the fullness of the moon. The centre line of Sisiutl's face becomes the knife-edge of a paddle flashing down, down upon him, the sound of its flashing ripping into him. He thrusts up his sword to ward off the blow and cries out . . .

Solomon's body plummeted from his bed onto the floor, and he awoke bathed in sweat, as another bolt of lightning tore through the night and flashed across the dark of the ceiling above him.

Downstairs, he opened the fridge door, took a bottle from it, and poured himself a glass of milk. His hand shook as he drank. He poured a second glass and then the fridge door closed, leaving him in darkness again. Walking silently into Cameron's study, he sat at the desk, listened to the rain splatter down upon the roof overhead, and looked at the print on the wall, dark in the darkness yet white within the lines of the face that looked down at him.

Sisiutl.

Alex took up the next thread of the story. Gawan wins the love of Orgeluse when he passes the last test she has set for him by leaping the chasm and claiming the wreath guarded by Gramoflanz, and by deciding he isn't going to let being in love with her push him around any more. Alex paused, as if he wanted that point to penetrate the room, then went on. The only trouble is that by winning Orgeluse, Gawan also has taken on the chaotic situation in the Land of Wonders she has helped bring about. Orgeluse hates Gramoflanz for killing her husband; Gramoflanz hates Gawan because Gawan, he thinks, has killed his father; Itonje, Gawan's sister, loves Gramoflanz and hates Orgeluse.

Solomon observed Alex as Alex spoke. Something had happened to him over the weekend. He had steadied down somewhere in himself and hardly looked at Sigune as he went on to tell of the unexpected fight between Gawan and Parzival, neither knowing who the other is, then about Parzival's fight with Gramoflanz the following day and Arthur's move to reconcile those at odds with one another.

"God, it's one big mess!" said Juliet. "Everyone is related to everyone else or in love with someone, and yet no one knows who anyone else really is. No wonder they're at each other's throats."

"Maybe being related to someone is not enough, in this story, to let you see who that person is," suggested Sandra.

"Could be," Anwar shrugged, "but it all sounds like life to me. People hurt one another; those who are hurt want revenge on those who hurt them and don't think twice about hurting others to get that revenge."

"But it doesn't turn out so badly in the story," Sandra said. "Once everyone makes up with everyone else."

"Except for Parzival," said Alex. "After everyone has made up with everyone, there is a big party that night, and those knights who don't have a lady in camp make sure they don't spend the night alone. Parzival is tempted to take a lady for the night so he can be happy, too, then doesn't, because he decides to be faithful to Condwiramurs."

"So what does he do? Go off and meditate?" Jason asked.

"No. He saddles his horse, puts on his armour and rides away," said Alex. "But it's his attitude that got me. He's not bitter that he's alone and he doesn't spoil the party for anyone else. He just accepts that things are the way they are and gets on with his life."

"That was good storytelling," Solomon said to Alex on their way back from the store. "You're in better shape than you were last week."

"Well, I decided to smarten up and put my head back on," Alex grinned.

"That's good," said Solomon. "I think she'll like you better with your head on."

"Parzival is riding along," Anwar began, "when he meets a very powerful knight whose surcoat is covered with gems, and the two fight. For once, Parzival has met his match. The other knight is winning, and Parzival is about to lose until he wakes up, calls out the name of his wife's city as a battle cry, and drives the other knight to his knees. Then Parzival brings his sword down for that last blow, and the sword breaks in two upon the other knight's helmet, the same sword Parzival had taken from his cousin, Ither, the knight he had killed in front of Arthur's court."

"Way back then? It took a long time for that to catch up with him," Lorne observed.

"Yes. And when the knight took his helmet off, he turned out to be Parzival's half-brother, the one who had been born in the East. His skin was even a mix of black-and-white patches, and he said that fighting Parzival had been like fighting himself. Actually, I'm glad he almost beat Parzival because I was afraid Parzival was never going to lose a fight." Anwar then told how the two brothers rode back to Arthur's camp and were welcomed, and how the following day, when they were both to become knights of the Round Table, Cundrie again rode into the circle on her mule, approached Parzival, and told him he was now the Lord of the Grail.

"Just like that?" said Astrid. Anwar nodded. "And that he was to go with her to the Grail Castle and take a companion with him. So he chose Feirefiz, his half-brother."

When Anwar had finished, Candace Waverly went to the blackboard, took a piece of chalk, then drew a thin crescent moon, and within it, a violet circle and a faint shining within the dark of the circle. "Cundrie's words to Parzival were, 'The inscription has been read: you shall be Lord of the Grail.' Now, I want us to look at what I have just drawn as an imagination of the Grail—not the Grail itself, but an imagination—and work with it for a few minutes. Has anyone observed what I have drawn, when you've looked at the evening sky?"

"Yes," Solomon said, putting a matter-of-fact tone into his voice. "It appears after the moon is made new, above the sun. When the sun has gone down, I mean."

"Good. And what have you observed about that first appearance of the moon?"

"A light goes right around the edge, like you've drawn it. And something tries to shine, there in the dark circle."

"You're a good observer, Solomon. Thank you. I'm going to call this a Grail moon, then ask you just where the name of Parzival might have appeared, if you can picture that."

The class studied the drawing. "When Trevrizent was speaking to Parzival, didn't he say the name of those who were called to the Grail always appeared at the Grail's edge?" Catherine ventured. "Which would be like the crescent in that drawing."

"But that's not where Parzival's name appeared," Solomon interjected, not knowing how he knew that but knowing it beyond question.

"Then where do you think it did appear?" Candace asked.

"In that dark place where the shining is. Because he came to the Grail a different way."

"How do you mean, different?" Anwar asked.

"I mean, he wasn't called the way the others were. He just decided he was going to find it again, and he did," said Solomon, leaning back in his desk seat and folding his hands behind his head.

"But how would they see his name there, if it's dark?" asked Astrid.

"But it's not completely dark," said Anika. As she spoke, Solomon could feel that her eyes were upon him and not upon the blackboard.

"Yeah, there's that shining there. What is that, Mrs. Waverly?" Izzy asked.

"The reflection of the sun from the earth, or to put it another way it's the earth shining upon the moon with the sun's help. And something more, perhaps, if we take this as an imagination."

After lunch the grade eleven class took up their paint brushes in the art room, ready to continue work on their veil paintings. Rebecca Edwards had something else in mind, however. "Put your veil paintings aside, please. We'll be working on wet paper today. You all need to loosen up and wet on wet will do that nicely. Make a colour circle, throw it into chaos, and see what comes."

"And that's it?" Izzy said.

"That's it. Now to work, please."

With the edge of his hand, Solomon removed the excess water from the paper, then began with the lemon yellow to the left of centre. The yellow deepened to gold at the upper corner, then into the orange-red along the top. Going the other direction, the yellow became green, then the prussian blue appeared along the bottom and would have taken the paper over if he had let it. Going into the bottom right corner, the blue deepened to ultramarine, then flowed into the cooler red to become shades of violet at the right side of the paper. He had to work to keep the colours where they belonged yet allow them to meet and reach into one another.

All about him, his classmates worked silently at their painting boards; Anika stood near him, concentrating, yet seemed to feel him looking at her. She glanced up and lifted her eyebrows. Solomon changed the water in his jar, returned to his board, and observed what he had done. A circle of colour around a white, open centre. Pretty enough as it was, but Rebecca wanted chaos. So, here goes chaos. He breathed in, dashed the brush down onto the paper, and threw the colours against and into one another until the paper looked like a sea of mud. He cleaned his brush and looked at the sea of mud to see if anything was living there. Dipping the brush down into the sea, he began to move it about, carefully, and found there was still colour related to colour beneath the mud.

His eye followed his hand then stopped its moving when the yellow-green of the crescent appeared. The space above the crescent was dark with the prussian blue he had pushed there when he was making chaos. Solomon touched the crescent again, working his brush toward one tip then the other. Something began to form as the right tip of the crescent became a tongue protruding from the head taking shape around it. Solomon swept his brush over to the left tip and found a head forming there as well, this one of fire red darkened down by the colour about it, in contrast to the blue-violet head forming about the right tip. Solomon lifted his brush away; his eyes widened at the crescent moon reaching up at either end to become the heads of—Sisiutl!

The room about him fell away from his consciousness as Solomon plunged himself into the working of his brush, now bringing fresh colour onto the paper, darkening even more the blue-violet of the right head against the lighter violet about it, then accentuating the stone-green about the left head and the horn-like gesture protruding up and back from it. He lightened the green of the crescent itself toward yellow, and then his eye moved into the dark blue space above the crescent. He cleaned his brush, changed the water in his jar, and stood a few seconds, looking into the dark space.

Lightly, he touched the tip of the brush into the circle of blue and began to lift the colour away. At the edge of his awareness of things, he felt Anika's presence as she stood, brush in hand, and watched him work. Then he felt others of the class gathering about him—Izzy, standing where he could look over Solomon's shoulder; Astrid, beside her board, looking over Solomon's other shoulder. One by one, Solomon's classmates put their brushes down and became absorbed with the movement of his brush. No one moved; no one spoke. Alex, with Sigune beside him, watched closely as Solomon's brush lifted a little more blue from the dark of the circle above the crescent. A curve of white appeared. Solomon lifted away more blue, and the curve became a beak, then the dark patch behind the beak became an eye as he lightened up the area around it. He moved the brush to the left, lifted away another patch of blue, and there was a wing drooping down from the dark knot of a shoulder. At the bottom of the circle, a hint of white tailfeathers appeared. Below the beak the brush revealed another wing, this one probing the darkness about it . . . He cleaned his brush again, then extended the yellow tongues of Sisiutl along the curve of the circle until they joined together at the top—the two heads of Sisiutl reaching toward one another from the tips of the crescent moon, their tongues meeting to become the thin curve of light encirling the darkness within, and the white bird-figure faint within that darkness.

Solomon's eye returned to the crescent itself. There should be a central face there, where the crescent bulged. His brush poised above his paints, he thought about drawing the face in, then stopped the brush from going farther. If a face was meant to be there, it would have come of itself. But it didn't, so leave it alone.

Solomon looked up, then about into the faces of his classmates. Rebecca appeared beside him and examined his work. "Put a touch of that blue in this eye, and this blue in that eye," she said, then walked away.

Izzy finished the story. Parzival arrived, with Feirefiz, at the Grail Castle and asked the question Anfortas had been waiting for. At once Anfortas was healed. Then Parzival rode to Trevrizent's cave and met his wife and two sons along the way because she had been coming to meet him. When they all met, Trevrizent said that Parzival had actually won his way to the Grail and forced God to acknowledge what he had done, which was a pretty far-out thing to do because nobody had ever done it that way. "And then they found Sigune again," Izzy said, "but she was dead now. So they lifted the stone lid of Schianatulander's coffin, placed her beside him, then closed the coffin up."

"And that was it for her?" Anika asked, with a glance at Sigune.

"It looks that way," Izzy replied.

Anika fell silent, and Sigune looked more thoughtful than usual.

When Izzy was done, Candace Waverly walked to the front of the classroom. "Let's look at the story as a whole. Any comments?"

"It took him a long time to get there," Alex said. "After he blew it on his first visit."

"It's a funny story, the way it moves along," said Sandra. "It starts out in a straightforward way, falls apart in the middle and goes two ways at once, then gets it together at the end."

"Yes," Candace agreed, "but remember that Wolfram warned us in his introduction that the story would dart, twist, and turn between shame and honour, raven and dove, felt together in one and the same moment, on the way to finding true inner security."

"But it sure takes a long time to get there," Solomon said, glad that this main lesson was about to be over.

"Yes, it does," Candace said.

SIX

When Paul Kane told Solomon it was time he chose a faculty advisor for his grade twelve project, Solomon was at a loss to know whom he should choose. Then, as he went through the teachers one by one, he realized that Darryl Storm was the teacher he wanted to work with—not because Darryl knew anything in particular about Bill Reid, but because Darryl was a eurythmist and seemed to be ready for anything. Surprised by Solomon's request, Darryl was also pleased and agreed to be his advisor. They began to meet during the fall while Solomon sorted out what he was going to do and how he would go about doing it.

Solomon had conceived the idea of a project on Bill Reid at Expo '86 that past summer, when he had been standing with Anika, Sigune, and Alex before *The Golden Hind*, the replica of Drake's ship. "It's tiny," Sigune said. "There's not even enough space to go to the bathroom."

"Or even to stretch," said Alex. "There's more room for that in the Haida canoe."

At the word, *Haida*, Solomon looked about at the fifteen-metre canoe that dipped and rose with the rippling of False Creek. Its long prow extended forward from the trim hull of the craft, filled with eyes, eyebrows, teeth, and a hand contained within the black-and-red lines of a killer whale. "Lootaas. Wave Eater. That's what Bill Reid named it," said Anika.

Solomon remembered Bill Reid's name from Cameron's prints. "I've heard of him, sort of. Who is he?"

"Bill Reid? He's the one who began the renewal of Haida art. He carved *The Raven and the First Men*, out at UBC."

Solomon stared back at her. "Where?"

"At the Museum of Anthropology. You mean you haven't seen it?"

Solomon shook his head and laughed.

"What's so funny?" Anika cocked her head as she spoke.

"Someone wanted to take me there once, but I wasn't interested." His eyes travelled along the Lootaas, from prow to stern, then came back to Anika. "I'm part Haida."

"So is Bill Reid. Perhaps he's someone you should get to know."

Borrowing some books from the library and from Cameron, Solomon started with Bill Reid's biography. Bill Reid was born in 1920. That would have been about the time his father was born, Solomon calculated. Had they ever met? Maybe, but maybe not, since Bill Reid had been born in Victoria, lived much of his life there, and didn't really go to the Queen Charlotte Islands until he was twenty-three. That would have been in 1943, when Isaac could have been fighting in the war.

Solomon was also struck by the way Bill Reid's mother had hidden him away from knowing anything about being a Haida, in the same way that Parzival's mother had hidden Parzival from knowing about being a knight. Yet Parzival ended up being a knight, and Bill Reid ended up becoming a Haida carver and artist.

One night, Solomon was reading through Bill Reid's telling of Raven stealing the light and calling forth the first human beings from the clam shell, when Cameron walked into the living room. Cameron sat down and Solomon read out a couple of passages that he liked.

"The Xhaaidla," Cameron said, when Solomon had finished.

"What's that?"

"It has to do with the way the Haida experienced the world. As I understand it, however much I understand it, the surfaces of the world as we see it—land, water, sky, objects—are like a skin that joins two worlds together, yet separates them. On this side of the skin—the Xhaaidla—is the world we see; on the far side is a world we don't see, but which is just as real. Perhaps more real." Cameron paused, and Solomon was struck by a flash of pain and longing that crossed Cameron's face.

"Animals can pass through the Xhaaidla into that other world where they shed their skins and assume human form, can transform freely, back and forth, but not we, it would seem . . ." Then Cameron lost his words.

Solomon rested his elbows along the top of the couch, remembering the ending of his father's story of Raven stealing the daylight, prompted by the question:

"Weren't the people happy when daylight came?"

"Not everyone, it seems. Some people were wearing animal skins and skins of birds, and couldn't get free of them soon enough. So they're in those skins even though they're our relatives and have places where they can take the skins off and dance and be human, like us."

Was it just the animals who felt trapped in their daylight skins? Solomon wondered. "The Xhaaidla sounds like the Tlaamelas," he said. "The Tlaamelas is like a screen and when a dancer comes past it onto the floor, he is coming from somewhere else."

"Yes," Cameron said, his eyes alight with interest. "Yes, the two concepts may well be similar. Margaret told me something about your dances when we first met. But not much since."

Then Solomon realized his brother-in-law wanted him to say more about those dances, that Cameron had been wanting Margaret to say something more. Solomon also remembered what he had seen in Margaret's eyes when he had asked her about the prints hanging all about the house.

"I think I'd better go to bed," Solomon said. As he stood and stretched, he spotted Bill Reid's print, *The Children of the Raven*. The little face in Raven's eye stared back at his.

He was still thinking about Cameron a few days later when he made his first trip to the Museum of Anthropology at UBC. He looked over the old totem poles that had been taken from the abandoned Haida villages on the Queen Charlottes—or Haida Gwaii, as Isaac had called the islands—but soon focused in on the large carving of *The Raven and the First Men* in yellow cedar that Bill Reid had completed three years earlier. Overwhelmed at first by the sheer mass and power of the work, Solomon had to walk around the carving a few times to sort out what he was seeing.

Six human figures emerged into the daylight from the clam shell, each with its own gesture. The first showed only her backside to the light, her knees still folded up against her belly as she slept within some dream of her own. The figure next to her, on the other hand, was caught fast in the act of seeing that light. Entranced? Mesmerized? Solomon looked again at the figure with one hand and one foot free of the shell and tried to decipher the expression on that light-struck countenance. Then he walked on around the carving.

The face of the third figure, upside down on its way out of the shell, was truly dumb-struck by the light flooding into her eyes, her hands clutching at the upper edge of the shell and giving no hint as to where they would go or what they would do next.

The fourth figure was coming out of the shell bum first, testicles first, soles of the feet first. That was one way of coming into the world, getting yourself right into it before you turned about to see what you had come into.

Her hands resting lightly, momentarily, upon the lower rim of the shell, the fifth figure gazed calmly into the light about her—bemused, pensive, reconciled, as if she had known, always, even in the darkest recesses of the shell, that one day the light would draw her forth.

The last figure held his attention the longest. One hand clutched upward at the shell, yet looked as if its grip was on the verge of relaxing rather than strengthening. The head was upside down and the eyes were half-open, half-closed, or about to close forever. Not eyes opening to the light out of the darkness, but eyes once open to something seen in the darkness and now being killed by the light. Eyes dying, dying into the light . . .

Solomon now stood at the back of the carving. Seen from behind, Raven's wings seemed to droop somewhat, as if in pain or from exhaustion, as if he wanted to fly off from the shell and what he had called forth from it, yet couldn't lift his wings enough to do that.

Starting another walk around the carving, he directed his attention to the face of Raven. He rounded the shoulder of the right wing and stopped. Raven gazed into a far distance, as if he beheld what could be but was not as yet. As Solomon stepped forward, the line that formed the vertical axis of Raven's eye came into view and with it a question from Raven to himself, as if he were troubled by the possibility he beheld and doubted whether he should bring it about.

Solomon stepped forward again, and Raven's gaze contracted back into his eye and hardened as it snatched the possibility inward. The lines of Raven's beak came into view, defiant and even cruel as they ran together at the tip: "To hell with doubt! Let's do it!"

And now Solomon could take in the whole of the right side of Raven's face, with a glimpse of the left side over the rim of his beak. He wondered at the change in Raven's expression. Gone was the defiance, the cruelty. Instead, Raven's eyes and the whole of his countenance showed a knowing sadness, a compassionate gazing into what had to be seen and done—what had been given to him, Raven, to see and do.

Then the expression changed dramatically as Solomon rounded the tip of the beak and stared Raven full in the face. Now Raven smiled at him, grinned at him, even winked at him. Raven the Trickster grinned his trickster grin. "Gotcha!" the grin said. "And you know I've got you!"

The smile faded as Solomon stepped forward again. Another question took its place, not from Raven to himself but now from Raven to Solomon: "And what are you going to do about it?"

"As if there is anything you can do about it. As if I even cared." And now Raven took no interest whatsoever in Solomon or in anyone other than himself. Even as his eye sought the distances it had glimpsed before, its gaze veiled over and faded away into the ovoid of yellow cedar. Then the eye itself vanished as Solomon stepped past the forward thrust of the left wing.

Solomon walked around the carving yet again to confirm what he thought he had seen then stood a long moment to take the whole of it in. The yellow of the cedar shone back at him in the afternoon light that dropped down upon it from the skylight above.

Yesterday morning Anwar had led off the review in their main lesson on optics. "So Newton didn't really see what he thought he saw when he looked into the prism and saw white light breaking up into colours?"

"Newton looked into the prism from one point of view," Paul said, "and observed what he observed. But there is more to light than that, as you have seen from our experiments and from Goethe's observations of colour. Newton concluded that all colours are contained in white light alone, whereas Goethe saw that colour comes about through a meeting of the light with the darkness."

"Why didn't Newton see that?" Sandra asked.

"Possibly because of the way he conceived the world—which may have come about as a result of what he observed but which may also have shaped the way he observed," Paul replied. "For Newton, darkness was simply the absence of light. Darkness in itself had no reality for him."

"So in Newton's world the darkness is shut right out?" Solomon asked.

Paul nodded. "Yes, you could put it like that."

Anika shivered. "It feels like a prison. Like living in a prison of light." Solomon looked again at the carving before him, now holding the last of the day's light about itself, and saw that trickster's grin looking back at him: "Gotcha!"

Anika stood with Solomon on the day of the Christmas fair as Margaret and Cameron looked around the hall of the elementary school. Boughs of fir and cedar had been draped about the hall the night before. Tables set up along the walls and in the centre of the hall held hand-made wooden toys, large soft dolls, straw stars, and other items crafted by parents of the school. From along the corridor came the sounds of a flute and violin and hand drum. "That's Astrid playing the violin," said Solomon, "and Juliet on the hand drum. They've put together the world's first violin and hand drum duo."

"With Catherine's flute thrown in," Anika added. "I have to go. I'm helping in the tea room. Come by there, if you need to sit and rest."

"She's a lovely girl, Solomon," Cameron said as Anika left them.

"Yes, she is," Solomon agreed, seeing what he had been taking for granted through another pair of eyes. "We're good friends."

He walked about the hall with Margaret and Cameron, and then they found their way to the tea room, set up in the grade two classroom. Paul Kane sat at one of the tables. "May we join you?" Margaret asked.

"Of course. It's good to see you both here."

"Well, we decided to get ourselves to a Christmas fair before Solomon is out the door and gone," Margaret said.

Most of the children's work had been taken down for the day, but a few paintings had been left on the classroom walls. One of them showed a saintly figure deep in conversation with a wolf. "That looks like St. Francis," Cameron said.

"It is St. Francis and the wolf of Gubbio," Paul replied. "Children feel especially close to animals at that age."

"That reminds me of some of the origin stories of my people where a wolf is like a guardian spirit that shows the people where they should live," Margaret said.

Solomon blinked as Margaret spoke. He had not heard her talk about their stories since he had come to live with her. Cameron also started, as if Margaret had suddenly opened a door for him. "It must have been a wonderful thing to have had that kind of communion with an animal," he said. "Where did it go? I think the aboriginal peoples may be one of the few who are still in touch with that world."

He looked to Margaret for confirmation, and Margaret shut right down. "Cameron, I am your wife. Your wife. Not a guide back into some aboriginal paradise you have dreamed up and which I have never known. And even if it did exist, I would not live there, or go there, even for the sake of taking you. I can only be your wife and hope that's good enough for you." She looked about the room. "This is a lovely fair and I want to see more of it before it's over and done with. Please excuse me."

"And please excuse me," Cameron mumbled when he had recovered enough from the shock of Margaret's exit to go and look for her.

"Are you all right, Solomon?" Paul asked.

Solomon ran his hand through his hair. "I guess I am. But maybe I'll sit here a while and make sure."

"Then I'll give you room to do that." With a light squeeze on Solomon's shoulder, Paul took his leave of him.

So, what do I do about all of that? Not much, Solomon concluded, though he knew that what had just surfaced between Margaret and Cameron was something he had felt as an undercurrent in their relationship ever since the day he had walked through the door of their house.

"Hi. I'm done for the day." Anika sat down at the table before she had fully taken Solomon in. "What's wrong?" she asked, once she realized that something was wrong.

Her eyes, still as direct as when he had first looked at them in that class photograph three years ago, unlocked the place where he kept all the things he didn't want to talk about. Words welled up and out of him as he told her what had just happened. "It's like she's shut the door on our village and everything that went on there and is never going back. I don't think she even wants to be an Indian, though I think he does for whatever reason."

Anika stayed silent for a moment, struggling with something in herself. "Are you going back? To your village?" she asked finally.

His eyes met hers. "I don't know."

"I think you should," she said. Yet as she spoke the words, Solomon could see that something in her didn't mean them. From the room next door came the notes of Astrid's violin and the beating of Juliet's drum.

"They play well together," Solomon said because he didn't want to talk about the other anymore.

"Yes, they do," said Anika.

"Our class trip," Paul Kane ventured at a class meeting in January. "Our last class trip. Any ideas?"

"What about Haida Gwaii?" Solomon said, from out of nowhere. They all looked at him in surprise.

"Where's Haida Gwaii?" Astrid asked.

"The Queen Charlotte Islands," replied Juliet. "The Haida call it Haida Gwaii."

"Isn't there a blockade going on there?" said Anwar.

"Yes, there is," Solomon said. He knew Bill Reid had stopped work on another, large-scale project to be cast in black bronze and placed in front of the Canadian Embassy in Washington, D.C. The Haida were trying to stop the logging on Lyell Island and to secure the southern part of Moresby Island where many of the old Haida sites were located. Bill Reid had put his project on hold in support of the Haida. Solomon knew that, but that didn't deter him from pursuing his suggestion. "We don't have to go where the blockade is," he pressed.

"Then where do you want to go?" Jason asked, in the way Jason often asked.

Solomon wasn't sure. He only knew he burned with the wish to go to the islands that had inspired Bill Reid, the islands his grandfather had sought out to find the People of the Raven, the islands that had been the birthplace of his father. He felt all of that, but didn't know how to say it. His classmates looked him over, uncertain as to how to take up his idea and his determination to make it happen.

"Your project is about Haida Gwaii, isn't it? Sort of?" Sandra said.

"Yes," he nodded.

"And Solomon is part Haida," said Anika. Alex, Sigune, and Izzy nodded to confirm what Anika had said.

"Well, why not?" Sandra said with a toss of her hair. "We can drive there, and the islands are beautiful, even the parts that have been logged. At least that's what my parents say."

"But how will we drive there? With all of us and all our stuff?" Catherine wondered.

"We have a van," Anika said. "My mother will drive it. And we've raised enough money to rent another one."

The class looked at Anika then at Solomon, thinking, maybe, that the two of them had planned all of this out. But he had said nothing to Anika.

"Well, the Queen Charlottes are closer than Australia," Lorne mused.

"That blockade still bothers me," Anwar said. "If I wanted to walk into a fight, I'd go back to the Middle East."

"Then we'll need to take care as to where we place our feet," Paul said. "What about it, grade twelve?"

From the moment everyone agreed, their plans fell into place. Nancy Hunter, Anika's mother, would drive her van and Paul would drive the other. Timing was the only matter that proved to be thorny. The weeks from a late Easter to graduation were filled with completing their projects and with planning for graduation itself. They considered taking some of their Easter holidays, but Astrid was scheduled for concerts during that time. She offered to withdraw from the trip, but no one would hear of it.

The class settled on the week before the start of Easter and hoped the weather would be with them. Leaving early on Saturday and driving north, they would catch the Monday night ferry from Prince Rupert for Skidegate Landing, and come back to Prince Rupert on the Thursday night ferry, then take the ferry south through the Inside Passage to Port Hardy on Friday. By Saturday night, they would be back in Vancouver.

They left just before dawn under a clear sky. At Hope the mountains flanking the Fraser Valley closed in upon them, then fell behind as they wound their way up the Fraser Canyon. They made good time going north on the Cariboo highway and camped west of Prince George that night. On Sunday, they travelled at a more leisurely pace along Highway 16 and reached the Skeena River that afternoon. As they drove along the Skeena, the river ever widening its grey coils as they went, Solomon's excitement began to build. His grandfather, he realized, might have come this very way looking for the meaning of the riddle that had troubled his sleep two nights before the battle of the Little Bighorn. That thought brought him back to his own riddle, akin to the one that had drawn his grandfather westward.

That night they camped within a half a day's drive of Prince Rupert. As the campfire drank in the gathering darkness, they joked about, told stories, and sang all the songs they knew. Then they crawled into their sleeping bags when they could no longer find a reason for staying awake. Only Paul and Nancy stayed at the fire.

"Goodnight, Paul," called Juliet and Astrid from somewhere down in their sleeping bags.

"Goodnight, Mum," Anika called from her tent. Moments later, the fire eating into a fresh chunk of wood was the only sound to be heard.

Solomon lay in a tent near the fire and was about to fall asleep when he heard Nancy Hunter's voice. "So, what will you do for entertainment, Paul, when this crew graduates?"

"Hope the incoming grade nine is every bit as entertaining. From what I've seen of that class, however, I'll have no worries on that score. But I shall miss these guys. They've been a very special gift to a first-time class guardian."

"I wonder where they will go from here?"

"Many places, I suspect. Some to college and university. Astrid, to the Academy of Music, and Anwar's father is talking about moving back to Iraq. And Solomon? Well, who knows where his searching out will take him? God knows, he's determined enough once he gets hold of an idea or an idea gets hold of him. Look how he pulled off this trip. I hope his determination doesn't trip him up one day."

"He's a fine young man," Nancy said. "I only hope Anika can get over him."

His eyes trying to pierce the wall of the tent, Solomon could see that the fire had almost died out. "We'd better turn in, too," Paul said.

"You've been looking up at those clouds all evening long. What's going on?"

"A sixth sense, perhaps. They have a nasty feel to them. I just pray that whatever I'm feeling is wrong."

As the firelight faded away, Solomon lay at the edge of sleep, wondering what it would be like to feel for no one else but Anika.

Well into the night, the front of the system that had been massing itself together out in the Pacific rounded the southern tip of Kunghit Island, joined forces with another system from the southeast, and stormed northward into Hecate Strait, piling waves upon one another. Late Monday morning, the *Queen of Prince Rupert* left Skidegate Landing and hugged the coast of Graham Island as far as Lawn Point. Then her skipper, a man with years of experience sailing those waters, took a long look out into the strait, turned his ship about, and fought his way back to Skidegate Landing. Once there, the *Queen of Prince Rupert* stayed in her berth for the next forty-eight hours.

Stranded in Prince Rupert while the wind howled out in the strait and everyone around them hunkered down to wait the storm out, the class of 1987 counted their cash to see if they could afford to be stranded. Then Solomon phoned Margaret, Margaret phoned her parish priest, and he phoned the clergy at the Anglican cathedral in Prince Rupert. There the class slept that night and nights thereafter while they came to know Prince Rupert better than they had intended.

Late on Wednesday, the *Queen of Prince Rupert* made her way across Hecate Strait, and on Thursday morning, an officer from the ship met the class at the Prince Rupert ferry terminal. "You're welcome to sail over if you want, but we'll spend three hours at Skidegate at the most before we head back for here, then down the coast on Friday."

"I have to go back," Astrid said, as they huddled together inside the terminal, "but you guys go ahead. It's okay with me, really."

"I don't feel good about that," said Juliet. "It's a class trip."

"And I told my family I'd be with them during the holidays," Anwar said. "Things aren't easy for my parents right now, especially my dad."

"Solomon, you could go over," Sandra suggested, "and do what you need to do. In fact, I'd feel better if you did because I know what this trip means for you."

Solomon looked at their faces and saw that everyone, including Juliet, agreed with what Sandra had said. He looked at Paul, but Paul's face gave no clue as to what he thought Solomon should do. Which was neither one way nor the other, he discovered as he listened to himself. "It's a class trip, and I'm a member of the class. We all go south together."

Jason found him outside moments later. "I'm sorry. I wanted this for you. We all did."

"It's all right, Jason. It's really all right."

And then, as the *Queen of Prince Rupert* sailed southward down the Inside Passage on Friday morning, Solomon worked hard to tell himself it was all right. Paul found him out on deck that evening when the ship had outsailed the rain and was chugging through an overcast silence of mountains and waterfalls on either side of her.

For a time Paul sat with Solomon and did not speak. "I once wanted something, very badly," he said at last, "and worked very hard for it. And then I didn't get it. Once I freed myself from my disappointment, I found that the energy that had been blocked from going in one direction was still there to go somewhere else, for something that proved to be as important for my life as what I had first wanted. I hope that will be so for you."

Solomon nodded, enough to let Paul know he hadn't spoken in vain, and then Paul left him to himself.

That night, the class bedded down in the lounges of the *Queen of Prince Rupert* along with others on board, spreading loose seat cushions out on the floor and then their sleeping bags. They gave themselves over to an exhausted sleep as the ship's engines churned away below the deck.

In the last hour of darkness, Solomon awoke. He sat upright, then stood to go out on deck. Stepping past Izzy asleep beside him, he paused at the doorway to glance over at Anika, but her eyes were closed and she did not stir.

A wind tugged at him as he stepped outside and leaned against the railing. He was looking eastward toward a range of mountain peaks wrapped in dark cloud yet with a hint of the dawn behind them. The ship had left the Inside Passage behind and was out in the open water north of the tip of Vancouver Island. Solomon looked more closely and knew, suddenly, why he had awakened here and now. He strained to see through the darkness, to glimpse, if he could, that one peak amid the others and then that one spot along the coast that had been his home. But Duxdzas had tucked itself away within the dark folds of cloud along the coast, and Duxsowlas, with Log Island and Sand Island, lay hidden beneath that darkest of dark times, the darkness before the dawn.

At first he thought the wet on his cheek was the start of more rain. Then he realized he was crying, for his mother, Adha, Frank, Peter, his cousin, and Hector, his friend, as well as for the warm bosom of Sadie Moon. Even the face of Uncle Charlie flashed before him, and at the last, the face of Naomi.

Standing on the deck of the *Queen of Prince Rupert*, the open Pacific to his back, Solomon sailed past the world he had once loved and had never wanted to leave. Inside the ship, his classmates slept. Out on deck, he stood alone waiting for a light to come yet knowing the dawn to the east would not bring that light, but only a darkness of its own.

"Say it again."

"*Auxw!*" Solomon repeated.

"Strange," said Darryl Storm. "It sounds almost like a straightforward *au*, and then a hard *ch*, as the Dutch say it. But there's something like a *w* in there that keeps slipping around."

"That would be characteristic of Raven," Solomon said.

Darryl laughed. "Try once more, please."

"*Auxw!*" Darryl made the gesture for *au*, one arm stretching outward from his shoulder at a slight angle from the horizontal, and the other bending upward and coming to rest above his head; then he moved both hands downward and drew them toward his chest, palms open as if to sweep something to him then let it flow past. Solomon spoke the raven's cry twice more as Darryl repeated the making visible of it in eurythmy, fine-tuning the gestures as he did.

"Does the palm overhead always turn outward, as if it's holding something away?" Solomon asked.

"No. You can turn the palm inward if you wish. So, that's the best I can do on the spur of the moment. I hope it proves useful."

"It will," Solomon said, "when I figure out what its use will be."

At seven o'clock that evening, a Wednesday in June, parents from the grade twelve class and from the whole school sat down in rows of chairs set up in the elementary school hall for the final evening of project presentations by the class of 1987. Solomon Jacob, the program said, would be the last student to speak that evening; the title of his project was, "From Raven to Newton: The Art of Bill Reid."

Solomon stepped to the front of the hall, half hoping that some of the audience would have left by now. But almost everyone had stayed. His eyes swept across the faces—Cameron and Margaret, his classmates, some parents he knew and others he barely recognized, and his teachers. Then he drew himself upright. Since his class had returned from its trip, he had put everything else in his life aside to finish this project, and now he had to pull it all together.

"*Auxw!*" Solomon gestured the sound in eurythmy as everyone woke up and took an instant interest in what he was doing.

"*Auxw!*" Solomon repeated the gesture, this time with the palm overhead turned outward. Then he dropped his hands to his sides and grinned. "That's the cry of Raven, just after he's turned daylight loose in the world and finds he's of two minds about having done that. Which is why I did the one gesture two different ways. I'm going to start by telling that story."

Solomon told the story, then something about the life of Bill Reid. Drawing upon some of Cameron's prints, illustrations from books, and his own observations, he went on to take his listeners along those paths into the art of Bill Reid that had interested him and elaborated his thoughts about what he had found, especially about *The Raven and the First Men*.

When he had finished, he stood and waited for any questions that might come. Nancy Hunter raised her hand. "Solomon, further to what you said about the Raven becoming black when he stole the sun, as a reminder perhaps that the darkness hadn't been driven out of the world altogether, do you see any connection between that and the use of black argillite by Haida carvers or the fact that Bill Reid is going to cast his next work in black bronze?"

Solomon considered a moment. "I hadn't thought about either of those things. But there could be a connection."

A hand went up on the other side of the hall, belonging to a man with three children in the elementary school. "There is a question I want to ask, if it's not too personal. Running through your remarks was the thought of a journey from the world of Raven stealing the sun to the world of Newton sealed tight by daylight. And yet Bill Reid, as an artist, had to start from the world of Newton and find a way back to Raven's world, and perhaps a world before Raven. Do I have it right?"

Solomon grinned, his hands in his pockets. "That sounds pretty good to me. You listened well."

The man laughed and turned to the woman beside him. "You see? At least one person thinks I'm a good listener."

Everyone in the hall laughed, and then the man continued: "My question then is, is Newton's world, and Raven's, a dead end or can one move on from there? I think I heard you asking that of yourself, and I wonder if you found any clues that could help that question along?"

Solomon followed the question back to the face of the man who had voiced it, a warm and honest face. "I guess that is a question I've been asking myself but didn't ask right out." Solomon looked at the floor a moment then back to the questioner. He felt Cameron's eyes on him as he spoke. "I think what my project did was help me find the question. Which is good. Finding an answer may be a lot harder."

A child in the elementary school, sitting with her mother, raised her hand and asked very seriously, "Are you a Haida?"

"Yes. Part Haida," Solomon answered, with equal seriousness, "and part Kwakiutl, and part Lakota."

"Oh!" the girl said, very impressed.

"Well, I guess I'll sit down and let you all go home," Solomon said.

"Not yet, Solomon," said Darryl. "Your artistic project?"

"My God, that's right!" Solomon exclaimed. "I'd forgotten all about that." He went to the table at the front of the hall, drew a cloth away, and a gasp went up from around the room as people craned their necks or stood to look at what he had done.

Carved into a circular slab of yellow cedar was a relief of a crescent moon along the bottom, with the two heads of Sisiutl extending upward along the curve on either side, their tongues joining together at the top and their heads closer to one another than they had been in the painting he had done during that art class a year earlier. The head of Raven emerged from the circle above the crescent, thrusting forward from the plane of the carving as if it were breaking free of it. Below the head, Solomon had carved in relief the wings, tail, and feet of Raven. In the body of the crescent below the Raven, the first hint of a central face of Sisiutl peered out at the faces that had come forward and were now gathered about the carving.

On his way forward, Cameron took Solomon by the hand. "That was splendid, Solomon! Just splendid! Thank you."

Solomon walked down the aisle to where several of his classmates stood, and received the hugs they gave him. "I'm just blown away!"

said Jason, and Solomon had to look only once at him to know he truly meant it.

"That was so good, Solomon," Anika said, her arm slipping about him. He slipped his arm about her as Izzy crowed, "And that's it! We're done, done, done!"

"That is very strange," Sigune said, looking past Solomon toward the front of the hall.

"What's strange?" Solomon asked.

"Your brother-in-law. Look at him, up there with your carving, pointing at it, and talking away. You'd think it had been his project."

Solomon let go of Anika's waist as Margaret came up to him. "I'm proud of you," she said to her brother. He put his arms about her, and she held him for a long, long moment.

"Done, done, done!" Izzy crowed again, the next day as class ended and lunch break began.

"Not yet," said Catherine, starting down the stairs. "We still have another week."

"Doing what?" Izzy asked. "Forget it! We're done." Anika and Solomon laughed, then Anika stopped short at the grade nine classroom. "The firepole!" They dashed through the doorway past a startled group of grade nines and were down the pole, one behind the other, before the grade nines could do more than cry after them, "Hey, you guys! That's our pole!"

"Possess-ive!" said Catherine as they walked out into the sunlight. Anika threw her hands into the air and spun about. "Glorious! I want to go, now, somewhere, anywhere. Anywhere but here!"

Solomon stared at her as she stopped spinning about. "Then let's go."

"You're kidding?"

"No, I mean it. Let's go, now, somewhere."

Anika stared at him. "You do mean it!"

"Yes, I mean it. What about you guys?"

"You mean, let's play hookey a week before we graduate?" Izzy said, as Catherine and he gaped at Solomon and Anika.

"I guess that's the word for it," Solomon said. Izzy shook his head. "I must be getting conservative or just lame in the foot, but no, I'm somehow not into that at this point in my education."

Catherine laughed. "Me neither, though it sounds like a neat idea."

"What about it, Anika?"

Her eyes gleamed back at him. "All right, let's do it."

"What'll I tell Darryl at P.E.?" Izzy asked.

"Tell him we became ill, suddenly, together," Anika said.

"Don't tell him anything," Solomon said, "except that you don't know where we are. He'll catch up with us if he wants to."

The sun had started its afternoon descent when Solomon and Anika reached Stanley Park and made their way along to Second Beach and then to Third Beach, stopping for an ice cream or two as they went. Laughing, they sat down in the sand, propped their backs against a log, and went on laughing and talking, until their laughter and words became silence.

"Do you know," Anika said, "that this is one of the few times you and I have talked together, really talked together?"

He shielded his eyes against the sun so he could look at the ships anchored out beyond the mouth of Burrard Inlet waiting for their tugs to take them into harbour. "With words, maybe. But we've talked with our eyes, Anika, many times. Your eyes talked to me before I met you, when I looked at the class picture during my interview."

"I had a dream about you, before you came to the school." Solomon kept his eyes on the ships as she continued. "You were sitting, alone in a canoe, like the one that Bill Reid made. It was so big, and you looked so alone in it as you tried to paddle it by yourself."

Now Solomon returned her gaze. "And I dreamed about you the night we came down from Prince Rupert on the ferry," she went on, "only this time there were people in the canoe with you. Some members of our class and others I didn't know. I woke up then, but you had gone out on deck. I wanted to come out with you, but something in me said no."

"I went outside just to see where we were," he said, wondering if Anika had seen herself in the canoe with him.

"Did you see your home?"

Solomon looked away. "We did sail past your village, didn't we?" she persisted.

"Yes, we did. But I didn't see anything. The sky over the mainland was too dark. Everything was too dark."

Anika fell silent and peered out at the setting sun from beneath her hand.

The night was well and truly dark by the time he walked in the door of his house. "Paul Kane called, hours ago," Margaret said, "to find out where you were this afternoon. Where were you this afternoon?"

"Playing hookey, with Anika. I'll call Paul now."

On Saturday morning Solomon and Anika stood with Paul in the grade nine classroom. At their feet were cans of paint, rollers, and brushes. "Do the four walls and the trim," Paul said. "That will be your gift to the incoming grade nine."

"And to you, Paul," said Anika, with a tiny smile.

Solomon rolled the first coat onto the walls, then helped Anika with the trim while the walls dried. After lunch, he started rolling on the second coat and arrived at a corner at the same time as Anika and her trimming brush. "I can't reach that spot up there," she said. Taking her brush, Solomon touched it down where she had pointed and handed the brush back to her. "You have paint on your nose," she said, her finger lifting the paint away as she smiled up at him.

"And you have paint at the corner of your mouth, right here." Solomon started to take the spot away with his finger, then kissed her instead.

"What are you doing?" Anika asked, as he drew his mouth away from hers.

"Just kissing the paint away. I'd better make sure it's all gone." He kissed her again, setting the roller down as he did so he could put both hands about her. One of her hands still held the brush but the other closed around his neck and she pressed herself against him as he drew her close. "What are we doing?" she asked as their mouths parted.

"Making up for lost time, I think," Solomon said. He took the brush from her hand and dropped it down into a spent paint can. This time she drew his mouth to hers. As he drank in her warmth and loveliness, the sheer sweetness of her body against his obliterated all thought of anything or anyone other than her.

The following Friday, the class of 1987 became the first to graduate from the Chinook Park Waldorf School. After Paul Kane had given the class their diplomas, Izzy made a speech on behalf of his classmates—the most coherent string of words his classmates had ever heard Izzy put together. Then Solomon and Juliet stepped forward and beckoned for Paul to join them. "Native people have a custom of naming a person who has given of himself in a special way," said Solomon, "and our class wants to adopt that custom and give you two names, Paul. The first is Siwayugila. In Kwakwala, it means Paddle Maker. The Paddle Maker is a master craftsman who not only can make good paddles for himself but can also teach his students to make their own paddles so they can go wherever they want to go. Which is what you have done for us. And with the name, we want to give you something to show what a good job you did."

His red hair touched by the stage lights overhead, Paul turned about as Anwar handed him a paddle, made and signed by every member of the class. "We also give play names," Juliet said, "so you won't take yourself too seriously. Our play name for you is He-Thinks-So-Hard, His-Head-Is-On-Fire. And here is a gift to go with that name."

Juliet handed Paul a portable fire extinguisher, and the hall erupted into howls of laughter.

When the ceremony was done, the class walked across the street to Chinook Park where tables were set up for a reception. Margaret, Cameron, and Solomon stood with Paul as he looked the paddle over. "Did you help Solomon with that name?" Paul asked Margaret.

"With the Kwakwala wording, yes. But the name itself and the paddle came from them, from all of them."

His diploma opened out in his hand, Solomon stared at the wording of his name. "The school office called me to make sure they had the right spelling of your name," Margaret said, "and I thought you might want the whole of it back one day. So that's what I gave them."

Deciding there was nothing he wanted to say about that, Solomon rolled up the diploma and walked over to Anika, who was standing by herself. "Congratulations," he said, touching her with his eyes.

"And to you. I think Paul liked the paddle."

"I think so, and the fire extinguisher, too. Anika, I want to give you something." He slipped his hand inside his jacket pocket, past the tie he had borrowed from Cameron, and withdrew the eagle feather. "My brother gave me this on my fourteenth birthday. It's one of the few special things I took with me when I left home. I want you to have it."

He placed the feather in her hands, and her hands trembled as they closed about it. "I don't know what to say, Solomon. It's beautiful and so special. But are you sure?" Her eyes sought his, frank and questioning. "Are you sure it's really for me? And not someone else?"

He took her by the hand and closed it tightly about the feather. "Yes, I'm sure," he said.

The party that night was held at Catherine's house in West Vancouver. "So this is your house!" Izzy said as Catherine met Solomon and him at the door. "Yes, this is my house," said Catherine, as she showed them inside, "and I'm glad it's going to be the scene of a real party."

"Hi," Anika said as Solomon stepped out onto the patio that overlooked the Lions Gate Bridge, Stanley Park, and Vancouver's West End.

"Hi." He slipped his arm about her, putting aside for tonight any thoughts of Duxsowlas. Anika's arm tightened about him, and they stood long together, looking down at the brightening of lights below. Back inside, Anika went into the kitchen, and Solomon found Alex sitting on a couch with Sigune curled up in his lap.

"You guys seem to be doing all right," Solomon grinned.

"You too," Sigune said. "It's about time the two of you got it together, if my eyes do not deceive me."

"Your eyes see pretty well," Solomon confirmed. He headed for the kitchen to find Anika. On the way he came across Izzy and Catherine going through a stack of records. "Real live records!" said Izzy. "I'll bet these go back some."

"Back enough," Catherine said. She placed a disc on the turntable and set the needle down. "I like this song, especially."

The first stroking of the guitar touched into Solomon as he started toward the kitchen. Then the words came.

> The first time
> > ever I saw your face

His body froze and the world about him came to a stop.

> I thought the sun
> > rose in your eyes . . .

Unable to move, Solomon saw nothing and no one—until he realized Anika was standing at the kitchen door, frozen in place by the look in his eyes. Solomon turned away from her, went out onto the patio, and sat on a stone bench. He gazed unseeing at the lights spread out below him. After a time he realized she had come outside and was sitting beside him. He turned to her, to tell her—to tell her what? That he no longer knew what world he was living in? But her hand covered his mouth before he could speak. "Don't. Don't say anything."

When they had sat long without speaking and he was able to put his arm about her, Solomon said, "It's crazy. I don't know what she thinks about me now, or if she thinks of me at all."

"If she's anything like you, she still thinks of you. That's why I didn't come outside that night when you were on deck. Because I knew you were looking for her. I've always felt you looking for her. And I felt her looking for you. Solomon, are you sure you want me to have that feather?"

"Yes, I am. Even more so, now. I've hurt you, Anika. I'm sorry."

Anika's hand moved to wipe the wetness from her eyes. "Other than, damn it all, and oh shit, what can I say? But you haven't hurt me in that way, Solomon, not by being true to yourself. As long as you do that, you won't hurt me or anyone."

Her head came to rest against his shoulder as the lights of Vancouver gleamed more fiercely into the clear summer darkness.

SEVEN

"Take out all twenty-one with one breath, and this next year will sit in the palm of your hand," said Margaret.

Solomon laughed then gathered the morning into his lungs. The flames resisted the first onslaught of his breath then gave way, right to the last candle. He sat back and grinned into the wisps of smoke rising up from the plate. "That's the first time I've seen birthday candles around a stack of hotcakes."

"That's as much as I can cope with at the start of this or any day," Margaret said. "But if you're lucky, there'll be a cake when you come home."

"Sounds good. By then I'll have had it with Yeats, or Eliot, or both, and be ready for something else to chew on."

"I'll give you a ride up the hill if you're going now," Cameron offered. "And I'll treat you to lunch at the pub."

"You're on for lunch, but it's too early for me to go up now. I'll work on an essay then catch a bus."

It was a need to think some things over, however, rather than an essay, that led Solomon to turn down Cameron's offer. A lot had happened in the three years since his graduation from high school, yet not much had happened. He was majoring in English at Simon Fraser University because Candace had prepared him well and he was good at English. Yet he had lost touch with many of his classmates. He still saw Izzy, now and then, as well as Alex and Sigune, who had an apartment in Kitsilano and were both struggling to pay their way through UBC. And he knew that Anwar had moved to Iraq with his family, but had heard little about anyone else and hadn't seen Anika since that last party at Catherine's.

And he had not returned to Duxsowlas, though he had intended to do so after he graduated. That last party, however, had thrown his intention into confusion once again. Having turned aside from Anika out of loyalty to Naomi, the thought had struck him that Anika might be wrong. Time moves on, and maybe no one at Duxsowlas, not even Naomi, cared any longer whether he still remembered his village or what he did about it. As the bus climbed Burnaby Mountain, Solomon remembered his mother also cooking hotcakes for him the day he had turned fourteen. Then he saw himself standing that last morning at the mouth of the river, the self he had discovered, or created, these past seven years falling from him like disease-stricken skin. Was this person named Solomon anyone more than the angry boy who had stomped out of his house to escape the truth of who his uncle was, and maybe a truth about himself?

When his class was done, Solomon found Cameron waiting for him at the pub sipping at a glass of beer, his second, if the empty glass on the table was also his. "Was it Yeats or Eliot today?" Cameron asked.

"Yeats. Lines and lines of Yeats."

Cameron laughed. "Order anything you want. I've covered the tab. Would you like a beer?"

Solomon shook his head. "No thanks. I'll swallow Yeats down with a strong cup of coffee."

Solomon brought his sandwich and coffee to the table, took out his volume of Yeats's *Collected Poems* and thumbed through its pages. "We read a poem called 'The Two Trees.' It might interest you." Finding the poem, he began to read through images of the holy tree growing in the heart, trembling flowers on holy branches, stars merry with light, sure and hidden roots, the flaming circle of loves and days, and the leafy ways of ignorant innocence. Parzival, before that first visit to the Grail Castle, when his heart was still free of doubt. Or Hamatsa, just before the forest about and within him disclosed that being that could split him right down the middle. But why was he thinking of Hamatsa or Parzival in the pub at SFU on his twenty-first birthday?

"The Tree of Life," Cameron said, "before Paradise ceased to be paradise."

Solomon nodded and went on reading, now drawing up from the page the fatal images of the bitter glass lifted up from the demons, roots half-hidden under snows, broken boughs, blackened leaves, and the ravens—the ravens of unresting thought, flying, crying to and fro, their claws cruel, their throats hungry, shaking their ragged wings and sniffing the wind, while the eyes of the beholder grow all unkind. Gaze no more in the bitter glass, but only on your own heart, said the poet to his beloved . . .

"But what else is there?" Cameron asked. "There is nothing but the bitter glass since your friend Raven filled the world with light. Surfaces that give back only your mirror image. A pane of glass that invites you to fly through it but kills you if you try. Ravens of unresting thought, driven by their own light into the bitter glass." Cameron stopped suddenly. "Why did you read that poem to me?"

"I thought you might be interested in it."

"And that's all?"

"That's all," Solomon answered, but he knew he was lying and suspected Cameron knew that, too. As his brother-in-law scrutinized him, Solomon realized he had been playing trickster, playing upon something that had surfaced in Cameron during the time Solomon was working on his Bill Reid project, especially that day at the Christmas fair. Cameron waited until he saw nothing more would be forthcoming. Then he said, "How did those lines go? The glass of outer weariness . . ."

"Made when God slept in times of old."

"Yes, that was it. Odd, that a poet can capture in a few lines what eludes most historians in pages. Broken boughs, blackened leaves, and threatened pines. I guess you know about Oka and what's happening there."

The change of subject was sudden and caught Solomon off guard. "No, I don't. Where's Oka?"

"In Quebec, near Kanesatake, where the Mohawks live. The mayor of Oka wants to expand his golf course of nine holes into another nine holes, right into the Pines that stand on land the Mohawks claim as theirs. Holy trees in Mohawk heartland. The Mohawks have said they're not going to let that happen, and the mayor of Oka doesn't seem to understand that the Mohawks won't let it happen. So the people of Kanesatake occupied the Pines ten days ago. I'm surprised you're not up-to-date on a subject such as that."

"I guess I'm not," Solomon replied, suddenly wary of Cameron because he realized Cameron was now playing trickster with him.

When Solomon arrived home that evening, he found Margaret sitting at the kitchen table, the day's dishes piled in the sink and no cake in sight. "Sit down. I have something to tell you."

He sat across the table from her and waited. "Mom died last night. Aunt Minnie called this morning after you left. They sang the memorial songs for her this afternoon, and they'll bury her tomorrow."

Several moments passed before Solomon could speak. "How did Mom die?" he asked when the words could come out.

"Her lungs fell apart. She had been coughing them up for years, Minnie said, and there wasn't much to her lungs to begin with. I guess what was left just caved in upon itself, and she stopped breathing. She wouldn't let anyone, Slim, or Sam, or Frank, take her out to hospital. She simply went to bed and stayed there until it was over."

"Why didn't you try to reach me at SFU after Minnie called you?"

"What for? What would you have done? What could you have done? I decided tonight was soon enough."

Solomon's tongue slipped numbly back to the roof of his mouth as his eyes moved about the room. They came to rest upon a calendar pinned to the wall beside the doorway. He stood and walked over to it. Margaret's eyes, vacant with pain, followed him. "What are you doing? Figuring out what day and world you're standing in?"

"It's nearly seven years since Dad died." He gave Margaret time to take his words in. Then he went back to the table and sat. "I waited too long," he said. "We waited too long. I took Mom for granted and thought she'd always be there. Dad's dying, that's what I've thought about these seven years, and I forgot that others can die, too, when they've decided there's no use waiting around any longer. Mom stopped waiting for us and died."

Margaret took his words in, then got up and went over to the sink. Drawing a stack of dishes to her, she turned on the hot water tap. The water ran across her fingers and from their tips until the heat began to bite. She turned the tap off suddenly. "I've never forgiven her."

"Forgiven her? For what? For not seeing what Harvey and Uncle Charlie were doing?"

"Maybe that, though she wasn't alone in turning a blind eye. No, it was her accepting what Dad did to her that I couldn't forgive."

"What did Dad do to her?"

His sister's eyes took him in. "You loved Dad, didn't you?"

He nodded. "Didn't you?"

"Did I? Yes, I suppose I did, once. And then I didn't love him very much, if at all, afterward." She blinked and shook her head sharply. "God, what am I doing? You're twenty-one; you're a man. You might as well know, and if you can't take it now, you never will." Margaret turned on the hot water then the cold, and her hands and voice settled down to business. "Do you remember a teacher who came to Duxsowlas? Grades one to four. You would have been three at the time, so maybe you don't. Anyway, she was from Wales and her name was Emer."

A picture rose up within Solomon of children circling, and then Naomi pulling him into the circle: *Fie, fie, fie for shame, turn your back to the wall again.*

"Yes, I do remember," he said. "She stayed in the village for Christmas. I had a dream about her. About her and Dad."

"Yes, she stayed for Christmas, spent time at our house and time with Dad alone, time enough for the two of them to get pretty close to one another while Mom watched from out in the cold. Then she left in March, in a hurry, with the tree of life sprouting in her belly. Which means, dear brother, provided she didn't miscarry into the Atlantic Ocean, that you and I and Frank have a brother or sister or something wandering about in the world, somewhere." Margaret took a dish towel from the rack beside the sink and tossed it across the room to Solomon. "Here, dry these, while I brew us a strong pot of tea."

He dried the plates, cups, cutlery, and two pots in silence while the kettle came to a boil. Margaret's words had numbed but not shocked him, for he had already known or dreamed the truth they told him, long before now. He returned to the table and the mug of tea Margaret had poured for him. The first sip of tea a wet fire about his tongue, his numbness gave way to a surge of feeling—anger on behalf of his mother, and shame on behalf of his father, yet a shame that wondered how a man who had lived as truly as any man Solomon had ever known could have done what Isaac had done. What meaning had that act of love within the whole fabric of Isaac's life or the life of Emer? And what of the brother or sister born of that union? And their family still alive at Duxsowlas?

"It's time we went back, Margaret," he said. "Before there's no one left to go back to. Adha, Frank, Lila, Sam, Peter . . ." The names came flooding to his lips, but he stopped pronouncing them as he saw the shadow cast down upon Margaret's face by the light overhead.

"Yes, Adha. Axilaogua, holder of great names and keeper of the tribal flame. God, I must have been a sadness to her whenever I put on my button blanket and tried to dance as she did, knowing she could see the blanket went only as far as my shoulders and back. She wanted a traditional granddaughter like your little friend Naomi, and she got me. No, Nathan Solomon, you go back to Duxsowlas if your mind and heart tell you to do that. For me the door is closed."

"How do you know what kind of a granddaughter Adha wanted you to be? And how can you say for sure the door is closed?"

"Because I know how tightly I closed it, and why." Margaret eyed him steadily across the rim of her cup, and Solomon set his down with a shrug. "Then maybe it's closed for me, too. I slammed the door pretty hard on the way out."

"But slamming a door isn't the same as closing it, and besides we're talking about two different doors, mine and yours. Duxsowlas is still your home, your real home, but it's not mine. My place is here, whatever being here may bring me." Margaret's cup stayed at the level of her mouth, but she did not drink from it. Solomon watched as her eyes left his and she went away from the world between the two of them into another world with a painful truth of its own.

He looked about the kitchen, his sister there at the table with him, but no longer there, and felt the absence of her husband. Where the hell was Cameron? It was close to midnight and Cameron had not come home. With a shock, Solomon realized there had been other evenings like this one, a number of them in recent months, only he had been asleep to what he had been seeing. Where is Cameron, Margaret? The thought felt its way to his lips and wanted to speak itself into a question. But Solomon held the question back.

Margaret set the cup down and stood. "Staying up all night isn't going to bring Mom back or solve anything else for that matter. I'm sorry I had to dump that other thing on top of her death, but I saw no point in keeping you in blissful ignorance any longer. It's turned out to be one hell of a birthday for you, but I guess you'll find a way of putting your shoulders under it. You seem to be good at doing that."

But he had one more question before going up to bed. "How did Aunt Minnie know where to reach you?"

"I phoned her as soon as you moved in, so she could tell Mom you were safe."

Upstairs, lying in his bed and staring into the dark of the ceiling, Solomon wasn't sure what he could shoulder. Above his head, touched by the light that drifted in through the window, the head of Raven protruded from the plane of yellow cedar encircled by the crescent moon of Sisiutl—just as he had carved it three years ago. Had anything in that picture or in him moved on since then?

He turned onto his side to sleep if he could and realized he was crying.

On a July afternoon, Solomon sat in a cafe in Gastown that led into a pub and ordered another grilled cheese sandwich. As he ate, he thumbed through a book on Mohawk culture and history. Cameron's question about Oka had goaded him into doing some research on Mohawk resistance to incursions upon their lands and their sovereignty as a people.

Aware that there had been a changeover in waitresses, he glanced in the direction of the voice that had not gone away, even when he had said no to a refilling of his cup. Juliet stood at the table, a pot of coffee in her hand. "Hello, Solomon. It's been a while." She glanced about the cafe. "I can sit with you for a minute if that's okay."

"Sure. It's good to see you. What are you doing here?"

"Making enough money to do something else. What are you up to?"

"Going to school for the summer term. Then I'm going home for a few weeks," he said, remembering that night in the Stein Valley, at the fire.

"That's good," she said. "That's where I'm going, too. As of today, we Indians need to support one another."

"What do you mean, as of today?"

"And where have you been?" Juliet asked, astonished at his question. "The Quebec police raided the Mohawk camp in the Pines at Kanesatake, early this morning. There was shooting and a policeman was killed. Then the rest of the police ran like hell, leaving cars and vans behind them. The Mohawks trashed several and used them to blockade the road. It's been on the news all day; everyone is having a bird about it."

"Christ!" Solomon exclaimed, as several hundred years of history came crashing into his life.

"There's a TV in the bar," Juliet said. "Maybe we can catch a newscast."

She was right; a newscast was in progress. Solomon and Juliet stepped into the dimly lit bar where several people stood, drinks in hand, their eyes fixed on the TV screen. He drank in the images that poured forth: reporters rehearsing yet again the drama as it had unfolded and continued to unfold; Warriors with their semi-automatic rifles at the high point of Mercier Bridge from Chateauguay into Montreal, the Warrior flag and that of the Iroquois Confederacy flapping defiantly from the concrete blocks into which they had been stuck; three Warriors riding high in the crib of the front end loader at Kanesatake, one with the rifle raised above his head in a gesture of triumph; the grim faces of the Sûreté du Québec, the masked faces of the Warriors, and the faces of the Mohawk women—defiance steeling the anguish that moulded, creased, and masked the faces of the women. And then Solomon saw the other faces, not on the screen, but in the bar, faces looking now at Juliet and at him as if the two of them were wearing masks.

Throughout July, he sat in front of the TV and watched the drama unfold. Reporters gathered at the blockades in the Mohawk camp and at Mercier Bridge. Human rights commissioners and international observers appeared on the scene; some of the key players welcomed them, and others harassed them. Corporal Marcel Lemay, killed in the Pines on July 11, was buried; it was not yet clear whose bullet had killed him. The Sûreté du Québec stood at the barricades and tried to stare the Mohawks into submission. Negotiations between the Mohawks and the provincial and federal governments started up, broke down, and began again. Crowds gathered daily and nightly at the Chateauguay end of Mercier Bridge and set about making life miserable for the police, stray Mohawks, journalists, and anyone else who seemed an apt target for their frustration and rage.

Support for the Mohawks swelled in native communities across Canada, and Solomon tried to go about business as usual. Yet even though he had no intention of joining those on their way to Kanesatake or of putting on a mask, people he met on the street, in stores, or on the bus looked at him as if he were wearing a mask. The looks were not necessarily hostile, especially during the initial weeks of the standoff when public sympathy was as much with the Mohawks as against them. But Solomon couldn't ignore what the looks told him. He was an Indian, as masked to those who met him as were the Mohawks in the Pines to the TV cameras.

Had it always been that way, and he simply hadn't seen or wanted to see it for what it was? He registered for his fall courses and promptly forgot them. In the evenings, he stared at the masks yet again, and the masks stared out of the screen at him and wouldn't let him evade what they wanted him to see.

One night he dreamed he was dancing in the big house at Duxsowlas. Naomi stood where Adha had always stood, her rattle moving to the beat of the log drum and her voice wanting to draw him toward her. A mask covered his head, but he could not say what mask it was or whose, only that the mask began to bear down upon his forehead, press in upon his face, and then his hands became frantic as they struggled to tear the mask away. Naomi's voice faded; the big house collapsed around him, fell away beneath him, and he could not breathe. He tried to tear the mask from his face, but the mask had become his face.

On August 20, the army replaced the Sûreté du Québec at the barricades and replaced the concrete blocks with razor wire. On August 27, the premier of Quebec asked the army to dismantle the barricades. The following day the prime minister appealed to the Warriors to take the barricades down as CF-5 fighters streaked across the sky above Oka and civil authorities advised residents to evacuate. That afternoon cars with Mohawk women, children, and old men and women left Kahnawake by Mercier Bridge. The crowds gathered at the north exit hurled stones, bricks, and debris at the cars as they sped past, while the police stood, watched, and did little else.

On August 29, the army and the Mohawk Warriors dismantled the barricades on Mercier Bridge. Solomon turned off the TV, closed his eyes, and rested his head against the back of the couch. It was over. The Mohawks in the Pines at Kanesatake might hold out against the army a while longer, but it was over.

Margaret walked into the room, a cup of tea in her hand. She had stopped watching the drama of the Pines some time ago. "When do you start classes?" she asked.

"Next week."

"What courses are you taking?"

"I don't remember," he said. Margaret's cup paused in midair. "You're starting your last year, and you don't know what you're taking?"

"That's about it. I've had other things on my mind these past few weeks, but I don't suppose you care a shit about that."

Her eyes widened. "What are you talking about?"

"You know, Mohawks in the Pines, golf courses on Indian land, soldiers ready to rush the barricades, and just plain being Indian. None of which fits into your nice white world."

Margaret's nostrils flared and her eyes flashed. "Or into your world, you arrogant hypocrite! I didn't see you lighting out for Kanesatake, so what the hell gives you the right to talk to me like that?"

"Living in this house and using my eyes. You'd walk right out of that brown skin of yours, Margaret, if you could. But skins don't shed so easily, and besides, you have a husband who wants to get inside brown skin and shoot himself upriver, back into paradise. But he's given up on the inside of your skin and is poking about elsewhere."

She gasped, her breath a knot at the back of her throat. "What are you saying? What do you know?"

Solomon got up from the couch and stretched toward the ceiling.

"Ask Cameron why he's not around much these days. Or hasn't that fact registered within your tight-assed world?"

Her hand snapped back and she hurled the cup at him. He turned his shoulder aside as the cup flew past, to crack apart against the wall behind him. Solomon saw the brown liquid staining its way across *Transformation #3*, along the lines of the figure in red feeling its way out of the black skin of Raven. He laughed softly. "Serves the stupid bugger right. He should have gotten out of there long ago. I think I'll sleep somewhere else tonight." He walked out on his sister without a further glance and made his way through the East End of Vancouver to where Izzy lived.

"Solomon! What's up?"

"I just had a fight with my sister. Can I stay here tonight?"

"Sure, come on in. Man, you look pretty raw around the edges." Izzy led the way into the kitchen. "Everyone else has gone to bed, but I just got in. Jason, Sandra, and I were at Stanley Park all day. They asked if I had seen you lately."

Solomon dropped wearily into a chair. "And now you can tell them you've seen me, whatever it is of me you've seen."

Izzy leaned against the sink. His eyes stayed upon Solomon. "Do you want something to eat? Or drink?"

Solomon shook his head. Izzy went on looking at him until Solomon came back from wherever he had gone and stared back. "What are you looking at?"

"You," Izzy replied.

"What about me?"

"It's hard to say at this time of night. But somehow, you don't look like the Solomon I know."

"Maybe I'm not the Solomon you know. Say, 'Duxsowlas,' Izzy."

"What?"

"Duxsowlas. Just say the word."

"Solomon, what the hell is this about?"

"Nothing much. Thanks for the bed."

Some hours later, the night narrow about him, Solomon got up from the mattress Izzy had laid down on the floor of his room and went into the bathroom. As he was about to turn the light out and return to bed, he caught a glimpse of his face in the mirror. Only it wasn't his face, but that of a stranger. He stepped forward to inspect it. Dark, with a savage light in its eyes, the face of the stranger looked out of the mirror. Yet it was his face, and it was insisting upon recognition.

He placed a finger down upon the surface of the glass as if to press through it and touch that other face, but the surface resisted him.

Upon awakening the next morning, he found a note tucked under his pillow:

> I've gone to work, but you can stay here tonight,
> if you need to.
>
> Your friend, Izzy

Solomon dressed, looked at the note again, then crumpled it up and dropped it into a wastebasket before leaving the house. After getting something to eat at a nearby cafe, he went to a phone booth.

"Hello."

"Hi. Remember my voice?"

"Solomon! Where are you?"

"Waiting to see you. Are you busy tonight?"

"No . . ." she hesitated, then said, "No, I'm not busy."

"Then I'll see you at Stanley Park. Third Beach. Okay?"

"Okay. Yes, I'll meet you there."

He reached Third Beach shortly before sunset and waited until she came into view, walking toward him across the sand. She stopped a few feet away from him.

"Hi, Anika."

"Hello, Solomon. My God, I still can't believe it's you I'm looking at. You're just the same, yet different somehow."

"Three years is a long time. How have you been?"

"Well enough. And you?"

"Pretty well. I'm going into my last year at SFU. Majoring in English would you believe?"

She laughed. "I believe you. You were always good in English. I'm slogging toward the finish of a BA in psychology at the other end of town."

"Have a seat. The sand is still warm."

"Thanks." She sat beside him and leaned her back against the log. "Why did you call?"

"I wanted to talk with someone. Someone I had been close to. I've thought about you these past three years."

She tried to veil the look in her eyes, but the Anika that was direct and clear betrayed her. Encouraged, he ventured further. "It's been one hell of a summer for me."

"Yes, I guess it would have been with the trouble at Oka and all. It hasn't been easy for Juliet, either."

Juliet? "Yeah, Juliet. I saw her the day the barricades went up."

"She's up at Mt. Currie on the blockade there. That's what Astrid told me last week."

He nodded. "That's good."

"Have you heard any news of Anwar?" Anika asked.

Anwar? Why was she asking about him? Then he remembered. Anwar was in Iraq, and Iraq had invaded and occupied Kuwait. "No, nothing. I haven't been in touch with anyone for a while."

She nodded and he glanced at her, her face aglow in the light of a sun about to set. The warmth of her grabbed at his insides and wouldn't let go. She had been on the verge of welcoming him inside her once. That would have been lovely then. It would be lovely now.

"Have you gone home yet?" Anika asked.

He shook his head. "No, I haven't."

Surprised by his answer, her eyes asked the next question. "Well, I decided my reasons for doing that weren't real reasons," he replied.

She turned her head away. He waited, then reached for her hand. "It's good to see you, Anika. To be with you again," he said, simply, yet moving silently within himself.

This time she did not try to veil her eyes. "It's good to see you. I've thought about you often." Then she reached with her other hand into her shirt and drew forth the eagle feather. "I've tried when I've thought of you to think this truly belonged to me. But I know it doesn't, even though it's from you and something special of you came with it."

He looked away from the feather and from her. "I guess it's too Indian for you," he mused.

Bewildered by his reply, she seemed lost for words. "That's okay," he said. "I think I understand. Would you feel better if I took it back?"

She nodded. "Yes, Solomon, I would."

"All right. Release it and let it fly home," he said, holding out his palm. She laughed and placed the feather there. He closed his fingers about it and tucked it inside his jacket. "There. You feel better?"

Her smile deepened. "I feel better. Thank you."

"Good," he said as he touched his hand lightly to her face then kissed her. With the second kiss, his arms closed about her, and he drew her down onto the sand just as the sun touched through the horizon line. Anika half-resisted him, then began to yield to the insistence of his body against hers, though he could feel a struggle continuing somewhere within her, not Anika against him but Anika against Anika.

The sun cast back a swath of golden-red light upon Third Beach where there was no human presence other than the two bodies feeling for, yet against, one another upon the gleaming sand. As if wanting to resist, Anika continued to yield to that in her which had once loved and wanted Solomon. Then, as his hand went to move her legs apart, his body pressed forward too insistently.

Slipping through the horizon, the sun exploded into a swirl of feathered light as Anika's body erupted up from the sand and her hands thrust him away. She gathered her shirt about her and stared hard at him, one knee upon the sand and the other beginning to straighten as she struggled to stand. Stark with what she knew, her eyes riveted in upon his. "You ravening bastard!" she gasped. "You were going to fuck me! Fuck me! And that was all, wasn't it?"

He reached for her. Her hand closed into the sand and then drew back. He reeled backward as the sand struck him full in the face, and heard her crying as she ran from him.

Then he began to run, and as he ran, the house and city that were no longer home fell behind him. By the time he reached the Trans-Canada Highway, his run had exhausted itself. Then he stuck out his thumb and took the rides as they came, until just east of Cache Creek, a long ride took him to Revelstoke.

Beyond Revelstoke, the mountains stayed with him, range upon range of them, as the long highway snaked through the Selkirks, around the northward thrust of the Purcells, and in that last darkness before dawn, into the Rockies. Curled down into the bed of a pickup that would take him as far as Banff, he was as afraid of the darkness without and within as he had been that night on Log Island when he had buried his body under a bush of salal. Yet he struggled to remember the name his father had spoken that last morning.

East of Banff, the mountains began to slide apart. In the front seat of a car, at the edge of sleep, he glimpsed the black sides of them going to indigo, and about the peaks the first pure blue of a dawning sky.

EIGHT

He lifted his head away from the window and shook himself awake as the highway flashed past the last of the peaks draped with dawn mist, past spruce and poplar spotted with wolf willow, toward the brightening of the sun. The mountains fell behind him except for a line of peaks to the north and the flat-faced sentinel that brought the line to its end where the foothills rolled up to it from the prairie farther east. When the highway reached the sign that read "Morely Road," the grey coupe took the exit. The driver slowed, then stopped. "This is it. Cross the bridge and go north along that road until you come to Morely."

He nodded and opened the car door. "Thanks, for the lift."

"The seat was empty. I hope you find the person you're looking for."

The car vanished down the ramp back to the highway, and he pulled his jacket close about him against a sharp wind from out of the mountains. He looked at the restaurant on the hill behind him, the gas station, then at the bridge spanning the highway. The sun newly risen in the east cast long shadows across this strange, open land. Then he began to walk. Crossing the bridge, he made his way along the road, glancing at his shadow as he went. Stretching westward, his shadow walked with him as his feet crunched into the gravel along the side of the road and urged him forward as if they knew of themselves what they were about. The rest of him knew and felt nothing.

At the crest of a hill, he met a woman going the other way. He stopped and the woman stopped. "Maybe you can help me. I'm looking for someone."

The woman's eyes considered his. "Yes," she concluded, "you certainly are. Who is this someone you're looking for?"

"A relative, going back to my grandfather and my grandfather's brother. They came here after the 1885 Rebellion. My grandfather went on, west, but his brother stayed. His name was Wounded Drum. I wondered if there might be someone here related to him and to me."

The woman put a finger to her lip as she thought about it. "Maybe he didn't stay around for long after your grandfather left, or else he lived and died without passing himself on. Or my memory is fading out because I can't think of anyone of our people with an echo of that name."

A truck came up the hill behind her and she flagged it to a stop. "Alec, this person is looking for a relative, going back to someone called Wounded Drum. I'm drawing one big blank. Help me, please."

Alec tapped his fingers upon the steering wheel; then he grinned. "Wesley Drum. Up at Big Horn."

The woman shook her head and sighed. "Of course. You want to take this young man with you Alec, if you're heading back?"

"I'm heading back," Alec said with a glance that was more than a glance. "Climb in."

Alec drove west to Banff, then turned north onto a road that ran between mountain ramparts on either side, the peaks rising up from the valley of the Bow and giving way one by one to others that emerged from behind, each locked fast in its towering silence.

At Saskatchewan River Crossing, Alec turned eastward. Now the mountains opened out to the south, revealing a plain of spruce and meadow grass. "The Kootenay Plains," Alec said. "It was our land, once. And still is our land."

Farther along, the road veered northward and came upon a lake to the east; then a dam appeared at the northeastern end of the lake. "Many of our people were buried here," said Alec. "Then the businessmen and government men who turn water into electricity decided they needed even more of our land. So they made plans to dam the Saskatchewan River, right here. We told them it was our land and that our people were buried here, but they went ahead in 1969, and started building their dam. They told us they'd see the grave sites were moved, and wondered why we still didn't smile."

1969, the year I was born, he thought, but said nothing. Alec drove on farther, then turned north, up a narrow, dirt track. "Our reserve is just down the road, and Wesley lives up here. He takes hunters out into the bush, loses them, then makes them pay double after he finds them." Alec grinned across his shoulder. "It's a living, I guess."

Alec's truck bumped up to a crest and over it; then he came to a stop before a log cabin. Beside the cabin a corral held some horses and two mules were hitched to the railing. The cabin door opened. A man stepped out onto the porch, nodding at Alec as he considered the other face before him.

"This fellow thinks he's related to you, Wesley."

Wesley chewed on that idea. "Then we'd better feed him, too."

Inside the cabin, a cast-iron stove burned wood, and a woman stood at the stove, cooking. "This is Sarah," Wesley said. "We sobered up together a few years back and decided it was too good to stop there."

He sat at the table with Wesley and Alec. Sarah placed a plate of bacon and eggs before him, then a steaming cup of coffee, and he ate without speaking or being spoken to. By the time he set his fork down and looked up, Alec had gone. Wesley sat near the stove, fiddling with a strap on a bridle. "You'd better take your jacket off as if you mean to stay a while," he said.

The eagle feather fell from the jacket as he undid the zipper, and he barely caught it before it hit the floor. Sarah let her breath go once the feather was in his hand, and Wesley watched him closely as he set the feather upon the table.

"So you're a relative of mine. I didn't know I had any of those left. Tell me how we're related."

"My grandfather had a brother called Wounded Drum."

"Then we are related. Wounded Drum was my grandfather. Do you come with a name?"

Do I come with a name? he asked himself as his heart sank the more toward the pit of his stomach. What do I come with? Nothing . . .

"Jacob," he said.

"Jacob. And that's it?"

"Yes."

"All right, Jacob. Tell me about any other relatives I might have, so I won't be so surprised if they drop in."

"My dad is dead. And now my mom. My brother Frank still lives in the village where I grew up with my Adha, and there are some aunts and uncles on Mom's side. And my sister lives in Vancouver."

"Anyone else?"

"Maybe. A brother or sister somewhere from my dad."

"And why aren't you out on the coast with your family?"

"Things stopped working out there."

"Well, things are still working here. There's a pair of boots standing by the stove and a hat on the peg over there. You can bunk down on that bed in the corner when we're back from this trip. You'll find me at the corral."

The boots fit and so did the hat. Out in the corral, Wesley had packed up one of the mules and was cinching up the canvas thrown over the pack saddle and gear on the other. "That one is called Easy Does It," he said, "and this one is First Things First. Watch that back hoof, or she'll kick your salvation right out from under your crotch. Pass the rope underneath that box and send it back to me. That's good. Are you running from the law?" The question came lightly but firmly across the canvas.

"No," Jacob said as he took the rope again. "No, I'm not running from the law."

"And if I hear someone pounding on my door late one night or early one morning and open it, am I going to find some woman's husband shooting at me in the hope of hitting you?"

Jacob tightened the rope along the canvas and returned it to Wesley. "No," he smiled, thinly. "There's an angry girlfriend, out west, but she won't bother to come looking for me."

"That's good because I wouldn't want to gain weight all of a sudden. Can you ride a horse?"

"I've never ridden a horse."

"Can you ride a horse is what I asked."

"I guess I can," said Jacob. And that's what he did the whole of that day. Once his legs had bent, then bowed, to the shape and sway of the saddle beneath him, there wasn't much else asked of him other than staying in the saddle. The horse did the rest. That night he left the fire where Wesley entertained two white hunters from somewhere else on the continent, crawled into the sleeping bag Sarah had given him, and sank into a numb sleep in which nothing stirred, not even a flicker of a dream.

In a silence that felt neither backward nor forward, Jacob followed his cousin into the days and weeks of autumn as the foothills yellowed against the first snows on the mountains to the west. He saddled horses in the morning, unsaddled them in the evening, and rode them through the hours in between, stopping to make campfires for lunch as well as first thing in the morning and again at night. He did whatever Wesley asked of him and then things he could see needed doing, grateful for the long hard days and exhausted nights that kept him at bay from himself. He said nothing of the life he had left behind him and gave no thought to where his life could go now. Space and time about and within him shrank to the present, and that became a world in which his life was still possible, though barely so.

One day at a time Wesley would say, as he tightened or loosened a cinch, to no one in particular and for no particular reason it seemed, other than the saying of it.

Late in September, a tall figure of a man stood in the doorway of the cabin. "Looks like we'd better warm up a seat and a plate for Leo," said Wesley. "This is Leo Many Hands. And this is my cousin Jacob from the west coast."

"I thought you had buried all your relatives," Leo said.

"So did I. But this one hasn't died as yet. So Leo, what's up?"

"The Mohawks walked out of the Pines, yesterday. They burnt tobacco, said their prayers at the fire, then tried to find a back door that would let them walk out with dignity. But the army didn't go along with that. So it ended with our sisters and brothers being seized, and punched, and knocked to the ground. They even roughed up a girl who was trying to carry her little sister out." Leo fell silent and sipped at his coffee. Jacob studied the length of rope he had been holding, aware that Leo was studying him.

"It's enough to make someone pretty angry," said Wesley, observing Leo's scrutiny of Jacob. "Especially someone like you."

"Especially someone like me," Leo agreed.

"And you've decided to come and be angry here," Sarah said, with a smile but not smiling. "And hope we'll get angry with you."

"Yeah, that would be all right, too. There should be enough anger to go around."

"Could be," Wesley said. "There are many things that might make me angry, but you have to be careful how you get angry if you want to stay sober. First things first."

"Except when first things come last. As the missionaries taught us so very well." As he spoke, Leo went on assessing Jacob until Jacob jerked his head upright and shot a glance back.

"What are you looking at?"

"You. I'm trying to figure out if you care."

"Why should I care?" As he snapped the words out, he asked himself if he had ever cared. "Have you seen what you want to see?"

Leo cocked his head. "I think I see a loser," he smiled.

Wesley sighed as he reached for his hat. "Well now, while the two of you are deciding whether you're going to like one another, you can help me bring down three horses I left in a corral above Bighorn Canyon because I think they would like someone to come and bring them down."

Late that afternoon, they led the horses through dense stands of spruce to the rim of Bighorn Canyon then along the rim itself. At first

Jacob thought Wesley was crazy to come that way, but neither Wesley nor Leo seemed to mind riding that close to the edge, and the horses didn't seem worried either. So Jacob relaxed into the saddle and let his horse take him even closer to the rim. Far below, the Bighorn River snaked down from the north, twisted about to the east, to the south, then to the east again. As the sun sank toward the mountains behind him, it drew the last of its light up the walls of the canyon, past layers of sandy, dark brown, brown, then red, rock until the river itself lay at the bottom of a pool of darkness.

Jacob reined his horse in. Wesley, Leo, and the two horses they were leading disappeared into a stand of spruce farther along the rim, and it was as if they had ridden right out of his world. Alone now with only the horse he rode and the horse he led, Jacob peered down into the darkness that crept up the canyon wall. Maybe the darkness was reaching up for him? The thought slipped into him and took hold. Maybe the darkness wanted him to join it, down at the bottom of the canyon and beyond the canyon bottom. Well, why not dive down into the darkness and put the light behind him?

He nudged his horse closer to the edge. The horse resisted the pressure against its sides until the pressure became too insistent to resist. Reluctantly, the horse stepped forward until Jacob was gazing right down the canyon wall. He drew in a last breath and straightened himself into the stirrups as he raised his hand above the flank of his horse.

The sound of a hoof against a fallen branch stayed the movement of his hand.

"That would be a mean thing to do to your horse." Wesley's horse stood a few spruce trees away, as did Leo's. "To both horses in fact," Wesley went on. "The one on the lead would probably follow you down just for company."

"We Indians are experts at turning our anger against ourselves," Leo said as Jacob's body slumped back into the saddle, "especially when it's all dammed up inside. Don't damn yourself, Jacob. Deal with the dam, instead."

Leo reined his horse about and followed Wesley toward the stand of spruce into which they had vanished earlier. Jacob drew his gaze up from the darkness below, reined his horse away from the canyon rim, and rode after them.

III

CAST

Wesley Drum, *in his early 50s*

Sarah, *about the same age as Wesley*

Leo Many Hands, *in his late 30s*

Nadine Stone In My Chest, *in her early 30s*

Jacob, *23*

Sundown, *maybe 20*

Caitlin, *almost 19*

STAGING *The audience faces north, looking upon a dirt road running past the head works of a dam site, east of the Canadian Rockies. A campfire burns at centre stage, half-circled by logs and rocks for sitting upon.*

To the west—stage right—two metal railings, about 1 ¹/₂ to 2 metres in length, 1 metre in height, and with a 1 ¹/₂ metre gap between them, extend from the backdrop at a 45 degree angle to the front line of the stage. This is the entrance to the head works, a pillbox of concrete and wood at the end of a concrete ramp running out into the lake behind the dam, and not visible to the audience. However, the audience does see a double wire gate between the railings, painted into the backdrop, maybe 2 to 3 metres in height and crowned with barbed wire along the top; at either end of the gate another frame of wire is painted into the backdrop, extending beyond the railing on either side. The effect is that of some winged metallic being standing guard at the entrance to the head works. To the west of the railings and gate, a wooden power pole stands, either beside the railing or painted into the backdrop.

Rock has been piled up behind the campfire area, a low level line of defence that can extend into the backdrop itself.

To the east—stage left—wood has been dumped into a pile. Between the rockpile and the woodpile the road itself is painted into the backdrop, winding up a rise in the land to curve away to the northeast. At the top of the rise, a large pylon is painted into the backdrop, standing east of the road. A police car is parked just off the road, beside the pylon. A second pylon emerges in the distance, northeast of the first one.

Rising up along the backdrop, above and beyond the setting itself, is a line of mountains.

LIGHTING *A large spread of light upon the campfire area, smaller circles of light, one to the west, upon the railings; one to the east, upon the woodpile; one to the south, upon the stage area in front of the campfire. A light off-stage from the west indicates sunset, and from the east, sunrise.*

At those moments when an actor leaves the campfire area for one of the outer circles of light or returns from them to the campfire area, he or she should make a complete counter-clockwise turn along the way, done discreetly or obviously, as the director sees fit in each instance.

ACT ONE

Sunset, September 26, 1992, the second anniversary of the ending of the Mohawk occupation of the Pines at Kanesatake. A faint light from the west onto a darkened stage and a drum beating tentatively as if the drummer is searching for something. The woodpile light brightens. Wesley Drum sits upon an upended log, listening to his drum as he beats upon it. The drum is very old with a small hole near its centre.

Wesley: *(Stops drumming and speaks to his drum, a laugh in his voice.)* So you're not going to tell me, are you? Not yet, anyway. Tell me the song my grandfather used to sing upon you, even though that song should be inside your skin by now.

(He drums softly, listens, then begins to chant.) You didn't listen—You didn't listen—You just didn't . . . listen! *(A short, sharp beat.)*

Hell no, I didn't listen, even though he lived past eighty. Outlived my dad and might have outlived me, if he hadn't died and I hadn't stopped drinking. *(Sighs.)* But it wouldn't have mattered how long he lived, because I just didn't listen to that song.

(He stands.) I did hear some of the things he told me, though. You'll have to remind them he said, remind them whose land this was and still is, and that we are here and have never been anywhere else but here. Because their memories work in a funny way, and they forget the things they said to us and promised us. I guess their minds are so full of what they're going to say next, they can't remember

the words they've already spoken. (*Light brightens upon the campfire area, where the rest of the cast is gathered around the fire.*) So that's why we're here today occupying this dam site, to help them remember and give them a few more things to think about.

Sarah: While we study this amazing dam they've built upon our land.

Wesley: That's Sarah. She and I live together. We sobered up together a few years back and decided if we could do that, living together could be even better.

Sarah: We came this morning, as the sun was getting out of bed. We brought wood in Nadine's truck and piled up these rocks in case we have to duck for cover at high noon.

Leo: Though these rocks won't do much for us if the cavalry does charge. But we needed the exercise, this place needed landscaping, and Sundown can sleep there during the day if he gets bored.

Nadine: Besides, you became good at piling up rock when you were in jail.

Wesley: Leo Many Hands. He says he's also been in many jails, on many blockades, and lived many lives, like a cat that can land anywhere without thinking much about it. Nadine has been with him for a while, I guess. We've been using her truck. It's the only truck I know that does the Grass Dance, moving or standing.

Leo: All of us may be dancing around a rockpile when this occupation ends.

Nadine: Oh, yeah? And how is it going to end, Leo?

Jacob: The way we agreed it was going to end. We walk out on the fourth morning when the sun rises.

Wesley: That's Jacob. We're related—cousins, from what he said and from what I could get. He walked through our doorway about two years ago with nothing much of him left in his eyes. Just the look of a person running from something he was on his way to meet. So Sarah fed him and then I took him with me, guiding. Jacob almost rode one of my horses off the rim of Bighorn Canyon one sunny afternoon. But Leo and I talked him out of that, and he talked himself into this instead. In fact, Jacob helped us scheme up this occupation. He's pretty smart in a way.

Leo: (*To Jacob.*) You still think we're just going to walk out of here on the fourth morning? I bet our guardian angel over there (*gesturing toward the police car*) may have other ideas.

Sarah: (*Quietly.*) The fourth morning will bring whatever it brings.

Sundown: (*Fingering a repeating rifle.*) It had better bring more than sitting on my ass and waiting for something to happen.

Wesley: Sundown. He's never done this sort of thing before. (*Chuckles.*) None of us has, actually, except for Leo. But I guess Sundown thought he was going to be at Wounded Knee or Oka. Instead, he's here on this dam site with a gun that has nowhere to go.

Nadine: What do you want to happen, Sundown?

Sundown: Whatever. As long as we do it.

Sarah: Well, while you're figuring out what it is you want us to do, please put that gun down. Your finger is making the trigger nervous, and that makes me nervous.

Leo: (*With a glance toward the police car.*) And it might make our angel nervous, which could lead to an unexpected turn of events.

Sundown: (*Laying down the gun.*) I just want this occupation to happen.

Jacob: It's happening, Sundown, so relax and wait for them to make a move, if they decide to move.

Sundown: Yeah, and what will we be doing? While they're deciding.

Sarah: We'll be occupying our ancestral land.

Wesley: By being here, celebrating the 500th anniversary of our discovery of Columbus.

Nadine: We're here because we've never left this or any of our land.

Sarah: Because this land has always been occupied. That's what we're doing here, reminding them of how things really are.

Leo: (*To Caitlin, who has been writing all the while.*) Did you get that, little lady? We're occupying our ancestral land. I went to school, so I can do a spell check for you.

Caitlin: (*Still writing.*) Thanks, but it might be like sending a blind man to buy paint.

Leo: (*Eyes widening, as everyone else laughs or chuckles.*) Hey, you've got a sharp tongue, little lady! About as sharp as your pen.

Caitlin: (*Backing off a bit.*) Never fear. Like alehouse talk, it'll get weaker with the night air.

Wesley: Now, that's Caitlin (*pronouncing it "Kate-lin"*).

Caitlin: Kat-lheen (*as she continues to write*).

Wesley: Right. And she's our journalist. An occupation of a dam needs a journalist to tell the world who's occupying what and why. Caitlin (*carefully sounding it out as Kat-lheen*) came walking down the road this morning at sunrise all the way from Wales, while we were unloading the firewood and piling up rocks. She'd gotten wind of an occupation about to happen, she told us, so she wanted to stick around and let the world know about it.

Sundown: And what have you been writing all day? Nothing's happened as yet.

Sarah: A lot has happened. We came and we're here.

Jacob: And we're staying until we leave. This is a serious occupation of this dam site. (*A touch of something in his voice, mockery perhaps, draws Caitlin's attention to him. She observes him with interest.*)

Sundown: (*Disgruntled.*) Get real. No one cares that we're here. Not the guy who came this morning, and not even him (*gesturing toward the police car*). We're just some Indians camping out on a dirt road.

Leo: He cares. Otherwise, he wouldn't be here, parked beside that pylon. We've got a cop and a journalist, so we're into a real occupation of this site for now.

Wesley: Yeah, that's our cop. We don't remember just when he drove up to that pylon. All we know is one moment we looked up and there he was. At least, we think he's there because we haven't seen anything of him as yet. Just the sunlight bouncing off his windshield. (*He leans his drum against the woodpile and walks over to the fire where he sits with the others. The woodpile light fades, as does the last light of the sun from the west. The light about the campfire brightens some more.*)

Nadine: (*After a brief silence.*) Well, guys, here we are, sitting upon 4,054,000 cubic metres of earthfill.

Jacob: (*A mocking tone.*) Imagine!

Sundown: Yeah, that's the word they used in that information house down by the river. Imagine!

Sarah: It was a good thing we went down there and had a look. We want to be informed occupants of this site.

Leo: Let's see now. There's 25 million tons of earthfill within this dam and it would take 160,000 box cars to haul it away.

Nadine: Imagine!

Jacob: And this dam generates enough horsepower to move fifty diesel locomotives . . .

Sarah: Pulling 160,000 box cars . . .

Leo: That are hauling the dam away . . .

Sundown: While the dam is generating enough power for those fifty locomotives . . .

Sarah: That are hauling it away.

Nadine: Imagine!

Wesley: And a person could stand by the track for four days while that train rolled past.

Sarah: If you wanted to wait around that long.

Leo: And all the concrete in this dam would build a sidewalk
            from here to the next town to the west.

Wesley: So why didn't they just build the sidewalk? (*Everyone
            laughs.*)

Nadine: And this dam is as long as 700 people in a movie lineup.

Sundown: Man, I wonder what was playing that night.

Jacob: And then there are the lightbulbs, which our visitor today
            was so worried about.

Sarah: How many light bulbs was it?

Jacob: 1,200,000 one-hundred-watt light bulbs. That's what this
            baby can light up in any given second.

Sundown: He was from the government, right?

Leo: He was so rattled he didn't know where he was from.

Sundown: Did he come before the cop came or afterward?

Leo: Who knows? And who cares? The two of them are just a
            right and left hand trying to get their act together.

Sarah: (*Taking her time and laughing as she speaks.*) And he said,
            "What are you people doing, camping here beside the
            head works of this dam?"

Nadine: And Jacob said . . .

Jacob: We are just occupying this dam site for a few days, to
            celebrate the 500th anniversary of our discovery of
            Columbus . . .

Leo: And the second anniversary of the ending of the Mohawk
            occupation of the Pines at Kanesatake . . .

Nadine: (*Looking up and about.*) It was about this time of night when
            they walked out, Warriors, women, children . . .

Wesley: And the twentieth anniversary of the completion of this
            very fine dam on Indian land.

Nadine: They walked out and the army was waiting for them as they walked out. (*Out of the flow and into herself.*)

Jacob: So you can see that such a triple occasion calls for our occupation of this dam site.

Sarah: "But you can't occupy this land," he said. "It belongs to the power company."

Jacob: It belonged to us before you put your hands on it. We want to remind you of that for the next few days.

Wesley: "But you're blocking the head works," he said. "What are you going to do with the head works?"

Nadine: (*Back into the flow.*) Well, I don't know. What could we do?

Leo: "You could shut the whole dam down," he said. "That's what you could do!"

Sarah: Ooh! We could do that? Well, thanks for telling us. We'll keep it in mind. (*She dissolves with laughter, as do the others.*)

Leo: (*To Caitlin.*) Are you getting all this down, little lady?

Caitlin: (*Staring hard at him.*) As sure as my pen can stay with your tongue.

Nadine: And then Jacob said . . .

Jacob: What would happen if we shut the dam down?

Sundown: "What would happen?" he squawked. "Don't you realize this dam powers 1,200,000 one-hundred-watt light bulbs throughout this province, and beyond?"

Nadine: No!

Sarah: No!

Leo: Imagine that!

Wesley: And Jacob said . . .

Jacob: Then do yourselves a favour and let us shut the damn thing down. No one needs all that light. Nobody can bear all that light.

Caitlin: (*Pen poised above her pad.*) That was an odd thing to say. Why did you say that?

Jacob: (*Returning her look.*) Because it was what I decided to say.

Leo: Then he jumped into his truck, cranked the engine, rolled down the window . . .

Nadine: So he wouldn't put his tongue through it . . .

Leo: And he said, "We'll deal with you people soon enough, if you stick around here."

Sundown: Then he gunned the engine, until it sounded like fifty diesel locomotives.

Sarah: About to pull 160,000 box cars.

Nadine: To haul the dam away.

Wesley: And with a hearty Hi Ho Silver, he was gone.

Leo: Leaving Tonto behind once again, to set up camp.

Laughter all around, gradually dying away.

Sundown: Man, what would they do if we shut down all their light bulbs?

Caitlin: Convert to nuclear power. (*They stare at her.*) That's right. One teaspoon of uranium can power a hundred-watt light bulb for seven years, rendering obsolete a ton of coal and this dam we're sitting on. Shut it down and you'll give them all the reason in the world to go radioactive.

Sundown: You mean something like, "Good morning, Sir or Madam. I am from the power company and I have in my hand a teaspoon of uranium for your hundred-watt light bulb with our guarantee that if your light bulb is not satisfied, you may lick the spoon and charge it to us."

Jacob: (*Laughing.*) But I don't think they carry uranium around in teaspoons, Sundown.

Caitlin: No, they use pylons, like those out there, with wires frozen to the underside of their arms as they march across the north of Wales following the tracks left by the Roman armies. The pylons march where the Romans marched.

Wesley: (*Musing.*) The pylons march where the Romans marched . . .

Jacob: And over here the pylons roam where the buffalo roamed. That's what we need, a few thousand buffalo to do to the pylons what they once did to the telegraph poles.

Sundown: What did they do to the telegraph poles?

Jacob: The buffalo would rub up against them for a good scratch, until the poles were lying on the ground. They sure scrambled up a few messages those buffalo.

Wesley: Yeah, my grandfather told me about that. Then the telegraph people decided to spike the poles up, down, and all around, figuring the spikes would keep the buffalo away.

Jacob: (*Drawing the others into his words as he speaks.*) But you know what those buffalo discovered? The sweet unbearable joy of those spikes scratching at their skins. They trampled over each other to get to those poles, climbed upon each other's backs for the ultimate scratch, until they rubbed their skins raw . . .

Sundown: (*Moving his back up and down as if scratching it against a pole.*) Yes, just do it!

Jacob: And the great North American prairie became one big graveyard for telegraph poles. Until they decided to kill the buffalo. (*To Caitlin.*) But we saved a few and we'll send them over to you to deal with your pylons.

Leo: (*With reserve.*) That's some story, Jacob. Where did you hear that story? From Wesley?

Jacob: (*Hesitating.*) No, it's something I learned at school.

Nadine: Yeah, sure. They taught you that in residential school?

Jacob: I didn't go to residential school.

A few seconds silence, as everyone stares into the fire and Leo makes up his mind about what he is going to say next.

Leo: Well, I did go to residential school. In fact, that's where I
           was given my name.

Nadine: Yeah? Leo Many Hands? In residential school?

Leo: You've got it.

Nadine: You've never told me that.

Leo: It didn't seem worth telling, until now. (*Pauses.*) I was
           about to live with my grandfather when they took me. I
           was nine, maybe ten. He was going to teach me whatever
           it is a grandfather teaches you. So I didn't have that kind
           of teaching, the way Wesley had . . .

Wesley: (*Quietly.*) They also put me in residential school.

Leo: But they didn't take your grandfather away from you. He
           died while I was there and they didn't even tell me until a
           year later. The bastards didn't even tell me my grandfather
           had died. (*He stares into the fire.*) Anyway, I was a big kid
           and an ugly kid with a big, loud mouth, and I made sure
           no one messed with me. Not the boys in my dorm, or the
           priests and brothers who messed around with the boys.

           *The firelight dims as Leo rises and moves into the brightening
           light circle at the railing. Caitlin also rises and moves into the light
           circle at the woodpile. The light brightens upon her when she
           speaks.*

           Then one day, this priest, Father Joseph, watches me
           as I carve into a piece of wood.
           "You have good hands, Leo," he says.
           "I think they could do many things. Many good things.
           I hear they're good at picking the lock
           on the food room, late at night."
           He's smiling at me the whole time, and I keep looking
           at my piece of wood and at the knife in my hand.

Caitlin: And a young man came to the door of the king
           of the Tuatha De Danaan.
           "Who are you yourself?" said the doorkeeper,
           "and in what are your hands skilled? For no one comes
           through this doorway without hands skilled in an art."

Leo: "I can teach your hands to do many good things,"
Father Joseph says. "And to be bold in what they do . . ."

Caitlin: And the young man said, "I am Lugh, son of Cian
of the Tuatha De Danaan, and of Ethlinn,
daughter of Balor, King of the Formor.
Question me, for I am a carpenter."

Leo: "So let me teach your hands, Leo," he says.
"But my name isn't Leo," I mumble.
"Ah, but you have a courageous heart, like the heart of a lion,
and your hands will become bold, too.
Yes, my son, your name is Leo."

Caitlin: "We don't want you, for we have a carpenter,"
the doorkeeper said.
"Then I am a smith," said Lugh.
"But we have a smith," replied the doorkeeper.
"Then I am a champion," said Lugh.
"Ah, but that is no use to us, for we have a champion,
the king's own brother," replied the doorkeeper.

Leo: Yeah, he was a good teacher, that priest. He taught my hands
to saw, and plane, and hammer, and chisel—funny,
that his name was Father Joseph—and then to wire
and plumb and fix . . .

Caitlin: "Question me again," said Lugh, "for I am a harper."
"That is of no use to us, for we have a harper ourselves,"
the doorkeeper answered.
"Then I am a poet, and a storyteller," Lugh said.
"We have all the poets we need," yawned the doorkeeper.
"Then I am a magician," said Lugh.
"But tell us," the doorkeeper asked, "what power can you
work that we don't already have?"

Leo: "You'll be Leo Many Hands when I've finished
teaching you," he said.
"And then you can open any door in the world.
Leo Many Hands, hands that can work wherever
they want to work."

Caitlin: "Then let me be a cupbearer," Lugh said.
             "We don't want you; we have nine cupbearers ourselves,"
             stated the doorkeeper.
             "Then," said Lugh, "go ask your king if he has any one man
             that can do all these things. If he has,
             you can close the door on me."

Leo: And then I turned sixteen. Leo Many Hands, ready
             for the many doors of that world they said
             was the only world left for us to live in.
             The night before I left, Father Joseph came to my bed
             and took me by the hand. He led me into a small,
             dark place, somewhere in that school.
             "Leo," he said, "there's something your hands can do
             for me, now. For me, Leo, please.
             For what my hands have given yours."

Caitlin: And the doorkeeper went to the king, and told him all.
             "There is a young man at your door
             whose name should be Samildanach, Lugh Samildanach,
             Lugh, the Master of all the Arts, for all things
             the people of your house can do, he himself is able to do,
             every one of them."

Leo: Then he lifted his cassock. (*Pauses.*)
             "Bless me with your hands, Leo," he said.
             "Yes, Father," I said, "for you have taught my hands
             to do all things."
             Then my hands reached for him, through the dark,
             into the dark and closed in upon him,
             closed in, closed in, and didn't let go.

             (*Fiercely.*) And I still haven't let go!

             The railing light fades as Leo returns to the fire, and the firelight
             brightens. The light upon Caitlin dims as Leo speaks.

Leo: (*As he sits.*) They charged me with assault. (*A cutting*
             laugh.) That was the first time I went to jail.

             Caitlin returns to the fire and sits, without speaking.

Sarah: You should tell us how you got your name, Wesley.

Wesley: It's not much of a story, after what Leo has told us.

Sarah: (*Pressing him.*) But it's a good story. It would be good to
           hear it about now.

Wesley: (*Smiling.*) I guess so. Why not? When my grandfather's
           people crossed the Medicine Line to join up with Sitting
           Bull here in Canada after the fight at the Little Big Horn,
           my grandfather carried the name Wounded Drum.

Sundown: How did he get that name?

Wesley: That's another story again. Anyway, after his mother and
           older brother had gone back across the line and younger
           brother had gone north and west—you remember, Jacob?

Jacob: Yes, I remember.

Wesley: Then Wounded Drum was left alone with the wife he had
           taken from among the Nakoda at Morely. And this
           missionary comes to him and says, "You need a name,
           now."

           My grandfather says, "I have a name," and speaks his
           name in Lakota. "No, no," says the missionary. "That's not
           a real name. You need a name like Peter Smith or Billy
           Brown. So white people like me will know who you are."

           "Well," my grandfather says, "then I want the name of
           that preacher you told us about, the one with the warm
           heart. John Wesley. That's going to be my name."

           "Oh, no!" says the missionary, dancing from foot to foot
           like a person with a rattlesnake in his boot. "You can't
           have that name. That name belongs to John Wesley
           himself."

           "Well, where is he?" my grandfather asks. "He's dead,"
           the missionary says. "Then he doesn't need that name
           anymore," my grandfather says, "and I guess he won't
           mind if I take it over from him."

           That missionary didn't know what to say then. So he kept
           moving his words around, hoping they'd figure something
           out, and finally he said, "Well, all right, you can take John

Wesley's name for yourself, but only as your first two names. You have to choose a last name that isn't his."

My grandfather laughed. "If it isn't going to be one of his names, it will have to be one of mine, so I'll just call myself John Wesley Drum." The missionary decided to quit while he was ahead or at least not so far behind, and that became my grandfather's name, John Wesley Drum. Then my father was born, the name was passed on, and my father became John Wesley Drum, Junior. Only people came to calling him not John or Wesley or even Drum but just Junior. Even white people called him Junior: Hey there, Junior. How's life out on the rez?

(*Knowing laughter from the others.*) Well, when I was born and my grandfather wanted to keep the name going and call me John Wesley Drum the third, my father growled, "No one's going to call my kid the third." So he broke the chain by slipping the first two names around one another and I became Wesley John Drum. No junior, no the third. Just Wesley Drum.

(*Pauses.*) Though when I was drinking, I wasn't even that. I didn't have a name at all, nothing but wino, drunk, or hey, Indian! There wasn't enough of me left to put a name to. (*To Sarah.*) Remember?

Sarah: How could I forget? There wasn't much to either of us when we first met. Not even enough to go to bed with one another. You know Wesley, you were the first man I met that I didn't go straight to bed with.

Wesley: (*Chuckles.*) I guess I was too drunk to find my belt buckle.

Sarah: It's a good thing you didn't find it. If you had, I'd have walked out on you the next morning, like I walked out on all the others. (*Pauses.*) You know, I've spent my life walking out of places and out of people's lives on and off the reserve. Grandmothers, aunts, uncles, foster homes—I've walked away from all of them. Maybe I was looking for the parents that were too drunk and too broken ever to come looking for me.

(*She looks about her, into the night, then up at the sky, before she continues.*) There was a missionary lady, though, who lived on our reserve. I stayed with her longer than with anyone.

Leo: You stayed with a missionary lady? No wonder you were messed up. That's all the missionaries were good for, messing us up.

Sarah: (*Quietly and firmly.*) She never hurt me. In fact, she was the one who told me about my name. "You're Sarah," she said, laughing as she said it. "That's your trouble. Sarah spent her life wandering about with her husband, Abraham." So maybe I've been wandering about looking for my Abraham. What about it, Wesley? Are you my Abraham?

Wesley: Well, I don't know. I'm trying to remember the story. Was he a good lover, this Abraham?

Sarah: I guess he was, but Sarah didn't have any children for the longest time. (*Laughs softly.*) Maybe that's why I bedded down with all those men, trying to do what that other Sarah couldn't do, have a child. Good luck to me! I think every one of them was sterile. After a while I stopped worrying about birth control. (*To Wesley.*) But I don't think you're sterile. You're just not Abraham.

Wesley: And maybe you're not that Sarah.

Nadine: I don't know that story. Did she ever have kids, that other Sarah?

Sarah: Yes, a boy named Isaac. When she was ninety.

Wesley: (*Laughing.*) Well, what do you know! There's always hope.

Sarah: (*Also laughing.*) We'll see. (*To Jacob.*) But if I had an Isaac, that would make me your grandmother.

Jacob: My grandmother? (*Pauses, then a restrained laugh.*) Yeah, I suppose it would if you went by the story.

Nadine: You know that story?

Jacob: Yes, I know that story.

Sundown: How does the story go?

Sarah: Jacob is the son of Isaac, the second son, and he steals his older brother's birthright.

Sundown: Rips his brother off?

Sarah: Yes. Then he runs for cover, all the way east to find others of his family to look after him. Until he has to go west again and face up to his brother.

Caitlin: And then he meets an angel at the ford of a river.

The others stare at her.

Sundown: You know this story?

Caitlin: Yes, I know this story.

Leo: A real angel, eh?

Nadine: Imagine that!

Caitlin: (*Looking across the fire at Jacob.*) And the angel wrestles with Jacob all night long, until the sun rises.

Sarah: Then the angel says, "Let me go back to the sun."

Caitlin: And Jacob says, "Not until you bless me."

Leo: So, have you been blessed, Jacob?

Nadine: Maybe Jacob hasn't let the angel go.

Leo: Or the blessing didn't take.

Nadine: Or he didn't take the blessing. That sounds like a missionary story. Did some missionary tell you that story, Jacob?

Jacob: My mother told me that story.

Leo: Then she must have heard it from a missionary.

Jacob: Maybe. They did come to our village.

Leo: They came everywhere and got to most of us. What did your grandfather say, Wesley? About the missionaries who wouldn't let him keep his name?

Wesley: (*Thoughtful.*) Not very much one way or another. But one time, I remember, we were sitting together somewhere and a priest walked past. My grandfather laughed to himself, kind of a gentle laugh, then said, "Consider the missionaries, Wesley. They neither sow nor reap, yet their god feeds them. So if you're ever hungry, go and become a missionary."

Laughter, during which Jacob rises and walks toward the light circle at stage front. The light brightens as he steps into it and the campfire light dims.

Jacob: (*Stands quietly before he speaks.*) Consider the ravens. That's how the story really begins, isn't it?

Wesley: (*Appearing at the wood pile as the light there brightens.*) How does any story really begin? But I guess that's a good enough beginning. (*He sits on an upended log and takes up his drum.*)

Jacob: Then tell me the story.

Wesley: I've told you the story.

Jacob: Tell me again.

Wesley: Why? Didn't you listen the first time I told it?

Jacob: I need to hear it again.

Wesley: From the beginning?

Jacob: Yes.

Wesley: Late in the morning, a Sunday morning, the soldiers rode into the valley of the Greasy Grass. Fast-riding horse soldiers throwing up the dust.

Jacob: But my grandfather had a dream in the same valley two nights before that morning.

Wesley: That's where his story starts. My grandfather's story starts when the old men cried, "Soldiers coming here! Soldiers are here!" Our great grandfather, Spreading Eagle, reached for his new, fast-shooting rifle, never before fired, then threw a handful of dust upon his horse and said to his oldest son, "Come, it is a good day to die, for everything we love is here."

The first soldiers rode down the valley along the river, dismounted to shoot, then scattered for the trees when they saw the power that was ours that day. And when the trees would hide them no longer, they became afraid and rode for the river. The oldest son rode with those of our people that cut the soldiers off there, knocking them from their saddles as they tried to jump the water where there was no place to jump.

"It is a good day to die," our great grandfather said, as the eagle bone whistles shrilled, calling the warriors to Crazy Horse, "Hoka Hey," and they rode down our side of the river to meet the soldiers that were seen going down from the bluffs on the other side. My grandfather, a boy of twelve, seized his drum, a good, new drum, for he had a strong song to sing for his father as his father went into the fight—a song as strong as an eagle winging up to the sun. He ran behind the horses, ran through the camp of the Cheyennes, the song ready to wing from his breast like a strong, young eagle.

At the crossing down the valley, four Cheyennes, their horses dancing together, held the soldiers back until Crazy Horse came, his warriors fanning out from him like the wings of an eagle. Our great grandfather was one of the first to cross the river, his rifle lifting into the sky above him, just as my grandfather reached the bank, his drum high above his head as he cried, "Hoka Hey!" And the soldier bullet lifted Spreading Eagle from his horse, until his body dropped down to our Mother, the Earth, and a bullet came singing through the skin of my grandfather's drum. He looked up, past the sting along his hand, through this hole (*as Wesley raises his drum overhead*) out into the sun. (*Pauses.*) Maybe it was the same bullet.

(*He taps at the drum.*) I asked my grandfather once if he remembered the song he was going to sing. "I can't find that song in my heart anymore," he said. "Not anymore."

Jacob: Only the song he sang to my grandfather, when my grandfather left.

Wesley: Yes, the little brother he loved.

Jacob: The little brother who had the dream two nights before the soldiers came. My grandfather.

Wesley: Yes.

Jacob: Tell me about my grandfather, about his dream.

Wesley: (*With a shake of his head.*) My grandfather never told me about the dream.

Jacob: But my grandfather told him. That's what my father said.

Wesley: My grandfather never told me.

Jacob: Then I'll tell you that story.

Wesley: You've told me that story, my cousin.

Jacob: I need to tell it again. (*Wesley begins to drum, softly, as Jacob continues.*) My father left me alone for three days and three nights on an island near our village. I was nine. The third evening, the sky was blue about the sun as the sun set and deep with the first of the stars. As I watched the sun set . . .

Wesley: (*Waits a few seconds.*) As you watched, my brother?

Jacob: I saw the first sliver of the new moon above the sun after the sun had set. The crescent gleamed back at me as the night grew dark, and within the gleam of it, a dark circle in the cradle of the crescent and a light gleaming all about the edge of the dark circle. And in that encircled darkness, another light gleamed and shimmered and tried to form itself—a white Raven, wanting to spread its wings yet not able to spread its wings and fly free of the dark.

I held that moon there above the horizon all that long night, until the sun rose upon me and my father came on the fourth morning and told me what I had seen that night was what my grandfather had dreamed.

Wesley: And your grandfather left my grandfather, the brother who loved him, to go and find the people of the Raven—a people who would know the story of his dream and a way to see through it.

Jacob: Then my father said, "A name is being held for you by your Adha, your mother's mother. Gwawinastoo, Raven's Eye—that will be your name when you see through to the Raven in the dark of that crescent moon."

Wesley: You didn't tell me that part of the story.

Jacob: No. I wonder how far through my grandfather saw.

Wesley: You were going to tell me about the sun going down.

Jacob: I saw the crescent moon.

Wesley: Before you saw the crescent moon.

           Jacob stands in silence, before he returns to the campfire. Wesley stops drumming and looks at the drum as the woodpile light dims to a glow and the firelight brightens.

Sarah: (*Yawning.*) Bedtime, happy campers. If we want to put in a full second day of occupying this dam site.

           Sundown has taken out a pair of binoculars and is crouched at the rockpile, peering over the top of it at the police car. Nadine looks over and notices him.

Nadine: (*With a playful backhand slap at his thigh.*) Hey, bimbo! What are you doing? Think you can see that cop in the dark?

Sundown: You'd be surprised at what I can see in the dark. (*Goes on looking.*) Man, that guy sure loves his cop car because he hasn't put a foot out of it since he drove up to that pylon. (*Laughs.*) Or maybe he's brought his girlfriend with him.

Nadine: Or maybe she's brought her boyfriend. Get with it, Sundown.

Sarah: Either way, they're bedded down for the night, and that's where I'm headed.

Leo: (*Also looking at the police car.*) Maybe someone should keep awake in case he doesn't stay bedded down.

Sarah: Don't worry. Wesley is still trying to find his song. He'll be up for a while, perhaps all night long. (*She takes up a blanket and goes to the woodpile, as Nadine and Leo unfold the blanket they will share.*)

Nadine: Don't you snore in my ear, Leo. I want some deep peace and sweet dreams for tonight anyway.

Leo: (*Settling down beside her.*) Then don't snore in my ear. Just give me your best side. That's all I want.

Nadine: It'll be my backside, tonight.

Leo: That's a good enough side. Any side of you is good enough for me. (*He pulls the blanket over them.*)

Sundown sets the binoculars aside and curls into himself at the foot of the rockpile. Jacob takes up a sleeping bag and comes forward to the front of the stage as that light brightens, and unrolls the bag so that its head is at stage centre. The campfire light dims down upon Caitlin. She sets her pen and pad down and just sits, not sure where to go next. The woodpile light brightens somewhat as Sarah settles down beside Wesley.

Sarah: Are you going to stay up all night? That song could wait until tomorrow. God knows, it's waited long enough, up to now.

Wesley: Too long. It's become caught in this drum because I didn't listen. A song needs to fly free like an eagle; otherwise, it'll die—die slowly, maybe, but for sure in the end if a singer's tongue can't find it.

Sarah: (*A knowing smile.*) First things first, eh?

Wesley: (*Returning the smile.*) Yeah, first things first.

Sarah: You're just like the mule you gave that name to. Okay, have it your way. Goodnight, Wesley. I'll be here, when you put the drum down.

Wesley: That's good. It's a good thing, knowing that you're there.

The light upon him dims to a glow as Caitlin rises, takes her sleeping bag in hand and walks to stage front. Jacob sits on his sleeping bag, looking out at the night. Caitlin unrolls her bag so that it is head to head with his. Wesley drums intermittently during the following interchange, pausing now and then to listen to his drum.

Caitlin: Do you mind? (*Waits for a response, then.*) It's okay. I don't bite, much.

Jacob: Why should I mind? It's a free campground.

Caitlin: Just thought I'd ask. Do the polite thing. (*She kneels upon her bag.*)

Jacob: Do the polite thing—is that what a journalist does when she's chasing after a story? And you seem to be full of stories, little lady.

Caitlin: (*Turning on him with fury.*) Don't you call me little lady! I won't take that from you!

Jacob: (*The breath knocked out of him.*) Well, pardon me! But you sure took it from Leo all night long. Why not from me?

Caitlin: Because you're not Leo. That's why.

Jacob: Are you sure about that? What makes you so sure about that?

Caitlin: I was listening to you, when you spoke. Whoever you are, you're not Leo.

Silence. Jacob looks away, then looks back.

Jacob: Who is Lugh?

Caitlin: (*Astounded.*) You heard me? (*Stress on "heard."*)

Jacob: You weren't the only one listening.

Caitlin: You heard me? (*Stress on "you."*)

Jacob: You weren't the only one listening. Who is Lugh?

Caitlin: Yes, who is Lugh? Well, Lugh is the son of Cian, of the Tuatha De Danaan. And who are they you are about to ask. The Tuatha De Danaan came to Ireland when the world was still young, through the air and the high air. It was out of the mist they came and they brought the light in the shining of their faces, and in the shining of the face of Lugh, above all the others. But Lugh also is the son of Ethlinn, daughter of Balor, king of the Formor—king of a people filled with darkness. Balor of the evil eye, the eye filled with darkness and with death. The light and the dark together, that's Lugh, behind the shining of his face, shining like the sun.

Jacob: (*As much to himself as to her.*) Light and dark—half dove, half raven. Sounds like Parzival's brother, Feirefiz.

Caitlin: Parzival? You know that story?

Jacob: I know that story. It seems you and I know a few of the same stories.

Caitlin: But how do you know that story?

Jacob: There are things I know. That story is one of them. Parzival, the Red Knight, charging about on his red horse and knocking other knights from their horses—and all the while, bearing the hatred of the sun.

Caitlin: Because he didn't ask the question of the wounded king in the Grail Castle.

Jacob: What ails you, Uncle? That's what he should have asked. But he didn't ask.

Caitlin: Though they all expected him to ask the healing question. But he didn't know . . .

Jacob: Didn't know enough to ask. Or didn't care. So on rides Parzival, knocking knights off their horses and dropping the reins of his . . .

Caitlin: And bearing the hatred of the sun, until one day he meets his half-brother, Feirefiz, and they fight.

Jacob: And they don't know they're brothers, as they fight, then knock each other off their horses.

Caitlin: And their anger rose and the earth shook under their feet, and their swords clashed, while overhead the ravens screamed.

Jacob: It was one hell of a fight.

Caitlin: Until Parzival drove Feirefiz to his knees, and then his sword broke upon the helmet of Feirefiz.

Jacob: And Feirefiz could have killed Parzival, but didn't.

Caitlin: Then they knew . . .

Jacob: You have fought here against yourself.

Caitlin: Against myself I rode into combat here and would gladly have killed my very self.

They fall silent, look at one another.

Jacob: (*Matter-of-factly.*) You're a good storyteller.

Caitlin: (*Likewise.*) Thank you. So are you.

Jacob: It's good to have a story to tell. They told stories to each other, Feirefiz and Parzival, about their father.

Caitlin: Whom they never knew. Did you know your father, Jacob?

Jacob: He's dead. (*Stunned by answer he has given.*) Yes, I knew him.

Caitlin: What was his name?

Jacob: Isaac.

Caitlin: Isaac! Imagine that. Then you really are Jacob.

Jacob: I was fourteen when he died.

Caitlin: I was fourteen when my mother died.

Jacob: He killed himself taking a man from our village out to hospital on a day no boat should have gone anywhere. A man who had abused just about every kid in the village— including someone I really cared about. I've been trying to understand why my dad did what he did that day, but I don't yet. Maybe I never will. (*Lies down on his bag.*)

Caitlin: But you knew your father, before he died . . .? (*Perhaps a question, perhaps not.*)

Jacob: (*Letting her words penetrate.*) Yes, I knew him. He taught me many things. And I think he loved me.

Silence, except for the sounding of Wesley's drum, very softly now. Caitlin looks away, all about her, then glances back at the figure beside her, now asleep.

Caitlin: Lucky you, Jacob. I never knew my father. (*Looks down at him before speaking again, now more to herself.*) Lucky you.

Lost in herself, she looks out at the night, then begins to sing to herself as the light at the woodpile brightens and Wesley stops drumming.

Sonny lives on a farm
and she lives all alone.
Her Daddy's a sailor
who never came home.

Nights are so long,
Silence goes on . . .

Wesley: That sounds like a good song.

Caitlin: It's a sad song. The Irish love sad songs.

Wesley: Are you Irish?

Caitlin: Yes.

Wesley: I thought you came from Wales.

Caitlin: I'm Irish, too. Welsh, Irish, and whatever else is in here.

Wesley: You think there could be something else?

Caitlin: There could be. But what I think doesn't matter much, does it?

Wesley: That sounded like a good song. It's good to have a song inside you.

Caitlin: It's a sad song. I can never play the sweet music or sound the sweet string. Whenever I'm sweet, I'm sad. If it's sweet you want, it's sad I'll be. If your river is running to sweet, I'll turn it to sad. (*Lies on her bag, head to head with Jacob.*) For me that sweet music is a long way off, sometimes north, sometimes east, and then it changes to the west. But in all the wide world, I do not know where it will come from. (*She sleeps, and the light upon Jacob and her fades out.*)

Wesley: (*To his drum, as the light upon him begins to fade.*) It's good to have a song under your skin, and a story, even if it's a sad story and a sad song. (*He drums softly, as the light upon him fades out.*) Listen, listen, listen.

ACT TWO

September 27, 1992, just as the sun is setting. The cast gathers about the campfire as the last light from the west fades and the campfire light brightens. Sundown, with his binoculars, is concentrating on the police car as the others find places to sit.

Sundown: (*Lowering the binoculars.*) Whooee! That guy is something else. Hasn't even stepped out the door to take a leak.

Nadine: He could have walked off somewhere when our heads were turned. Or maybe he's died on the job.

Leo: My head hasn't been turned, not once. He's too busy watching us to worry much about whether we can see him.

Nadine: Why are you so worried about him?

Leo: Because he's there, that's why. As long as he's there, I'll worry about him.

Sarah: Then we should move our camp up there. It might make it easier for him to keep an eye on us, and for you to keep an eye on him. So you won't worry so much.

Leo: And abandon the head works of this dam? I don't think so. As long as we're here, we have our finger on the throat of 1,200,000 light bulbs (*strikes a pose*) throughout this province and beyond. I like having power over that kind of power. (*With a glance at Jacob.*) That might come in useful before we walk out of here. Who knows?

Nadine: (*Wanting to keep the mood on the light side.*) Or maybe we could invite him down to our fire for another day of learning about native culture from Sarah. We might send him home a changed man.

Sundown: Tell me about it! Man, somebody should hand me a degree or something when we walk out of here.

Nadine: (*Playful.*) Ooh! Poor baby! Your sore head is breaking my heart. (*Looking into the fire, then at Sarah.*) You're a good teacher, Sarah. I learned a lot today.

Sarah: Funny. I don't think of myself as a teacher. Just a person who has started late and is running hard to catch up. (*To Wesley.*) I guess that goes for the two of us, eh?

Wesley: (*Who sits quietly, listening, as do Jacob and Caitlin.*) Pretty much. Except when I'm running, I sometimes think I'm doing so with one leg tied behind my head. Unless I'm on a horse and the horse is doing most of the work.

Nadine: (*With a laugh.*) Then let the horse do the work, if you're lucky enough to have a horse under you. You're still good teachers, both of you.

Sarah: A teacher is only as good as the ears willing to listen. Besides, you know a few things yourself.

Nadine: My grandmother was a good teacher, too. My mother's mother, old Annie Stone In My Chest. (*Pauses, then decides to go on.*) Funny, how we got that name. It came from her father. He had a trapline along a river valley, going back for generations in our family. Then one winter morning, he went out to check his traps and found someone had bought up a big chunk of the valley and had torn out the line. Grandfather took it to court and lost. The judge said, "Well, do you have anything else to say?"

My grandfather stood so very still, without a word. The judge said, "Well?" And my grandfather murmured, "There is a stone in my chest and I cannot get my words past it."

The judge laughed and said, "That would be a good name for you, old man. A good Indian name—Stone In My Chest." After he had looked long at that judge, my

grandfather said, with great dignity, "Yes, I think that
would be a good name for me." So from that day on, his
name was Stone In My Chest.

Wesley: You took your name from your mother's people?

Nadine: Anything worth having came to me from my mother's
people, and from her. All I ever got from my dad was a
beating.

She stands and goes to the railing; the light brightens upon her.
The firelight dims as Caitlin goes to the woodpile.

My dad had gone to town to drink that night.
It was late when he came home, though none of us
had gone to bed. We knew there was no point in doing that
until he came home. I heard his truck bumping
along the dirt road and up to our shack.
Funny, it used to sound just like my truck sounds.
Maybe that's the one thing I did take from him,
a truck that sounds like his.

He kills the engine. We hold our breath, and wait.
But for the moment, nothing happens. We hold onto
our breath, waiting . . .

Caitlin: (*As the light brightens upon her.*)
The pylons march where the Romans marched, across
the north of Wales to the stretch of water
where they could look across to Ynys Mon,
the Isle of Anglesey.
Across the water and along the beach stood the Druids,
their warriors, and the women . . . the women . .
the women . . . .

Nadine: Those moments scared me the most, waiting
for him to leave the truck then kick his way
through the kitchen door. Knowing
he was sitting out there, his anger
boiling to a rage.
That night his foot takes the door
right off its hinges. My mother puts me, my sister,
and my two little brothers behind her back,

and meets him at the centre of the kitchen.
She is crying already, but stands her ground
and meets him.

Caitlin: The Druids raised their hands in prayer to the heavens,
pleading, pleading to the gods, and all along
the beach the women keened and wailed,
their hair and their voices reaching
into the wind. Oh God,
how the women wailed . . . wailed . . .

Nadine: He just stands there, at first, stunned
by my mother's rage and fear and helplessness.
For a moment, I thought he was going to leave.

Caitlin: The Romans fell back, at first, to the bank along
their side of the water, thrown into confusion
by the power in the keening of the Druid women.
Afraid of that power, naked, vulnerable,
that cried out from the Druid women.

Nadine: Then I see the change in his eyes.
His hand starts to lift . . .

Caitlin: And then some centurion or other cried out,
Come on, boys! They're only screeching women.
Let's go get them!

Nadine: I watch as she falls,
falls . . . falls . . .

Caitlin: Come on, boys!

Nadine: And then I'm standing over her,
my fist clenching at the air.

Caitlin: Let's get them!

Nadine: And I hear my voice cry,
Don't hit her . . .

Caitlin: Go get them!

Nadine: You're angry at yourself! You're just angry
at yourself! Don't hit her!
Please, don't hit her.

Caitlin: Get them!

Nadine: I didn't even see his hand coming,
             until it struck me.

             *Silence. With dignity, Nadine walks slowly back to the fire and
             sits. The firelight brightens with the dimming of the railing light.*

Caitlin: (*Quietly.*) And when the Druids were done down, the
             Romans set to work and laid waste all of the oak trees.

             The woodpile light dims as Caitlin returns to the fire.

Nadine: (*After a pause, and pointing to her mouth as she speaks, matter-
             of-factly.*) See this tooth here? The chipped one? That's the
             night I got it. I've had to be careful about biting into a
             carrot ever since. I stick my teeth out even now whenever I
             eat one. The kids at school used to tease me and call me
             Bugs.

             (*A few chuckles around the fire. Then Nadine continues.*) I saw
             my grandmother that next summer. "There's a big stone in
             my chest," I said to her, "and it's never going to go away.
             What can I do about this stone in my chest that will never
             go away?" I asked my grandmother.

             "Ooh! Then make that stone into a story-stone," she said,
             and told me about a people, once, who found a big stone
             in the forest. The stone knew their story, knew of a world
             before this world where all the stories began, where their
             story began, and it told them all the stories they knew.
             "Make that stone in your chest tell you your story," my
             grandmother said, "and that stone will live and not be a
             stone any more."

Jacob: (*From out of nowhere.*) The Grail is a stone.

             *Puzzled looks all around, except for Caitlin, who seems more
             fascinated than puzzled.*

Leo: What did you just say?

Jacob: The Grail. It's a stone. A stone that feeds people. And
             things go to ashes there and are reborn. That's what the
             story says.

Leo: Oh yeah? And what else does this stone do, besides giving feasts and raising the dead?

Jacob: (*As much to himself, as to the others.*) Funny, that stone. Whatever you need or want to eat it gives you. Even more than you want or really need.

Nadine: I like that kind of stone. I'll have a deluxe burger with fries, please.

Leo: And a sixpack to go.

Sarah: A sixpack of what, Leo?

Leo: Whatever. Whatever this Grail stone happens to have in cold storage.

Wesley: I sure would have liked to have had a stone like that when I was drinking and my supply had run out and it was two a.m. on a Sunday morning. Though maybe it's a good thing I didn't have such a stone around. But tell us more about this wonderful stone, Jacob.

Leo: (*On edge and pushing at Jacob, despite his show of humour.*) Yeah, tell us more, Jacob. Tell us that story, since you seem to know that story.

Jacob: (*Back to here and now.*) I don't think I'll do that. Not tonight, anyway.

He falls silent and the others with him. Sarah, who has been watching Sundown, leans over and nudges him.

Sarah: Then let's have a story from you, Sundown.

He looks back at her, deciding.

Sarah: Please. It would be good to hear a story from you, and maybe good for you to tell it.

Sundown: (*Bringing his gaze back to the fire and stretching a little.*) What the hell, why not?

Well, I was adopted by a white family and for a time, a long time I guess, it was okay. They took care of me and maybe they loved me, or wanted to, at least. And then I turned fourteen.

Jacob raises his eyes, straightens, and listens intently.

And found there were some kids in the town where we
lived who had decided they didn't like me very much.
They never told me why they didn't like me and maybe
they didn't even know themselves. Anyway, not liking me
was reason enough for them to come after me. They were
bigger than me and more than me, and there wasn't
enough of me either way. I didn't have a hope in hell of
standing my ground.

*The firelight dims as Sundown stands and walks to the woodpile.
Caitlin stands and goes to the railings. Again, the light
brightens upon her when she speaks.*

They beat me up only once, just off the school grounds,
but they took their time, worked me over good,
really good, and made sure they hit all the right places.
"If we ever catch you in the daylight again," they said,
"we'll beat what's left of the light right out of you."

I never went back to that school. When I left my house
the next day, I went outside of the town, out
onto the prairie, and waited for the dark to come.

Caitlin: On a night late in the fall when no moon is in the sky,
the shearwaters fly down onto the rock cliffs
and ledges, into the cracks and crannies
of Bardsey Island, off the tip of the Lleyn
in North Wales. It's from the islands west of Scotland
they come and they come at night
when there is no moon to betray their coming
because they know the ravens are there, waiting.

Sundown: I came into town after the sun went down, along
the back roads and alleys. For a long time
my foster parents didn't know what was happening.
The school never missed me.
Nobody seemed to miss me. Then one night,
as I was coming in from out on the prairie,
I saw the truck at the edge of town, waiting.

Caitlin: During the day, the shearwaters lie low,
rest, nurture their young, and stay out
of the light, out of the sun
and the light of the full moon.
Holding the night close about them,
they wait for their young to grow.
Close in their darkness, they outwait the ravens.

Sundown: I backtracked, crept along the town's edge
and tried another street. They were waiting there,
too, and at the next street, and the next.
There wasn't a street into town
where the truck wasn't there, waiting for me.

Caitlin: But some among the shearwaters do not dive down
into the dark of the cliffs, ledges
and crannies. Caught instead in the beam
from the lighthouse on Bardsey Island,
they follow the beam in until they hurl themselves
against the glass, into the light,
crushing themselves against the light.

Sundown: I didn't go home for a week. Seven nights I stayed
out there, until it started to snow
and I had to come in. So I came in,
came in . . . came in . . .
toward the light in a drugstore window
and threw myself into the glass.

Caitlin: Crashing against the light until they fall,
the shearwaters, one by one down into the dark
at the foot of the lighthouse
where the ravens wait . . .

Sundown: They sent me home that first time, to my foster parents.
So I went through the glass again, and again,
until they gave up on sending me home
and sent me to jail instead.

And then I felt safe . . .

*The light fades from both Caitlin and Sundown, and each
returns to the campfire circle as that light brightens.*

Sundown: (*As he sits.*) One of those nights out on the prairie, I met an old man out walking from where he lived at the edge of town. "We never see you around in the daytime anymore," he said. "Maybe sundown is when you wake up. Maybe that should be your name, Sundown."

"Yeah, sure, I laughed." And then I thought, "What the hell, why not?"

Sarah: The light of day can be cruel to a person sometimes.

Wesley: (*Laughing softly.*) There was a long stretch of years when I didn't care much for the daylight. But daylight comes when it comes and there's not much you can do about that, is there?

Jacob: Wrong. You can shoot the sun out of the sky. (*He looks around, matter-of-factly, as the others stare back at him.*) That thought has never crossed your minds? Well, there's nothing to it. If you want out of the daylight, you just take Sundown's popgun in hand, aim, squeeze off a few rounds, and bye-bye, sun.

Nadine: (*Uneasily.*) You're in a weird way tonight, Jacob. That is for sure.

Jacob: So it would seem. I think I'll go for a walk. Find a place where I can ambush the sun tomorrow morning when it gets out of bed.

He rises and walks to the railings; the light brightens to a glow upon him. He leans his backside against the inside of the railing nearest the campfire and searches out the night. His presence is more felt than seen during what follows.

Leo: (*After a moment.*) If we hear a splash, I guess he's walked off the dam and into the lake.

Sundown: Maybe the cop will get him. Maybe they'll go to town together in the cop car.

Sarah: (*Also wanting to ease the tension.*) Or perhaps Jacob will put his head down and go to sleep somewhere, wherever the earth decides to be good to him. And now I'm going to give the earth a chance to be good to me. Goodnight, all.

Leo: Not yet. There's a story we haven't heard. (*To Caitlin.*) What about you? How did you come by your name?

Caitlin: My mother gave it to me when I was born. And that's about it. Not much of a story, I'm afraid.

Nadine: A journalist should have a name with a story to it. I think we should give you a story-name before we walk out of here.

Wesley: (*Chuckling.*) How about Caitlin Many Pens? I've never seen a person lose pens the way you do. Do all journalists lose pens the way you do?

Caitlin: (*Trying to laugh with them at herself.*) I can't speak for other journalists, but I've never been able to keep a pen in my hand or my pocket for more than a week, if that long.

Sarah: Well, you're about to break that record here. You'd better hold onto that one. We've one more day to go, and we're about out of pens to give you.

Nadine: For sure. I didn't even know we had so many pens between us until you started hitting us up for them. (*She turns to Sundown and hugs him.*) Hey, night crawler, do something radical and go to bed for a change.

Sundown: Okay, just for you. When I'm finished here.

Nadine: You just want to wait up for that cop, when he finally steps out to take a leak.

Leo: (*Bedding down beside Nadine.*) If he does step out, make sure that's all he does.

Sarah: (*Unrolling her blanket by the fire.*) And what about you, Wesley?

Wesley: Soon.

He gets up and walks to the woodpile. Upending a log and sitting upon it, he takes up his drum and cradles it in his lap without playing it. Caitlin takes her sleeping bag to stage front and unrolls it there as the light brightens upon her and the campfire light dims down though not out. Caitlin starts to sit on her bag, then after a glance over at Wesley, she walks to the woodpile. The stage front light dims down.

Caitlin: Are you going to play your drum? I like listening to your
             drum.

Wesley: My drum is listening. Listening for your story.

Caitlin: It will need a long wait for that.

Wesley: (*Passing by her response.*) There's always that other name
             we look for, maybe in a vision. Or it could be that name is
             looking for us and bringing a story with it. (*Pause.*) Or
             maybe the name has already found us and we don't know
             what to do about it.

Caitlin: And then there is the name that goes looking, looking for
             its story.

             *She walks forward a few steps, looks out into the night as she
             speaks.*

             We were twelve, Erin and I, the day Uncle Sean took us
             walking in Snowdonia. Erin is my sister, my twin, and we
             climbed with Uncle Sean up the trail that leads out of
             Llanberis, alongside the railway track, until we stood
             under the long, high ridge and peak of Snowdon itself. I
             walked with my eyes fixed upon the high air, searching
             the sky for an eagle (*laughs*), which was stupid of me
             because there are no eagles left in Snowdonia or in the
             whole of Wales.

Wesley: (*Startled.*) There are no eagles?

Caitlin: There are no eagles, not in Wales nor in Ireland. We killed
             them off long years ago. Though one came to visit us the
             fall I was fourteen. A young bald eagle that flew out of the
             Atlantic mist from somewhere over here and landed in the
             southwest of Ireland. The Irish fed him and sent him home
             on Aer Lingus, first class, a month later.

Wesley: (*With a delighted laugh.*) A first-class eagle. That's good. It's
             good the Irish did that.

Caitlin: But there were no eagles to look for that day, even though
             we call Snowdonia *Eryri*, which means eagle. Perhaps I
             didn't know there were no eagles or didn't believe it if I
             knew, so I looked as I walked and Uncle Sean asked,

"Caitlin, what are you searching the heavens for?"

"An eagle, Uncle Sean." At which Erin laughed, "You're daft, Caitlin. The eagles have gone away from here, forever."

Wesley: Is she like you, your sister?

Caitlin: She's like herself. No, we're not alike, my twin and I. Strange that she was given the Irish name, and I the Welsh. Erin has no love for Ireland. Not so, my mother or myself.

Wesley: Your mother, she was with you that day?

Caitlin: No. She rarely came with us. Uncle Sean said nothing after Erin had spoken, though we went on standing there under the ridge of Snowdon, with the heather and gorse fresh with springtime about our feet and the ravens skimming along the ridge and out into the high air above it. But not an eagle was to be seen.

Yet I went on searching the sky as we walked down the trail and then I saw the feather, a feather I had never seen the like of, falling out of the sun, falling through the high air and toward the reaching of my hand.

"Uncle Sean, look! The feather of an eagle!" My eye staying with the turn and twist of its falling, my feet moving without my knowing, until my legs went red from the gorse thorns biting at them, and my eye taking my hand with it, the both of them reaching . . . reaching out.

And then my hand closed about the air, but there was nothing in it. Nothing . . .

I turned, weeping, to my uncle. "I did see it, Uncle Sean, I did! An eagle feather, falling from the sun." While Erin stood, her face gone ghostly pale and looking at me as if I had just come out of the Sidhe, from spending a time with the fairy people.

"Ah! So you did, Caitlin," said Uncle Sean and smiled, as if a moment long awaited had come. "Yes, an eagle feather falling from the sun and bringing your name with it. Pluen

Eryr, Eagle Feather. Now that would be a good name for you, Caitlin."

Wesley: Pluen Eryr . . . (*Sounding the name to himself and within himself.*)

Caitlin: Erin said little as we went on walking down the trail, nor did I speak. When we had come through the last of the metal gates and stood under the first green of an oak, Uncle Sean said to her, "There's a name for you, Erin, as well. A name someone has left for you."

"There is?" she said. "Yes," he replied. "In Welsh, it could be Llygad Cigfran. But the Irish would be better. Súl an Fhiaich, Raven's Eye. That will be a good name for you on a day when you're ready to take it."

"And when will that day be?" she asked. "When another eye of the Raven comes from across the sea looking for you," said Uncle Sean.

"And who is the someone that left me that name?" said Erin. "Someone who was close once to your mother," he said. "And does Mother know about this name?" she asked, kicking a rock out of her path.

"Ah, she could well know," Uncle Sean said, looking out at the sun trying to open up a bank of cloud. "But for now, we'll keep both the names a secret between ourselves."

Erin kicked out at another rock. "I don't think I want that name," she said and walked away from us down the road and into Llanberis.

Wesley: And your mother never found out about your names?

Caitlin: No, neither of us spoke to her of that day, ever. She died two years later when we were fourteen. Of a broken heart, Emer died. Of a heart long ago filled to the breaking.

Wesley: That was her name? Emer?

Caitlin: Yes. I never knew my father's name.

The light at the railing brightens upon Jacob. He becomes aware of Caitlin and Wesley and listens closely to what follows.

Wesley: Pluen Eryr. An eagle feather from the sun.

Caitlin: Falling from the sun.

Wesley: Yes, falling, like the life of a warrior fallen in battle. When a feather fell in battle, my grandfathers would stop fighting, to take up that feather from the earth. But only a warrior who had been wounded and who had become strong in his wound, strong and straight in his knowing of himself through being wounded—that warrior alone could take up the life of a fallen warrior, touching the feather with his right hand, then lifting it up from the earth with his left to take the spirit of the fallen warrior home.

Yes, I too think that's a good name, Pluen Eryr. A good name for you, Caitlin.

Wesley rises. Leaving his drum behind, he goes to the fire and lies down beside Sarah. Jacob now looks intently at Caitlin as she speaks to herself.

Caitlin: There is a strangeness upon me and a sorrow and a longing and a seeking out . . .

Turning, she sees Jacob gazing at her from the railings. Suddenly, she feels vulnerable. Very vulnerable.

Hello . . .

Jacob: Hello.

Caitlin: You were listening.

Jacob: I guess I was. But only just now.

Caitlin: You scare me when you listen. What did you hear?

Jacob: Oh, something about a feather falling. An eagle feather, maybe.

Caitlin: Maybe?

Jacob: Maybe. I'm not an expert on eagles. They've never come down far enough for me to study them thoroughly.

Caitlin: They've never come down . . .?

Jacob: Nope. Eagle never comes right down. So said someone I once knew.

Caitlin: (*Suddenly finding herself moving from a defensive stance toward an offensive one.*) Well then, if it's not eagles, what are you an expert on, Jacob?

Jacob: Raven.

Caitlin: Ah, ravens?

Jacob: Raven. (*Stressing the singular. He eyes her carefully, before continuing.*) Consider Raven. He neither sows nor reaps, yet makes sure someone is going to feed him, anyone he can con—gullible bears, deer, gulls, killer whales—anyone with a fire and a pot on it. Or Raven just takes what he wants, when he wants it. Though he lost his gizzard once doing that. Did you know Raven lost his gizzard?

Caitlin: No. I'm not on familiar terms with Raven's gizzard.

Jacob: I guess not, because you don't know that story. Some people tore Raven's gizzard out of his ass end when he was sleeping after he had eaten all their salmon, and used it for a soccer ball. Raven got it back in the end, but had a hell of a time digesting from then on. (*Pauses.*) Maybe that's why he never stops being hungry because he can't take what he does eat all the way into himself . . .

    (*As if remembering something he has heard once.*) Hungry is this great Raven! Hungry for men, and for women, too . . .

Caitlin: Ah, hungry for women, is he?

Jacob: Why not? Food is food, and a feast is a feast. Raven is an expert at going to feasts, though not so good at giving them. He tries, and bungles it every time. He feeds off others but doesn't let them feed off him, doesn't know how to do that, because all his eating never feeds him. Consider Raven . . .

Caitlin: I know about Raven.

Jacob: You? What do you know about Raven?

Caitlin: Cigfran. Meat scavenger. Fiach. Deer slayer.

Jacob: You know nothing about Raven.

Caitlin: You know nothing of what I know. Raven, feeding on chopped flesh as the field of slaughter reddens. Raven, gnawing at men's necks, blood spurting in the battle fray, hacked flesh, battle madness, blades in bodies, bright faces pale, confusion on clear wits, shadows over grey eyes, and in the high air above, the ravens groan and scream. Death of sons! Death of kinsmen! Death! Death!

(Now, with a deliberate, measured cadence.) Begin, murderer; pox, leave thy damnable faces, and begin. Come—the croaking raven doth bellow for revenge. *(Pause, to let the words penetrate. Then, calmly.)* Hamlet, Act III, Scene II. The play within the play, as Hamlet contemplates killing his uncle.

Jacob: *(Also calm, though intense.)* I know the play.

Caitlin: Do you, now? *(Pause.)* Why Jacob, you seem pale. Are you contemplating the killing of an uncle?

Jacob: You know nothing about Raven.

Caitlin: No? Did you know Raven picks the light from the eye of the lamb?

Jacob: Of course. The eye is the first thing Raven pecks out, and stealing light is his speciality. Anyway, the eye is only a wound the light makes when it comes stabbing into us. Do you know who brought the daylight into this world, Caitlin? Raven, that's who.

(Waiting for her to respond.) Ooh! Another story you don't know. Well then, the daylight with the moon and the stars was hidden away in the house of a man at the head of a river. Maybe the river where I was born and maybe not. The man was a chief, or fisherman, or some big name, and he didn't think letting the daylight loose on the world was such a good idea. But Raven found his way into that house and played the man for a fool by becoming his grandson. Soon enough Raven booted the stars up the smoke hole, then the moon. When he got his claws around the sun, he

257

went up the smoke hole with it, tossed it into the sky and hello, daylight! Whether the world wanted it or not.

"Come on out, folks!
Come out of your little clamshells!
Have I got a treat for you—
A whole bunch of daylight for a rock-bottom
price you can't refuse."

"Hey, Raven?" they ask.
"What is it going to cost us,
this daylight you've brought?"

"Well now," Raven says, "that's going
to be a surprise. But don't you worry.
You won't know about that right away
and by the time you do,
that's just the way it will be
and you'll have forgotten how things were
once, or won't give a sweet damn about it.
For now, nothing down and a hell of a long time
before the first payment is due."

So out of their clamshells they come, out of their dark, warm clamshells, wide-eyed, wounded-eyed human beings struck dumb with Raven's light.

And now Raven sits on his clamshell in the Museum of Anthropology, University of British Columbia, Vancouver, maybe wondering himself if all this daylight was such a good idea. But what the hell, a fellow has to see to live and eat, and a sun is a sun, right? So let's get on with it, whatever it happens to be or can be when you're sitting on a clamshell in the Museum of Anthropology.

Caitlin: That's not where Raven is sitting.

Jacob: (*With a start.*) Oh yeah? And what do you know?

Caitlin: What I know. (*With conviction.*) Raven sits on Cuchulain's shoulder—poor, dead Cuchulain, strapped to a rock in the Dublin General Post Office—gazing serenely through the window at all the tourists gawking back at him.

(*Waiting for him, then.*) Ah! A story you don't know. Cuchulain, hero of Ulster, holding the men of Connacht at bay from river to river, from ford to ford—Ath Gabla, Ath Froich, Ath Meislir, Ath Taiten, Ath Lethan, Ath Ferdia. (*Pause.*) Yes, Ath Ferdia. Cuchulain, killing each of them at the ford and naming the ford with the name of each one killed. No man could withstand Cuchulain at the ford. Cuchulain, son of Lugh . . .

Jacob: (*Suddenly interested, in spite of himself.*) Son of Lugh? The one you told me about yesterday, whose face was full of light—

Caitlin: And the dark in the light. Or is it the light in the dark of him? Lugh came to Deichtine when she had swallowed a mayfly that floated past her lip from a cup of water, came to her as a dream, saying she would bear his son, ". . . for I myself was the mayfly coming inside of you from the cup."

Jacob: The chief's daughter at the head of the river, she swallowed something as she drank from the river—a hemlock needle, or pine needle, or spruce, something—and then she gave birth to Raven, in that house where the sun was hidden away.

Caitlin: Then Lugh took her away in the guise of a flock of birds to Brugh na Boinne and into the Sidhe to be among the Tuatha de Danaan, now the people of the fairy. After a year's time, Cuchulain was born in a well-lit house but with not a sign of his father anywhere. Poor Cuchulain, no father. But never mind, for he is a tough lad and good with a sling, killing off birds with it, then squirrels, charioteers, a pet bird from the shoulder of Queen Maeve, jesters, the sons of kings and queens, harpers, satirists, and fools. Many, many fools. All in good time, of course. You can't stone the world to death in a day.

Jacob: (*Quietly.*) He should have gone right for the sun instead of messing about with what the sun leaves scattered down on the ground.

Caitlin: In time, Jacob, in time. A hero must have training before he takes on the sun. Find the hero-light about his head before taking on the light itself. So Cuchulain crossed the sea to train with Scathach, the Shadowy One, and learned he could not put a quick end to the sun with a sling, as if it were but a nagging fly or mosquito. No, but now he had to learn the feats that would release the sun in him—stepping on a lance in flight and standing erect on its point, the stunning shot and cry stroke, the apple and thunder feats, his hero scream, and his salmon leap, from the end of the bridge to its middle, from the ground into the yew tree, from holding the edge of the sea-cliff with a single hand up onto the path, where he struck dead the one-eyed, bird-headed hag.

Have you ever found yourself hanging from the edge of a sea-cliff, Jacob, hoping there was a salmon leap left in you before you fell?

The question is addressed to him, but not to him. He waits for her to continue.

Then, at the last, the Shadowy One taught him the use of the Gae Bolga, the javelin with the many barbs tucked into it, that would ray open like a burst of the sun into every bone and sinew and limb of whomever it struck, and out of her foresight she said to Cuchulain, "You'll live a hero's life, you sweet, bright, shape-changing man. But not for long."

So, there you have it, Jacob. Poor Cuchulain, dead in the Dublin General Post Office from taking on the sun and trying to take it in, with your Raven sitting on his shoulder.

Jacob: (*Turns away and tries to shrug her off.*) You know nothing.

Caitlin: Ah! I've bored you and you've gone slack on me. So, how to firm you up? (*Looking him up and down.*) Yes, Cuchulain's wooing of Emer. That will do it.

Jacob: (*With a start.*) Emer? Who was she?

Caitlin: Well now, it seems I have indeed pegged a story for the taking up of your slack.

Emer had the six gifts Cuchulain wanted and wanted badly—beauty, voice, sweet speech, needlework, wisdom, and chastity. So he came to her in the Garden of Lugh and spoke to her in riddles. She then riddled him until, gazing upon her lovely face and the plain of her breasts, he said, "I see a sweet country. I'll rest myself in that sweet country."

"Ah," she said, "no man will travel in or rest in my sweetness until he has proved how firm and fitting he would be. First, he must do the salmon leap—"

Jacob: (*Breaking in, abruptly.*) Yeah, Raven figured that one out, how to get the salmon leaping upstream to where they could spawn. He put this good-looking woman with big teats at the head of the stream and said, "You stay there, Woman-with-big-teats-floating-around-in-the-water, and those salmon will be right up, spawning as they come, once they know what's waiting for them."

It sounds as if your hero Cuchulain would fit right in with those salmon, spawning himself to death as he leaps—

Caitlin: (*Her head cocked to one side.*) Are you pissing on my story, Jacob? And on me? You must have gone slack again to be able to piss on me.

(*She observes him more closely.*) Or is it because you're blushing? Why yes, I do think you are blushing, Jacob.

Jacob: (*Fiercely.*) You know nothing!

Caitlin: Don't I, now? I like it when you blush, Jacob. You remind me of Deirdre when she saw the raven drink the calf's blood up from the snow. "I could want a man with those three colours," she said, "with hair the colour of the raven, cheeks like blood, and his skin like snow."

Jacob: (*A sharp laugh as he looks at the backs of his hands.*) I guess that disqualifies me. Snow-white skin has never been a speciality of mine.

Caitlin: But you do have the hair and the cheeks, Jacob. Especially the cheeks. You're blushing still, aren't you?

Suppose, Jacob, just suppose, I were to do with you what
Deirdre did when she saw the man she wanted. She took
him by the cheeks and the ears, and put him under a bond,
a geasa, saying shame and mockery if you don't take me.

What would you do, Jacob, if I took you by the cheeks and
ears, saying (*crouching and making as if to rush him*) shame
on you if you don't.

Jacob: (*From the railing, to which he has retreated, his eyes wide upon
her.*) Don't . . . what?

Caitlin: "What sort of man is this Cuchulain?" Queen Maeve asked
Fergus. "This ravening hound that tears my army apart
from ford to ford? Is he the toughest they have in Ulster?"

"He is," Fergus replied. "There is none more tough than
he. No warrior more hard. No point more sharp, swift,
slashing. No lion more fierce. No raven more flesh-
ravenous."

"Ah, then," Queen Maeve said, "he should spend a night
between my friendly thighs for there is flesh aplenty there."

So then, Jacob, what would you do if I took you by your
blushing cheeks and bound you to a night between a pair
of friendly thighs?

He stays put, leaning against the railing, his face averted from hers.

Surely, it wouldn't be the first night you've spent between
a pair of friendly thighs?

*She takes in the whole of his gesture. A look of wonder appears
on her face.*

Or would it be? (*Pause.*) Are you a virgin, Jacob?

*No answer. Her baiting of him gives way to astonishment. She
sits, slowly, upon Wesley's upended log.*

Sweet Jesus, you are! You're a virgin. (*Now she looks away.*)
And I've made you ashamed of it. (*Another pause, then she
laughs a little, at herself.*) Like wolves, women tear at their
own shadows. Irish women, especially.

You know, Jacob, someone should give you a decoration or something and send you on tour. You're a rare phenomenon these days.

Jacob: (*In charge of himself once again, and laughing softly.*) Sure. Or put me in a museum, somewhere, on a clamshell, where I could sit like Raven and look at my admirers. Only I wouldn't deserve the admiration or qualify for your decoration. (*Looks over at her, deciding; then.*) There was a girl in my high school class who loved me and trusted me. One night, after the Mohawks took down the barricades on Mercier Bridge and I knew the Indian summer of 1990 was about over, and was angry at everything under the sun, we met on a beach in Vancouver. I took her love for me and would have raped her with it, only she was on to me and out of there before I could pull my zipper all the way down.

Abruptly, he goes to the fire, finds his sleeping bag and walks to stage front to unroll it. The light brightens upon him and fades out at the railings.

So, Caitlin, does that leave me a virgin? I hardly think so.

Caitlin: (*Not looking at him.*) I don't know. Perhaps. If there's a place inside you still that hasn't been violated or that you haven't violated. Something of you that you're keeping for someone, someone who is not just anyone.

Who have you been keeping yourself for Jacob? The girl you nearly raped?

Jacob: No. Not her. But I'm not sure anymore.

Caitlin: Well, whoever she is, I think I'm jealous of her.

Jacob: What does it matter? She may be dead by now. (*Returning Caitlin's stare.*) Yeah, and my father is dead, and my mother, and my older brother. Many people I love are dead. That's the way it often is with us.

Caitlin: (*With wonder.*) But you're still faithful to her. She must be someone special, whoever she is.

Jacob: (*To himself, remembering.*) Eagle never comes down, not right down. She was the one who said that, once, when we both were little.

Caitlin starts, looks away. Jacob sits on his bag, his back to her, looking to the west.

You were coming onto me pretty strong, Caitlin, weren't you?

Caitlin: Yes. Yes, I was.

Jacob: Why were you coming on to me like that?

Caitlin: (*With a laugh.*) Why? Well, you do have raven hair and red cheeks. And I suppose I was sussing you out, trying to find a way through a few of your riddles. A woman does that to a man sometimes, to coax the inside out of him or find a way into him. There's a truth a man will tell a woman in bed that he won't tell anywhere else.

Jacob: (*Smiling to himself.*) And you know that, for sure?

Caitlin: (*With a look in his direction.*) Yes, I know that for sure. (*She looks out into the night.*) It's long the clouds are over me tonight. It's long last night was; it's long this day was, and yesterday was longer again to me; every day that comes is long to me . . .

Jacob: (*Suddenly.*) You remind me of her.

Caitlin: Of whom?

Jacob: A woman who came to our village when I was little. She was a teacher and spoke like you speak.

Caitlin rises from the log and takes a few steps to the east, while listening intently.

When she spoke, it was like waves with light on them, but sad somehow, washing up on a beach at the other side of the world. I would listen to her words, then my dad's words, and it was like two oceans meeting, each speaking itself yet wanting to reach into the other.

She stayed in the village that Christmas, and she and my Dad . . . they got pretty close to each other. Then she left, all of a sudden.

I dreamed about the two of them one night, about them being together, and then my mom standing somewhere else. I've tried to understand how he could have hurt my mom the way he did. I guess that woman touched something in him, and he in her—touched where no one else had ever touched. (*Pause.*) The way you nearly touched into me.

Caitlin: (*In a whisper, almost, as she gazes over at him.*) What was her name?

Jacob: (*With a shake of his head as he turns half about.*) What did you just say?

Caitlin: (*Gazing back.*) Nothing.

She finds her sleeping bag. Bringing it to stage front, she unrolls it head to head with his. With a look at Jacob's back, she sits upon her bag and then places her back against his.

Do you mind?

Jacob: (*Feeling her against him.*) No. No, I don't mind.

Back to back, back of the head to back of the head, they rest into one another. A few seconds of silence.

Caitlin: A penny for them?

Jacob: For what?

Caitlin: The thoughts I feel in your head. (*Pause.*) A pound then. Irish or English, take your pick.

Jacob: A pound. That sounds like a lot of money.

Caitlin: I suppose, if you need it and don't have it. But less than I was preparing to pay a few moments back.

Jacob: Well, I was thinking about the moon. The first crescent of the moon will show itself in the west tomorrow night. A Grail moon, one of my teachers called it.

Caitlin: How do you know it will be tomorrow night?

Jacob: Because I keep my eye on that kind of thing. The moon rolled past the sun last night. Funny, how the moon rolls past the sun and across it, now and then, like a stone rolling across the mouth of a tomb. The sun takes on another light when the moon rolls across it and even grows wings like an eagle. Or an angel, maybe, before the moon rolls away.

Caitlin: The Grail is a stone.

Jacob: And then the moon rolls on up the sky until it's just above the sun. That's when you can see the thin crescent of it, holding that dark circle.

Caitlin: Where Parzival's name was hidden.

Jacob: Hidden where no one could see it. Tucked away in all that darkness. (*With a chuckle.*) Yeah, I know that story.

Caitlin: We know that story. "So," they all ask Parzival, "what makes you think you can find the Grail again or the wounded king? When you botched it up the first time around." All the wise men, the king's horses and wise men, saying, "You'll not see the Grail again."

Jacob: You need a name to find the Grail.

Caitlin: A name to see through with to your name.

Jacob: Yeah. Well, good luck. I'm tired of trying to see through riddles and I've about run out of names.

Caitlin: (*At the edge of sleep.*) Cuchulain was tired and riddled through and through, the night he stood alone at the ford. A solitary man came to him, saying, "I will give you aid, now, for I am Lugh, your father, from out of the Sidhe. Sleep then, my son, and let your riddles heal, for I shall stand for you throughout the long night at the ford. I myself shall shine in the dark about you, until you awaken and can arise into the sun." (*Her head drops a little, as she sleeps.*)

Jacob: (*A hesitant, yet resolved whisper.*) Caitlin . . . her name was Emer, the teacher who came to my village. What was your mother's name?

(*He waits for the reply that doesn't come; then.*) Yeah, sure. Dream on . . .

(*Gazing into the night above him as the light above dims to a glow.*) What are
you looking at, Raven?

I'm looking at you, Raven.

Why are you looking at me,
Raven?

Who else is there to look at,
                Raven?

And what do you hope to see,
Raven?

Why, the Grail, Raven . . .

But is the Grail looking for you,
                Raven?

The campfire light brightens some. Sundown crouches at the rockpile, binoculars in hand.

Sundown: Psst! Jacob . . . are you asleep?

Jacob: Yes. (*Laughs softly.*) I'm asleep. What about you?

Sundown: No chance. I'm waiting for that cop to crawl out of his car and go for the leak of the year. Man, that guy is something else! Maybe it's part of their training.

I think I'll sneak up on him in midstream where he's standing under the stars watering down a wolf willow, and tap him on the shoulder. "Excuse me, sir, but you're pissing on a relative of mine." (*Laughs to himself.*) At least, that's what the Elders tell us. Is that what you think, Jacob? That everything is related to us?

Jacob: (*At the edge of sleep.*) Yes, everything. Even what we piss on.

The light upon Jacob and Caitlin fades to a soft glow, as they sleep, back to back.

Sundown: I guess it is that way. Or should be. Maybe I'll just walk right up to him and say, "Man, I'm glad you're doing this. We were getting worried about you."

Then I might join him, the two of us looking up at the stars and letting it all run out. "How are you guys doing down there?" he might ask.

"Well, you know how it is. If you occupy one dam, you've occupied them all. It must be boring for you, having to keep an eye on us."

"No, I'm not bored at all. You guys are doing a pretty good job of occupying that dam. So quiet about it, you've kept me wondering what's going to happen before it all comes to an end. Keep me guessing; that's a good strategy, and I've ridden shotgun on a few occupations in my time. You're doing a first-rate job. Stick with it."

"That's good to know," I'd say. "Well, I should go back now, take up my binoculars, so I can keep on watching you. But I'm glad you finally came out of that car. You'll have a better night for it."

"So am I," he says. "You guys have a good night. See you in the morning."

(*He laughs, and tosses a stick onto the fire.*) But what the hell, why not?

The campfire light fades out.

ACT THREE

September 28, 1992. *The last light of sunset still lingers. The cast sits about the fire except for Jacob. He stands at the railing, a dim light upon him, gazing at the sky to the west. The west light fades as he speaks.*

Jacob: What are you
             looking for, Raven?

             For my name on the Grail,
             Raven.

             And what do you see, Raven?

             Not much.

Nadine: What are you up to, Jacob? Hanging out with the stars?

Sundown: He's thinking about becoming an astronaut.

Leo: Or he's waiting for the Second Coming. That's tomorrow
             morning, Jacob. Or should we call it the Second Leaving?
             First, the Mohawks at Kanesatake, and now us. Only I
             guess there will be a bit less drama about our going, about
             as much as we've generated up to now. Unless we decide
             to liven things up.

             *He looks around at the other faces for glimmers of response, but
             sees none, except for a flicker from Sundown. Jacob turns and
             joins the others at the fire as the firelight brightens fully and the
             railing light fades.*

Wesley: (*Gazing to the west.*) Now that is some new moon. Look at the ring of light about the dark circle in the crescent. As if some person dipped a finger in the sun, then ran it all the way around.

Leo: (*With a glance over his shoulder.*) Hardly enough for Coyote to howl at if you ask me.

Wesley: Then we'd better look for another trickster.

Leo: How about Jacob? Is that what you were doing, Jacob? Howling at the moon? Maybe you're a trickster in training, hiding away up there in that darkness.

Nadine: (*Contained, yet on edge.*) Let it go, Leo.

Leo studies her as Sarah places a stick in the fire.

Sarah: We should smudge this place one more time before we walk out. How is your sweetgrass holding out, Wesley?

Wesley: We have enough. (*Chuckles.*) We could smudge the cop car, too. Leave him with a blessing.

Sarah: And then see if we can find Nadine's truck. Where did you park your truck, Nadine?

Nadine: Where I left it, wherever I left it. Finding the truck is the least of my worries.

Leo: Then what are you worried about?

Nadine looks back at him, but does not answer.

Sundown: We should give the cop an Indian name while we're at it. Stone Bladder. Tell him he's set the world record for fluid control.

Wesley: Maybe he's been ordered to keep his bladder on reserve, in case we shut down the head works. By that time he'd have built up enough pressure to provide an alternative power source.

Leo: Then let's shut the head works down and find out what he can do.

A count of ten.

Nadine: That's not a funny idea, Leo.

Leo: I'm not joking. (*To Caitlin.*) What about it, journalist? Some real action to spice up your story.

Caitlin: (*Sitting, her pad open on her lap, but not writing.*) I can spice up a story on my own, if need be.

Leo: I just bet you can. But we haven't given you much of a story, yet, to spice up.

Caitlin: There's always story enough, if you've an eye and ear for it.

Sarah: Give the head works a good night's rest, Leo, and let's leave here in peace.

Leo: Leave here in peace? Do you really think they're going to let us walk out of here in peace? That our cop is the only cop around? There'll be enough cars waiting for us over the hill, around the bend, and down the road tomorrow to make him look like a tourist out for three days of sightseeing.

 They're going to scoop us, all of us including you lady journalist, before we ever reach Nadine's truck, wherever Nadine's truck is.

Nadine: Then why are they waiting? Why didn't they clear us out of here the first day?

Leo: Suspense. Drama. Let's play watch the Indians play at occupying a dam site. Then when the Indians stop playing around, our playing around can start.

 When we stop and try to walk out, they begin. But for now, it's keep us guessing, and we'll keep you guessing. So let's not disappoint them. (*To Jacob.*) Well, Jacob, what about it?

Jacob: (*Looking into the fire.*) What about what, Leo?

Leo: Don't bullshit about with me. You're the one who schemed this occupation up. It's time to let them know we mean business.

Jacob: Shutting down the head works wasn't part of the scheme.

Leo:	Then update the scheme and deal with what's happening and not happening, here, now.
Jacob:	What's not happening, Leo?
Leo:	This, damn you! This isn't happening. Sundown was right. All we are is a bunch of displaced Indians with a journalist camping out under the power lines. Who knows we're here? Who cares we're here? And who will ever know or care, journalist or no journalist?
Sarah:	We know we're here, and we cared enough to be here.
Wesley:	(*Glancing at the police car.*) And he knows and cares, enough to stick around for three days, dammed up waterworks and all.
Jacob:	And all those cop cars waiting for us just over the hill, the ones you told us about. I guess they must care something fierce . . .
Leo:	Don't you fuck about with my head! You especially! Two years ago you were hunched down in your saddle, ready to boot your horse off the canyon rim and ride a light beam all the way down to the dark at the bottom. You were as messed up as any person I'd ever met. This occupation saved your ass. So do it justice, Jacob.
Jacob:	No, you do it, Leo. Bust your way past that fence and do it. It's a free occupation. No one can tell another person what to do, right? You want to shut the head works down? Then shut it down!
	They stare at one another across the fire.
Sarah:	(*Raising both hands, as if to part them.*) We must not do this to each other.
Leo:	You don't see it, do you? You really don't see.
Sarah:	We must not do this.
Leo:	Who cares afterward if they throw us all in the can? We've put their light out for a day, half a day, an hour . . .
Sarah:	Not to each other.

Leo: We've shut their power down, for ten minutes even.
            Shown them we can shut their power down. Shown them
            what a big nothing they are, without their power.

Sarah: And not to ourselves. Especially ourselves.

            Silence, as Leo looks about for some flicker of support. Nothing,
            except from Sundown who now is about to burst from something
            building up inside of him.

Leo: (*With anger, yet a note of defeat.*) It's a good thing you didn't
            live a hundred years ago Jacob, because you know what
            you would have been doing? Riding scout for the cavalry,
            leading the Blue Coats to Sand Creek, the Washita, and
            down the valley of the Greasy Grass. (*Pauses.*) We should
            have let you ride off the rim of that canyon.

Sundown: (*Looking around at their faces, then at Jacob.*) Leo's right,
            Jacob. Let's do it! 1,200,000 light bulbs, poof! All that light
            going down at once. Let's do it.

Jacob: (*He has managed to hold together what composure and maturity*
            he has, face to face with Leo. But Sundown slips through the
            crack in his mask. The words following should fall in upon one
            another like a house coming apart because it is divided against
            itself—revealing the speaker to be poised still, on the rim of a
            canyon somewhere, deciding whether he is going to die or live.
            The rest of the cast stares as Jacob speaks, not fully grasping
            what he means yet sensing that what is behind his words will
            affect them. Caitlin alone does not look at him but at the pad in
            her lap, as if she is awakening to what he truly is about.)

            1,200,000 light bulbs—Christ! You know what's wrong
            with you, Sundown? And with you, Leo? You think too
            small. You don't see the big picture. The Big Picture!

            You want to shut down the light? Then go for the source.
            Go for the sun! Forget the damn head works, forget the
            dam. This dam is only trafficking in the light. You want to
            shut the operation down for keeps? Then go for the
            supplier, go for the guy at the top. Go for the sun . . .

            (*Stands.*) Don't sit there looking at me as if a bird just shit
            on your head. Get rid of the light where it starts slashing

and hacking the world into bits and pieces and things and spaces, scattered all to hell. Light scattered into wires and bulbs and sockets and generators, and little flashlights that go click-click in the night.

(*Makes the gesture of snapping on a flashlight and shining it in the face of each person about the fire.*) Click! Boo! Click! Boo! Click! Boo! Click! Boo! Click! Boo! Click! Boo!

Too big a project for you, Leo? Sundown? Going for the sun? Then let me show you how. (*Taking up Sundown's rifle.*) You wait the night out, right here, and watch for the sun to come up. Then you draw a bead on the first curve of it—like so!—and wait until it's all there, its ass parked on the horizon like a clay pigeon ready to fly. Then squeeze off a few rounds, though one shot will do the trick if your aim is good, and you'll blow that sucker right out of the sky and back into the night.

So there you go, Sundown. (*He releases the rifle with a short, sharp throw to Sundown, who just manages to catch it.*) Do it. You know, just do it?

(*Sundown gapes at the rifle, then back at Jacob. Sarah is the first to regather her wits.*)

Sarah: Go for a walk, Jacob.

(*He looks down at her and does not move.*)

Walk the walk, Jacob. Now, please.

Jacob turns and goes to the railings. He leans against the inside of the near railing, grips it with his hands and stays put, in a dim light. Wesley rises as the campfire light dims, and goes to the woodpile. Sitting as the light brightens upon him, he takes up his drum, makes as if he is about to play it, then lowers the drumming stick. He is deeply troubled as he speaks.

Wesley: I think you should tell me that story.

Jacob: (*As the light brightens upon him.*) What story?

Wesley: About the sun and what happened to it as it set.

Jacob: I told you. The sun set and then I saw the crescent moon above it, the way it was tonight. Only both moons are gone now. Neither moon is there anymore.

Wesley: Something happened to the sun, before it set.

Jacob: Ooh! You really want to know what happened to the sun? All right then, I'll tell you what happened to the sun. It blew up. Blew up into a sky full of feathers—

Startled, Wesley clutches at his drum and listens intently as Jacob continues.

It fell apart into feathers of light, floating out into the sky as the sky became very blue, and deep, then dark, until the feathers were eaten up by the darkness. My grandfather saw the sun do the same thing in his dream that night, two nights before the fight at the Little Bighorn. Just as he dreamed the crescent moon I saw, a white raven in the dark of it.

He stops speaking. Wesley waits.

Wesley: Go on with the story.

Jacob: That is the story. I've told you the story.

Wesley: (*Firmly.*) No. Not the whole of the story.

Jacob: You want the whole story? (*Waits for Wesley to respond.*) Well, why the hell not? Sure, Wesley, I'll tell the rest of the story. (*Stepping away from the railing and ranging back and forth within the circle of light.*) I was fourteen that spring and my uncle said to me, "I'm giving a potlatch and I want you to be there." He said no more, but I knew what he meant. I was going to become Hamatsa, in place of my older brother. David had been the Hamatsa in our family until he set fire to himself one day and took a whole island with him, the same island on which I had spent those four days.

Well, we buried David, and now I was to become Hamatsa. Go out into the forest for another four days, wander about among the trees, sit on the bank of our river and . . .

(*Stops short; then.*) Do what? Christ, what was I supposed

to have done? Become Hamatsa, I guess. (*His voice changes, as if he is remembering something he has been taught.*) Hamatsa, the one who bears the knowing of the fullness of who he is. So my Adha, my grandmother, taught me. The one who goes into the wild and comes back to his people filled with dreams and visions, with darkness and light, then dances the last of the wildness out of him inside the big house. And everyone inside the big house looks upon him, and they all see themselves, mirrored in Hamatsa, because in meeting Bakbakwalanooksiwae, Hamatsa has met himself.

Do you know who Bakbakwalanooksiwae is, Wesley?

Wesley: I haven't heard that name before. But I might know something about him, under another name.

Jacob: Yeah? Then you're doing better than I am. All I know about him is that he has no mask. My people have no mask for Bakbakwalanooksiwae. Some things are too big, too close, too naked to be masked.

I did put one of the Humsumth masks on, though, when I was twelve. Huxwhuxw, Crooked Beak, and Raven—the Humsumth, huge birds that are sort of like guardian angels of Hamatsa, maybe. They come to you during your four days in the forest and you see them out of the corner of your eyes, in and out of the shadows. And you're not sure about them, whether they're against you or for you. Are they going to bring you back whole or eat you up along the way? (*Again, remembering.*) Very hungry for men is this great Raven.

The Raven mask was the one I tried on. Two friends and I found it in a chest, in my uncle's house, when he was somewhere else. My uncle caught me with the mask on my head. I was dancing about, playing Raven and snapping the beak, making Raven noises—Haap! Haap!—and having one hell of a good time, when he walked through the door.

He shamed me for that, in the big house, before the whole village. Son of a bitch! I could have killed him, right then, but he was too big, too much a heavyweight guardian of the tradition for me to think long about doing that. So I settled for hating him, half-hating him, until I turned fourteen and he told me about his potlatch.

Everything seemed better, that spring. I worked on a pole with my dad and told my girlfriend I loved her.

Jacob pauses as the pain of remembering strikes into him. Wesley continues to listen with every fibre of himself as if his listening would give Jacob the courage to continue.

Then she came to me, that night in June, told me her dad was starting to abuse her. The next day he put a screwdriver through his penis, working on his boat, drunk. The whole village stood there watching him bleed into the sand, ready to let him go on bleeding. They knew what he had done to his children and theirs.

My dad was the only one who would take him out to hospital, in my uncle's boat, into the rising wind and water. Funny, I knew they had died, somewhere out there, before I tired of watching the wind and water and went home.

"Go up to your uncle's place and bring your little brother home," my Adha said. So I walked, in the rain, up the steps, and pushed the door open. There he was on the couch, about to come on to my little brother. My dad is out there floating in the water, and my uncle, my traditional uncle who shamed me for wearing his mask, my uncle is about to abuse my little brother.

A plane brought the two bodies home the next day and the whole village went to the big house to sing the mourning songs for my dad and for the abuser he had tried to save, and my abusing uncle was to lead in the singing . . .

I waited outside until the big house door had closed, then took my dad's boat, and a gun.

Do you want to hear about that gun, Wesley?

Wesley: Do you want to tell me about that gun, my brother?

Jacob: Do I have a choice, now? It was our great grandfather's
gun, the gun Spreading Eagle was lifting into the sky
when the soldier bullet lifted him from his horse. My
grandfather took it west, and my dad brought it with him
to our village and hung it on the wall of our house. I took
it and bullets enough and went up the river to the point
where I had seen the twelve eagles.

I'd thought it was the eagles I was going to kill, but when I
got out of the boat and stood among the snags, I knew it
wasn't the eagles, but the sun.

(Pause, then, as if he is somewhere else.)

Don't ask me if I love the light;
blind I am, my seeing gone.
What I once saw, I see no more;
my seeing died, when daylight dawned.

All my life, I'd been watching the light, observing how it
worked, beating up on the shadows and driving them
under bushes and trees and inside people's skins. Ever
since Raven carved eyes in my head, Raven Sir Newton,
I've been watching the light work.

Raven came and brought the sun
and kicked the shadows all about
and with the sun, Old Raven brought
the day and dawning of my doubt.

Light is cruel, as well as kind
and is not gentle with the night.
So understand if I rage, rage
against the coming of the light.

(With a laugh at himself.) I wrote that in high school, grade
ten. Stole the last line from a Welsh poet, Dylan Thomas.
Probably stole the whole thing from him. You should ask
Caitlin about that poet, Wesley. She's Welsh, when she's
not busy being Irish.

(Now back into himself, with a measured intensity.)

I load the gun, taking my time because I don't know

where I am going when I'm done there.
Then I throw the lever, the light all about me flashing
out from the feathers of the eagles, up at me
from the snags, from every pebble lying about the point
and I'm sick of seeing all that light, sick of the light
making me see, so I let the sun have it,
squeeze, and again squeeze, reload,
squeeze again, and again, and twelve bullets are on
their way, the eagles screaming as they circle up,
up, up, until they fly into the sun,
the sun explodes—and the feathers begin to fall . . .

(*His hands upraised as if to catch them or ward them off.*)

        falling
falling, all about me . . .

(*His hands drop to his sides and he laughs.*) But I guess I
wasn't such a good shot after all. The sun was back the
next day, the day I flew out of my village.

Wesley: You flew out and left your brother with your uncle? (*But it
is not a question and Wesley's pause is more to gather himself in
than to await any answer from Jacob.*)

I was six the day my grandfather died. It was a summer
morning, 1945, and I woke up in the dark before the dawn
because I heard him groaning and turning in his bed as the
sweat poured from his body.

"Grandfather! What's wrong with you?"

He came back slowly from wherever he had been that night,
as if he didn't want to come back. "Wesley," he whispered,
his eyes opening, "they've just blown up the sun."

"No, Grandfather," I said. "The sun is about to come up,
there through your window."

"No, Wesley. They blew it up, just now. I saw them do it.
They've forgotten how to see the sun inside the sun and so
they blew it up." He closed his eyes then, and died.

Tell me my cousin, my brother, is that the only way to find
the sun inside the sun? By blowing the sun up?

The lights at the woodpile and railings dim, leaving Jacob with his head bowed and Wesley sitting at the woodpile, drum in hand. As the campfire light brightens, those sitting there are feeling the impact of Jacob's words to Sundown, who still holds the rifle.

Sundown: Weird, man! Maybe our brother Jacob is training to be a trickster.

Nadine: (*To Leo.*) And what are you listening for?

Leo: The splash, that'll tell me he's walked off the dam into the lake.

Nadine: That was funny, last night.

Leo: (*Prodding her.*) So why aren't you laughing now?

Nadine: Because . . . because it's tonight, that's why. And we're walking out of here tomorrow morning and I'm scared.

She puts both hands to her face, her elbows resting upon her knees. Sarah comes around behind her, kneels, and wraps both arms about her, rocking her to and fro, gently.

Sarah: (*Quietly.*) What's scaring you, Nadine?

Nadine: I don't know. Something's happening here, something I don't understand. Or maybe I'm just not made of the stuff that occupations or blockades are made of. (*Raises her head and leans back into Sarah.*) You know, I felt guilty because I didn't go back to Kanesatake that summer. Come on, I told myself, you're part Mohawk. Get yourself into the Pines with those people. But it didn't happen and now I know why. I was afraid to go and would have been more afraid if I had gone and tried to stick it out. God, I'd have freaked the first time I saw a gun, no matter who was carrying it. That gun of Sundown's is bad enough.

(Sundown looks quickly at the gun he holds, then lays it down against the rockpile. Nadine gazes into the fire as she continues.) They were brave, those Warriors and women in the Pines. Really brave.

Sarah: And scared. They were scared, too, Nadine.

Nadine: No, they weren't scared. Not the way I am, right now.

Sarah: They were scared, one time or another. Most brave people get scared on their way to being brave.

            Silence. Leo looks across the fire at Caitlin, who sits, hands on her pad, staring into the fire.

Leo: Well, I trust you've written all of this conversation down. It should make for one hell of a story—the occupation of a dam: the human drama. Or something like that.

Caitlin: (*As she realizes he is speaking to her.*) I'm sorry. I was somewhere else. What did you say?

Leo: Ooh! Asleep on the job, eh? You'll never get a promotion that way, little lady.

Caitlin: Don't call me little lady.

Leo: Sorry, I didn't hear you, little lady. I must have been somewhere else.

Caitlin: Don't call me little lady!

Leo: Ooh! Sorry, sorry, sorry. I'd forgotten. You're not a little lady. You're a little journalist, trying to grow up to be a big journalist. And maybe you'll get a job with a big paper when you grow up to be a big journalist. By the way, what paper are you working for?

Caitlin: (*Now evasive.*) I don't write for a newspaper.

Leo: Then what do you write for? A magazine? Or are you going to look beautiful for a TV camera somewhere?

Caitlin: I don't work for anyone . . . just yet.

            Everyone stares at her.

Leo: Hold on. I want to do a hearing check, to make sure I'm all here. You don't work for a newspaper? Or a magazine?

Caitlin: No . . .

Leo: Or a television network, or an open line show?

Caitlin: (*Tight lipped.*) No.

Leo: Then are you even a journalist?

Caitlin: I'm training to be a journalist.

Leo: Oh, I see. A trickster in training, and now a journalist in training. Well, well, this occupation is just one big training ground, it seems. And what are you going to do with this story of yours, when the dust of this occupation has settled?

Caitlin: I'll sell it, somewhere, to someone.

Leo: *Maclean's? The Globe?* CBC? Or some two-bit paper, somewhere, where no one knows how to read? Little journalist in training, you're as big a con artist as any I've met. And you've had the gall to sit with us for three days, taking part in our ceremonies, eating our food and acting as if you were someone we could trust. Jesus!

He starts to stand, but Nadine reaches over and lays her hand upon him.

Nadine: Leo! Don't!

Leo: (*Sitting back down, then breathing out. He laughs.*) Why, you're not even writing this down, little journalist in training. I bet you've lost your last pen.

Caitlin: (*Stands.*) As a matter of fact, I have. Excuse me, while I go and look for it.

With a turn, she walks to the woodpile, past Wesley, to stand at the front of the stage, just within the brightening circle of light.

Back at the fire, Leo picks up a stick, looks it over, then throws it onto the fire.

Sarah: Respect the fire, Leo. No matter what else is happening.

Leo lapses into a sullen silence and does not look at her.

Sundown: Some occupation this is turning out to be! Our journalist isn't a real journalist and maybe we haven't even got a cop. (*He lies back against the rockpile.*)

Leo: We have a cop. He's just drowned in his own urine, that's all.

Sarah: Or maybe he's in training, too, as we all are. Including you, Leo.

Leo: What do you mean, including me?

Sarah: Including you. This is your first occupation, or blockade, or whatever, isn't it? That's why you're so on edge. Somewhere in there, you're as scared as the rest of us.

Nadine: (*Looking at Sarah, then at Leo.*) Is that so, Leo? That's not the impression you gave us.

Leo: Now tell me, Sarah, what makes you think I'm green, or scared?

Sarah: It's all over you. It's been all over you ever since I've known you. You don't have a mirror that works, that's all.

Leo does not respond. Nadine observes him closely, then with a sigh, she leans back into Sarah.

Nadine: My, my. So this is one big training ground all around. Maybe that's good, learning together, being scared together, and learning together, how not to be scared.

Leo . . . (*She leans over, to touch him.*) It's okay, Leo. The first time can be a good time, maybe the best time. It was for us, remember?

(*He doesn't respond to her.*) All right, be the way you have to be. I've become used to having stones in my life. (*Pause.*) But not in my chest. I don't want my heart to be a stone, ever again.

Sarah: Let's try and sleep now. Morning is coming soon.

Nadine: I don't want the morning to come, Sarah. I'm afraid of what the morning will bring.

Sarah: The morning will bring whatever it brings and we can't do much about that. Except to ask our grandmothers and grandfathers to be with us, then meet what comes with whatever is best in ourselves. Until then, let's sleep.

The light fades out on the campfire and comes up on the woodpile. Troubled, Caitlin stands and looks out into the night.

Caitlin: (*Softly.*) Bless to me the thing of my desire, the thing whereon is set my mind, my love, my hope. Bless to me mine eye . . .

Wesley: (*Looking up from his drum.*) It seems Jacob isn't the only person searching out the stars tonight.

Caitlin: (*Snapping back to herself.*) I'm looking for my pen. That's all.

Wesley takes a pen from his shirt pocket and holds it out, until Caitlin becomes aware that he is doing so. She takes it from him, looks at it.

Wesley: It told me it belonged to you when I found it. I don't think it lied to me.

Caitlin: It's mine. Where did you find it?

Wesley: Where you left it. But you should give it a long rest and let your ears do the work. You have good ears.

Caitlin: And what makes you think I have good ears?

Wesley: You're filled with stories. A person filled with stories has good ears.

Caitlin: (*With a dry laugh.*) To be sure that's me. Caitlin, you're filled with stories my mother used to say and sorting them out is work enough for a lifetime. But the one you've just told me is a lie. Not a story, Caitlin, but a lie. I was nine, perhaps ten, the day she said that.

My pen may not lie, Wesley, but I did. To all of you, when I told you I was a journalist. I'm not a journalist.

Wesley: No? Well, you could have fooled me. I'd always thought a journalist was a person in search of a story and that's you, Caitlin.

Caitlin: Ah! That's a nice way of padding a broken bone. However, you needn't bother. The story is outrunning me and I don't know where to look next.

Wesley: Then stop running after it and listen inside of you. Maybe that's where the story is.

Caitlin: (*Slowly, as she gazes at him.*) You know, don't you?

Wesley: I'm not sure what I know.

Caitlin: Yes, you know. You do.

She draws her gaze from him and searches out the night above her.

Erin and I had just turned sixteen, three years ago tomorrow— tomorrow is my birthday, Wesley. Strange, I had forgotten that—and we were on a school trip to Paris. It was a Sunday, the first day of October, and we were coming from the Place de la Concorde after staring up the Obelisk of Luxor at Ramses etched in stone below the peak of it, the world at his feet. Over the Pont de la Concorde and across the Seine, the four stone men sat in front of the National Assembly, two of them bearded and bald, the other two curled and shaven, their laps filled with law and learning, their hands all quilled and scrolled, their stone eyes full of enlightenment.

We came up to the bridge and were about to cross when I looked down the river to where the Eiffel Tower scraped at the clouds as they scudded over the top of it, then along to Le Pont d'Alexandre III—the bridge of the four golden horses, two at either end, winged Puckas with their heads rearing and their nostrils flaring back at the sun. At their sides the four golden women, their breasts afire, hold the bridles of the Puckas, making as if to restrain them, yet ready themselves to be taken up by those flaming wings.

Along both banks the trees go to gold and rust, and shiver with a touch of the wind, and then from out of the shadow of the bridge, the canoe appears. Paddling into the light, it passes the long boats filled with sightseers and takes command of the river.

The sounding of the drum stops me, a few steps onto the Pont de la Concorde. Long and black, its prow filled with eyes and teeth, and red tongues curving up and back upon themselves, the canoe takes command of me.

In the prow, a man sits, wearing the mask of a bear and the drummer wears an animal skin about him, while

others sitting further back are robed in dark blankets
rimmed with red, one wearing a headdress of white fur.
On either side of the canoe the paddlers strike down into
the Seine, their faces alight with a knowing of themselves.

"What are you about now?" Erin's hand tugging at my
sleeve. "We'll all be gone from this earth before you catch
up with us, if you stay standing here." But I pull myself
away, looking still into those faces, searching them out,
face by face, and then I see hers. She sits amid the other
faces, almost hidden away, yet once my eyes find her, they
will not let her go for it is my own face I am seeing,
looking for me.

"What cheek!" Erin spurts out. "One of them has a camera
and is photographing us."

Then one of our classmates came along the bridge to look
for us, a boy filled with languages and reading the
newspapers every day. "Who are they?" I asked him,
knowing he would know. "The Haida," he told us.
"Indians from the west coast of North America in a canoe
made by one of their artists."

"Wonderful," said Erin. "Now let's get out of the ford before
it floods us over." It was then I turned to her and said,
"I'm in that canoe and so are you."
"And what do you know?" she flared. "About yourself
and about me to tell me where my self might be?"
"I know what I've just seen," I said. "As I'm standing here,
I know."
"Then build yourself a boat, like Brendan, cross the sea,
catch up with yourself and great good luck to you, if you
must when you can, but not today. Come on!"

I turned about for a last look as she pulled me away, but
the canoe had vanished into the darkness under the Pont
de la Concorde, taking me and my story with it.

(*Pauses. Now, more to herself.*) I take the way as it turns. Do
you think I don't know every winding way I take? Life
winds; only death is straight, straight as a spear, straight to
the story's ending.

Whirling about and dropping to her knees, she clasps Wesley's hand in both of hers, a gesture of supplication.

The story is here, Wesley, isn't it? And you know, you know the rest of the story. Please tell me, please.

Wesley: (*Troubled as he speaks.*) What person can say how much of a story he really knows? Or what part of a story is his to tell? My grandfather knew about such things, but I didn't listen so very well and I didn't ask, soon enough. (*Looks at her.*) Maybe time will tell you the rest of the story. Tell you better than I could or should. Time is a good storyteller, I think.

Caitlin looks back at him, then withdraws her hands from his. As she stands, her voice lightens, becomes almost playful, the sun playing upon the back of a river on its way to the lip of a falls.

Caitlin: Indeed. Time is the best of storytellers. We have that saying, too, in Ireland. You'd make a good Irishman, Wesley.

Wesley: (*Chuckling.*) Maybe that's what I'll become when I die, an Irishman.

Caitlin: Then you could come back in your next life as my father. Have you ever fathered anyone, Wesley?

Wesley: (*With a touch at his drum.*) No, not that I know of. My seed got tired of waiting for me to sober up. I might pull off an Abraham with Sarah, but I don't think so. I seem to be lean on relatives of any kind in this life. Only Jacob, and he didn't drop by until a couple of years ago.

The light brightens upon Jacob at the railings as Wesley finishes speaking. Jacob is gazing at a feather he holds, from the wing of an eagle, its base wrapped around with faded blue felt, a leather thong dangling from it. As Caitlin speaks he turns and walks with deliberation into the brightening light at centre stage front. The railing light fades out.

Caitlin: Yes, Jacob. That's another story, isn't it?

Wesley: Maybe. And maybe not . . .

Jacob: Caitlin . . . ?

Caitlin: (*Turning toward him, as if in a dream about to come awake.*)
            Yes . . . ?

Jacob: This is for you. (*He holds the feather out to her. She stares at it
            and does not move. He continues, feeling his way very, very
            carefully.*) My little brother gave it to me when I turned
            fourteen . . . just before I left my village. I tried once before
            to give it to someone, the girl I almost raped. She wanted
            to tell me then, the day we both graduated from high
            school, that it really didn't belong to her, but I wouldn't
            listen. That night we met on the beach, she gave it back to
            me. Maybe that's why I tried to rape her, because I was
            full of anger about being an Indian that summer, and it
            hurt, her giving it back to me.

            But she was right. It didn't belong to her. It belongs to you.
            I've never known anything so clearly as I know that,
            tonight. This is yours, Caitlin. Take it. Please, take it . . .

            *Caitlin steps forward, into the circle of light she now shares with
            Jacob. The woodpile light dims down to a glow upon Wesley.
            Caitlin reaches for the feather, her hand closing about it slowly,
            as if knowing a fateful course will be set once the feather passes
            from his hand to hers . . .*

            *Feather in hand, she turns counter-clockwise, away from him
            until she is facing stage front and looking at the feather she now
            holds.*

Caitlin: It's long the clouds are over me tonight . . . longer still the
            rising of the sun, and this day coming.

            *A sharp downbeat from Wesley's drum as she whirls, counter-
            clockwise, right about until, facing Jacob, she begins to circle
            him, counter-clockwise, slowly, as the drum goes on beating,
            softly, relentlessly, throughout what follows.*

            What are you running from, Jacob?

Jacob: (*Stunned by the transformation in her and turning to stay face
            to face with her.*) What are you talking about?

Caitlin: There's a shadow on your tail, Jacob. Is that what you're running from?

Jacob: What the hell are you talking about?

Caitlin: You know what I'm talking about. Or perhaps it's the light you're on the run from. Is it the light that's shadowing you, Jacob?

Jacob: Who the hell are you to say that? Who gave you the right to talk to me like that?

Caitlin: (*Brandishing the feather.*) You did, just now. Stop running, Jacob, and face me.

Jacob: You? Who are you?

Caitlin: Who am I? I am the brother you won't go home to meet. I am the uncle you want to kill or heal. So why haven't you healed me, Jacob? Or killed me? And why did you leave me at home?

Jacob: (*Softly.*) How do you know this?

Caitlin: Don't you care enough even to kill me?

Jacob: (*Emphatically.*) How do you know this?

Caitlin: Because I know. I know you—

Jacob: You don't know me. You know nothing!

Caitlin: Yes, I do know you. I am what you are looking for, Jacob. (*A deep breath.*) I am the Grail, I am the stone you can't walk around, anymore. Trip on me, Jacob, or crack your head open, but you're not going to walk around me.

Jacob: You're crazy, you know that? Gone, gone, gone . . .

Caitlin: I am where your name is hidden, Jacob. The dark place in the moon where your name is hidden.

Jacob: (*Lunging for her, frantically.*) Give me that feather! How did you get that feather? How?

Caitlin: It fell into my hand from the air and the high air, and higher than the high air. All my life I've waited for this feather to fall into my hand.

Jacob: (*Lunging again.*) Give it to me!

Caitlin: Then come for your name, Jacob, if you want the feather.
           I'm at the ford, Jacob, waiting for you, with the feather and
           your name.

           *Both Caitlin and Jacob whirl about and now circle together,
           counter-clockwise, face to face within the circle of light. Sarah
           walks out of the dark at the campfire to the railings, kneels there
           facing front centre stage. The light brightens to a glow upon her.
           Nadine, Leo, and Sundown rise from their sleep to kneel on one
           knee at the campfire as that light glows upon them, intent on
           what is about to unfold.*

Sarah: And that night Jacob was left alone.

Caitlin: When morning came, the first day, Ferdia, foster-brother
           of Cuchulain came first to the ford and had the choice of
           weapons until nightfall. That long day Cuchulain and he
           hurled darts and spears at one another, then kissed one
           another at its end. Their horses passed the night in the
           same paddock and their charioteers sat beside the same
           fire.

Sarah: And one came to wrestle with Jacob, all the night long,
           and Jacob had never wrestled with anyone so strong.

Caitlin: The second day, it was the big stabbing spears they fought
           with, and on the third day with the great stroking swords,
           the day's shadow long over them and within them until
           the night parted them. And it was not in the same paddock
           their horses stood or by the same fire their charioteers sat.

           *A downbeat brings the drumming to a stop. Jacob and Caitlin
           turn again so that they are back to back, almost touching, with
           Jacob facing toward stage front.*

Jacob: The last night is the longest of all. Deep into the cedar and
           salal and darkness and lost in himself, Hamatsa fights
           back the hunger, the hunger black and tearing at his
           stomach. Oh, how heavy with hunger is Hamatsa as he
           stumbles, staggers, crawls toward the river, toward the
           meeting at the river. Hungry for the meeting at the river is
           Hamatsa, and afraid—

Downbeat, as the two whirl about and circle face to face to the beating of the drum.

Sarah: Yet Jacob is also strong. Ooh, he is so very strong, strong as the one he wrestles. Jacob, that one says, it's good you're so strong. Come, and show me what you will do with all that strength.

Caitlin: The fourth morning Ferdia came early to the ford, a great stone fixed to his chest, in dread of Cuchulain's javelin of many barbs, the Gae Bolga.

Downbeat, whirl about, and the drum stops, with Jacob and Caitlin back to back, as before.

Jacob: What ails you, Uncle? What the hell's wrong with you, Uncle? Ask? No, I didn't ask! What have you to do with me, Uncle, that I should ask anything of you?

Downbeat, whirl about, and the drum continues with Jacob and Caitlin circling face to face.

Caitlin: And they fought, Ferdia and Cuchulain, that long morning, fought their way into the sun, hacking, hewing, striking, the one at the other until their heads and feet touched, their shields split, and they drove the river from its bed.

Wesley: And then the soldiers came, riding down the valley of the Greasy Grass, riding hard and fast along the bluffs above and down to the ford where the warriors met them.

Downbeat, whirl, and the drum stops, with Jacob and Caitlin back to back, Jacob facing east and Caitlin facing west.

Caitlin: It's against yourself you fight . . .

Jacob: Against myself I ride . . .

Caitlin: Against yourself, for yourself . . .

Jacob: And would gladly kill my very self . . .

Downbeat, whirl, and the drum continues, with Jacob and Caitlin circling face to face.

Sarah: And then the other one struck Jacob to the ground . . .

Wesley: It is a good day to die . . .

Sarah: But Jacob would not let go . . .

Wesley: A good day to die . . .

Sarah: And the other one said . . .

Wesley: Everything I love is here . . .

Sarah: Let me go, Jacob. The sun is coming. Let me go . . .

Wesley: Everything I love . . .

Caitlin: And at the last, Cuchulain, the light burning about his head, reached for the Gae Bolga . . .

Wesley: And Spreading Eagle rode with the warriors into the ford, his gun lifting into the sky, lifted up from the drum and the song at his back. Like a winged eagle, the sun filled his body . . .

Caitlin: And the Gae Bolga struck Ferdia full in the chest, shattered the stone into three parts, and filled him with its barbs . . .

Wesley: As the soldier bullet lifted him from his horse . . .

Caitlin: Filled him full of the sun . . .

Downbeat, whirl. The drum stops, again leaving Jacob and Caitlin back to back, as before.

Caitlin: Take your name, Jacob, and bless me.

Leo: But the blessing didn't take.

Nadine: Or Jacob wouldn't give the blessing.

Sundown: Do it, Jacob.

Caitlin: Bless me, Jacob. Tell me your name and bless me.

Leo: So Jacob held on and the Angel wouldn't let go.

Nadine: Until the blessing was given.

Sundown: Do it . . . Do it!

A commanding downbeat. Jacob whirls away from Caitlin, and she whirls away into the darkness that falls upon the campfire as all lights black out, except for the circle at stage front, where Jacob stands alone.

Jacob: Hungry for men . . . is this great Raven! Hungry for blessing . . . is this great Raven! Hungry for me . . . is this great Raven—
Feed on me, Raven.
Feed on . . . my hunger. Feed . . . !

Now wrestling deep within himself, wrestling for something from deep within himself.

I am . . .

Nu gwa am . . .

I . . . am. I . . .

(*He whirls about and stands facing east, both fists clenched.*)

Haau!
(*From the pit of his stomach, the cry of the Hamatsa splitting open the last moment of the night. From the east, the first glow of the rising sun.*)

Haau—!

With the second cry, the campfire light floods down upon Leo, Nadine, and Sundown. Half-kneeling or crouching, they start awake as from a deep sleep and gape at Jacob as he whirls about once again and snatches up Sundown's rifle. At the railing, Sarah raises both her hands, palms upward, in a gesture of both supplication and support.

Sarah: Let me go, Jacob. Back to the sun.

Jacob places the rifle to his shoulder, cocks it, and aims as if following a winged creature in flight.

Sarah: You're blessed now, Jacob. Let me go—

Jacob holds his aim a second longer, ejects several bullets from the rifle. He steadies his aim once more.

Sundown: Do it, Jacob . . . Do it!

Sarah: (*Quietly.*) Bless me, Jacob, and let me go.

Jacob ejects one more bullet. Slowly, he lowers the rifle. Fully risen now, the sun shines in upon him. He looks down at the rifle, places it into Sundown's open hands, then drops to his knees, exhausted with his eyes closed, and his face lifted into the light. Sarah drops to her knees behind Jacob, and Wesley sits down on his upended log, gazing at his drum. The rest of the cast sits, slowly, about the fire. Sundown looks down at the rifle in his hands.

Wesley: I think that song my grandfather sang is going to wake up, now. Yes, I can hear it coming.

Nadine: (*Looking at each of them as she speaks.*) It's the fourth morning, guys. We've done what we came to do, so let's walk out, now. Wesley . . . Sarah . . . Leo . . .

Leo: It's a good thing you didn't pull the trigger, Jacob. You might have hit it. You should give yourself an Indian name when you go home, if you ever go home. A name like Raven's Eye.

Nadine: Jacob . . . Caitlin . . .

Wesley: That is Jacob's name. Raven's Eye. His grandmother has been holding it for him.

Caitlin: (*Staring at Wesley.*) What? What did you say?

Wesley: Raven's Eye. That's Jacob's name.

Caitlin: (*Dropping to her knees before Jacob, her back to the east.*) Jacob, look at me!

Nadine: Leo . . . Jacob . . . Sundown . . . Let's walk out, please, now . . .

Sundown: (*Looking down at his rifle.*) Sun up, sun down . . .

Caitlin: Look at me, Jacob. (*As Jacob opens his eyes.*) Look at me, please . . .

Sundown: Sun up, sun down. What the hell, why not?

He stands abruptly, aims at the sun and fires. The light from the east blacks out, as do all the other lights, except for a dim light upon the campfire. An answering shot comes from the direction of the police car, whines past Sundown, and ricochets from a railing end.

Caitlin starts, then falls, her body twisting so that she hits the ground face upward. The feather drops to the ground beside her.

Sundown: (*Still looking where the sun had been and thrown into confusion.*) Holy Christ, that was a short day!

Then he sees Caitlin's body. The rifle slips from his hand.

Jacob: Caitlin . . .? (*He reaches out with his right hand, but does not touch her.*) Caitlin!

He looks up, sees Sundown, and goes for him.

You shithead!

Leo intervenes, knocking Jacob away with the back of his hand. He seizes the rifle, cocks it, and places the muzzle against Jacob's left ear.

Leo: Now I don't know what's left in here, but if I need to find out, your ear may end up on the other side of your head next to its friend, unless you listen.

Jacob gazes down at Caitlin's body. His shoulders go slack and he sags back into himself. Leo lowers the rifle.

That's better.

Jacob: (*Quietly.*) And what about her, Leo? What about her?

Leo: (*Also quietly, with conviction.*) She was a warrior, Jacob, in her way, and she chose to be here. So did you.

Nadine: Leo, look!

Along the backdrop, a show of lights flashing, as if more police cars are approaching. The pylon and the car beside it stand forth starkly from the lights behind them.

Sundown: Holy Christ, what do we do now?

Nadine: (*As Leo scrambles over to the rockpile beside Sundown and her.*) We have to end this, Leo. Now—

Leo: (*The rifle still in his hand.*) Or we start it. Start it for real, now.

The campfire light fades from the three of them, and also the lights along the backdrop. The three lights at centre front stage, the railings and the woodpile glow upon Jacob, Sarah, and Wesley.

Wesley: (*Beginning to drum softly.*) Yes, I hear the song coming, like a bird flying free and filled with the sun. Listen! (*He starts to chant, softly, as if feeling for the opening words of the song itself and continues to do so to the end.*)

Sarah: When a feather falls, the wounded warrior puts his own battle aside and his wounds, and gives himself—all of himself—to the lifting up of that feather . . .

His eyes upon Caitlin's body, Jacob reaches forth with his right hand and with great inner effort touches down upon her.

With his left hand, Jacob reaches down, lifts the feather from the floor—a gesture again filled with inner effort and with devotion—and places the feather upon Caitlin's breast. Then he slides both arms beneath her body and begins to rise up, lifting her with him.

Jacob: Nu . . . gwa . . . am—

His body stands erect as the light of the rising sun shines in upon him from the east and the other lights begin to fade out. Wesley's chant strengthens.

Nu . . . gwa . . . am—

The drumming stops, and the chant. Jacob stands, facing the risen sun.

Jacob: Nu gwa am . . .

The light from the east fades out, leaving the stage in darkness.

IV

ONE

They buried Caitlin's body in a spruce grove beneath the peak of a mountain, overlooking the valley of the North Saskatchewan. "I buried my grandfather near this place," Wesley said, as he covered the grave over so that no one would find it who did not know what to look for and where.

"A person of great spirit among our people is buried upon a mountain, so that her spirit can see into the future," Wesley continued, as they rode back to the cabin.

By that time the inquest had disintegrated into the dust. The bullet taken from Caitlin's body had nothing to do with the rifle Sundown had fired, and the constable on the hill swore that he had never discharged his weapon. Angry native leaders rose up in protest when the constable's superiors stood behind his testimony, but there was no evidence, the RCMP said, that any weapon of his had been fired that morning. The inquest concurred, and then had nowhere to go.

"And maybe our cop is telling the truth," Wesley speculated, as he went through what he had taken from Caitlin's body, found the name and address of her uncle and wrote a letter. Some days later, an answering letter found its way into his hand.

Eglwys Lleu
Trwyn y Gwyddel
Aberdaron
Pwellheli
Gwynedd LL53 8YZ
U.K.

Dear Wesley Drum,
Thank you for writing and telling us of Caitlin's death. It is hard to find words with which to respond. However, I concur with your

wish to bury her where she died and shall write the meddling powers that be to that effect. I think Caitlin knew she would not be returning to us, though she did not speak that knowing into words. Given my knowledge of my niece, I shall find my way to bear the loss of her, as hard as that will be. However, I cannot speak so for Erin, her sister. Her passage through Caitlin's death may be more dark than I would wish.

If your cousin is willing to bring Caitlin's personal effects to us, he would be most welcome, whenever he can undertake such a journey. He should make his way to Aberdaron and someone there, practically anyone, will be able to direct him on to Eglwys Lleu. Again, thank you for acting as you have and for the consideration you have shown in contacting me.

Yours very truly,
Sean Davies

"You picked up the feather," Wesley said, as he took the letter from Jacob. "Now you have to take it back to her people."

When the inquest came to an end and he was free to get on with his life, Jacob found a rancher Wesley knew at the south end of the Kootenay Plains and spent the long winter months herding cattle from one snowbound range to another. He saved every dollar he could from what he earned and took each day as it came. The inside of him ached as he lay awake on those nights when sleep wouldn't come, but it wasn't the dull ache of death in life that he had felt when he first came to live with Wesley and Sarah. The pain within him now was alive, spurring him toward that long journey eastward, and he fought against anything within or without him that would deaden the pain. Yet alongside the living pain, something was working to weigh his spirit down. What? What was it that still wanted to clog up the pores of his life?

When he came back to Wesley and Sarah that spring, they reminded him that he needed a passport to get out of the country, then back in. In the end, he wrote Aunt Minnie and asked her to send him proof that he had been born. A notarized copy of a birth certificate arrived from Port Hardy soon afterward.

On an overcast morning close to his leaving date, Jacob rode out to track down a horse that had let its hooves go to its head the night before. The track led over a ridge, then along the bottom of a valley and across a fast-running creek still swollen from the never-ending melt-off of snow higher up. Over another ridge he rode to where the mountain wanted to ease out into the foothills, intent upon the fast-fading track. The clouds low about the peaks after two days of rain and the air cold about him as his horse skidded down a long slope, through stands of spruce and then aspen, Jacob felt the ground beneath him go to mud. His horse slid its way to the valley floor, and he rode through more aspen until he ran out of track to follow.

Jacob reined his horse in. He was in a clearing, the aspen standing silent about him. No touch of wind stirred the leaves or his hair as he lifted his hat away to cool his forehead. Then he felt the first flakes of snow upon his skin. Within moments the world about him vanished as the whiteness of the snow erased all sense of direction and then of the place itself. He reined the horse about and tried to ride out of the clearing, back the way he had come, but there was no trace of a way back or a way forward. He reined the horse about again, and again, then again, until the snow beneath the horse was but a maze of hoofprints turning in and in upon themselves. When there was nothing left to turn into, the horse stopped turning, simply stopped and stood breathing itself out into snow about its nostrils.

In that instant, Jacob knew what was holding on to him. Fear. Resolved though he was, he was also afraid of boarding that plane, of meeting Caitlin's people, even though his other self was utterly given over to doing that. His residue of fear, however, had clamped itself about that other self. The world without him a seamless curtain of white, Jacob gripped the reins in his hand and kicked at the ribs of his horse. The horse shuddered from the blow but did not move.

Quok . . .!

From under the rim of his hat Jacob peered into the whiteness, saw nothing, yet felt the sound of wings closing in upon him. Beating the snowflakes aside, the wings brushed against the back of his head, took hold, and then Jacob felt the fire licking down upon him. The fever worked its way through the pores of his skin and he began to swim within it. His shirt soaked through to the inside of his jacket, Jacob shuddered and let the reins slip from his hands.

The horse shivered as the reins fell slack about its neck. The weight of its rider slumped forward in the saddle as the hands grasped at the horn. The horse made for a break in the whitened wall of aspen, picked its way along the valley floor, and started to climb. The man in the saddle closed his eyes, leaned into the ascent of the horse, and let the fever and the horse take him until he felt hands draw his body from the saddle and place it into bed.

Contained by layers of blankets, the fever winged its way into, then along, secret passages that led toward another fire locked within the drum of his heart. Like a summer storm breaking after lightning has cleared a path for it, the sweat poured forth from his body and the fire within followed after, scouring the fear from the marrow of his bones. Then the fever spread itself into flaming wings that condensed to wings of metal as they lifted him from the earth, up, upward toward the waiting stars . . .

The beating of Wesley's drum from the hood of Nadine's truck, with the chant Wesley wove into it, followed the plane as it climbed, until the sun dropped behind the line of mountains and the plane curved eastward into the continent-long night. At a height far above the earth, his flight path levelled out and darkness closed in about him. Yet the chanting stayed with him as the night deepened, sounding at first in the voice of Wesley, then in the voice of Isaac, from those four days on Log Island.

High above the plane, the stars flashed forth as they passed overhead and drew the night in their wake—the Great Bear making its circle about the North Star, the Hunter with his Dog, and the Twins above them:

> *The Creator put
> them there to remind us that nothing is ever alone,
> that every being has a twin somewhere . . .*

Embraced by the stars and the darkness, the plane held its course as he peered through the window beside him. Then the morning star appeared in the east, and light gleamed up from the horizon beneath it.

"Good morning."

"Good morning," he said to the stewardess standing in the aisle.

"Are you ready for the challenges of this day?"

"I hope so," he replied, meeting her gaze.

"Well, the day is making itself ready for you. We'll be serving breakfast soon."

The plane started to descend, and the earth again took hold of him, pulling him downward toward the light spilling through the horizon to the east. He looked out the window, down thousands of metres into the waters of the Atlantic. As the light extended its reach from the horizon, he saw far below him fingers of land reaching out into the grey-black sea that washed up about them. Behind the reach of those fingers, some barren mountains emerged and then a stretch of land behind them, the green of it brightening as the morning touched down upon it.

Now the land below him seemed to reach upward, as well as out into the sea, to draw him down, down, down—and then the sun crested the horizon and came flooding in upon him.

TWO

Prestatyn . . . Rhyl . . . Towyn, and then on to Colwyn Bay. The towns and their signs flashed past the window as the train sped on its way west along the rim of North Wales and his tongue tried to taste that other language in green lettering above the black letters of the English. To the north the rain lashed down into a grey expanse of water and onto beaches abandoned by the summer tourists, and whipped at the windows of the train so that he could almost feel the sting of each drop as he went on watching the signs come and go.

Cyffordd Llandudno. At Llandudno Junction, he boarded a train that put the sea behind him as it sped southward up a long valley until it snaked along Afon Conwy—the river Conwy. To the west, the first mountains of Snowdonia gathered together and drew nearer as the valley of the Conwy narrowed into them. Sheep grazed along the valley floor and upon the green of hillsides punctured by outcroppings of rock. Hedges and fields flashed past him, then a little cemetery tucked into the side of a hill. Suddenly he straightened in his seat. Peering intently through the window, he glimpsed a patch of tall pink flowers alongside the track, a shaft of sunlight upon them as cloud cover overhead broke open for an instant. The flowers flew past him, but another patch appeared, then another. Pink flowers, their forward petals reaching for the four directions as the back petals formed themselves into a cross.

Fireweed . . . The first living thing to grow back from the wreck of everything else around. He closed his eyes, to remember the words more clearly, then looked again. Yet another patch of fireweed flashed up from the side of the tracks. As the weight upon his heart began to lighten, he leaned back into his seat and smiled, to himself and at himself.

A last patch of fireweed appeared, and then the train plunged into a corridor of darkness. The world beyond its windows suddenly obliterated, the train kept plunging forward along the length of the tunnel, and the tunnel went on lengthening before it toward the brightening circle that appeared in the distance. The train slowed as it cleared the southern entrance of the tunnel, then wound its way alongside a mountain of slate until it came to a stop at Blaenau Ffestiniog.

Now Bus Gwynedd took him down grade after long grade toward Tremadog Bay, the road twisting in and out of itself as the bus traded turn for turn. The southern slopes of Snowdonia drew nearer, pressing at him then withdrawing somewhat to become the granite flanks of a field. Fists of rock thrust up into other fields, hips and shoulders of rock from the side of the road—as if, beneath the covering of grass and oak, beech and hazel, another being wanted to declare itself, its bones of granite struggling to awaken from a long sleep.

The bus rolled to a stop in Porthmadog. Passengers got off and got on, and he sat where he was, listening to this other language sounding all about him. A group of teenagers sat a few rows back as they sat on buses in Vancouver, joking about in Welsh, flirting with one another and insulting one another in Welsh, completely at home in their words. As he listened, the words that had awakened from their sleep within him rose to his lips and formed themselves: Nu gwa am . . .

From Porthmadog, the bus sped past more groves of beech and oak until it reached the coast of the Lleyn Peninsula at Criccieth. A shaft of sun bounced from the walls of a castle near the water, and the clouds over Snowdonia fell away behind him. Winding its way out onto the Lleyn, in and out of the shadows cast by the trees, past more fists and hips of granite, the road took him toward the sea, then away—as if there were no other way for you to arrive at your destination than by winding about as best you could, into yourself, then out, in, then out, down the reach of the peninsula toward its end.

The bus pulled into the square at Pwllheli and stopped. "Thanks," he said to the driver.

"Hwyl!" the driver replied.

"What does that mean?"

"What does it mean? Cheers! That would be close, I'd say."

"And how do you say the name of this town?"

"Pwllheli."

"Say it again, please." The driver repeated the name and he listened closely. There was something almost familiar in the thrust of the "ll." "Pwllheli . . .?" he ventured.

"Not quite. Pwllheli," the driver repeated. That was it, the "tl" sound in Kwakwala. He touched the tip of his tongue to the front of his palate and tried again. "That's close," the driver said. This time he flattened his tongue somewhat against his palate and pushed the sound forth. "Yes!" the driver exclaimed. "Almost spot on!"

"Good. Where do I catch the bus to Aberdaron?"

Leaving Pwllheli, the bus stayed with the southern coastline until the road spun inland to Sarn Meylltern, then veered southwest once more. The bus stopped; two old women got off and a family climbed in. The bus stopped again. The family got off and an old man climbed the steps. He stood beside the driver and talked to him as the bus went grinding up a long rise of land in the way Old Man Williams used to talk on one of his walks through Duxsowlas to anyone who would listen.

The bus crested the rise and the mountains of Snowdonia to the north vanished. Up ahead, the land bent due south toward the town tucked down into its curve, as if held within the sweep of a crescent. Beyond the town, the Lleyn ran toward an end not yet visible except for a hump of land that stood forth in the far distance as if arising from some depth of water beyond the land's ending.

Bus Gwynedd wheeled, bumped, and rattled its way down to Aberdaron. It stopped near a grocery store and a whitewashed bridge crossing a stream. He walked over the bridge, past the little hotels and restaurants that made up the centre of Aberdaron, turned two corners and came out at a long beach. A church stood to his left, its cemetery about it. Waves rolled up onto the sand, the light still bright upon them even though it was well after six in the evening.

Well, here I am. Now then, where am I, and where do I go from here?

He walked back along the street until he met a woman in front of one of the hotels who looked as if she might know something he didn't know.

"Excuse me. I'm looking for Eglwys Lleu." He spoke the name as clearly as he could, exploiting his discovery of the "ll" sound.

She blinked at him. "Well now, you said it well enough. But are you certain you know what it is you are looking for?"

"Yes. Sean Davies is the person I want to find."

She laughed. "Then it's Eglwys Lleu you're wanting to get to. Now then, how to get you there . . .?" She looked about her, up and down the street, to where a van was parked beside the store. "Cross over the bridge," she said, "and wait beside that van until its owner comes out of the store. His name is Dafydd Jones. He'll be the best one to direct you on to Eglwys Lleu."

Crossing the bridge, he waited by the van. A short man with a barrel chest bursting through his plain cotton shirt walked out of the store, his gumboots scraping the earth aside.

"Are you Dafydd Jones?"

"I am. And will be a while longer, I hope."

"I'm looking for Sean Davies."

Dafydd Jones appraised him, one hand shading the sun from his eyes. "Indeed, it would seem you are," he said. "And you want to be steered the right way about. Well then, come with me." Dafydd led the way until they stood beside the bridge. "Now, you see this road?"

"Yes."

"Follow it up the hill and stay with it whatever it does, until you come to Uwchmynydd."

"Where?"

"Uwchmynydd. There'll be a cluster of houses as the road climbs and then it will bend to your right and you'll see the second chapel and a public phone with a letter-box beside it. Handy if you decide to call home or post someone a letter. All this after you pass the concrete pillar-box on your left. Are you with me?"

"I think so."

"Then the road will bend about to your left and a public footpath will veer off to your right. That would take you up to Anelog from where you can see the sweep of the Lleyn, right out to Bardsey Island with the sea washing up on both sides. But don't take that path. Follow the road around to the left until you see a metal gate on your left and then another one. But don't take either gate. Stay with the bending of the road to the right, then left again past a long whitewashed house until you see a metal gate on your right. Don't take that gate, either. Just carry on and follow the road up the next hill to where it will bend about to the right again. On your left you'll see a grassy footpath, between a lane and a metal gate. Take that path and stay on it, keeping your eye on Mynydd y Gwyddel straight before your eyes. Trwyn y Gwyddel and Eglwys Lleu are tucked away behind it. Stay with what you see then and you'll find your way from there."

"And what is Mynydd y Gwyddel? And Trwyn y Gwyddel?"

"The Mountain of the Irishman and Nose of the Irishman. A good place for Sean Davies as things have turned out."

He drew a deep breath and tried to remember what Dafydd had just told him. "Thanks for the directions," he said.

"Glad to be of help. I may see you in the next day or so. I call in on Sean from time to time. Hwyl."

"Hwyl."

Dafydd glanced back at him from beside the van, eyebrows raised. "Hello, now! You have a ready enough tongue about you."

"I learn some things quicker than others. Thanks again."

He headed up the road, shifting his pack as he climbed until it was well placed against his back. The road crested the hill and wandered its way along an edge of land thick with gorse, bracken, and blackberry that dropped away to the beach below before turning inland past more banks of blackberry bushes. A field opened out on one side of the road then the other; wire fences ran along both banks while farm buildings scattered themselves about the dip and roll of the land.

Up a hill, past a chapel and some houses, he rounded a bend until he saw the pillar-box to his left, then the phone booth, letter-box, and the second chapel with the words A.D., Uwchmynydd, 1904, written upon the front of it. Leaning against the pillar-box to catch his breath, he scanned the next stretch of fields and the line of the hill behind them. The hump of land beyond stood forth more clearly now, its bulk framed on either side by houses along the hill line.

Staying with the road, he followed Dafydd's directions and avoided suspicious-looking public footpaths and metal gates until the road took him up its next bend to the right and to the grassy footpath between the lane and the metal gate. He checked the path out to convince himself it wasn't one of the paths he was not supposed to take. Then he started walking through long grass that nearly covered the path over, the stench of earth and manure biting into his nostrils.

Passing through a metal gate, he closed it behind him and followed the path as it widened around to the left; stepping over the remnant of a barbed wire fence, he found himself in a field filled with sheep. As the sheep bleated warily, he saw a mound of land rising before him that he supposed was Mynydd y Gwyddel. Beyond it, that other hump of land, now clearly an island, lifted up its back from the sea about it. The sea itself was a sheen of glass, yet alive and moving in upon itself beneath the smoothness of the light upon it.

He followed the path around the edge of the field, the bracken and gorse close about his ankles, until he came to a dirt lane. He tried to squint the light away; then his eye went with it out toward the tip of land that had emerged from behind Mynydd y Gwyddel and just to the south of it. Tucked into that tip of land—Trywn y Gwyddel?—was a hint, a suggestion, of a man-made form.

Eglwys Lleu? He tried to glimpse the form more clearly, yet the light concealed as much as it disclosed. Looking left along the dirt lane, then right, he decided going right made more sense. He opened, then closed, yet another metal gate and walked on until he came to a paved road. A car drove by him. He glanced along the road in the direction from which the car had come, and it struck him that this probably was the same road he had put behind him when he had taken the grassy path. Why, then, had Dafydd Jones sent him along the grassy path?

He tucked the question away and walked westward, to where the road curved about sharply and started up the side of another steep hill. Right in the curve a track ran off to the left toward the sea. He took the track until he came upon a broad path leading up through the heather toward the crown of Mynydd y Gwyddel.

The track he had been on continued down the slope between the two hills, and he saw two people walking up it. "What's down there?" he asked.

They stopped to catch their breath, and then the man said in a very English voice, "St. Mary's Well. At least, the maps and guidebooks say there is a well down there. Good luck to you, I say, if you try and find it. We didn't."

"The path runs down to the rocks, then into the sea," said the woman. "We went as far as the rocks."

"However, the sea was welling up about the rocks," the man said. "So perhaps we did see a well, without knowing we were seeing it. The Welsh have an odd sense of humour." They walked on, and he stood looking down the track. The well could wait for another day, he decided. He started up the broad track and soon reached the crown of My-nydd y Gwyddel.

The far slope of Mynydd y Gwyddel ran down to his left out into an arm, or nose of land, up to another outcropping of rock, and then a short distance beyond. Right at the tip between two last bristlings of rock stood a small stone building. He made his way down the slope through violet and purple hues of heather until he saw what the building was. A church. Eglwys Lleu was a small stone church.

Amazed at what he had come upon, he dropped his pack from his shoulders and took things in. An outhouse of more recent construction stood east of Eglwys Lleu. Beyond it Trwyn y Gwyddel dropped down to the Irish Sea, and the Irish Sea surged past the dropping down of the land, in toward the black cliffs of the yawning V that separated Trwyn y Gwyddel from the next stretch of the Lleyn.

A tank of fuel squatted at the northeast corner of the church, its line disappearing into the hole in the stones just below a small window in the north side, covered over with a sheet of plastic. A column of smoke rose up from the slate roof into a waning ray of sunlight. Walking around the corner to the east end, he spotted a heavy oaken door with two black bands of iron holding its planks together and a black iron ring for a door handle. He raised his hand to bang it against the door but realized what an unnecessary act that would be. Taking hold of the door handle, he turned it and pushed the door open.

He stood for a moment within the dark of the nave until his eyes widened enough to take in the space about him. Then he pushed the door closed. To his left lay a mattress, tucked into the southeast corner of the nave. West of it, another mattress had been thrown down upon the stone floor. The wall along the east end, on either side of the door, was lined with shelves attached to it and a few cupboards beneath the shelves. The shelves held dishes, cups, a flower vase, a few pots, and some personal effects.

A man sat on a wooden pew before a fire burning within a ring of stones placed just before the chancel step. Other pews stood about him, not in rows as in a working church but close upon one another. The back was chopped out of one of them, and pieces of pew wood were stacked beside the fire. An axe leaned against the pew on which the man sat, its head at rest upon the stone floor.

"Are you Sean Davies?"

"I am. Take a pew and put the length of the day behind you."

"I'm from Canada," he said, as he sat in a pew close to the fire.

"Yes, I know. Wesley's cousin. I've been expecting you."

Expecting him? How long had this man been sitting around a fire in an old church at the tip of Wales expecting him? "My pack is outside," he ventured. "Caitlin's things are in there."

"Leave them for now," Sean Davies said. "It's time for a cup of tea. Or are you an inveterate North American coffee drinker?"

"I drink tea," he replied. While Sean made the tea, his eye followed the smoke as it drifted up from the fire, then out through the hole cut in the roof. A rough-and-ready hole it seemed. "I should make you a proper smoke hole," he said, for no good reason that he could think of. "Covered over, like the one in the big house at my village."

"And what would be the name of your village?"

"Duxsowlas. On the west coast of British Columbia—"

"Beside a river, with a mountain behind it. Duxdzas."

His gaze swept down from the wooden rafters along the underside of the roof to meet that of the man putting a cup of tea into his hand. "Yes, I know of your village," Sean continued. "And what do you call yourself?"

For a moment the snapping of the fire as it licked into a fresh bit of pew was the only sound to be heard. An interesting question, he thought, since he had truly run out of names. Except for one, maybe.

"Gwawinastoo." The name had not yet been given to him, but no matter. He was thousands of miles from the big house and any naming ceremony, and there was no other name to hand. "It means Raven's Eye," he added.

Sean became very still. "Yes, I suspected it might mean that. It's been many years since I've seen Isaac. How is he doing?"

"My father?" His ears couldn't believe what they had just heard, but his tongue seemed ready to believe anything. "He's dead."

"As I had thought. When did he die?"

"Ten years ago, the summer I turned fourteen."

"Then you must have been Nathan once," Sean remarked.

"Yes, that was my name once upon a time. I've gone through several names in my life."

"Most of us have, whether or not we change about the names given us." Sean stood, crossed the stone floor to one of the shelves along the back wall, and returned with a photograph.

He recognized the photograph as soon as he took hold of it. It had stood on a chest in his house beneath the rifle hanging on the wall. He remembered the cold January day he had first looked at those faces, still feeling the shame from Uncle Charlie's words in the big house and confused by his mother's drinking. His father, in uniform, gazed out at him as did the other young man in uniform, his eyes laughing and his hair flopping down across his forehead. And the girl with them, fourteen or maybe fifteen. Looking up at the face of the man seated before him, he saw that it was half a century older and there was little hair left to flop around, yet the eyes were still laughing. "Your dad and I were together for a time during the Second Great War, in the south of England, and elsewhere," Sean said. "The girl was my sister."

"And Caitlin's mother?"

"Yes. Her name was Emer."

A crack of light splashed across the photograph as the oaken door behind them creaked open. He turned about in the pew and tried to make out the figure standing in the doorway, the last of the day's light filling the frame of stone about her. Then she closed the door and walked forward to the fire.

"This is Erin, Caitlin's sister. And this is Gwawinastoo, from Canada. He was with Caitlin when she was killed. He's brought her effects over to us. Gwawinastoo means Raven's Eye."

The firelight flickered against Erin's face then away. She stared at the young man seated before her, and he stared back. She was darker than Caitlin had been, nearly as dark as he was; looking into her face was almost like looking into a mirror, but for her eyes, the deep blue of them reminding him of the eyes of Alex. The shock he saw in them mirrored the shock he felt within himself. "Please hand the photograph to Erin," Sean said.

She took it and glanced at it. "Why show this to me? I've looked at it countless times."

"But you've not seen it. Or wanted to see it," Sean answered. "The man standing beside me and with your mother is Gwawinastoo's father. And yours."

Her eyes bored into her uncle's, and he made certain she understood. "His name was Isaac Jacob, and he was your father. Gwawinastoo is your brother."

"Sweet mucking-about Jesus!" Erin tore the photograph in two and threw both halves into the fire. With a quick turn, she vanished into the darkness at the back of the nave. The door creaked open, then crashed shut.

He reached into the fire to rescue something of the photograph. "Let it burn," said Sean. "It's done its work."

So he let it burn. "What do we do now?" he asked.

"We wait a while, now that the thunder has come and gone," said Sean. "Sometimes Erin sleeps out in the heather when she gets her temper up. Or the gorse if she's really in the mood for a fight. But tonight she just might forget about that and come back here to sleep. We'll see. If she doesn't return, you can take her mattress for the night."

He considered a moment. "I'll unroll my bag next to that other wall."

"A stone floor is a cold, hard place to spend a night when there's little between it and you."

"I've slept many nights on cold hard ground, and I've enough padding to put between me and the floor. I don't want to sleep in her bed."

"A stone floor can be harder than cold ground, and colder, but as you wish."

"So Caitlin was my sister, too."

"Yes, Caitlin was your sister."

"I think she knew that just before she was killed."

"I hope she did," Sean reflected. "Given what she put herself through to find you. Go out and breathe the night air a moment. Erin won't be in a hurry, if she does come."

The night outside Eglwys Lleu was still evening, though the sun was well down in the west and the clouds above were massing together once more. To the south, a last glow of light lay upon the Irish Sea between the tip of the Lleyn and the island west of it. Bardsey Island, he supposed. Beyond the dark hump that seemed to be the island's backbone, the lighthouse flashed once, again, then again, yet again, and then a space of time before the beam of light swept in once more from the sea . . . the light beam into which the shearwaters flew to their death, as the sister he had never known to be his sister had flown to hers: "I am what you are looking for, Jacob . . . the stone you can't walk around, anymore."

Aok!

He listened.

Aowk . . .!

The call came from the dark cliffs rusted over with lichen where the sea made its V into the tip of the Lleyn. He could see nothing, but there was no mistaking that call, even though the tuning was a bit different here. Then the only sound he could hear was the sea murmuring against the rock far below him.

It began to rain as he entered the church, and Sean had placed more pew wood on the fire. "It can chill you when it rains here, even in late summer," Sean said, "so take the axe and go to work on the rest of that pew."

He did as Sean had asked until the seat of the pew had been reduced to more firewood stacked beside the ring of stones.

It was late, very late, when the oaken door behind them creaked open. Steps sounded on the floor in the direction of Erin's mattress, and then Erin herself appeared. She shook the rain from her hair, wrapped a blanket around her and curled up in a pew near the fire. Sean waited another long moment until the snapping of the fire had become a single sounding with the falling of the rain upon the roof. Then he placed a piece of pew wood on the fire and began to speak.

THREE

Very few of us who have fought in a war want to talk much about it. It is enough that we are alive now, when so many others were killed on either side of us. Being alive is enough and I have not spent any amount of time asking why it was that I lived and not others. Although I now have an understanding of things karmic that could be a doorway for such a question, I have not put it to myself about myself. About the lives of others, yes, from time to time, that I might better understand them. But not about myself. It is enough that I am sitting here tonight, telling this story to the both of you.

I was barely eighteen when I joined the armed forces late in 1939. I left my family's farm—the farm where Caitlin and you used to come with your mother, then later on your own, and where Dafydd and his family live now—knowing little about the first Great War, or Versailles, or how Hitler came to power, or Hitler and Chamberlain, and Munich. All I knew was that a darkness had been looming up all over Europe and was menacing the little part of the world where my family lived. If that darkness threatened to reach right to the end of the Lleyn itself, then I would not wait for it to come to me but would go out to meet it.

So by the spring of 1940 I was attached to a unit in the south of England and there I met my first Canadians. They were barracked at Aldershot, had been there since early in the year and were spoiling for a fight, which they got, more than they had bargained for, two years later at Dieppe. But some of them and some of us were given the opportunity for an excursion to France that very summer. Only days after our troops were rescued from the beach at Dunkirk, Churchill decided to send a force into Brittany, from a Canadian Division and a British division, to delay the German advance and hold a last bit of Europe for ourselves.

We sailed from Plymouth on June 13 and into Brest to meet the dawn the next morning. Little did we know the Germans would enter Paris that very day, that all resistance in France was at an end and that the French government was just days away from an armistice with Hitler and capitulation. We knew none of this as we changed from ship to train, myself and a few from my unit sandwiched here and there between several carloads of Canadians, some of whom acted as if they were on a bit of a holiday while others still looked green about the gills from our crossing of the channel.

By afternoon, we were away from Brest, puffing happily into a countryside fresh with summer. Trees sprang up alongside the tracks or stood on their own against the skyline, and then a church spire would grow up out of a field young with corn. Through villages we chugged, passing the backs of houses, their shutters closed, open, half-opened, as faces stared with unbelieving eyes into ours. Most of those about me, however, paid scant heed to the disbelief in those eyes, but were more interested in the cheap wine that flowed into the train at every stop.

Except for one Canadian. I came upon him on the platform between two cars, standing quietly and watching the single and double chimneys of the houses slide behind us until we were in the country again, the slopes of a little valley running down toward some tree-lined secret at its bottom. "Hello. A pleasant little outing, this," I said.

His dark face smiled. "So far, anyway. We'll see how long it keeps being pleasant."

"Your mates don't seem concerned about what might be up ahead."

"I guess they aren't. I hope they're right. We have only fifty rounds of ammunition, each of us."

"You're joking, of course."

"No, I'm not joking. My people back home have forgotten more about preparing for a war than this army has ever learned."

"Perhaps your army should take on some of your people as military consultants."

His smile saddened. "I don't think that would be a good idea. As I said, most of them have forgotten what they once knew."

An old man swept into view, along the side of the track. He also stared at us, before we rounded a curve and passed beneath a stone bridge.

"Who are your people?"

"The Haida. They live on what are called the Queen Charlotte Islands, off Canada's west coast. We used to call the islands Haida Gwaii. Some of us still call them that, those who haven't forgotten."

"Then you would be a seagoing people."

"Yes. We once had big canoes that spent long days riding the back of the Pacific."

I laughed. "Then that explains it."

"Explains what?"

"Why you're not green in the face like the rest of your Canadians, from crossing the channel."

Then he laughed. "That wasn't much of a crossing. You should have seen us out on the Atlantic, coming over. Even my stomach wondered what the hell was going on. But you're a seagoing person, too, I think."

"That I am. At least it's in my blood, even though I've spent more time on a farm than on the water. My name is Sean, by the by."

"I'm Isaac," he said.

We spoke nothing more yet stayed with one another as our train pulled into St-Brieuc. People crowded the station platform, wanting to go somewhere yet with little idea where in the world they could go. Then our train rolled on. The land about us flattened and widened, though the corn still stood in some fields while cows lay in others and the church spires went on growing up in between as if they wanted to pierce a hole through the silence that held the Breton countryside in its grip.

Isaac and I honoured the silence, exchanging glances only now and then as we looked out at the dark clouds coming together in the sky up ahead.

A few miles from Rennes, the train ground to a sudden stop. We saw a small armoured car parked near the train, with an officer sitting toward the front of it and another man stationed at the machine gun. A sergeant walked from the car to the train, boarded, spoke to someone in command, then shouldered his way down an aisle, looking from man to man, until he came to the platform where the two of us stood. "You, and you, off you come, with your gear, now," he barked, in a very Scottish voice.

"All oatmeal and salt, that one," I growled, as we left the train.

"I think we've just volunteered for something," Isaac grinned. And so we had. We were now part of a five-man reconnaissance into the south of Brittany. The train pulled away and neither of us saw it again. The following morning it would arrive at Laval and be on its way back to Brest in no time at all, once those on board learned that German troops were only forty miles away and that they would be fighting those troops on their own with no other support.

We, in our turn, wheeled down a road to the south. The sergeant drove, swearing under his breath that this was a damn-fool mission, while the lieutenant sat upright in his seat and looked as if he were on an outing with the Boy Scouts. The man at the machine gun scanned the road up ahead and hoped he would know what to do when the time came for something to be done.

After a time we came out on a road nearer the coast that ran southeast and northwest. The lieutenant ordered the sergeant to turn southeast. "I don't think this is a good way to go," Isaac breathed in my ear. The sergeant didn't seem to think it was a good idea, either, though he barked at us over his shoulder and kept on driving.

The road ran up a hill and we went with it, only to screech right around once we were at the top. Driving up the hill toward us was a German reconnaissance, two or three armoured cars in strength.

We sped back along the road as fast as our car could go. But Brest was a long way off, and we were certain they had seen us. The evening began to darken, but the sergeant drove without lights toward the last light to the west, an eerie orange softened from above by powder blue sky and then massed over by great, black sheets of cloud that draped down to the earth—a sky silent and unmoving before the onslaught of a storm.

The sergeant barrelled through Vannes, past a road that turned off to the south. The lieutenant wanted to turn off with it, but the sergeant resisted. He'd looked at a map he bellowed, and that road would run us out to the end of the peninsula. The man at the machine gun sat, mouth shut and teeth on edge, as did Isaac and I. We came to another road turning off to the south. This time, the lieutenant got his way. The sergeant made the turn but cursed the lieutenant for being a fool and continued to curse as he drove down the rapidly darkening road. Scots pines swished past us on either side, the one sight and scent of loveliness in the compounding mess into which we hurtled ourselves.

I learned later that the sergeant had been right. We were on our way to the Quiberon Peninsula, though we only suspected it at the time. All I knew then was the first bite of salt air into my nostrils. "I smell the sea coming up, fast," I murmured.

"Very fast," Isaac agreed.

In the meantime, the sergeant went on arguing with the lieutenant as we came up in the dark to a crossroad and ran smack into a German armoured car. All three men in front of Isaac and me were killed upon impact, as were those in the German car. All save one.

I lifted my face from the pavement onto which I had been thrown, then brought myself to my knees. He had propped himself against the side of his car even as it caught fire all around him, and his rifle was trained right on me. I think he was dying even then and knew he was dying, but we were at war and he wasn't intending to die alone. I gaped back into the one eye, opened wide as he sighted along the barrel. The other eye was shut tight, squinting half the world away from his seeing as his finger fumbled for the trigger, then found it.

As if held by the eye of a cobra, I froze within myself, certain I was going to die. Then his head snapped back, the rifle dropped from his hands, and his body slumped over the side of the car. Blood spilled from the eye that had held me in his sights.

When I could bring myself about, I saw Isaac on one knee lowering his rifle from his shoulder. Then his hand reached for my shoulder. "Let's go, Sean! Now!" He yanked me to my feet, thrust my rifle into my hand, and we started up the road in the direction from which we had come. Then we glimpsed the beam from the oncoming headlights, still distant but coming quickly. We froze against the bank at the side of the road and knew there would be no escaping those lights once they reached us. I looked down at my hand and saw it was resting on stone steps, set into the ground and barely visible. I drew back the tangle of gorse and ivy beside them, then grasped Isaac by the collar and pulled him up onto the bank then down into the darkness after me.

The thorns tore at my hands as I yanked the gorse back over the hole, and then we sat down on the wet earth of a passage grave, propped our backs against the upright stones of its sides and listened.

Headlights flashed by us, and the armoured car screeched to a stop. Excited voices shouted to one another, though we couldn't make out the words. Perhaps they would conclude the dead in the two crashed cars accounted for all who might have been present. Isaac must have read my thought for I saw him shake his head as our eyes sought one another out within the dark of the tomb. The soldier with the bullet through his eye would suggest otherwise.

The search began. Feet tramped up the road, then back, then tramped up onto the ground around the grave. Voices sounded all about us, then faded away, only to come pressing in again. But no hand reached for the gorse branches that shielded Isaac and me from the feet and voices in search of us.

A second armoured car careened down the road and stopped. Now a number of voices debated among themselves, then fell silent. Both cars started up and drove south toward the Quiberon Peninsula. The sound of them faded into the distance until we heard only the silence of the pines overhead and the grave in which we sat, and then the beating of our own hearts. My arm went slack and my rifle slipped from my hand as the back of my head came to rest against the upright stone.

"Are you all right, Sean?"

"Yes. Thank you. I'm sorry you had to kill him to bail me out."

"So am I. It's the first time I've killed a man in this war. But I knew there would be a first time, sooner or later. Unless someone put a bullet into me first. It would be good if it could be the last time I killed a man, but war doesn't seem to work that way. I just hope no one ever looks down the barrel of a gun at me the way he was looking at you."

"Odd, the way he looked at me. It reminded me of . . ."

"Of what?"

"Of something from an Irish hero tale. But you probably wouldn't know of it."

"Try me. I might surprise you, the things I know."

"All right, then. The tale is about Cuchulain, the terror of Ulster—at least my Irish mother said it like that—because he could fight with just about anything: spears, javelins, swords, even a slingshot. Either side in this war would pay him in spades to take up arms for it. But what made him truly terrible was his anger, or warp-spasm as it's sometimes called." I stopped speaking, not sure that I wanted to remember the story.

"Go on."

"Well, when the warp-spasm overtook him, Cuchulain's face became a mask, a hideous mask. One eye squinted itself closed, so tightly closed, the eyeball was forced right to the back of his head, while the other widened almost to the width of that side of his face. The one eye shutting the light right, out and the other not able to take enough of it in. The rest of him turned inside out and round about as well, but it was that face and my mother telling me about it that sent shivers through me. I hoped I would never see such a face in my lifetime, but I just did moments ago when he sighted along his rifle at me. One eye squeezed shut and the other stark and staring into mine, looking where best to put that bullet through me."

Rain started to fall. Down upon the earth over our heads, onto the gorse covering the entrance to the grave and onto the road beyond, the rain fell from the clouds above us, the black of them putting the finishing touch on a night black enough in itself. As well, the rain found a hole or two down into the back end of the grave, and the wet ground on which we sat became wetter.

"Anyway, that's why I couldn't move, even though he was about to kill me. Isaac, what's wrong?"

He stared at me through the darkness, yet not at me but at something far beyond and away from me. "I saw it, too, just before I shot him; I saw what you saw." He said nothing for a time, then started to speak.

"I told you I was a Haida, but that's only half true. My mother was a Haida, and my dad . . . my dad came from the land east of the Rockies and before that, from the country of his people, the Sioux, south of the American border. When my dad was seven, he had a dream, two nights before the Sioux and Cheyenne fought Custer and his soldiers at the Little Bighorn. A crescent moon appeared in his dream, holding a dark circle ringed about with light like a thread of gold. In the dark circle, my dad saw a white raven trying to fly free of the circle. At least, that's what he thought it was trying to do.

"My grandfather was killed in the fight with Custer, and his oldest son, One Eagle, had to care for the family—my grandmother, my dad, and a brother in between, the one my dad felt closest to. After surviving for two years by hunting what was left of the buffalo and outrunning the soldiers, they escaped into Canada and joined up with Sitting Bull and his people.

"That would have been the summer of 1878. The next summer my dad went on a vision quest with Sitting Bull as his guide. 'Go and find the people who know the Raven and the Raven's story,' Sitting Bull had told my dad, the day after his first dream. But my dad now wanted more than that dream; he wanted a vision to guide his next step and to show him what he should do to make a medicine bundle for himself.

"Funny, my mother was born that same summer, though Dad knew nothing of her then. In fact, he was only ten when he went into the Cypress Hills for those four days. He found a place in a grove of aspen on the south side of the hills with pines round about and plenty of sun. From there, he could watch the sun walk along the sky to the south. Only it was summer and the sun was very high, so he had to squint hard to see what it was doing.

"After they had made a place for him to be, set up the centre pole and a pole in each of the four directions with the offerings tied to each pole, his helpers left, and Dad spent two days and nights doing what Sitting Bull had suggested he should do. But no vision came to him, not even the dream he had dreamed three summers earlier. On the third morning, he knew he had to find someplace else in the Cypress Hills for his third night. He wasn't supposed to do that, move from the place where he had been, but he woke up the third morning as if a voice had been speaking quiet words into his ear: 'Go and find the crescent moon,' the voice told him.

"So Dad left the aspen grove, taking only the pipe Sitting Bull had filled for him, and he walked to the northwest because Sitting Bull had said once, 'You must go north and west to find the people of the Raven.' Sometime after noon, he found the place he wanted—a great north-facing crescent cut right into the Cypress Hills, all the way down to the prairie floor far below. He stood at its rim and could see where the earth had fallen away a long time ago, to roll out to the north like humps on the backs of the buffalo.

"Dad walked the crescent, first to the west, back around to the east, and then from the east tip of it back to its centre where he sat and watched the sun go down, far to the northwest. As he looked at the sun's going down, he found he no longer needed to squint the light away to see the sun as he had had to do in that other place. It was as if the sun were letting him have a good look at it with wide open eyes, and saying, 'You can look me in the eye, if you're ready for that.'

"That night, Dad slept right at the rim of the canyon, as if along the edge of the moon itself, and that night he did dream, of a face carved in stone. One eye of the face squinted shut, wanting to push the light right out, and the other eye opened wide to let the whole of the light in. Just before he woke up, a voice whispered, 'This is my human face; take care of it for me.' And he knew it was the voice of Raven.

"The next day his helpers came for him and found him at the place where they had left him. Dad rode down from the Cypress Hills with them to tell Sitting Bull what had happened. But when he tried to put a medicine bundle together, nothing walked into his hand. The only thing he found was a buffalo skull with one of its eye sockets crushed closed by something that had stepped on it. When he brought the skull to Sitting Bull, Sitting Bull laughed. 'You'll need a big medicine pouch for that,' he said, 'but if you look beyond the skull, you might be closer to your medicine bundle than you think.' He was right; soon after, my dad found a flat stone, the shape of a human face. A big enough stone, Sitting Bull said, for Dad to carve into it the face he had seen in his dream."

The rain had stopped, but the runoff from it went on dripping down into the grave. A sound from the south cut through the night, and an armoured car came up behind it, passed by the grave with a sweep of its lights and drove on to the north. We listened for the approach of the second car but heard nothing. "Looks like we're not going anywhere yet," Isaac said.

"No, it would seem not." I pushed back the gorse at the grave entrance to look for a first trace of the coming day. No light was showing. I sat back against the upright stone and must have grumbled under my breath because Isaac started to chuckle. "At least we're both alive, so far."

"Yes, so far."

"Some years later, my dad started his journey north and west. He must have been sixteen by then. He took his time going through the Rocky Mountains and across the north of British Columbia, working here and there, learning to speak English and carving the face into his stone. Well to the west, he met the first people who knew what Raven was about and spent time with them. Just after this century was born, he reached the Pacific coast and crossed over to Haida Gwaii. He had finished the carving by that time and had wrapped his medicine skin about it.

"My mother was living in Skidegate on the east coast of the north island. After all her grandparents had been killed by smallpox, sometime in the 1860s, her parents moved from their ancestral village of Chaatl on the west coast of the islands to a village called Haina. Then they moved again to Skidegate and died there of influenza when my mother was still young. She was the only child born to them and had no living relatives. So the missionaries raised her, taught her English and everything else they knew, and thought they knew—certain she would become one of them or something close to it.

"But she met Dad and left the missionaries standing with their mouths open when Dad and she found a boat that would take them through the narrows and back to Chaatl. Chaatl had been abandoned by the time they moved there, except for a few houses left standing and the totem poles round about them. By the time I was born, when they had almost given up hope of having a child, the forest was moving in upon the houses and taking them over. Seeds fell on the heads of the poles, and trees grew down over them and up through them until only a couple were left to stare out through the forest and across the channel. But we lived as best we could. Dad learned to fish, went on learning how to carve from what the poles said to him, even as they fell from his view, and my mother taught me English and whatever else she decided was worth my knowing, about being Haida and about the world of the whites.

"I was twelve when my mother died, 1933 by the calendar. We placed her body on a platform, in the trees, the way we had once buried our dead. Then Dad and I moved to Skidegate."

Isaac stopped speaking. I parted the gorse branches once again and glimpsed the first light of day. But we heard nothing of that other car, to the south of us.

"Did you ever see the stone face your dad carved?"

"Only half of it, the half with the wide-open eye. He gave it to me just before I left Skidegate to join up with my unit."

"You mean he broke the mask in two?"

"Yes, that's what he had done. He told me the story of the mask and how he had come to be where he was. And he gave me a Haida name, that night: Xuuyaa Gut-ga-at-gaa."

"I'm trying to sound it to myself, but my tongue's about to give up. What does it mean?"

"Raven Splitting-in-Two. 'I want you to come back from the war,' he said, 'and take me to Chaatl so I can die there. Carve a mortuary pole for my body and put my medicine bundle in it, too. If you need the other half of the mask by then, take it. If not, leave it in the pole for that part of you that will come looking for it one day.'"

"What are you going to do, now, with the half he has given you?"

"Damned if I know," Isaac laughed. Then he said, "I've never told this to anyone before now."

The day was upon us. We waited into its first hours for that car to the south to drive back up the road, then out of our lives. But no sound of it reached our ears, and we had to make a move, whatever might come of it. "We'll be putting this grave to work if we stay any longer," I said, then led the way out into the light. Standing on the bank by the road, we could see the two armoured cars, crashed together with their dead still in them. The morning had nearly gone and it was close to noon, with the sun high above our heads in a sky cleared of clouds.

"What is that?" I heard Isaac ask. I turned about and saw what he had seen."

"For the love of Jesus! It's a dolmen." And so it was, two dolmens, in fact, the one leading into the other. "We have them in Wales, and there are plenty of them in Ireland."

"What are they for?" He walked toward the south-facing entrance of the smaller one as he spoke.

"They were graves, as I've been told, dating back several thousand years."

Fascinated, Isaac started to walk around the stones in the direction the clock turns.

"Walk the other way, against the clock, three times," I blurted out. "Especially if you've a mind to go inside."

Bemused, he looked over at me. "Why that way?"

"Because it's the way my mother told my sister and me to go. That's all I know."

"Then that's good enough for me," he grinned, and started to walk about as I had said. The smaller dolmen to the south was capped by a couple of stones that let the sun beam through the gaps between them. The larger dolmen to the north had a single, large capstone and was well shadowed. "I'll take you home to Wales, and even to Ireland, if you want to study one of those," I said, "but for now, let's get ourselves back to Brest as best we can."

And then the sound of the armoured car whining up the road from the south closed in upon us, too rapidly for us even to consider making it back to the passage grave. Isaac dived down into the south entrance to the pair of dolmens, and I followed at his heels. We crawled through the smaller dolmen, the sun striking full upon our backs, and into the shadow of the larger one. "Don't worry," Isaac whispered in my ear. "I walked around for both of us."

In a space almost big enough for us to stand, we crouched back to back, and listened. Then, as I took a look at where we were, my heart sank. At the north end, a single upright stone took the weight of the capstone. The gaps between it and the nearest standing stone on either side were wide open to a pine forest smitten with daylight. Only a blind man or a fool could miss seeing us here. Yet, looking behind me, I saw a single standing stone that marked the transition from one dolmen to the other and caught the sun like a mirror, as if to deflect it from the shadow within which we crouched. Isaac faced the gap to the west, and I the one to the east, our rifles at the ready.

The car stopped. Voices bantered back and forth. For certain, they had given us up and would drive on. But no, their feet came stomping along the road then up onto the bank. The voices became the more excited, and I pictured hands pulling at the gorse that had not quite settled back into place.

Then their voices fell to a hush as their steps drew closer, coming on carefully now. We saw their boots, a set of them standing at either side of the north upright stone.

Over the years since that moment, I've sometimes thought how I would tell what happened next, when the time for telling came. There are things almost too real for words to grasp. Nonetheless, I shall find what words I can, as best I can, to tell you that the two of us found ourselves wrapped about with light—not the daylight of the sun outside the dolmen, but another light as old as the beginning of the world itself, and older, that touched down through the stone over our heads and took us into itself. I knew Isaac saw it as clearly as I because of the way his back came alive against mine.

Dismayed by whatever it was that was about to betray us, my finger tightened on the trigger and the press of Isaac's right elbow into my back told me his finger was doing the same. In that same instant, the two sets of boots became two faces, peering into the dolmen from either side of the upright stone. Your father looked directly into one pair of eyes, and I into the other. Yet we didn't shoot for the light would not let our fingers move.

"Was siehst du?"*

"Nichts. Und du?"

"Gar nichts. Es ist viel zu dunkel da drin."

"Ja, genau! Schwarzer als die Nacht selbst."

Two pairs of eyes continued to peer into the light-drenched shadow in which we crouched, yet seemed to see nothing. Unable to move and barely able to breathe, Isaac and I stared right back.

"Also, was machen wir jetzt?"

A breeze blew up all of a sudden, stirring at the needles on the pines all about the dolmen.

"Lass uns gehen und lass das Dunkel dunkel sein!"* The two faces vanished, then the pairs of boots. The armoured car started up, a voice laughed, and then the car drove on to the north. The breeze brushed against my cheek, and the light that had enfolded us was gone. I looked at Isaac and he looked at me, and we both knew, though we understood nothing of what we knew.

We made our way along the little roads that led north until we reached the road running up and down the coast. There was no sign of a German reconnaissance, only the horse-drawn carts filled with families fleeing the advance of the Germans. Many gaped at us, not understanding why we had appeared in their midst yet knowing fully the gravity of our situation. From out of the chaos of carts there appeared one with a motor attached to its front end—I can describe it in no other way!—and a

* see glossary

cab thrown around the motor. The driver braked sharply when he saw us, exclaimed this and that, then threw us both into the cart and into a mess of squawking chickens. Pushing the motor as much as he could, our saviour wove a path in and out of the continuing chaos of carts while his chickens screeched and defecated, squawked and defecated some more.

That night we stopped at a farm, well off the road. Isaac and I slept in the cart, while the chickens emptied themselves upon us and all about us, and at dawn we were off again.

Late in the afternoon the cart came gasping into Brest, found the harbour, and expelled the two of us onto the dock, an hour before the last of our ships was to sail for Plymouth.

"Privates Jacob and Davies, reporting back from reconnaissance, Sir," we blurted to the first excuse for an officer we could find. The officer returned our salute, gagged, and summarily ordered us to immerse our dung-caked and feathered selves in the Atlantic until the stench of us was gone.

And so it was that your father and I met. Our meetings continued over the next two years. Inexplicably, we would find ourselves on the same train to London or in the same pub in London, and soon we began to plan weekends together. Then, in the fall of 1940, I came up with the idea of a three-week leave in Wales.

I brought Isaac home to our farm. Emer had just turned fifteen and her eyes would not leave this Canadian who she knew at once was more than just a soldier, even though he came from a world she barely could imagine. Always it was the three of us walking together up and down the Lleyn, now climbing up to the remains of the stone fort at Tre'r Ceiri or taking the path along the coast out to Pen y Cil. As the oak and beech leaves went to gold, then to rust, I teased her about wanting to be with us, but could not tease her away from us. Our mother smiled and worried some, while our dad scratched at his neck and made himself busy with the few sheep we kept. Isaac, in turn, simply accepted her being with us and seemed to make nothing more of it than that.

The day before we left, our dad took a photograph of us, Isaac and I side by side, and Emer with us, holding our dog and wanting so much to become a woman . . .

Isaac and I tried for another leave together, in 1941, but with no luck. Then the spring of 1942 was upon us and he said to me one weekend, on our way back from London, "A few of us are being transferred to the 2nd Division, because we've had experience in the field, as they put it."

He laughed. "Some experience that was!" Then his laugh faded away. "They're cooking something up, something more than war games between ourselves. I can see it in their eyes."

The night of August 18, some 5,000 Canadian troops sailed for France, and the next morning they swarmed onto the beaches of Dieppe. Your father was among them. When the shooting and dying came to an end, the ships brought him back with others who had survived. There was a steely piece of Germany in his leg, not enough of a piece to cripple him, but enough to take him out of the war. It wasn't the wound in his leg that needed healing, however, but the one in his eyes and in his heart. "Go to the farm," I told him, my hands gripping at his shoulders. "Go to my family, before you think about going anywhere else, and stay as long as you have need of us."

So that was where your father went, the fall of 1942, and he stayed through the winter. By early summer he had left, before my dad died and I went home to help bury him, and I never saw Isaac again. But I did see Emer and hardly recognized her on her way to being eighteen. She no longer was a girl wanting to be a woman but had become a woman.

Our mother said little to me about the months Isaac had been with them and I knew better than to ask. By then I had loved some myself, in the way love sometimes comes about when a war makes any moment stolen from it the more bittersweet for having been stolen.

The next summer I was among those who landed on the beaches of Normandy. During the long months I spent fighting through France and into Germany, I sometimes had the feeling Isaac was beside me. And there were nights I sat, keeping myself awake because others depended upon my staying awake, and felt the press of his back against mine, if only for that fleeting moment.

In the years after the war, we heard nothing of Isaac or from him. Emer worked at several jobs, one after the other, then decided to become a teacher. She finished her training, began to teach, but never married. Men fell in love with her and wanted to love her. She, however, loved none of them, and they soon gave it up.

Then, in the spring of 1972, in a Church of England newspaper, she saw an ad tucked away on a back page. The ad was for a teacher in a small native village on the west coast of Canada. The name of the village was Duxsowlas. She applied for the position, got it, and left for Canada at the end of the summer. There was no reason in the world for her to hope that Isaac would be living in that village, but, indeed, there he was when she arrived.

The following March she returned. She could have stayed, she told me. Isaac would have stood by her, and her child would have been welcomed into the village. However, she could see nothing but pain coming from that and had chosen to leave. In September, on Michaelmas Day, Caitlin and you were born. "Here," your mother said, that same day, handing me one half of a stone mask. "You know what this is about. You decide which of them shall have it, when the time for that comes."

She did not speak of Isaac again, ever, to me, or to Caitlin or you, to the day she died. But I know in my heart her silence was not one of hatred for your father, but of a life that knew and accepted what it had called to itself. Beyond that knowing, there was never a need for her to say a word more.

Tonight, however, Emer's silence and mine has come to an end.

Yet the silence lasted a moment more as the fire flickered down to its embers. He didn't look at Erin, and she did not look at him. Then Sean reached across the fire and handed something to Erin. "It's stone," he said, "so I doubt it will burn as readily as the photograph."

Erin's fingers closed upon the half-mask with the wide open eye. She stood, drew her blanket about her, and walked to her mattress. Lying with her face to the wall, she curled up into the folds of the blanket, and then she slept.

He sat with Sean and gazed into the embers, warm upon the stone, until the last glow of them was gone.

FOUR

The Irish Sea lapped at the last, jagged reach of the rock on which he stood, a few steps beyond the path that had ceased to be a path.

"Go on," Sean urged.

Go where? He thought of the man and woman who had come down here, not even this far probably, and had turned back because they could see no point in going farther. Now he could understand why they had turned back. Yet Sean called out again, "Go ahead, right to the water, then look to your right."

So he followed the path that wasn't a path, one hand on the rise of rock beside it, and then he saw the ledge that ran along the rock face to his right to where the cliff bent around to the west. "Make your way over to the well," said Sean. "There's room enough for the two of us to stand once we're there."

He started along the ledge, and indeed there was rock enough for his feet to take him to where the cliff turned then caved inward at its base. He stood shoulder to shoulder with Sean, and they peered down into the little pool of fresh water that peered up at them.

St. Mary's Well. Tucked under and within the rock face before which they stood and fed by streams of water that trickled almost imperceptibly from the rock itself, it mirrored their two faces and the sky beyond as well as revealing its own bottom, strewn with tiny bits of rock and with coins.

"One of our poets hints that we should see beyond our own image when we look to what the well can give us," said Sean. "I don't agree. The seeing of my own face has become part of what the well wants to show me. The coins are another matter."

His eyes searched the surface of the pool, the surface that was both a mirror and a window. The pool gazed back at him, what it mirrored becoming as real as the well bottom that showed through the image of his face and the sky beyond. "At Samhain, the first of November, the lakes of Ireland turn to glass," Sean said, "and you can see right into the other world. But there are the wellings of water, here and there, that need not wait upon Samhain to do that for us. Try and hold it all together in one act of seeing."

The Xhaaidla. The skin through which everything passes into another world where it becomes what it really is. The thought came to him as Sean spoke again. "Let's walk on, out to Braich y Pwll."

They went back up to the paved road, then up and along the side of the high hill called Mynydd Mawr, the Big Mountain. The whole reach of Bardsey Island came into view, from the high hump at its eastern end, through the abandoned farms that had once been its heartland, then out to where the island broke up into rocky fingers extended into the sea. The lighthouse blinked seaward then back toward the Lleyn, and they continued on until they came to an arm of land that became the western tip of the peninsula.

Sean led the way along a faint track that ran down onto Braich y Pwll, the Arm of the Pool, then sat down amid the heather and gorse. He sat beside Sean, avoiding the yellow blossoms of the gorse, and letting his body down with care. Sean had been right.

The stone floor had taken its toll on him before the night was over. Bringing his knees up enough so that he could rest his elbows upon them, he looked out at the sea. Below its surfaces, rough here, smoother there, currents turned ceaselessly. Mynydd y Gwyddel was visible around to the south, but not Trwyn y Gwyddel or Eglwys Lleu. It was as if neither existed any longer, not from where they were sitting. Suddenly, the question he had put aside yesterday rose up within him. "Why did Dafydd send me the way he did, instead of by the road?"

"What did you see coming the way you did?"

"What did I see? Metal gates, long grass, and sheep. A lot of sheep, and baled hay, along with gorse, and then . . ."

"And then?"

"Then I caught my first glimpse of Eglwys Lleu. At least, I thought I saw it, though the light out here took away as much as it gave me. I looked and Eglwys Lleu was there, then again and it wasn't."

"Braich y Pwll was the ending of the pilgrims' road, once," Sean said, after a moment or two. "As early as the fifth century, perhaps, they started to come to Bardsey Island and kept on coming for the next thousand years from all over Europe. They would wait here for the boats to take them over. Our name for Bardsey is Ynys Enlli, Isle of the Currents. The currents were fierce then and are mean enough still. So there might be a wait here before they undertook that last leg of their pilgrimage."

Sean stopped speaking. He shaded his eyes and gazed out at the slashes and circles of light that dropped down upon the grey of the sea through the breaks in the clouds overhead. "Many did cross over," he continued, "but I imagine this one pilgrim, whoever he or she was, and whatever year or century it was, becoming fed up with waiting for the boat and wanting to take a look about. Perhaps our pilgrim walks to a place to the east of here, not far, where the eye might have glimpsed something on the way down to Braich y Pwll but passed the glimpse by because it was occupied with arriving somewhere else. Or perchance our pilgrim comes for the first time upon that place where the eyes can just spy out the tip of Trwyn y Gwyddel. The pilgrim blinks to confirm what the eyes suddenly see. For there Eglwlys Lleu has appeared, not yet in stone but in the play of the light itself, the form of it revealing to the pilgrim what it might become if stone were brought to it. So when the next boat leaves for Bardsey, our pilgrim is not to be found but instead takes on the building of Eglwys Lleu. The form seen in the light is framed in stone, and in time it is only stone the eye sees. Except for those places where the eye can glimpse, if only in a flash, what our pilgrim first saw. The spot where you first saw Eglwys Lleu is such a place."

As he turned Sean's words over, another thought struck. "When those German soldiers looked into that dolmen, they said something about it being too dark to see anything. Then as they left, one of them said, 'Let the dark . . . be dark?'"

"Leave the dark to the dark. To itself."

"But it wasn't dark for the two of you, inside?"

"No," Sean smiled, ruefully, "far from it, though it wasn't daylight light that we felt upon us."

"Then what sort of light was it?"

"Well, now, that is a question. It would depend, I suppose, on what you think passage graves and dolmens are really about, other than places to bury the dead. I've reason to suspect our Druids saw something of another, perhaps older, light within the stones of a passage grave or the shadow cast by the capstone of a dolmen or even the shadows thrown by standing stones in a circle—those stones holding the daylight at bay and letting the other light shine through for those with the eyes left to behold that shining."

A light before Raven's world . . . The thought of it grasped him as firmly as he grasped hold of it. "And you think that's what you saw that day? You and Dad? The stone shutting the sun out so the Germans couldn't see you, yet letting this other light in?"

"Perhaps," Sean said. "Though what happened that day, and why, remains a riddle for me."

"Did you ever go back there?"

And now Sean laughed. "Once, sometime after the war ended. The dolmen's name on the guide maps is Dolmens de Mane-Kerioned, but it's known locally as La Butte-aux-Fees, the Fairies' Mound. That name may suggest little to you; for a Welsh-Irishman, however, a fairy mound is where the Tuatha de Danaan retreated, after they were defeated by the invading Celts."

"The Tuatha de Danaan? Caitlin told me about them. Lugh was one of their leaders, Cuchulain's father. His face shone like a god's face."

"It seems the two of you covered a good stretch of ground during those three days," Sean observed.

"So what happened when you went back to that dolmen?"

"Nothing. I sat down in it, then sat some more. A few people came along for a look at the dolmen and found me there, sitting. Shaking their heads and asking themselves, probably, who this fool was, and why, and where from, they went their ways and left me there, still sitting. Fortunately, I didn't open my mouth but just sat. That's the last occasion I've spent any length of time in a dolmen. But then, you'll want to see that for yourself, won't you?"

"See what?"

"Whatever the thought that's just gotten hold of you wants you to see. After all, your name is Raven's Eye."

The image of a raven's eye rose up within him as Sean spoke and suddenly, the pit of his stomach became a yawning abyss, like the darkness at the bottom of Big Horn Canyon. "There's no raven's eye left to see with," he blurted forth.

"And how is that?"

"Because I shot it out of his head." His own head dropped into his hands as the import of his words struck home. Then he pulled himself upright and told Sean what had happened, as he had told Wesley that last night at the dam—Uncle Charlie's shaming of him, his night meeting with Naomi, Isaac's deed of compassion, Uncle Charlie and Frank, Isaac's dead body being pulled from the plane, and his trying to shoot the sun from the sky at Snag Point—but now without the rage that had filled his telling of it to Wesley.

Gathering his breath in once more, he then told Sean what he had not told Wesley or anyone, until that moment: "I heard him calling me, 'Quo-k,' when I had lowered the gun and the last feather had come down. 'Quo-k' . . . and there he was, waiting for me in the shadow of a big cedar. When I saw him, I thought I'd look into that eye of his and just see my own face looking back, like another time I looked into his eye. 'Gwaau' . . . he coaxes me forward, then his eyelid opens but there is no eye, only the raw socket where his eye had been, as dead and empty as the full moon I saw later when I lay back in my dad's boat all that night long, feeling as if I, too, had just died."

Out on the Irish Sea, another orb of light touched down upon the grey, smooth yet troubled surface, then lifted away. Now there, now no longer there. "What about the other eye?" Sean asked. "Assuming that your raven started life with two eyes. Would I be right enough, assuming that?"

"I guess that would be a true enough assumption," he replied.

"Good. Then there is and always has been an eye left in that raven's head."

"But one eye isn't enough," he insisted.

Exasperated, Sean threw up his hands. "Ears, man! God gave us ears to hear with! One-eyed is crippled seeing but not stone blind. Have you considered there might be another eye somewhere waiting for yours?"

Now he became exasperated. "What the hell . . . What other eye?"

"Who, not what. Your sister, that's who. Erin was also named Raven's Eye, by me, on behalf of your father, when she was twelve—once I knew for certain it was to her and not Caitlin that the half of the stone face should go. Súl an Fhiaich her name is, in Gaelic: Raven's Eye. What do you think your father's Haida name was all about? Raven Splitting-in-Two: one eye of the Raven was born with you, while the other was born here. Each of your eyes needs the other."

Then he remembered: Uncle Charlie's potlatch and the button blanket his dad had worn, with Raven splitting apart from the tip of his beak to either side of the blanket. And the half-mask of Isaac's glugwe, the black half-face with the single eye showing. Why had the other half been covered over with the blanket? Because it couldn't be shown yet? Or because there had not been anything there, as yet, to show? His shoulders relaxed some. "All right. What do I do about that?"

"Ask your sister to go to Ireland with you."

"Why Ireland?"

"Because the passage graves and dolmens there will best give you what you need to see. And Erin knows where to find them, more so than she might want to admit."

He shook his head. "Somehow, I doubt that will happen. She won't want to go to Ireland with me."

"At the outset, no. But your asking her is the only chance Erin has of discovering what she might really want. Besides, you have no choice, if your pilgrimage is to go anywhere from here. You need the seeing she has and the eye she is alongside of yours."

Now it all seemed so simple, yet impossible. "I don't know how I would ask her that," he confessed, "or even where to look for her."

"The second may not be that difficult," said Sean. "She often walks to the top of Anelog and sits the day out there. There's a path to the top at Uwchmynydd, one Dafydd probably told you not to take. As for the first, well, that will be up to you, won't it?"

He spotted the little dance in Sean's eyes, then had to laugh. "Yes, I guess it will be. But there's something I want to give you before I go looking for Erin." He drew the eagle feather from his jacket. "My brother, Frank, gave it to me. I tried to give it away once, but it came back to me and asked me to think again, though I wasn't thinking very well at the time. But then I gave it to Caitlin and she took it, truly took it. It was in her hand when she died. I picked it up from where she had fallen and so I'm responsible for bringing it home to you. You're the person it belongs to, now."

Sean took the feather and did not speak.

"Pluen Eryr. That was Caitlin's other name, I think."

"Yes," said Sean, stroking the feather lightly. "Yes, that was Caitlin's other name."

Nu gwa am.

A movement along the slope of Anelog caught his eye. The bird hovered in the afternoon light, held there by the steady beating of its wings as it waited for something down in the heather to move. A hawk, maybe, unable to do anything but wait until something other than itself moved.

Nu gwa am.

He had climbed up here just after noon, taking the footpath from Uwchmynydd. As he climbed, his eyes took in the sweep of Wales right down to the Pembroke coast, as well as the Irish Sea along the north coast of the Lleyn, a rougher, heavier sea than that off the south coast.

Sean had said he might even see a hint of Ireland if the day was clear enough, but no hint of Ireland was visible. Nor could he see anything of the tip of Trwyn y Gwyddel or Eglwys Lleu.

Erin was sitting where Sean had said she might be sitting as if she were waiting for him to appear. But he didn't think she was doing that. "Hello. Mind if I sit down?"

"Suit yourself."

So he sat, then sat some more, as he wondered how this conversation could begin. First words needed to be good words, and true.

"Do you hate me, for being your brother?"

For those were the truest words he could find. He wondered if she would blow up and storm off somewhere, taking the mountain with her.

"How could I hate you?" she replied, after considering a moment. "For what? You were but three or so when my mother came home carrying us. It's just that I can't think of you as my brother. That's all."

"And what about Dad? Do you hate him?"

"I don't know. Perhaps I'd like to hate him, but I haven't adjusted, as yet, to the idea of having had a real father somewhere in the world." She sat calmly as she spoke. Whether or not she felt calm inside herself, he couldn't tell.

"Maybe I feel the same about suddenly having another sister," he ventured. "We have a cousin in Alberta named Wesley, and it shook him a bit when I bumped into his life. He wanted to know how many other relatives might come wandering through his door because he likes to prepare himself. I guess I didn't give you a chance to do that."

A bittersweet smile touched down upon her mouth. "Indeed, you didn't."

"Erin, would you go to Ireland with me? Please?"

Her eyes started; the smile faded from her mouth and her face shadowed over. "Why do you want to go to Ireland?" So he told her about his talk with Sean. "Oisin," Erin breathed when he had finished.

"Who is Oisin?"

"You, perhaps," she sighed. "And Caitlin, and our mother, once. And who knows, even Uncle Sean, in his own dear way."

"So, tell me about Oisin."

"You should have asked Caitlin. She was the storyteller."

"I know. She told me some stories. We told stories to each other. But I can't ask her about that story."

"No, you can't, can you?" Something flashed up within her as she

335

looked at him, but she pressed it back down as she drew her knees to her breast. "All right, then. Oisin was the son of Finn, when the time of the Fianna was nearly done and a mist lay over Ireland. One morning a woman rode out of the mist from the west, a queen's crown upon her shining hair. She had come she said to give her love to Oisin and take him with her back to Tir-nà-nOg, the Country of the Young—where no mortal ever wasted away, because there was no wasting away of time itself. So Oisin went with her, first to the strand, then out into the sea on the back of his horse until he rode beyond the mist and into Tir-nà-nOg. There he stayed and should have stayed, having ridden there, but he longed after a time to see Finn again. His queen told him he would not find the Ireland he had once left and warned him not to set foot on the soil if he wished to return to her. Oisin rode away on his white horse, rode throughout Ireland, and saw nothing of the land he had known, only waste and nettles. But in the end, he did see a stone trough of the Fianna and forgetting the warning, dismounted to drink from it. He withered in an instant and became an old, old man. The rest of his days he lamented his loss: 'It is long the clouds are over me tonight . . .'"

Then Erin drew in her breath and looked at him. "Why is it we can't let what has been lost alone? When we know for a certainty that it has fully gone? Yet there my mother would stand at the west of Ireland, whenever we went there, as if to see through the mist to some lost and light-filled place beyond. And Caitlin? She flew west of the mist in search of a brighter part of herself and ended up like Oisin, crumpled on the ground. Do you understand what I'm saying? The Tuatha de Danaan have gone into the Sidhe—the ring forts, graves, and fairy mounds—and for a reason. Why can't we just leave them be and let that world go?"

Suddenly vulnerable, her eyes looked back into his. He wanted to look away but did not. "You're also a storyteller. But I'm not Oisin."

"Are you sure about that?"

Her eyes stayed with his as something in them and in her words sliced close to the bone. But he stood his ground. "I'm not Oisin," he reiterated, "though I have a brother-in-law who might be. Anyway, I'm asking you to go with me to Ireland and no farther. Right to the west of Ireland, maybe, but not into the sea."

"Why me?" she persisted. "You're all grown up. You can read a map, and I suspect you know what you want to find. Why do you need me?"

"I'm not sure I do know what I want to find. And I need someone to go with me who is not just anyone."

And now her eyes broke from his and sought out the hump of Bardsey Island. "I can't decide that here and now. I'll think on it and let you know tonight."

Then she left him sitting there.

He looked again to where the hawk had been hovering, but it was gone, and he didn't know if its waiting had come to anything. Unzipping his daypack, he took out a pad of paper then a pen. First, Sean's address at the top of the page, then the date, and then he wrote in earnest:

Dear Margaret,

Forgive me. I was aiming for me but took a shot at you, instead. Not the first time I've done that. I don't know what I knew about Cameron, but it wasn't enough that night to make of it what I did.

A lot has happened since my leaving you, but, yes, we do have a sister somewhere and somewhere is right here in Wales. Her name is Erin. Her twin, Caitlin, was killed a year ago when she and I were occupying a dam site in Alberta. It was all over the news, so you probably know about it. We also have a cousin, Wesley. As he says, just when you think you've run out of relatives, some more turn up. Erin and I may be going to Ireland soon. I don't know what will happen after that. Maybe I'll come back here and figure what to do next.

I love you and Cameron, too.

Your Wandering Brother

He folded the letter and placed it in one of the two envelopes he had already addressed and stamped. Then he began a letter to Anika.

At Uwchmynydd, he dropped both letters into the postbox beside the phone booth and headed back to Trwyn y Gwyddel. On his way down the slope toward Eglwys Lleu, he met Dafydd Jones. "I've brought a mattress for you to spare your back," said Dafydd.

"Thanks," he said, "and tell me, why is Sean camping out in a church?"

"Ah, I was wondering when you might ask."

"What made you think I'd ask?"

"Because you'd need to be blind and dumb not to ask. The authorities are pulling down several churches around here. The one up at Sarn is already gutted out; the roof was falling in they said, and there was no money to keep it and the rest in repair. Sean took on saving Eglwys Lleu by moving in. I put in the little window and the fuel line, and punched a hole through the roof for a chimney. It looks as if Sean'll stay put for a time until he runs out of pew wood to burn."

"I told Sean I'd build him a real smoke hole, like those in our big houses," he chuckled. "Maybe I should make good on that offer."

Dafydd's eyes twinkled. "The chimney hole I made leaks and so does the roof, so I'll hold you to that when you're back from Ireland."

"We may get to it sooner. I don't know if I'm going to Ireland."

"You'll go," said Dafydd. "Hwyl."

After chopping into another pew, he waited with Sean for Erin to return. Eventually she pushed the oaken door open and walked straight to the fire. Squatting down she picked up a stick of pew wood and poked about in the flames with it. "We can catch the early bus out tomorrow," she said, "and make our way to Bangor. We'll take the train from there to the ferry at Holyhead and be in Dublin by evening. I hope you've a pound or two in your pocket. Travelling in Ireland can become a costly business."

"I've a pound or two," he replied. "Thanks."

She nodded but in a way that told him she didn't want any more talk about it.

It rained again that night, but at dawn there was only cloud overhead as the two of them put Eglwys Lleu behind them. He turned, once, to look back at the little stone church and saw it now for what it had become—not the embodiment of a light-filled form that might have hovered here once, but just old stones placed one upon another, worn and grey from the years upon them. That and nothing more.

The morning light was still very young when they reached Aberdaron and the bus stop. Erin dropped her pack to the ground, sat with her back against it, and pulled the hood of her jacket down over her eyes. "Where's the bus?" he asked.

"On its way here, I suppose."

He paced over to the bridge then back. The main street of Aberdaron was empty of people almost, except for one or two bodies that barely seemed awake.

"Maybe it's late."

"It's not late. It's just not here. Go for a walk on the beach, will you, and let me sleep? Or I may change my mind about all of this." So he walked down to the beach, listening for the bus as he went, then gave that up once he was walking along the sand with the sea at his ear. As he turned back, the sun rose up behind him. His eyes followed the high banks that overlooked the beach until they came to a fence post stuck into the earth right at the topmost edge.

A raven sat upon the post, its black wings glistening in a sudden shaft of sun upon them.

FIVE

Dun Laoghaire. The evening light about them was soft yet lucid, and the sky, pink tinged with orange and sheeted over with cloud, as they followed the crowd from the ferry terminal and caught the train into Dublin. After checking in at the youth hostel on Mountjoy Street, they sat in the hostel cafeteria to figure out what would happen next.

"Céad míle fáilte," Erin said. "A hundred thousand welcomes to Ireland, though one is all I need or want. Well, I suppose you want to get down to sussing out passage graves and dolmens, preferably ones that are dark and filled with secrets."

"Why not?" he grinned, almost liking the sweet barbs in her words. "Where do we start?"

"Newgrange, perhaps. Just to say you've been there if for no other reason. The line-up shouldn't be that bad now that it's September and most other seekers of secrets have returned to their ordinary lives. Can we afford a car for a day or two?"

They decided they could, and Erin made the call to secure one for the next day.

He went to bed early that night, fell into a deep sleep, and awoke with a start into an after-midnight darkness, nearly cracking his head against the bottom of the bunk above his. The cry sounded again from the street below the half-opened window next to his bunk, assaulting the brick walls of the hostel. Rage, pain, then more intense rage filled that voice, as if a hand at the throat were choking it back then releasing its grip suddenly so that ferocity of the rage and pain became the greater for their having been choked back. There were words as well, words the voice cried to someone who had been there and gone, or who had never appeared at all, words cursing the very name they cried for. But it was the rage and the pain that he heard.

It was not the first time such a cry had awakened him. About a year before Old Man Williams died, he had come awake in his bed at Duxsowlas. The party up at Ed William's had ended, or maybe Amy had simply kicked Ed out. In any event, Ed began to rage up and down the village, starting at Sadie's and ending up on the Jacobs' porch steps. Ed sat on the steps, cursed Amy, then Isaac and Edith, then Uncle Charlie, then Adha, and the darkness and light themselves, along with the world that stumbled stupidly from one to the other. Well through the night until nearly morning, Ed had raged and cried.

Lying in his bed then and listening, he had wondered why neither Isaac nor Edith left their beds and told Ed to get the hell off the porch and go home. Now as he lay and listened again to the cry that tore the night open, years and miles from Duxsowlas, he understood why his parents had left Ed to his rage and his pain.

Some hostellers were up and gone by the time he awoke the next morning, while others lay sleeping. Erin and he ate the breakfast of juice, rolls, and coffee that went with the cost of the bed, waited around the hostel until noon, then left to pick up the car. He followed her along Mountjoy Street to Blessington, then down Frederick to Parnell Square. As they walked past an opened set of iron gates, he glanced through, first at the cross-shaped pool that centred the space inside the gates, then toward the large sculpture standing before a white marble wall at the far end of the square. "What is that?" he asked, as he stopped for another look.

"The Children of Lir in the Garden of Remembrance," Erin answered, walking on. "A monument to the Easter Uprising of 1916."

"There'd be a story, then, relating to it?"

"Yes, there would be. There's always a story here relating anything to everything or to nothing," she replied, as they crossed a street and kept on walking. He said nothing more but made a note of the square and where it was in relation to the hostel.

They continued along what now was O'Connell Street, a street more crowded than those along which they had walked. As people strolled past them, he could recognize the German words or accents, something that might be Dutch, then voices speaking in Italian. Those who lived in Dublin threaded their way through the visitors and went about their lives that day, or lounged with their backs against the walls of the shops and buildings, the better to look the visitors over. Erin clutched her daypack more closely to her, and he could feel his hand tightening upon his packstrap. Then they walked past a large plate glass window before which a knot of people stood, gazing through the glass.

He stopped and this time he did not move on. Eventually, Erin turned about, walked back, and stood beside him.

"So that's Cuchulain," he said, looking at the bronze sculpture that stood just behind the glass in the General Post Office. Cuchulain's body slumped to his left, his head now a leaden weight against the left shoulder from which an arm dangled down to the shield the hand no longer grasped, though the shield was still strapped to his wrist. The right hand clutched limply at Cuchulain's sword, and his legs were about to buckle out from under the body kept upright only by the strap around the rock at its back.

Raven perched on Cuchulain's right shoulder with the right leg forward, his eyes staring into a distance far from where the talons gripped firmly at Cuchulain's skin. The expression on Raven's face almost mirrored the face that looked into a similar distance from atop the clamshell thousands of miles to the west: "Well, that's another one gone. Too bad . . ."

He glanced at Erin and caught the little smile that played at her mouth. "Another one of Caitlin's stories?"

He nodded. "Poor Cuchulain, dead in the Dublin General Post Office, was how she put it."

"Not dead," Erin said. "Not yet. Just dying."

"He looks pretty dead to me," he observed.

"Almost, but it wasn't until the raven settled on his shoulder that the men with their swords knew it was all up with Cuchulain. It was then that Lugaid struck Cuchulain's head from his shoulders and the hero light faded away from about it."

"So it was Raven that let them know Cuchulain's light was coming to an end?"

"Yes, if you want it that way. The raven's landing was the tip-off. The Goddess Morrigan as the Raven of Battle."

His eyebrows lifted as he glanced down at the words set into the base of the sculpture, then the seven names below the words. "The leaders of the 1916 Uprising," Erin said. "The post office was one of their main strongholds until the British shelled it." Her voice sounding a different note again. Where the hell is she coming from? he wondered.

They picked up the car at the rental office just off O'Connell Street. Erin sat herself behind the wheel and he sat beside her, after he had figured the side of the car in which he was supposed to be sitting.

The haze that had settled down upon Dublin stayed with them until they were well north of the city on the road to Slane. Beyond the haze, green fields and their stone walls stood out in the light of a clear day. They crossed the Boyne and turned east into Brugh na Bóinne, the valley of the Boyne. A few more turnings in the road, and they pulled up at Newgrange behind a large touring bus. "Thank God, there's only one," Erin said, as they bought their tickets, then pushed through the wooden gate to join the next party on its way into the tumulus. "You can stand here for hours during the summer and think this might be where you'll crumple up and die, by the time you're through the entrance."

Massive and walled up with white quartz all around, and grassed over on top, the mound of Newgrange made a striking impression as they walked toward it. Their guide gathered all of them around her, said her introductory words, telling them Newgrange was five hundred years older than the pyramids, then led them inside and went on talking. She told them the interior of the tumulus was cruciform in shape but that didn't mean anything, then cast them into darkness for a simulation of the sun shining through the roofbox above the entrance way on the day of the winter solstice. She turned the lights back on, gave them a few minutes more to look around, then escorted them outside.

It was over and done in twenty minutes. "That was short and sweet," Erin said. But he was studying the entrance stone that had received but a passing glance from him on their way in. Erin stood beside him as he puzzled over the spirals that curved into and out from one another. Then he took note of the straight line etched downward from the top part of the stone, just left of the midway point. "What's that about?" he asked.

"Use your eyes. The spirals change direction when they cross over that line. See, the ones to the left spiral inward in a clockwise direction, and the ones to the right spiral outward clockwise, marking the changing direction of the sun at winter solstice. That's one of the wisdoms about it, anyways."

Bending down, he looked more closely. Cross the line and the spirals to the left become their own mirror images on the right. He focused in on a particular spiral to the left, then another on the right, to ensure that he was truly seeing what he had just glimpsed. He straightened up and sought out the roofbox above the entrance to the tumulus. "She said they may have built this especially to catch the sun at winter solstice."

"Uncle Sean also said something about that, once," said Erin. "Newgrange and Cairn T, only Cairn T lets the sun in at the equinoxes."

"And where's Cairn T?"

"At Longcrew near Kells. We could overnight in Kells and go there tomorrow. In fact, we're less than two weeks from the equinox and we might even catch something of the sun on the back stone, if we're early enough. That should excite you."

"Maybe it would. Let's find out."

Several hours later, they stood before the Tower Cross in the Church of Ireland yard right in the middle of Kells. They had wandered into there on their way back to the hostel and now gazed up at the east face of the cross. Seven half-spheres clustered together at its centre where the shafts from the head and arms met, and the centre itself was encircled by a ring of stone that brought head, arms, and the downward shaft of the cross into a whole. His eye ran down the cross, making out the stories in stone that followed one upon another, stories worn down over the centuries yet still able to speak. The fall of Adam and Eve, maybe, above the intricate knotwork at the very bottom. The left arm held what might be the sacrifice of Isaac, and he spent a long moment looking at it, before his eyes crossed over to the right arm. Two men, with a bird hovering between them.

"St. Paul of Thebes and St. Anthony, if I have my stories straight," Erin said, anticipating his question. "And that would be a raven giving them bread from heaven."

He started to laugh.

"What's so funny?"

"Him. This really is another side of him. The Raven I've known would have eaten that bread up as soon as he cleared the gates of paradise. Those two would have been lucky to get a crumb between them, let alone a whole loaf. How did they go about making these crosses?"

"With much sweat and blood, I would think," she replied. "First, they had to cut out the sandstone, or granite, where there was no sandstone, and then bring the rough stone to the place where the cross was to be erected. Then the carver would smooth the surface down with an adze."

"Until the master carver was satisfied the stone was ready to become a cross," he continued. "Then the master carver would sketch in the stories and the knotwork, maybe letting an apprentice do some of the initial carving. When it came to the finer details, the master would take over, always keeping his chisels sharp. Then, when the cross was to be erected, the community from round about would come and raise the cross with a ceremony of some kind."

Erin stared at him. "Go on," he urged.

"Why should I, if you know so much about it? And how do you come to know so much?"

"Because that's how our carvers worked on our totem poles, and these are your totem poles," he said. He walked over to another high cross, part of which was broken away. Along the east face braids, knots, mazes, and spirals formed patterns of interlocking lines and curves, each pattern wanting to affirm its kinship with the others.

"Everything is related," he murmured.

"What in the name of God are you muttering about?" Erin asked, hands on her hips. But he left her there and walked over to a cross that stood nearer the church itself. From the centre of the east face, Christ opened out his arms to the world. The west face, however, was completely blank with only blocked out panels suggesting an intent to carve them. Nor had the north arm of the east face been carved, or the shaft of the cross, or the south and north sides of the shaft. He walked about the cross again and wondered what had been envisioned, once, and by whom, and why the vision had died before it left the carver's hand, for the blank panels could not speak for themselves. Or perhaps the vision itself had never fully formed? Like the last stretch of a pole left unfinished in their father's shed at Duxsowlas.

Then he saw that the church yard was fast becoming dark and that Erin's patience was wearing thin.

The next morning, they awoke well before sunrise, made coffee and ate some bread rolls, then set out for the Longcrew Hills—Slieve na Calliagh, the Hill of the Witches, as Erin called it. Within an hour's drive and under a clear sky, she turned into a narrow road that ran up a hill and stopped before a house. "I'd almost forgotten about the key," she said.

"What key?" he asked.

"The key we need to let ourselves into the tumulus. The key I'll have to wake this man up for if we're to have it."

"It's a bit early to wake up anyone," he ventured..

"It is. But that's what I'm about to do. If I'm not back soon, very soon, you'll know this wasn't the best of ideas."

Five minutes later, Erin climbed into the car, key in hand. "What did the man say?" he asked.

"Nothing much I could quote. It was all in Irish. Rough-and-ready Irish."

The car bumped up the narrow road as Erin gunned the motor and turned with the curves until they came to a parking area, near a gate that led onto a hillside heavy with sheep. The sheep scattered as they climbed Slieve na Calliagh, and then Cairn T emerged as the top of the hill appeared. Perhaps it, too, had been stoned together with white quartz once, but now Cairn T was a mass of loose grey stones held in place by the limiting wall that encircled it. Erin headed off to the left, while he, without realizing why at first, started around to the right, countering the visible movement of the sun.

"Where are you going?" she called.

"Making sure I go inside the way I should," he called back.

"Jesus!" she exclaimed, threw up her hands, then followed after him.

He completed his three circuits and stood at the entrance, looking through the black bars of the gate that would not let him go farther. Erin walked up and handed him the key. The dawn light sharpened along a hill to the east as the sun made ready to rise. They hadn't arrived any too soon. He reached for the brass padlock that appeared to be securing the iron gate, but the key wouldn't go in. He tried again, then again;the key refused to fit. He looked helplessly at Erin. Erin cursed under her breath, then said, "All right, I'll run down, drive down, and try to put it right. Tell the sun to hold off, if you can."

Then she was gone. He stared through the bars into the tumulus, still dark within, though he could make out a sillstone where the passage from without reached the central chamber and then another sillstone where the head chamber began. At the back of the head chamber was a stone covered with symbols, petroglyphs not discernible as yet, yet which seemed to be like the pictographs he had once seen in the Stein Valley.

The light about Cairn T brightened the more and then the sun rose. Instinctively, he stepped to one side of the entrance, dropped to his knees and peered through the bars as the sun's first rays swept past him into the tumulus. The light lengthened right to the backstone, taking in the top portion of the sillstone just before the head chamber. Upon the backstone itself, a rectangle of light exposed a humanlike figure to the far left, then two ladder forms, two sun symbols maybe, then the lower part of an eight-petalled flower with a circle about it. The sun's ray shifted to the right as the rectangle began to shrink, moved right again, then more to the right, and the rectangle went on shrinking until it lit only upon an encircled six-petalled flower. The rectangle shrank to a small square, a speck of light, then a dot.

By the time Erin finished her run up the hill, the light had vanished from the backstone altogether and moved to the standing stone at the northwest angle of the central chamber.

"No luck," she puffed. "Either he left when we did or he went back to bed and that was it. I should have booted this key back through the mail slot for all the use it is to us."

But he barely heard her because his eyes had seen something on the other side of the iron bars. Reaching through them, he dropped his hand down until his fingers closed about a second lock, as black as the iron of the gate and tucked away inside it.

"May I have the key, please?" He took it from Erin, slipped it into the lock, and gave it a turn.

"I suggest," said Erin, as he gazed at the lock in his hand, "that while you're looking for whatever it is you're looking for, you make some use of the light that's right here." She turned and walked down the hill toward a cluster of stones to the east. He watched her go, then pushed the iron gate open.

Half-crouching, he crept along the passage and over the sillstone until he could half-stand inside the central chamber. Then he knelt before the sillstone at the head chamber and gazed at the backstone. Rich in pictures, the stone drew his eyes along its surface to eight-petalled flower suns, an eleven-petalled sun, as well as the six-petalled sun where the last finger of the sun from without had touched before withdrawing. There were the ladder forms as well, and the petalled human form, along with jags of lightning and what looked like two nests of bowls or crescent moons, out of reach, it seemed, of the sun's path along the backstone.

His eyes full of what they had tried to take in, he sat back against the northwest angle stone and surveyed the central chamber, the sting of Erin's words still with him. So, what was he looking for? The light before Raven's world? That was the idea that had seized him when he and Sean had talked as they sat together at Braich y Pwll. But what was he actually seeing, here and now?

He ran his eyes along the corbelled stones above his head, then along the standing stones supporting them. The corbelled ceiling at Newgrange had towered over him on a grand scale, whereas Cairn T was much smaller, more intimate and wonderfully balanced with its three chambers at the head and arms and the four supporting stones at the northeast, northwest, southeast, and southwest, along with the sillstones at each of the chamber entrances and the entrance from the passage way.

And all for the sake of letting the daylight in, a little at a time, at certain seasons of the year? That thought nagged at him as he looked again at the backstone, and then pulled a postcard from his jacket pocket. The postcard pictured a three-fold spiral he had glimpsed on a standing stone in the head chamber at Newgrange. The Tri-spiral, it was called. All three spirals moved in the same direction—with the visible sun as they wound into their centres, and counter to its movement on their way out. He was struck by where it had been placed in Newgrange, not on a stone facing east, from where the light entered the tumulus, but on a wall in the head chamber facing west. Which meant that the sun could touch that symbol only if the backstone of the head chamber at Newgrange were torn away to let in the sun from the west . . .

After sitting for he didn't know how long, he put the card back in his pocket, stood, crouched, then replaced the lock. Pocketing the key, he went to look for Erin.

They walked down the Hill of the Witches to their car. As he opened his door, he turned to her and asked, "Did you see that other lock, before you went down to get another key?" He knew it was a cruel question as well as a stupid one, and regretted having asked it as soon as the words were out. Erin's eyes iced over. "If I had noticed, for sure I wouldn't tell you now."

The day grew hot and sticky as they drove back to Dublin, even though it was mid-September. He could feel the heat building toward the kind of thunderstorm that could cloud over a sultry day on the Canadian prairies then split it wide apart moments later. Maybe storms in Ireland didn't work like that, but if so, a big one was putting itself together out there in those powder blue-grey clouds to the west.

Erin drove in silence, except when she cursed under her breath at the traffic going into Dublin and at the two accidents that kept the engine turning over while the wheels went nowhere.

It was well into the evening by the time they returned the car, then found a pub off O'Connell Street. Two fiddlers, a guitar player, an accordion player, and a bodhran player very much at the end of their season played gamely to a pub filled with ears that could have cared less. They sat at a table towards the back, ordered something to eat and a pint of plain each. After they had eaten, Erin ordered another round, and another.

It had been a long time since he had done this kind of drinking, he realized. A few parties in high school, a few times when at SFU, but not that often. The memory of Edith cracking ketchup bottles open on their sink at home and of Ed Williams on the rampage had woven too tight a net about him for him to feel good about letting alcohol take any liberties with his life. But he felt compelled to stay with Erin and wondered where that was going to take them.

"Dia dhuit." The voice came from the table next to theirs. The two men looked as if they had been there for some time, though he hadn't noticed them until now. He looked at Erin for a translation, but she kept her eyes focused in the direction of the band.

"It means, God be with you," the one who had spoken said. "And you reply with, Dias Muire dhuit. God and Mary be with you. Now, where would you be from?"

"The west coast of Canada," he answered, sipping at the pint in his hand.

"You look like a red Indian," said the other man, suddenly. "Like the ones in the movies."

"You and your red Indian movies, O'Doud! You're leaping to conclusions and you've too long a face on you tonight," laughed the first man

"As a matter of fact, I am a red Indian," he said, setting his pint down and interested in what his candour would bring.

"I told you, Dennis!" O'Doud blurted out, as if he were deciding whether he would defend his scalp or his pint. "And would you be one of those Sioux?"

"You're a discerning person. I am part Sioux." He caught the eye of the man called Dennis, and Dennis started to smile.

"One of those Sioux that did Custer down and all the Irishmen with him," O'Doud pressed, making as if to attack while retreating.

"Right again. My great-grandfather was among the Sioux who fought Custer. But one of your Irishmen killed him before he fired a shot. Besides, it's the first time I've heard about Irishmen being there at all."

"It was so," Dennis observed. "The Seventh Cavalry was salted and peppered with Irishmen."

"Miles Keogh was Irish and a Carlow man," O'Doud glowered. "It was a bloody sad day when the Sioux did him down."

"O'Doud's a Carlow man, one or two lifetimes back, so he looks out for his own," said Dennis.

He toyed with his now empty pint. "Who knows? Maybe I was an Irishman, one or two lifetimes back, and your friend here was a red Indian."

O'Doud snorted and Dennis laughed. "Now that would raise the wick of history, wouldn't it?" he said, and then looked over at Erin. "And what about you? Are you from Canada, as well?"

Erin ignored the question and him, and Dennis let it go. O'Doud, however, was too drunk to let anything go. "For certain, you're also one of those Sioux."

"And Slán leat to you!" she snapped.

Dennis laughed again. "Do you hear that, O'Doud? Go for a piss, will you, and clear out your head."

"No pissing now, Dennis; this is serious!" O'Doud exclaimed. "There are two Sioux sitting beside us and one of them is speaking Irish."

Erin's gaze swung about, riveting in upon O'Doud. "It seems I am one of your Sioux. So was my sister. Finding that out bloody fucking killed her!" She kicked her chair back from the table and was out the door of the pub before any one of them could blink. By the time he was out the door, the storm building overhead had broken wide open and rain poured down upon him. There was no sign of Erin.

He made his way up O'Connell Street, past the walkers that had taken shelter from the rain against the sides of buildings, in shop doorways, or under an awning. Swathed about by the night, Cuchulain's dying body gleamed out at him from behind the window of the General Post Office, though Raven was completely swallowed by shadow.

O'Connell Street became Parnell Square, then Frederick, then bent to the left to become Blessington. He turned onto Mountjoy Street and his feet came to a stop outside the hostel. He was about to go inside to look for her, then knew that she wasn't there and that she would be all right. Like Cuchulain, Erin was into her warp-spasm, and he wouldn't give one or a hundred Irish pounds for the life of anyone who laid a hand on her right now. He brushed a puddle of water from the hostel steps and sat.

The rain withered to a drizzle, then stopped altogether. Now there was only the drip, dropping of water from the angles and corners of the hostel down onto the sidewalk. Two hostellers walked up, rang the bell beside the door, and waited until the responding buzz told them they could enter. Then there was no one else on Mountjoy Street.

He let his head rest against the wall. Closing his eyes, he went back through the events of the day, starting with the pub, then the drive back from Cairn T, then the time at Cairn T itself. When he opened his eyes, he saw a familiar form walking along Mountjoy Street. He stayed sitting until Erin had walked right up to the hostel steps.

"What are you sitting around for?"

"Waiting for you."

"How lovely! The gallant knight waits for his lady to favour his favours."

"I'm not asking for favours. I just want you to know the truth."

"And what is this truth you want to favour me with?"

"That you are my sister and I was Caitlin's brother, and all of us had the same father. She died knowing that. And I knew it, too, though I couldn't get at what I knew."

"You knew nothing of her!"

He sprang to his feet, his eyes blazing back into hers. "Yes, I did! Maybe things you didn't know about Caitlin and didn't care to know. She was ready to find out who she was."

"You go to hell!"

"No, you go to hell, Erin! If that's what it takes to slap some life back into you."

She swung at him, but he stepped aside, catching hold of her hand then releasing it. She was crying now and so was he.

"You killed Caitlin, damn you!" The words sobbed past the fury and pain that glazed her eyes over. "You killed my sister!"

He drew his breath in. "No, I did not kill my sister. She chose to be there. And that's the truth, Erin."

Their faces inches apart, their eyes stayed locked together some seconds more. Then their thumbs jammed the doorbell back against the stone wall.

He was awakened by the voices of the two Americans, the only ones left in the dorm midway into the morning other than himself.

"God, what a night! Did you hear those two screaming at one another?"

"Tell me about it. The night before, one drunk on the street; last night, two drunks on the street. I'm glad we'll be somewhere else tonight. Give me New York any day."

He dressed, shaved, went downstairs for coffee and something to eat, and waited for Erin to show up. Then he gave up waiting. Sometime after noon, he walked in the direction of O'Connell Street and let his feet take him where they would.

His feet took him to Parnell Square and through the gate of the Garden of Remembrance. The cross-shaped pool had been drained for cleaning and the blue-green tiles showed clearly their patterns of old Celtic weapons. He walked down the steps, alongside the pool, and up another set of steps toward the white marble wall and the sculpture before it standing in an oval pool of its own.

The Children of Lir, whoever they had been. Three of the enormous human figures cast in bronze were right at the front of the sculpture, while a fourth was hidden away behind the three. The body of the boy to his right, nearly prone and lifeless, was about to splash down into the water. A swan was rising up from between his shoulder blades.

The boy in front of him was in the act of falling. His arms reached out toward the water, his head dropped downward, taking the rest of him with it. A swan was taking wing from between his shoulder blades.

Their sister, to the left, had begun to fall. Her eyes only now had closed and her arms had just gone limp from her shoulders while her body turned toward the direction in which it would plunge. A swan was giving birth to itself from between her shoulder blades.

But it was the figure hidden behind the other three that fascinated him. He started to walk around the pool to the right, making a counterclockwise turn as he went—as if he were about to emerge from behind the Tlaamelas onto the floor of the big house or vanish from the big house floor into the world behind the Tlaamelas.

The third brother was not yet falling. His left arm reached up from his shoulders and his left hand seemed about to grasp hold of the tail feathers of the swan rising out of his right wrist. The boy's face was concentrated fully upon the swan and barely visible.

He walked around the back of the pool to the poem set into the marble at the wall's south end. His eyes scanned the opening line of the Gaelic, then found its English counterpart:

i ndorchacht an éadóehais´ rinneadh aisling dúinn . . .

In the darkness of despair we saw a vision. We lit the light of hope and it was not extinguished . . .

His feet took him around the sculpture a second time. The sister beginning to fall . . . the brother falling . . . the brother nearly fallen, the beak of the swan rising out of him opened wide. A cry of release? Triumph? What?

And then the brother not yet falling. He seemed to be winning his battle to stay upright, if one looked at him face on. Seen from behind, however, the hand wanting to pull the swan down to earth was itself at the point of dropping earthward.

Transforming, all four of them. But out of what and into what? He glanced past the figures at the front of the pool and saw Erin standing before them. She looked back at him, then walked to where the poem was written into the wall and where the wall curved forward to become a marble seat. He walked over and sat beside her. "What's their story?" he asked.

"Lir's wife died, and Aoife became the stepmother of Lir's daughter and three sons," Erin began, without preliminary. "Out of jealousy, Aoife took the children to Loch Dairbheach, the Lake of Oaks, and changed them into swans, leaving only their human voices, the music of the Sidhe, and their noble selves to them. Nine hundred years they spent on the world's waters—three hundred on Loch Dairbheach, three hundred on the seas between Ireland and Britain, and three hundred on the Bay of Domnann. At the end, their skins fell away and they were nothing but three withered old men and a withered old woman. They were baptized and they died. End of story."

He stood and read the poem through again:

> We sent our vision aswim like a swan on the river. The vision became a reality. Winter became summer. Bondage became freedom . . .

Turning about, he stared long at the sculpture. Not swans of bondage, here and now, but swans of freedom—"They've turned the story inside out and stood it on its head!" he exclaimed, his mind's eye remembering the change of direction in the spirals at Newgrange as they crossed over that line . . . past the Tlaamelas? . . . through the Xhaaidla? Everything turning itself inside out as it crossed . . . the darkness to light—or the light to darkness?

"So it would seem," Erin said. "It's a very Irish way to take something up, standing it on its head."

They fell silent. "Where do we go from here?" he asked, when he had tired of just sitting. For all he knew, she might be ready to go back to Wales.

"There's a dolmen south of here, near Piltown. Leac an Scáil, it's called. The Stone of the Shadow; another of Uncle Sean's finds. You can spend time crawling about in it, if you like. Then we could make our way west."

"And how do we get there?"

"I've snagged a couple of bikes. We can throw them underneath Bus Eireann when we get tired of pedalling."

He wanted to thank her, but it was clear she didn't want any of that. "Then I guess we might as well get going," he said, giving the Children of Lir a last look.

"We might as well, indeed," Erin replied.

SIX

Leac an Scáil . . . the Stone of the Shadow.

"Up the road a bit more, then go where the sign points. At the edge of a field," the man on the tractor said. "You're nearly to it."

Erin led the way along the narrow road, the sides of it thick with trees and lined with fences. Hidden by the trees that had grown around it, the dolmen did not reveal itself until they had almost walked right up to it. Then Erin gasped and so did he. As if the forward standing stones had erupted up from the earth and the capstone had been dropped down on top of them from some great height, the Stone of the Shadow towered above their heads.

Leac an Scáil was almost a double-dolmen. A smaller capstone extended itself horizontally over some smaller standing stones, teetering almost precariously upon one stone at its south end. That capstone, however, was held in place by the great capstone that angled up from it to reach, then overreach the tall standing stones at the front of the dolmen.

He leaned his bike against a tree, did his walkabout, and then squeezed his body into the chamber made by the horizontal capstone. Erin didn't follow him inside, though she crouched down and peered into the space where he sat. A few moments passed and he neither saw nor felt anything of significance. So he crawled out of the dolmen and looked about him.

To the west was a field filled with ragwort. To the east lay a field bordered by a wood and wire fence, while trees crowded in from the north and west, trees that would not have been there when the dolmen had been erected. A wind touched down into the trees and the clouds brooding overhead parted to let the light from the south fall upon the great capstone.

He walked around to the north end. Erin stood beside him, looking with him at the standing stones supporting the overreach of the capstone. The two at either side pushed their ends forward and another stone behind spread itself between them, while the overreach of the capstone completed the enclosed space. "That's almost a chamber in itself," he said, "and that's where something might have happened."

"Such as?" She folded her arms and waited for him to make himself clear.

So he told her what Sean had told him about a dolmen holding the daylight back, yet letting another kind of light shine through the capstone. "In the summer, when the sun is as high as it would have been when Sean and Dad were in the dolmen in France, this stone would throw a deep shadow right down into this front chamber and even beyond it, and cut the daylight right out."

"And then?"

"Then maybe someone standing here would have seen the light Sean and Dad saw in that dolmen."

Erin chewed the words over. "That's Uncle Sean, sure enough," she mused, "but you're also chasing some idea of your own or perhaps its chasing you and will start chasing me if I let it. But if you're on the track of these dolmens as a way of shutting the daylight right out, for whatever reason, wouldn't it have made sense for them to have blocked the daylight out altogether by covering this over?"

He stood in silence and didn't answer her. Somewhere across the field a dog barked, and then they heard the lowing of cattle from a nearby farm. The Stone of the Shadow, in turn, kept to its own silence.

An tIarthar . . . the West.

Bus Eireann cruised along beneath branches of oak and beech that arched themselves together from either side of the road, making the road a tunnel of greening shadow laced with shafts of light.

He straightened up and looked out the window toward the Blackwater Valley to the south—a green meadow, a line of trees, then more meadow, and then the land thick with trees and rising. Above all of that a black speck soared. There was little hint of a wind, yet the black speck had found something way up there that it could ride as its wings spread wide, then closed in, suddenly: "Ghe-la-kasla," he half-whispered.

"What is that about?" Erin asked.

"Just greeting an old friend."

"Ghe-la-kasla," she repeated.

"It's Kwakwala. It means . . ." and then he thought about what it could mean. "Hello-from-the-heart. That's pretty close, anyway."

Erin nodded and looked out the window again, but the black speck could no longer be seen.

"What did that man in the pub, Dennis, say to me?" It was the first time he had spoken anything about that evening.

"Dia dhuit. It means, God be with you."

He tried to sound the words out and she spoke them again. "Dee-a-gwitch. And the reply is Dee-as-Muir-a-gwitch. Or close enough, as you would say. If you want to practise some Gaelic, the Dingle is as good a place as any. Get a few words right and a drunken Irishman might think you belong here despite your looks."

He leaned back in his seat. "Funny you should say that. Because if you walked off the plane and into Duxsowlas, people might think you were someone coming home for a visit. Until you opened your mouth. But if you kept it shut, put a few more years on you, and changed the colour of your eyes, you might even pass as Margaret."

Erin flashed a glance at him. "And who is Margaret?"

"Our sister," he replied, deciding there was no more point in treading delicately around the bush. "She left Duxsowlas when she was seventeen, for what she decided were good reasons, and she's never gone back. Which is all right, I guess, only she's cut herself off from something of herself."

Erin drew back, then looked right into him. "And when did you leave that village?"

He heard the hesitation in his voice. "When I was fourteen."

"And have you been back?"

"No," he said.

"Then why don't you look to rowing your boat instead of rocking mine."

Now he flashed a glance at her, but her head was fast against the seatback, and she had closed her eyes.

An Daingean . . . the Dingle.

He dismounted from his bike, again, and wheeled it up the corkscrew of a road into the mist that rolled over the mountains all around them and into the boulder-strewn valley to the south with its lakes thrown down beside one another. The whole of it looked thrown together, as if some creator pressed for time had said to another creator, Where can I dump this? And that other creator had said, I know the very place.

Stopping yet again, he sucked the air into his lungs. To the northwest, Brandon Mountain thrust its height up into granite-laden slopes and lifted them steadily through the mist toward its peak. Bleak, yet beautiful. Like what he'd seen of Erin's soul thus far.

He looked up the road. She too had dismounted but had kept on climbing and had vanished into the mist that grew thicker by the moment. However, when he reached what he hoped was the summit, she was waiting for him.

"You're good at picking interesting routes," he puffed, as he wheeled up to her. "You should go to work as a tourist guide."

"I'll keep that in mind."

"So, where are we?"

"Connor Pass, the highest in Ireland. 1,500 feet; 456 metres. You can have it either way, as with much else here. The town of Dingle is down at the bottom, where I'll meet you. If you make it. Slán agat."

Then she was onto her bike and off into the mist, hurtling herself downward into the curving of the road. What the hell is this about? he asked himself as he sped after her. Then that question and all thought blew right out the back of his head as the road down from Connor Pass took charge. Faces of rock swept past, and the mist became a single sheet of white streaming up at him from the southern flank of the Dingle. The bike went whizzing about a curve to the left, another to the right, then continued to curve down and around wherever the road curved, whenever the road curved, and he gave up figuring out which side of the road he was on.

The mist thinned, thickened, and thinned again, then a last thickening before the mist came apart right at the tip of his nose and the sun struck him nearly blind. He braked, braked the more, then again, and finally rolled to a stop beside Erin just outside of Dingle town.

Erin leaned over the handlebars, breathing hard. "What was that about?" he asked when he had his breath back. She lifted her head, to let the sun warm her face. "Caitlin and I made this trip once, when we were fifteen, on bikes. We came to the top of the pass, and she dared me to do what we just did. But I didn't take her up on it. I've wondered ever since what it would have been like if I had."

He laughed. "Well, you can stop wondering. Are we going to do that kind of thing again? I'd just like to be ready for it, that's all."

"No," said Erin. "No, I don't think we'll do that kind of thing again."

They rode through Dingle town, on to Milltown, then took the road that led toward Ballydavid Head, even though Erin had said the hostel they wanted to find was out on Slea Head to the west. But the day was holding itself warm and clear, and the sun would set in its own good time. She seemed in no mood to hurry, and neither was he.

At the town of Ballydavid, they came upon a beach where three men winched their big speedboat up onto a trailer. Just beyond them, a family—father, mother, and two children—were climbing into a curragh. Once the children had taken their places, the father and mother, one seated behind the other, lifted their sets of oars free and slipped lightly over the first of the swells that came to meet them.

"I've never seen oars like that," he said. "Nothing but straight sticks all the way to the end of them. There's no blade at all."

"It's all in how you take to the sea and the timing of it," Erin replied. "And little to do with just pulling and pushing at the water with your oars."

At the western edge of the town, they found a path along the cliff that Erin remembered. Long grass parted as the path meandered along, adroitly skirting the places where the cliff simply dropped away into the Atlantic. After a time, they came upon a place where the cliff extended a little farther out and made a level plane of long grass back to the fence line. Dropping her bike down, Erin sat close to the cliff edge, and he sat beside her.

To the north, Ballydavid Head reached out into the indigo waters of the Atlantic. Opposite them, across a stretch of water, stood the peaks called the Three Sisters, one rising up behind the other until the last of them peered down at the passing swells. Only days away from the equinox, the sun lingered in its setting, glowing gold becoming a vibrant orange as if to hold to itself the last hours of summer.

It was Erin who broke the silence. "Why did Margaret leave Duxsowlas?"

He was chewing at a blade of grass when she put the question. Drawing it from his teeth, he tossed it aside. "Sexual abuse that was going on in the village. She saw it going on but didn't think anyone else cared enough to see. One afternoon she confronted my mom about it and didn't hear what she wanted to hear. So she left and eventually moved to Vancouver. My counsellor tracked her down after I had been in a group home there for a few months. She'd married a man who teaches history at one of the universities. A good man, only something in him wants to become an Indian and something in her doesn't want to be an Indian. So that's made life tough for both of them."

"How well did you know my mother when she was there?"

He reached for another blade of grass and plucked it free. "Well, as you put it once, I was only three, though closer to four by then. I remember the way she spoke, something like Caitlin's voice, and yours. Something like the way the sea here rises and falls, and goes in and out of itself, especially off the Lleyn. And I remember a circle game she used to play, with the grade one and two kids usually, but sometimes she would let us play with them."

"What was the game?" she asked, her voice knotting up all of a sudden.

"It went in a circle and there was a song to it: 'Water, water, wallflower, growing up so high'. . ."

"'We are all God's children and we all must die,'" Erin sang, as the sun went from orange to the edge of red. "Yes, I know that game. Mother would do it with the two of us and our friends, sometimes. Caitlin loved it and was into the circle like a flash, every time. I always held back, and she had to pull me in."

His eyes sought hers. "Yes, it was that way for me one time. I didn't want to go into the circle, but Naomi—she pulled me right into it, then she went to the centre and your mother sang, 'Except for little Naomi, the fairest of us all . . . She can dance, she can sing, she can wear a wedding ring'. . ."

His voice fell away, like the cliff face just feet away from them. He didn't tell her who Naomi was and she didn't ask.

Down in the water below, a curragh bobbed up and down while a fisherman hauled in one of his nets. "Do they ever fall out of those?" he asked, matter-of-factly, as if they had been speaking of nothing else.

"Yes; they fall out. Not often, but there's always that one wave out there waiting its turn, and when it does come in to meet the cliffs, it will reach into the boat to take a life with it."

"They must be good swimmers."

She laughed. "Not a bit of it. No seaman along this coast learns to swim. If you fall into these waters, it's more sensible to drown and be done with it."

He looked long at the curragh and at the fisherman hauling at the net. "That's how Dad died," he said. "When a wave reached into his boat."

Then he felt her eyes telling his to go on. Tell me, please, without making me ask.

So he told her of the very special girl who had once pulled him into her mother's circle game, and the girl's father, the village abuser . . . their father, standing on the beach and saying, 'I'll take him out, if none of you will' . . . the long wait throughout the day as the wind and waves told him not to hope, then walking into his uncle's house that night, and the question he had refused to ask: the question, he called it now . . . then going up the river in their father's boat, the eagles screaming into the sun as the last bullet cleared the muzzle of the rifle . . . the air crashing about him with a sound that wouldn't stop, then did, leaving only the falling of the feathers and the red eye-socket of the raven . . . and the long night beneath the vacant stare of the moon . . .

"And then I left." He lay back into the long grass. The sun had become a thin red coin slipping through a layer of cloud at the horizon, and he watched it until it set.

"Maybe we should look for that hostel," he said, after a time.

"It's too late to look for that hostel. But we can find a bed and breakfast."

"Let's save a pound or two and sleep out tonight, right here."

Erin tested out the long grass beneath her back. "All right," she said. "Why not?"

The following morning both of them knew why not. His back groaned as he rolled out of his sleeping bag, and she looked as if her insides were moving in a funny way. He watched as she dug into her pack, then went along the cliff until she disappeared for a brief time.

Another clear day and very warm. Hedges of fuchsia lined the roads of the Dingle, and the red-belled blossoms with their touch of deep purple underneath were laden with bees eager for the last nectar of the season. The humming of them danced about their heads as they pedalled along the road. He stopped and waited for her. "We don't have to do this today," he said. "We could go somewhere and not do much of anything until you feel like moving around."

"And how do you know about such things?" she probed, once she understood what he was saying.

He shrugged. "Growing up with a sister, I guess. Then living with her later on. And having girls as classmates and going on trips with them."

"I'll make out well enough," Erin said. "Let's see what's along this road."

Another hedgerow of fuchsia and they came upon some parked cars, and then the path signposted, Oratory of Gallarus.

An upside-down boat formed entirely of stones. So it appeared to him as they sat with their backs to the stone wall encircling the grassy area in which the little chapel stood. Erin closed her eyes, and he drank in the humming of the bees. Then he stood, walked across the grass, and stooped to pass beneath the teal green lintel stone above the entrance.

Standing right in the middle of the chapel, all ten by fifteen feet of it, he gazed at the opening in the east wall, the only opening other than the entrance way to the west. Opening, in fact, was the only word he could find to describe what he saw, for it was not much more than the size of a human head.

Although the sun now was well above the line of the opening, he tried to picture what he would see if the sun had just risen and were shining directly through. Then he examined the way the opening bevelled in from the inside of the wall toward a smaller opening on the outside and made the picture again. The light would ray in from the east at sunrise, slide along the floor toward the east wall as the sun went on rising, and then there would be no direct light for most of the day while the sun was overhead—not until the light rayed in through the doorway in the west wall at the end of the day.

So how did this little oratory relate to Newgrange and Cairn T? The light of the sun entered Newgrange once a year at the winter solstice, twice a year at Cairn T at the equinoxes, and twice a day here.

He sat down on the dirt floor, dazed as the thought struck him. Erin had been right; gripped by the idea that the dolmens and passage graves here might have been a way of holding onto a light that had been before Raven stole the sun, he hadn't been seeing what they might really be about: a way of letting the daylight in, different ways of letting the daylight in.

Erin's form filled the doorway, and then she sat beside him. "What is your head full of now?"

So he told her what he had just been thinking.

"You don't let go of a thing, do you?" she said. "Once it's bitten you and you've bitten into it."

"I've had my teeth into this all my life. And now some pieces seem to fit. Even our big houses were built with no windows; only the fire burning in the middle and only a smoke hole in the roof to let light in or out because that's the hole through which Raven took the sun out into the world. The people who first built them and those who built your passage graves and dolmens knew the daylight had to come, but wanted to let it come in slowly."

"What now?" she asked, because yet another thought had stopped his words in midstream.

"While holding on to that older light as long as they could? Maybe even letting the two kinds of light talk to one another?"

Erin thought that over. "Light speaking to light? Well, perhaps that's how it was. Why not? It makes about as much sense as there is sense to be made of such things."

Then he chuckled as he thought about it. "That must have been some conversation. I wonder what those two lights said to each other?"

Suddenly, Erin stood and pulled him to his feet. "Let's find out. You be one light, and I'll be the other." She walked to the middle of the oratory and stood, her arms folded.

"You're serious about this, aren't you? All right, I'll play the old light."

She considered that. "No, I don't think that's a good idea."

"Maybe not. So I'll be the new light, and you can start." Now he stood with his arms folded, waiting.

"Ah! I don't hear a choice in that. It seems our play has begun." Erin started to pace the dirt floor of the chapel. A cat beating the bounds of a trapped-in world, she began: "So, this is what you've left for me to shine in. A grave or two, a scattering of dolmens, dark corners of dark chapels. How very kind of you!"

"I just thought . . ."

"You thought? You're fond of that word, aren't you? And just what did you thought?"

"I thought we could do this thing together. Seeing that I have to come."

"Did you, now? Why don't you tell whoever let you loose in this world to take you home and stuff you back into your box?"

"I have to come and you know that."

"Do I? And who asked you to come?"

"You did. You just don't remember."

"Ah, you're right about that! I've forgotten more of the light I was, once, than you'll ever show. The world I lit up was bigger than what you've pieced together—everything leading on and back to every other thing. And nothing of things apart."

"Until you started to come apart."

"I? I started coming apart? Oh, no! No, no, no! You began to pick me apart."

"That's not how it was."

"That's how it felt! Pick, pull, tear, dissect—and toss the pieces outside until there's no inside left. Because you certainly couldn't handle me as I was."

"You didn't want to stay as you were, but you don't remember. That's why you're fighting me now, because you just don't . . ."

"I'm fighting you now because I know now what I didn't know then! Because I've seen how you go about what you do. And by God, or whatever gods or goddesses are left, I'll hold on to every grave and dolmen and refuge I have left to me for any in this world who grow sick of your seeing."

"The blind leading the blind, eh?"

"And what is that wisdom supposed to mean?"

"That there's no going back to you, as you were, whatever the dark places you keep for yourself. There's no going back and that's the truth."

"And what about you is true?"

"I do what I do, and I show what I show. That's my truth, for anyone with guts enough for it."

"And only a man truly blind could think your truth is truth enough."

"Maybe. That's beyond me. But whatever is beyond me, the seeing of it has to go through me."

"Then what need do you have of me?"

He stopped his circling of the oratory, and she stopped, too, standing before the opening in the east wall, the light from it shining about the dark of her head. The dark of the moon eclipsing the dark of the sun.

"To become the darkness." As he spoke, his inner eye glimpsed Raven wrestling the sun through the smoke hole of the big house, the white of his feathers burning black.

She began to move once again. "You mean, I should darken down into the stones, wood, and things of this earth, just so you can shine off of me and find out what it's like to be you?"

"Something like that. It's like a game of tag, and it's my turn to be it, for a while."

"Ah, there! I don't have a choice, do I?"

"Or maybe I'm the one who doesn't have a choice, except to go on doing what I do, wherever that takes me."

"You're wrong. I'd say that seeing choice is about the only thing you have going for you."

And then the flow of words ended. Erin released her breath and laughed. "Perhaps that's why Uncle Sean is busy setting fire to all those pews. To let that old light out."

Her laughter faded and she reached for his hand. "What's the matter? You look as if something's walloped you in the groin."

"David," he gasped, choking on the words. "Maybe that's what he was trying to do."

"Who is David?" Her voice urgent now, but she had to wait for the words to come, her hand gripping his.

"The brother I haven't told you about. Our oldest brother. He burned himself up when he was twenty-one. He couldn't see a life for himself and wanted to go somewhere different. So he set the darkness on fire to start him out."

And then the whole story poured forth. After he had finished the telling of it, he withdrew his hand from hers and wiped at his eyes.

"We don't seem to have many relatives left between the two of us," Erin observed quietly.

"There's still Wesley, who feels the same way," he said, with a hint of a smile. "And Margaret and Frank."

"The brother who was about to be abused."

"Yes. He was born three months after Caitlin and you were born. Maybe Frank was Dad's way of letting Mom know he still loved her, or her way of letting him know she still loved him. Though I'm not sure she ever forgave him completely. She started to drink a few years later."

Erin kept the silence for a time as if wanting to find the courage for her next words. "You asked me once if I hated you because your father was the father I never knew. Now I have a like question for you. Do you hate me because of what my mother did to your mother?"

"No, Erin, I don't hate you. I really don't. But I sure as hell could use a cup of coffee right now."

"And I, a strong cup of tea," she said. "We've earned it and we deserve it, the both of us."

Northwest through County Clare they rode, into a landscape paved over with limestone slabs, where the small grasses, plants, and flowers exploited the cracks in the slabs and the long fissures that ran between slabs. Here and there a granite boulder perched on top of the limestone, an exile from Connemara to the north since the last ice age—each boulder aloof from its fellows and pretending to be right at home where it sat and to have been there always.

From Galway, they cycled west along the north coast of the bay, the Aran Islands gleaming along the horizon to the southwest, and followed a gentle river, the trees at its bank throwing shadows from the last green of their leaves down upon the black water. Then they turned northward to Connemara, into open country where granite boulders poked themselves up through the bogland and, here and there, a father and son were hard at work footing the last of their turf into pyramids of six or seven sods each to let the drying wind do its work.

In the dying light of the day, they wheeled into the Inagh Valley, now drenched in the shadow thrown across the valley floor by the Twelve Bens to the west and up the flanks of the Maamturks to the east—stark, barren slopes and peaks but for the plantations of spruce along the valley floor contained by wire fences. The whole of it stark yet hauntingly beautiful.

He rounded a bend in the road, and an old man wearing a tweed coat walked past him slowly, feeling out the side of the road with his walking stick. The look in the old man's eyes was not a looking at him or at anything in this world for the old man was staring right through him as if he did not exist. I may see you, the ancient eyes said, but you are not in my world. In the world I know and see, you are not.

"Did you see what I just saw?" he asked Erin as she rolled her bike up to his.

"You mean the way he looked at me, but didn't see me?"

"Yes. As if his world had no place for us. There was an old man at Duxsowlas who could look at you like that, though it was a look he saved for visitors who sailed in on their big boats and tied up at our landing. Old Man Williams—the Old Man we called him. I used to imitate the way he walked, and he would threaten to whack me between the eyes as he would whack Sisiutl between the eyes if he ever met him."

"Sisiutl . . . the two-headed sea serpent you told me about?"

"That's the one. I could imitate the Old Man's walk, but never that look of his. The visitors would stroll through the village on their way to somewhere else and tell us how lovely and quaint and aboriginal it was, and we were—not in those words, but that's what they were saying. Then the Old Man would walk past them and look right through them as if they didn't exist. Others could pull that look off, too, if the occasion called for it, but the Old Man held the patent. I didn't think anyone else in the world could do it the way he did until that old man walked past us just now."

"It could be he does see another world," laughed Erin, "as did your Old Man."

"And suppose he does?" he wondered, as the laugh died in her throat.

"I don't like that look in your eye," she said, "and I could kick myself for saying what I just said."

They travelled all the way east . . . they travelled all the way west; they followed the rising sun . . . they followed the setting sun; they never ate more than one meal at the same table or slept more than one night in the same bed until the days slowed right down, and they stood one afternoon in a little grocery store waiting to pay for the fruit they had bought. The owner stood at the phone engaged in conversation with someone, though she glanced over at them now and again to let them know she would be there as soon as she could.

"Well, you are in a heap," the woman said to the someone at the other end of the line. "And what do you want me to do about it?"

"Fresh weather is expected for most of the day," announced the voice on the radio. He glanced at the calendar tacked up below the shelf on which the radio sat and saw it was the day of the equinox.

"That's right," said the woman into the receiver, "and that's the way of it, whether or not it sits right with you. Now then, I have customers, and a business waiting on me. Your business can wait until the end of the day."

Click went the receiver, and then the woman rang the coins Erin handed her into the register. "Taking a man out of the bog is one thing," she observed. "Taking the bog out of the man is something else again. Are you on holiday?"

"Just travelling," Erin said. "To nowhere in particular."

"Ah," said the woman, "then you have all the time in the world and that's well."

Erin pocketed her change, took the fruit in hand, and they walked up the hill from the store to where they had left their bikes.

"What are you looking at?" she asked, as he stopped walking. He pointed past her and down the hill. Toward the bottom, not far from the store, there stood a grey bricked garage with two creosoted doors. Up on the tar roof, along with a scattering of pebbles, a pair of red gumboots lay in a pool of water, their soles facing up the hill and their toes turned outward from one another—as if the wearer, all of a sudden, couldn't decide in which direction to walk and simply had stepped out of the boots rather than continue struggling with the question. There was no clue as to where the wearer of the boots had gone.

"Is that what it feels like?" she asked.

"Pretty much," he replied. "You were right. There's always been light enough for me to make my choices if only I had faced up to them. Even that night I walked in on my uncle about to put his hands on Frank, even then there was light enough for me to see what I might have said or done other than just walking out the door and out of his life."

"Perhaps," Erin said, handing him an orange. "But you were only fourteen, so stop thumping your craw about it. What else is eating at you?"

He took the orange but didn't answer her question.

"Well then, what do you want from the few days we have left? More graves or another dolmen? There's a big one up in Donegal. We might make it there before the cauldron of plenty runs out."

He shook his head. "No, I don't need another dolmen."

"What, then?"

"The dark. To go right into the dark, just once, and see what's there," he answered, remembering the eyes of the old man in the Inagh Valley.

"Good God, how much of the dark do you need? After what we've done?"

"Enough to shut the light right out."

"Ah, I see we're back to Oisin once again," said Erin. "Well, as I remember, it gets dark at least once a day. We call it night."

"Yes, I know, but even the night doesn't shut the light right out. I found that out once when I was on a three-day vision quest that I didn't know was a vision quest but ended up being one. The first night, I slept under a salal bush, and the night around me was as dark as night can get. But there still was a touch of light in it."

Erin tossed her head in exasperation. "You know, we could have found the dark you're looking for without ever leaving Wales, down in the bowels of a slate mine. But if you're in earnest about this thing, have you considered blinding yourself? That would deal with the daylight, once and for all."

He blinked as he realized she might be more serious than joking. "I guess that could do it but maybe not. It could be like castrating yourself because you can't handle sex, only to find out you've brought about the opposite of what you'd intended. You know what I mean?"

"No and yes," she replied, her head cocked and an imp in her eye. "But I can't think of any other way, now and here, to conjure up the dark you're wanting."

"Then let's go where the day takes us," he said, "and see what we find."

That afternoon they came upon a small lake and an old van parked beside the road. As they rode up to it, the sound of a fiddle came to meet them. Stopping at the van, they left their bikes and walked past the beech trees to the lakeshore. A woman squatted before an open fire, cooking, while another woman sat on a rock, bowing at her fiddle.

The fiddler's eyes twinkled when her tune came to an end. She handed the fiddle and bow to Erin. "How did you know?" Erin asked.

"I've a fairy feeling for certain things," the fiddler answered. Erin put the fiddle to her chin and began to play, a bit of a reel at first, then leading the bow over into a slow air. "Buiochas," she said, handing back the fiddle and bow. "It's been a while."

"But you've still a good touch in your fingers," said the woman at the fire. "You'd better take care, or they'll come for you from Sidhe whenever they need a fiddler."

Erin's eyes flashed. "Slán agat," she said, "and thanks again for more than you know." Taking him by the arm, she led him up to their bikes.

"That was a sudden goodbye," he said. "Where are we off to?"

"To find your darkness. Come on!"

There was nothing leisurely about the way she pedalled now, farther along the road to the west until they had put the lake behind them and Connemara opened out toward a last barren line of hills before it ran into the Atlantic. As he pedalled to keep pace with her, he felt her watching for the landmarks—the farmhouse to the north with the blue gables, a single oak to the south, and then the high hump in the land rising up ahead of them.

"We can leave the bikes here," she said. They climbed the bank beside the road to a stile, climbed it, and started across a pasture of short grass and rushes. Another fence appeared, but the stile was covered over by a large blackthorn tree, bent in an eastward direction by the relentless wind from the west. "This was smaller when I last saw it," Erin said, "and I wouldn't have taken its thorns on then. Let's brave the barbed wire farther along."

Erin walked on west, held the wire apart so that he could squeeze through, then squeezed through herself.

Mist rolled in over the grey hilltop then parted suddenly and a wave of light came rippling down the hillside—came, then went as the mist took command once again.

Sheep grazed at the foot of a large grass-covered mound that ran out from the hillside, then around and back into it in the shape of a half moon. They scattered as Erin climbed the mound and he climbed after her. Once she was on top of it, she paused and looked about her, as if to be sure they were where she hoped they would be.

"This is a ringfort," Erin said, "but they only needed half of the ring because of where they put it. We're standing on the rath, and the lios is the space inside, where they lived—men, women, children, dogs, cattle, and whatever else. What we're looking for is over there in the hillside."

She led the way until the two of them stood before a stone lintel very low to the earth with an entrance into the hillside beneath it. The stone was cracked, and it sagged somewhat but had not yet broken apart. A large ash grew up right beside it, its trunk blocking part of the entry into the passage. "This is a souterrain," Erin said. "A back door out of here, in case too many unannounced and unwelcome guests arrived at the front door."

"How did you know about this place?" he asked.

"We were nearly ten, Caitlin and I, and we came past that lake with Uncle Sean about this time of year. A tinker's caravan was camped there, and the tinkers told Uncle Sean about a fairy rath nearby."

"Fairy rath?"

"That's right. The home of the fairy people, or the Tuatha de Danaan as you know them. We're standing at the doorway. The ash was tiny then, and the way in completely unfettered. Caitlin wanted to go inside, and Uncle Sean was game, too."

"And you?"

"I would have none of it then. So no one went in."

"And what are you suggesting we do now?"

Erin looked up at the mist pouring over the hilltop, then back at him. "I'm suggesting we do whatever you're ready to do, before that ash grows any more and covers the entrance right over. It's as dark a dark in there as any you'll find on this earth, and I'll even lead the way in. What about it?"

He looked at her, then at the entrance to the souterrain. "Yes, I know," she said. "There's a fool born every minute and most of them live, including the two of us."

A smile spread across his mouth. "All right, Erin. Lead the way in."

SEVEN

He waited for her feet to disappear, then he followed after them. There was just enough room beneath the cracking lintel for him to squeeze himself into the passageway. His face right to the earth and the earth dry upon his fingers and strong about his nostrils, he inched his belly, thighs, and knees forward into the darkness that embraced him. Light enough filtered past his shoulders for him to see her feet up ahead. But that light was quickly fading away.

Feeling his way along the passage floor, he listened for the sound of her body moving into the darkness ahead of him. The earth beneath him began to rise, slightly, then sharply. A last gleam of light rayed up to that sharp rising of the earth, and then the light vanished.

He wriggled onward, and could no longer say how far he had come. A sense of distance needed light, and there was no light left. Then she stopped, and he stopped right at the soles of her shoes. He sensed her hand reaching through the dark and finding something unexpected.

She crawled forward again, and then his hand also felt the stone along the side of the passageway. Not just earth but stone. He spread his fingers in the other direction and found stone there, too. He tried to lift himself onto his knees and couldn't, but the height of the passageway had grown, and his back touched against a lining of stone in the dark above it.

Whatever a souterrain is, that's not what we're in . . .

The passageway continued to grow above their backs and the earthen floor rose steadily from the east as he crawled behind her, now on his knees. Crawled through a tunnel not of earth, but of stone. His fingers felt at the passage sides again. Not just stone, but standing stones, and the ceiling above, corbelled. Erin stopped yet again. He crawled up beside her until his hand came up against a stone and rested there, alongside hers. A sillstone blocking their path . . .

"Gwawinastoo . . ."

"Hello."

"Guess what?"

"What?"

"We're inside a passage grave."

"Then let's go right inside."

"Do you think that's a good idea?"

"What's not good about it?"

"You know what we might find? Because I doubt anyone has been inside here for a long, long, very long time."

"Ooh! I see. Actually, I can't see a damn thing, but that's something else. So, should we knock?"

He could feel the laughter rising up within her. "No, that wouldn't accomplish much." And then her laughter subsided into a pool of silence. "All right, let's go inside and take our chances."

She lifted herself over the sillstone and crawled into the central chamber of the grave. He followed behind, and then they lost touch with one another all of a sudden. He stopped and she stopped.

"Where are you?"

"Over here."

"Where is over here?"

"Where I am."

"Yes, and over here is where I am, but we'll have to do better than that."

He laughed, and she inched backward toward the sound of him laughing, while he backed himself toward her. Then their backs met and they squatted in the centre of the chamber, back to back, until they both sat, their backs still touching.

Silence closed the darkness about them and they continued to sit. Then he spoke. "So, is this in the same shape as Newgrange and Cairn T? Two side chambers and a head chamber?"

"It could be, but it's hard to tell, from here."

"Then let's find out. You go that way, and I'll go this way, and we'll meet back here."

"And where are that way and this way, let alone back here? But if we must, reach carefully when you put your hand past the sillstone if there is one. The remains of one of our hosts may still be there."

"And what am I likely to find?"

"Bones, probably. They cremated the bodies down to the bones, then put the bones in the grave."

"Ooh . . .!"

"Well?"

"All right. See you in a moment or two."

He dropped to his knees, and her back parted from his as she moved forward, then forward, and forward again until her hand felt the face of a standing stone. Which way from here? She moved her fingers to the left and kept on moving them until they parted from the edge of the stone. Feeling into the darkness before her, she dropped her hand, slowly, until it came to rest upon a sillstone.

His hand upon the sillstone opposite hers, he thought a bit about waking up the dead even if there wasn't much of them left to awaken. The same thought came to her, her hand still upon the sillstone. There were stories about curious mortals wandering into caves and such and awakening those sleeping within, and the awakened ones not responding well to that.

His fingers reached past the sillstone and dropped down toward the chamber floor. A curve of stone rose up to meet them. A stone basin, like the ones at Newgrange.

Her fingers moved carefully from the edge of the basin toward its concave centre, then stopped.

His fingers stopped as well. Then he withdrew his hand and crept backward toward the centre of the central chamber until his back touched hers once again. "What did you find?"

"Nothing. Just a basin."

"Same here. Only the basin."

"Perhaps they moved out. Decided they didn't like it here and went looking for another grave."

"Or maybe they never moved in, at all."

"That's a strange thought. A brand new rock tomb, thousands of years old. But why?"

His back and head still touching hers, he closed his eyes, though there was no need for him to do that, and thought about why. Maybe this really was a grave for the old light, the light before Raven's world began. Then he saw himself standing at Bone Spit that day, wanting to shoot Raven's world into oblivion. Sun up . . . sun down.

"Erin . . ."

"Yes?"

"I did kill Caitlin. Not directly, but I set it up, the killing of her."

Then he told her about the three days at the dam and the fourth morning. "When Sundown raised his rifle and pulled the trigger, just as Caitlin was about to tell me she knew who I was and who we were, it was as if I had put his finger on the trigger and said, 'Do it.' And then he did."

His words reached for her through the darkness, and waited for her words to answer him. "That bullet found her because I had shut her question out of my life and wouldn't admit that it was my question, too."

Then she told him about a day in Paris when the Haida paddled their canoe up the Seine. "Caitlin saw herself in that canoe and knew then who our father was, though she didn't know where he was or his name. She had wanted to know, always, and had wanted me to want to know. But I wouldn't give her that, ever, and so she had to take the whole of it on herself. If I had asked that question along with her perhaps I'd have been the one that bullet struck."

"Yes, it could have been you. But she chose to be there, and that's also the truth, Erin."

"I know that, now. And it would seem the two of us have chosen to be here. Did Dad ever say anything about fathering Caitlin? Or me? That you can remember?"

"No, though he might have said something if he had lived. But he kept that photograph of Sean and your mother and himself on the top of a chest in our house, right below the rifle I used to shoot the sun that day, the rifle our great-grandfather carried at the Little Bighorn. God, how it all twines and knots together, like those braids and knots on a high cross! And there's something else I understand, now."

"What?"

"Why something of him was never there, fully there at Duxsowlas after your mother left. Something of him was somewhere else, always, and I think it was over here, with your mother, and with Caitlin and you, even though he never knew you. He started carving a pole for David when I was fourteen, just before everything fell apart. Raven at the bottom, then Sisiutl, and the last blank stretch of it at the top. He kept looking at it as we carved, trying to figure out what should be there, but he couldn't see it. My cousin's uncle came by and said, 'What's going to happen there?' And Dad said, 'We'll see.' But he couldn't see it because what he was looking for was over here with you. Maybe that's why he chose to die when he did because his seeing had run out and he couldn't take it any further."

"You loved him, didn't you?"

"Yes, I did. And you might have loved him, too."

He could see nothing of himself or her in that darkness wrapped about them, not even the finger he rubbed against his nose. But that was of no importance.

"You said something back at the store about a vision quest that you didn't know was one but really was."

"Yes."

"Tell me about that."

So he told her about those three days on Log Island, his seeing of the Grail moon that third night and his holding of that moon within his seeing all the night through. Then in the morning their father had told him that what he had seen was what their grandfather had seen that night in the valley of the Little Bighorn.

"And the Raven looked as if it were trying to fly free of the dark circle?"

"Yes."

"That's what you saw?"

"That's the way Dad described it when he told me about Grandfather's dream. And that's the way he described it to your uncle, when they were in that passage grave in France."

"That may be what our grandfather saw, or the way Dad described what our grandfather saw, but what did you see? Because the picture I got from what you said wasn't a picture of Raven trying to escape from the circle. Make the picture again, now, and I'll try, too."

He closed his eyes, then opened them as he called up the picture—the gleaming crescent and the dark circle cradled within; the ring of light bright about the circle and then the shining figure forming itself within the encircled darkness. He held the picture within his inner seeing and searched out what it wanted to show him . . . "You're right!" he exclaimed. "Why didn't I see that before?"

"You did, but you didn't pay enough attention to what you saw. Neither did I to other things. But perhaps some things that want to be seen have to wait until their moment in the story comes."

"Yes. And then it comes time for the story to move on. I guess we should start crawling our way back through that passage."

"I don't want to go out that way."

"Then which way do you want to go? Up through the roof?"

"Not likely, but not the way we came in either. That's not the way they would want us to go from here."

"Who?"

"The ones who shaped this grave. And that's not what we pictured just now."

"Maybe not. But I don't see another way through, if seeing has anything to do with it."

"Maybe it does and maybe it doesn't, but let's sit a while longer, and something might show itself."

But what? he wondered. What would show itself to them as they sat, in the dark, in the heart of a passage grave?

The heart . . . Yes, that was where they were sitting, he realized, because the grave was shaped in the form of a human being. Head chamber, arm chambers, and the heart . . .

Nu gwa am. I am . . . As the words came to him, he pictured the last of the three crosses in the churchyard at Kells: the west face waiting to be carved and the east face with the figure of Christ stretching out his arms. From the heart of the cross. And then he remembered their father's words: *The one they talk about, listen to him* . . .

Nu gwa am: I am . . . the light. The light of the heart rising up to meet the daylight. Where? Where did heart-light and daylight meet?

Yes . . . ! They moved as one toward the head chamber of the grave. He was over the sillstone first, then she knelt beside him and their hands felt for the backstone. Only it was not a backstone, not a standing stone, but a leaning stone that had been set into the side of the hill. He put his back to it, his feet against the sillstone and started to push with all the strength in him. She placed her shoulder beside his and brought herself to bear against the stone. Of course—the thought came—if this worked, the whole of the hill might come pouring in upon them.

The stone began to move. They pushed relentlessly and the stone moved again. Earth began to fall through the widening crack between the stone and the hillside about it. And then the stone broke loose, came upright for an instant as the earth sank in upon them, and the light came reeling in. Back, and back the stone leaned, all the way back, until it fell away from their hands

down

down

down

down down

down

several hundred feet

to splash, then vanish into the Atlantic Ocean.

They were kneeling almost at the edge of a cliff where the west side of the hill they had come through dropped down into the tossing, crashing water below. On either side of them, the ocean had carved the land into a deep V into which the Atlantic rolled and pounded. Wave followed wave, and each wave gnawed and licked at the ledges, crevasses and caverns of layered rock before withdrawing seaward to regather its forces. High in the air above the ocean, the mist streamed, thickened, then broke open as the sun worked to take it apart.

Glancing over his shoulder, up the hillside, he saw they could make it. Work together, take our time, and we'll make it. He stood and balanced, reached for her hand and they started to climb.

Gripping her hand, he drew her toward him. She climbed on past, then reached for his hand, the blue of her eyes searching out the brown of his. Light finding light as their hands crossed over one another with each new foothold. Up, up, and up, one hand knotted into the other as they struggled through the mist until the sun stood before them in the heavens to the west and the mist was no more.

He stopped climbing where the angle of the hill began to ease off and he could see its crown, sat down in the heather, and she sat beside him. His face full of the sun, he reached out, put his arm about her and told her the story . . . "It was the third day. The Wanookqway were lost in the mist, and they were cold, even though they had Grizzly's skin to wear. Eagle's light was way up the mountain behind them and so was Mountain Goat's. Now there was nothing but mist and darkness, and they were getting sick of it. Everyone was getting sick of it, the whole world over. And most of all, Raven was sick of it. The hell with this, he said, and off he flew, to look for the sun . . ."

EIGHT

The water fell from his lips like a prayer as he dipped his hand into it, cupped it, and raised the cup so that he could drink from it again. Then he uncupped his hand and let the last drops fall back into the well. The face of the well wrinkled with ripples running out from the splash of the drops, colliding with one another, and the skin of the water shivering. Then the face of the well was calm and clear once again.

At the top of the grassy path, he met a man and a woman, each with a guidebook in hand. "It's down there," he assured them, "if you go all the way down."

Then he continued on up the path that took him around Mynydd Mawr to Braich y Pwll, the arm of land that extended westward. Finding a place part way out on the arm where he would be protected from the wind that blew over from the north side of the peninsula, he sat and waited for the sun to set.

It was the third Sunday in October. The sky had stayed clear the whole weekend while Dafydd and he had worked to secure the slate around the smokehole of Eglwys Lleu. Friday had brought the new moon and tonight would be the night of the first crescent.

He took out the letter from Margaret and read it again:

Dear Wandering Brother,

You may have been aiming for you, but you sure hit me where it hurt. I've been trying to forgive you, and I guess I've covered some ground in doing that.

Along the way I've had to face some things, too, about Cameron and me. I don't know how far I've gotten with that either, but it's time I looked at it straight on and asked what, if anything, we have going for us. So much for where I'm at and what I know about anything.

Some other news, not good. Aunt Minnie phoned a few days ago to tell me Adha isn't doing well at all. Minnie is bringing her down to one of the hospitals here sometime next week. I'll know more then about what's happening.

Well, Wandering One, you have a few things to come back to whenever you decide to come back. But there's something I need to tell you now. Do you remember the day when your class had its pool-shooting crisis? That night you said something about Uncle Charlie abusing David as well as coming on to Frank. I don't know where that came from, but the only abuser I knew of when I left Duxsowlas was Harvey; he was the one who had abused David. I never warmed to our uncle, and he was a grouch much of the time, but an abuser? I wonder about that, now.

So, we have more relatives? I guess we'll have to throw a potlatch when they show up on our doorstep to sort out who's who.

Until then, or whenever,

Margaret

He looked once more at the early September date before folding the letter, the only one that had been waiting for him when Erin and he returned from Ireland. Anika had not written.

The sound of footsteps touched into his ear. Without a word he handed Erin the letter and sat silently while she read it. From the darkening silhouette of Bardsey Island, the lighthouse winked at him.

"Start asking who your family is and what they're up to, and you will receive," she mused. "I only hope I'm up to meeting all of this when the day comes. I'll think that over during these next months."

"When do you go?"

"Right now. The job I've found wants me there at once. I'm staying with Dafydd at the farmhouse tonight."

"Well, tell Dafydd to get back here once you're on your way because I'm not going up on that roof again without him."

She laughed. "Come on! He's impressed with the work you've done. Very impressed!"

"He'd better be. I nearly fell off that roof twice today keeping him impressed."

"Well, you won't have to impress him much longer. When will you be done?"

"By the end of the week. Then I'll fly home." He squinted back at the winking of the lighthouse. "My pilgrimage is at an end, Erin. And I won't even make it to Bardsey to keep all those saints company."

"Not all the pilgrims got to Bardsey. For some, getting here was enough."

"I hope it proves to be enough," he said, "for what I need to start doing, once that plane lands. I wonder when I'll see you again."

"Before too long," said Erin.

"What do you mean?"

"I mean that I intend to work until I have money in my pocket to make a pilgrimage of my own to Haida Gwaii and to Chaatl, to look for that pole and the other half of that stone mask. Dad gave me the one half, remember? So it's time I started being Súl an Fhiaich. I'll go to Chaatl, find whatever is there to be found, and then I'll find you."

"That's good, Erin," he said. "It'll be good to see you again, whatever you find. Ha-la-kasla, Súl an Fhiaich."

"Goodbye, from the heart?"

"Yes."

"And Ghe-la-kasla to you, Gwawinastoo," she said. "Slán agat." She walked up the slope of Braich y Pwll and then was gone.

The sun sets with solemn dignity. His eye eclipses the shining disk as much as is needed to let him gaze into its encircled radiance. The light and the silence, and that is enough, as the Atlantic Ocean opens at the horizon, receives the sun's setting, and he waits, seeking out that place above the sun where the gleaming crescent will appear.

As the blue about the crescent deepens, the shimmering form in the dark circle makes itself known—not struggling to fly free of the dark, but going through it. Raven winging homeward through the dark of his . . . of her own eye, while all about the Grail moon, the stars begin to twinkle like buttons on a blanket.

V

I climb the steps to Uncle Slim's and Aunt Minnie's house and raise my hand to knock at the door; then I laugh at myself, open the door, and walk in.

Uncle Slim sits in a big, stuffed rocking chair near the window overlooking the bay and dozes. Aunt Minnie sleeps on the couch and snores as she sleeps.

"Yo, Uncle."

He starts awake. "Yo, Nephew!" he blinks. "Do you need another birth certificate? Because that's the last time we heard from you."

I laugh again. "No, Uncle, I don't need one of those."

Aunt Minnie's snoring changes pitch as she adjusts the couch to her sleeping body. I look at her and Uncle Slim looks at her, and we both grin.

"She's still saying her prayers," he says.

"Then you'd better turn her over, Uncle, before the volume increases."

And my eyes fill with tears. I start to shove them back under my eyelids, then stop shoving and let them come. I look at my uncle and see that he is crying, too.

Aunt Minnie snorts once, then awakens. She sits up on the couch and stares over at me, her eyes trying to understand who it is that sits in her living room, blubbering away. Once the understanding comes, I walk over and put my arms about her.

"Whew! I guess I'd better put on a pot of tea," Uncle Slim says, finally.

"You burnt the bottom out of the last kettle you put on," Auntie replies. "Leave the tea to me."

"Your Adha died at Duxsowlas," she remarks, as she puts the water into the kettle.

When she tells me the day and time, I go to the calendar on her wall and turn it back to September to find the date. The equinox, just about the time Erin and I were going through the passage grave.

"We buried her next to our dad," Auntie continues. "Your mom and dad are buried nearby."

"Is there anyone left alive at home?" I ask, after I swallow down the first mouthful of tea, and immediately regret having spoken like that. But Aunt Minnie and Uncle Slim walk right past my irony as if they hadn't heard or seen it, or had seen right through it—the way Old Man Williams used to see through people, and that old man in the Inagh Valley.

"Frank is staying in your old house," Aunt Minnie says. "He has a woman with him, a person he met when he was at college for a year in Nanaimo. She's older than Frank and has a boy by a white man she was with. Gina is her name."

"And Uncle Charlie?"

"He's still staying in his house," says Uncle Slim.

"Staying there and keeping himself alive, just," Aunt Minnie adds. "I guess I'd better fix a bed for you, in your old room."

I shake my head. "Don't bother, Auntie. I'm going over tonight. Have you got a boat I could use, Uncle?"

"Well, yes, I do," Uncle Slim replies. "A new boat, almost. I bought it a couple of years back, thinking I might take a trip around the world in it. But the world's moving too fast for me now, I guess."

"It's going to be dark in a couple of hours," Aunt Minnie observes.

"I know, but there'll be a full moon tonight and I know my way."

"You haven't gone that way for a long, long time," she counters.

"I still know my way, Auntie. What about it, Uncle? Can you spare your boat for a few days?"

"I can spare it for a few months," he laughs, "for all that I do with it."

Down at the boat, we check out the engine and the fuel tank. Then Uncle Slim points to the canoe paddle lying across one of the seats, a plain, sturdy paddle with no nonsense about it.

"That'll come in handy if the motor conks out and you still want to get somewhere. You'll be able to go round in circles, at least. Or you may bump into Sisiutl and need to crack him one over the head," my uncle grins.

"I'd just as soon Sisiutl stayed underwater until I'm home," I grin back. "But I'll keep the paddle close at hand, just in case. Ha-la-kasla, Uncle. Wish me well, you and Auntie."

"We always have," he says, as he helps me push off. "Tell Frank and your uncle it's time for a potlatch, now that you're back. Ha-la-kasla!"

I turn the key and the engine roars awake. With a turn of the wheel, the boat speeds toward the mouth of the bay, toward the deep black water and the high moonlit sky waiting for me in the night to come.

Aunt Minnie was right enough. It has been a long time since I travelled these waters. But I stay in the shadow of the island until I cross the strait to the mainland coast, then I keep the land in sight as the sun falls away beneath the Pacific horizon and the moon rises up over the coast mountains—a full but small moon far away from the earth tonight, its light cool, yet the more intense because of its distance from me. Light floats upon black water as the boat's headlamp probes the night air and guides me northward.

An inlet opens up on my right, then narrows into the land beyond, and I know that Thumb Harbour lies hidden away along the north side of the inlet's darkness. Knowing these waters I relax a little, and it's only a matter of fighting back the fatigue that wants to shut my eyes right down. So I keep awake by thinking of those in the boat with me, the dead that live on in me and want me to remember—Dad, Mom, David, Adha, Caitlin, and Emer.

Feeling my way through the night, I remember the dead in the way Sean had suggested, as being, each of them, on yet a farther journey, yet caring still about those of us with our feet on the earth, or for me travelling a moonlit night on black water and preparing myself to meet those waiting at the water's end. Or those who have long given up waiting. It would be the same, either way, as Sand Island looms up out of the moonstruck water ahead, a giantess stirring herself out of a long, drugged sleep.

Then Bone Spit. I ease up on the throttle, and the boat slows, slows, until the black water laps fragments of the moon softly against the sides of the boat. I silence the engine altogether and slip through a last length of darkness until the boat noses gently onto the cold, pale sand.

Why here? Then the dead tell me. It is they who have brought me this far, who have never left my side, and who must be the first to welcome me home.

I step into the water, pull the boat farther onto the beach, then secure it to the snag end of a well-worn log. The tide is right out, and I can see the neck of sand that leads over to the village.

A totem pole stands at the graveyard's edge, facing south toward open water. Not a well-carved pole, my hand tells me, and hacked up by someone's knife where there should be no mark. And someone has been taking pot shots at it, too, my fingers discover as they feel at the hole in Grizzly's face.

The paddle still in my hand, I walk into the graveyard, in among the Sitka that, like the Druid oaks, hold the space sacred, and there I stand

in a depth of shadow. In the distance the Giant burns, and the burning light licks at the blood-red armour that chains me about.

I swing right around, but to the north Log Island lies dark and still under the light of a cold moon. My hand clutches at the paddle as I look for my granddad's grave

my right hand heavy with the red sword it holds, and my left, shaking the rattle, softly . . .

I shake my head to expel the dream from my memory as I kneel before the grave of Puclalas and the moon lets me read the words on the headstone. Then the words on Adha's headstone, beside his:

Blaze Watson
1910-1993
Axilaogua
No Names Withheld

When I have looked long at the words, I step out of the shadow to find the grave of my parents

out onto the moonlit beach. My uncle kneels before me, a button blanket about his body, a crown of cedar upon his head, and he trembles as he prays. The crest upon his blanket stares out at me . . .

But the beach is empty of anyone and anything other than the moon-washed sand and the darkness beneath, which the moon can't reach. Drawing aside the salal that has grown over them, I read the words on Dad's headstone:

Isaac Jacob
1921-1983
Xuuyaa Gut-ga-at-gaa

And then Mom's headstone:

Edith Jacob
1936-1990
Now, through a glass, darkly
Then, face to face

And now David's, to remember how it was that day, only I
discover that the graves of our parents are not beside David's grave,
though all three lie within the burial area of the Watsons. And why is
that?

I make myself stop at Harvey's headstone. Are you among my
dead, too? Because you sure drove a spike into my life, as well as a
screwdriver into yours. But who were you? And why did you screw
up your life and the lives of others as badly as you did?

As I read the stone-held words, I lift my paddle to raise up the Sitka
branch that shadows them over, lift my paddle

into the full moon, to
drive it between the eyes of Sisiutl and into my uncle's heart. Then from out of
the blanket Sisiutl rises up, the knife edge of a paddle flashing down—

The moonlight strikes down upon the headstone, and I see the long,
thin shadow striking down upon me.

I roll. The paddle
burns the air at my shoulder, cleaves open
the space where I had been, and the earth sprays
up about it.

I roll as the paddle flashes moonward,
hungry for me, the face gleaming out from the blade
hungry for me. Sisiutl!

Into the shadow of a Sitka I roll
but the blade seeks me out. The bark flies apart
in my face as the teeth of Sisiutl rip into the trunk
where my head has just been and then there is nowhere
left to roll.

A headstone trips me as I try to stand
and the paddle slices along my shoulder blades,
touching enough to pull a scream

from my throat. Struggling to come upright,
I break free of the headstones, the shadows, and reach
open sand and then a foot hooks into one of mine,
drops me face forward, Uncle Slim's paddle still in my hand,
the sand in my teeth, and the moonlight raw
upon my back, and then I roll, come to my knees
as his shadow drops down upon me and covers me over.

   High above his head, his hands fast upon the handle,
   the blade flashes for a last attack, and down
   Sisiutl comes

             down

      down

      down

             down

     down.

         My hands spring up to meet the blow,
the shaft of my paddle between them. Sisiutl sinks his teeth
deep into the shaft, and his eyes strike
fully into mine. Everything stops
as I stare Sisiutl through . . .

             Crack!
goes the neck of Sisiutl, and his bite upon my paddle
breaks. His head spins up and up,
then drops

     down

     down

onto the sand and does not move again.

   Stunned by the onslaught, I blink up at the shadow towering over
me, my paddle battered, but intact. The shadow stares back. The hand
holding the shattered paddle drops down, and the broken shaft falls
to the beach beside its blade.
   "Nathan?"
My hands let go of my paddle.
   "Frank?"
   "Yes . . ."
   I stand, dazed, and then we stand together, arms about one
another. He isn't as tall as I am, my brother, but he's stocky and
strong.

"Remind me not to visit the dead ever again when you're standing guard," I say, as our bodies slacken, then collapse onto the sand where we sit together.

My eyes take him in, but my brother is still too choked up to speak. Then he wipes his hand at his eyes.

"We carved that pole for our family, Peter and Sam and I, because we needed something, and no one felt up to tackling the pole Dad and you had left behind. So we did what we could and raised it, but visitors in the night have a habit of taking shots at it and of trying to improve on our carving. Their last attempt was in August. I decided I was going to do some carving up of my own the next time I heard a boat out here. Your paddle had been standing against the wall for ten years, beneath where the rifle used to hang, and it was the nearest thing to my hand."

"Where did the rifle go?"

"We buried it with Dad."

There's a story about that rifle you didn't bury, I want to say, but that can wait. He scoops up a handful of sand. The sand slides through his fingers as his fingers open to let it slide through.

"The day after you left, I took Dad's boat and went up to Snag Point. Mom didn't want me to go there, but I went anyway. When I tied the boat up, I thought Christmas had come because the point was all white with something, and I couldn't figure out why it had snowed in June, there, and nowhere else. Then I saw what the snow was.

"I took the whole day and picked up every one of those feathers, then all of the down, from off of the snags and the tree trunks, and out of the branches. If I had to climb to reach it, then I climbed as high as I had to go. I gathered it all together and we've been using it ever since—giving the feathers to visiting elders, and members of the soccer team when they do well, and we've used the down for the Peace Dance, year after year. We even have some feathers left. I'm holding them for the time when Uncle Charlie dances again."

"Uncle doesn't dance, at all?"

"He hasn't danced or drummed since you left, except for the one potlatch he gave. When Mom died he stopped going to the big house altogether."

Moonlight, soft on black water. Pale light lying upon a surface of darkness it cannot yet comprehend.

"Will you go with me, Frank, to Uncle's house?"

"Now?"

"Yes, please. If he's awake."

"He'll be awake. He never sleeps, not really. He just lies on the couch with his back to the door, all night long and much of the day, now, hoping no one will come through the doorway. And no one does, except for Lila, and me.

Fie fie fie for shame
turn your back to the
door again—

The words of the circle game play about within me as we cross the neck of sand and walk the moonlit length of Duxsowlas—Sadie's, Hazel's, Hector's house, and Peter's, and then the soccer field.

Adha's house is dark and closed up, but a light gleams from Uncle Charlie's window. The steps groan with our weight and the door creaks as Frank pushes it open. His back to the door, our uncle curls his body away from the wounding world. Against the wall where the mirror hangs, the chest filled with Humsumth masks is closed fast and locked because of our uncle's shame—"because I am tired of being ashamed."

"Ghe-la-kasla, Uncle."

He turns toward the voice he hears, but can't yet comprehend, as his face, then his body, comes about on the couch.

"Ghe-la-kasla, Uncle. It's been a long, long time."

I kneel, and Frank kneels beside me. Taking my uncle's hand, I meet his unbelieving gaze, and my heart begins to form the words:

How is it with you, Uncle? What wounded you, Uncle? And what wounds you, still? For your sake, and mine, for the sake of us all, tell me, please . . .

In that last hour before the sun rises above the crown of Duxdzas, I sit at our kitchen table while Frank makes coffee.

"Did you have any idea about David and who he was?"

"Our brother who wasn't our brother? No, I didn't. I wonder who did know?" he says, and hands me a filled cup.

"Dad and Mom for sure, and Adha. Margaret? I don't think so. The rest of our family? Maybe. Maybe everyone else in Duxsowlas for all we know. The open secret no one ever told: Uncle Charlie's son. Who was she, I wonder?" Putting my question to Frank as I put the cup to my lips and let the coffee warm me.

"David's mother? The woman Uncle couldn't stand by or who wouldn't stand by him? He didn't tell us that, and would you want to know, Nathan, really? Because I'm not sure I want to know. And what does it matter, now?" Frank replies.

Possibilities carouse about in my head, but I know he is right. There are secrets within secrets better left in peace.

"But what Uncle did tell us sure makes sense of many other things," Frank continues. "David's anger, and his rejection of Uncle, the father that wouldn't admit to being his father, even though Uncle would have given him just about anything else. Do you think David knew?"

"What is knowing? Yes, somewhere in his bones David knew. And then there was Harvey's abusing of David! No wonder Uncle was ready to let Harvey bleed himself to death that day."

And then Frank's eyes tell me he has something more to say. "You asked me if I knew who David was, and I said no. But I always felt something about him, even when I was little. That he didn't have a home, really, even though he lived with us. And sometimes I could feel what Uncle Charlie felt for him, without knowing what that meant, because when David died that feeling started coming toward me. I think Uncle thought he should feel for you that way, when he was going to make you Hamatsa, but it was to me he turned. That's what was happening the night you walked through the doorway. I could feel all his love for David flowing over me, like the river when Duxdzas melts into it in the spring, a flood of love, and it scared me."

"Was Uncle about to put his hands on you that night?"

"I don't know, Nathan. I don't think he had ever abused anyone before then, though from what he just told us, he sure took a lot of abuse in residential school. But that night? Maybe and maybe not. Anyway, we'll never know, for sure, because you opened the door and then Mom let him have it, after you left."

"Mom let him have it?"

"Like Grizzly and Wolverine and Sisiutl, all rolled into one. You're not going to make Frank into another David! That was the gist of it."

"And how have you gotten on with Uncle since?"

"Good. Once the ground rules were clear." Frank leans back in his chair, mug in his hand and weighs up his next words. "In fact, when Uncle went ahead with his potlatch that fall, I became Hamatsa."

I let his words go inside and find me.

"That's good, Frank. I'm glad Uncle did that."

"You look wiped, Nathan," he says.

Yes, I'm wiped, but there's so much I want to tell Frank—about Erin, our sister, and Caitlin, her twin, and how she died, and Wesley and Sarah, and Sean, Margaret and Cameron . . .

You'll tell me, Nathan. In time, you'll tell me, his eyes reply.

The bedroom door opens, and a woman appears in the kitchen, rubbing the sleep from her eyes.

"This is Gina. We've been together for awhile," Frank says.

Her smile, like the coffee, warms something within me. "And you're Nathan, I'll bet."

"Yes. But how did you get there so soon?"

"Frank has talked so much about you, I feel I know you already. Besides, Adha told us before she died that you'd be home soon. You look hungry."

"Me, too," says Frank.

"God, you're always hungry! I'll cook up some hotcakes for your wandering brother and give you what's left."

Another door opens, and then a boy of eight or so stands beside his mother, staring at me. Dark face, dark eyes, but his hair is shock blond and sticks out from his head like the sun gone wild.

"This is our son. Sunny, we call him. And this is your Uncle Nathan," Frank says.

Sunny's eyes grow big as he tries to fathom the uncle who has just walked into his life. Gina smiles at him. "You want a hotcake, too?"

"Yes. That's why I got up," he says, shyly.

The hand holding my fork has become heavy by the time I've downed the last hotcake. Sleep would be good now, but I can't sleep yet.

"Yo, Sunny."

"Yes," Sunny says, not sure of me yet.

"So, you're my nephew?"

"Yes . . ."

"Has your Dad told you about what nephews do for their uncles, among the Wanookqway?"

He looks at Frank, then back at me. "No . . ."

"In the old days, nephews used to carry important messages for their uncles. Right, Frank?"

Frank's eyes search me out as he nods. "That's right. It was a great honour among the Wanookqway for a nephew to be chosen to carry an uncle's message. In fact, a nephew had to go through a long ceremony to make ready for that. Though I kind of forget what that ceremony was."

"But today I'll give you the honour without the ceremony," I say. "Would you please run down to Hazel's and tell . . . tell Makwalaga I'm home and that I'll be down to see her, soon. Very soon."

His eyes filled with questions, Sunny turns to Frank.

"Naomi," Frank says. "But we'll save Sunny that run, Nathan. Naomi isn't here. She went to Vancouver when Adha went, and then stayed."

"Maybe I could run to Vancouver, Uncle," Sunny says.

"I don't think so, Weesa. It looks as if I'll have to deliver the message myself."

I try to lighten my voice, yet feel it betray me as my eyes fill with questions. I know my brother sees them though he doesn't answer me at once.

"She didn't say when or if she'd be back. But I think she wanted to look for you."

Which is all he can say, as he holds my eyes to his until he knows I understand.

There are those, Adha told me once, who can look the centre face of Sisiutl in the eye right from day one and not blink, as there are those who never leave home yet shine as they move, in whatever way they move. Such a one is my brother, Dzulhdzulas: Where you go for feathers.

Frank stretches and yawns. "I should go to bed for the rest of the day, now that you're finally back. But it's Halloween tonight, and I've got to help decorate the school for the party."

"Halloween tonight and Samhain tomorrow," I say, thinking now of a tiny well thousands of miles from where we sit.

"What's that?"

"An old Celtic feast, when the lakes of Ireland turn to glass."

Frank laughs. "That sure would shock the hell out of a duck coming in for a landing."

We step outside together as the sun rises far up the valley of the river, while the river itself murmurs close to its bed and waits for the first rains of winter.

Auxw!

I follow my old friend's call right over to Log Island. Raven perches atop the green thrust of cedar growing up from the burnt-out crown of the Giant.

Frank smiles. "It'll grow right down the trunk and become the Giant, one day. I hope you're here to see that, Nathan, because you've been gone long enough."

"Maybe too long, Frank."

"Long enough, I think." Then he heads off across the soccer field.

Gwaau . . .?

And what do you want from me, now? Then I realize I am looking right at the carving shed and at the pole covered over with a tarp. Sunny appears at my side, hands in his pockets, and waits for me to do something.

"Help me take this tarp off, Weesa."

The pole has gone grey from neglect, but its surfaces are as Dad and I had left them. Dad's box of tools is at the back of the shed where I find the Raven-shaped D-adze. Taking it in hand, I go straight to the figure of Raven that anchors the pole.

Maybe I should warm up on something else, my mind suggests, but my hands intend otherwise. The sun splashes down upon the pole, down upon the eyes of Raven, the one clearly formed and the other as yet a hint of what it will be.

Sunny climbs up onto the pole and sits astride the Sisiutl face.

"Uncle Nathan?"

"Yes?"

"Are you going to stay here with us? Forever?"

I look into the eyes of my nephew and know how important it is that my words be true words.

"Forever is a long time, Sunny."

"For a long time, then?"

"Yes, a long time sounds more like it. Now, shift yourself one way or another because you're blocking the light."

My hand closes about Raven's body and I lift his beak for that first bite into the eye that will be. My hand starts to fall, and I feel her presence at my back, strong and straight, as Raven cleaves his eye open, going for the sun inside.

GLOSSARY

of Haida, Irish, Kwakwala, Lakota, and Welsh words in alphabetical order

Adha (Kwakwala) a revered grandmother

Axilaogua (Kwakwala) Woman who holds; used as woman who holds names

Bakbakwalanooksiwae (Kwakwala) often interpreted as Cannibal at the North End of the World; called the Spirit of Being by Ernie Willie

Braich y Pwll (Welsh) Arm of the Pool

Brugh na Bóinne (Irish) Valley of the Boyne River

Buiochas (Irish) Thank you

Céad míle fáilte (Irish) A hundred thousand welcomes

Cigfran (Welsh) Raven

Dia dhuit (Irish) God be with you

Dias Muire dhuit (Irish) God and Mary be with you

Duxdzas (Kwakwala) Sees all things; clairvoyant

Duxsowlas (Kwakwala) See through

Dzulhdzulas (Kwakwala) Where you go for feathers

Eglwys Lleu (Welsh) Church of Lleu (cognate of the Irish "Lugh")

Fiach (Irish) Raven

Ghe-la-kasla (Kwakwala) A greeting, "from the heart"

Glawemth (Kwakwala) Those who attend, guard Hamatsa during his dance about the big house

Glugwala (Kwakwala) A gesture with both hands enacted, standing, by the women in the big house at the culmination of the Hamatsa dance: a gesture of treasuring Hamatsa

Glugwe (Kwakwala) Treasure, referring to the dances an individual or family can show during a potlatch

Gwawinastoo (Kwakwala) Raven's Eye

Haida Gwaii (Haida) Islands of the People, the Haida name for the Queen Charlotte Islands

Ha-la-kasla (Kwakwala) A goodbye, "from the heart"

Hamatsa (Kwakwala) The pivotal dance of the Kwakwaka'wakw (Kwakiutl) Red Cedar Bark Ceremony (T'seka); the focal figure in the dance

Hiligaxstay (Kwakwala) The "conscience" of Hamatsa; danced by a female relative

Humsumth (Kwakwala) The three mythical bird masks of the Hamatsa dance: Huxwhuxw, Crooked Beak, and Raven

Huxwhuxw (Kwakwala) One of the three mythical bird masks of the Hamatsa dance

Hwyl (Welsh) Cheers

Kisoowaci (Kwakwala) Treasure; Kisoowaci Xwagwana (Kwakwala) His Canoe Holds a Treasure

Llygad Cigfran (Welsh) Raven's Eye

Makwalaga (Kwakwala) Moon Woman

Mynydd y Gwyddel (Welsh) Mountain of the Irishman

Pluen Eryr (Welsh) Eagle Feather

Samhain (Irish) One of the four principal pagan Celtic feasts, observed on the first day of November and pronounced as "Sau-in"

Sisiutl (Kwakwala) Double-headed Sea Serpent

Siwayugila (Kwakwala) Paddle Maker

Slán agat (Irish) Goodbye, from the person leaving to the person staying

Slán leat (Irish) Goodbye, from the person staying to the person leaving

Súl an Fhiaich (Irish) Raven's Eye

Tatanka Yotanka (Lakota) Sitting Bull

Tlaamelas (Kwakwala) The screen in the big house that separates the world of the big house floor from the world out of which the dancers come

Tla'sala (Kwakwala) The dances of the "light side" of a potlatch

Trwyn y Gwyddel (Welsh) Nose of the Irishman

T'seka (Kwakwala) The Red Cedar Bark Ceremony; the "dark side" of a potlatch

Tuatha de Danaan (Irish) People of the goddess Danaan; People of the gods of Dana; the Men of Dea: The people who came "from the north" or "through the air and the high air," and who dominated Ireland before the coming of the Celts

Wakan Tanka (Lakota) The all-encompassing or "great" spirit

Wanbli Galeshka (Lakota) Spotted Eagle

Wanookqway (Kwakwala) People of the River

Weesa (Kwakwala) Used as a name of endearment for any young boy

Xhaaidla (Haida) Skin, membrane, boundary, separating the visible, surface world from another world beyond the boundary

Xuuyaa (Haida) Raven

Xuuyaa Gut-ga-at-gaa (Haida) Raven Splitting-in-Two

Xwagwana (Kwakwala) Canoe

A colloquial rendering of the dialogue in German from page 325:

"What do you see?"
"Nothing. And you?"
"Nothing at all. It's much too dark in there."
"For sure! Blacker than the night itself."
"So, what do we do now?"
"Let's go and let the dark be dark."

ACKNOWLEDGEMENTS

Where to begin?

The Musqamagw Tsawataineux of Gwa Yee (Kingcome Village) took me into their community on many occasions from 1974 to 1977, and again for their Heritage Week in the summer of 1992. My thanks to them for all they have given me from their stories, dances, traditions, and struggles. Duxsowlas is not Gwa Yee, yet without Gwa Yee, Duxsowlas could not have been. A special thank you to Beverly Lagis, Thompson, her husband, now deceased, and their family for the times they opened their home to me.

My debt to Ernie Willie (Yah-Xath-anees), a friend, colleague, and fellow traveller within the human journey for many years, is incalulable. As one who delved into the culture and spirituality of his people, the Kwakwaka'wakw Nation, he shared with me many of the insights and meanings he had discovered. He read the manuscript of *Raven's Eye* in its early stages, and his critique of Part I prevented some wrong turns that could have taken the story off its true course. In the end, it's your story, he said to me, yet without Ernie's generosity, the story could not have been truly born. Ernie, with his brother Frank, died in a boating accident on the Kingcome River in June of this year. I and many others shall miss his warmth and wisdom.

Ernie also made it possible for the class of 1988 of the Vancouver Waldorf High School, with Martin Driehuyzen and me in tow, to spend two weeks in Heiltsuk community of Waglisla (Bella Bella). Our experience of three potlatches, the last in the community of Klemtu, the death of David White, and the ceremonies surrounding that, as well as the many meetings with those who opened their homes and lives to us, has also leavened the writing of this book. My special thanks to the Newman,

Windsor, and White families, and to David Gladstone for the welcome they extended.

Others among the Kwakwaka'wakw people who helped in forming this story are Bob and Donna Joseph, Ralph and Katie Adams, Louena Walkus, and Daisy Sewid-Smith, who gave me many of the Kwakwala words I needed. Thanks also to Jill and Dave Pearce for hospitality during the days I spent in Port Hardy early in 1993.

In Haida Gwaii, Eleanor Russ of Skidegate gave me the Haida words used here, and Clifford and Lloyd Moody shared their experiences as participants in the journey of the *Lootaas* and Bill Reid to France in the fall of 1989. Poul Lutzen took me to Chaatl, and with his wife, Bonnie Wasyleski, extended hospitality to me on two occasions.

Farley Wuth, then archivist at the Nakoda Institute of the Wesley First Nations, Morely, Alberta, gave generously from the institute's resources during the fall of 1992 and of his own time, out of his genuine interest in my research. Ken and Marea Craig loaned me their camper van for those two weeks, which enabled me to stay on the grounds of the Institute. The staff of the Custer Battlefield National Monument in Montana contributed to my understanding of the events of June 25, 1876, during the day I spent at the battlefield site, and the conveniently placed information building at the Big Horn Dam site in Alberta provided some useful statistics for Act I of Part III.

In Ireland, Ray McGrath provided a first-hand experience of Ireland's west coast, introduced me to a number of the stories and Irish words I have used, and has maintained an interest in this story. In Wales, Charles Lawrie, Dafydd Hughes, and Jean Lynch gave generously of their time, insight, Welsh wording, and friendship, while Alison and Martin Duncan provided their trailer at Penrhyndeadraeth for my base of operations.

Closer to home, Bob Waite of North Vancouver provided a valuable point of reference for the story in Part IV of the Canadian expedition to Brittany in 1940. I also am indebted to my friend, Seis'lom (Glen Williams), for what he has given me out of his experience of the spirituality and struggles of Native peoples in this country and for extending his friendship in recent years to my colleagues and students.

Among the many tellings I have heard and read of Raven stealing the daylight, I am particularly indebted to *Raven* by Dale De Armond (Anchorage: Alaska Northwest Publishing Company, 1975), *Totem Poles: According to Crests and Topics* by Marius Barbeau (Canadian Museum of

Civilization, 1990), *The Raven Steals the Light* by Bill Reid and Robert Bringhurst (Vancouver/Toronto: Douglas & McIntyre, 1984), and *Who Shall Be the Sun?* by David Wagoner (Bloomington & London: Indiana University Press, 1978).

My mother-in-law, Mary Stronach, introduced me to Richard Wagner's opera, *Parsifal*, at her Waipatiki beach cottage in January 1976. Ron Jarman, Francis Edmunds, Norman Davidson, and Rene Querido have enriched my understanding of Wolfram Von Eschenbach's *Parzival*. I am also indebted to the adults and grade eleven students to whom I have taught the Parzival story for the past seventeen years for what they, in turn, have taught me. The translation of *Parzival* by Helen M. Mustard and Charles E. Passage (New York: Vintage Books, 1961) is the one that I have worked with most extensively.

I turned to Lady Gregory's *Gods and Fighting men* and *Cuchulain of Muirthemne* (Foreword copyright for both volumes, Colin Smyth Ltd., 1970) to aid me in telling the Celtic stories and am directly indebted to Thomas Kinsella's translation of the *Táin Bó Cuailnge* (Oxford University Press, 1970) for its influence on some of Caitlin's lines in Part III (Used by permission of Thomas Kinsella).

Among the many books I have read on the way to and during the writing of *Raven's Eye*, the following were significant for the development of the story: Daisy Sewid-Smith, *Prosecution or Persecution* (Nu-Yum-Baleess Society, 1979); Douglas Cole and Ira Chaikin, *An Iron Hand Upon the People* (Vancouver/Toronto: Douglas & McIntyre, 1990); Franz Boas, *Kwakiutl Ethnography* (University of Chicago Press, 1966); Aldona Jonaitis, ed., *Chiefly Feasts: The Enduring Kwakiutl Potlatch* (Vancouver/Toronto: Douglas & McIntyre, 1991); Harry Assu with Joy Inglis, *Assu of Cape Mudge* (Vancouver: University of British Columbia Press, 1989); David Neel, *Our Chiefs and Elders* (Vancouver: UBC Press, 1992); Ulli Steltzer and Robert Bringhurst, *The Black Canoe: Bill Reid and the Spirit of Haida Gwaii* (Vancouver/Toronto: Douglas & McIntyre, 1991); Doris Shadbolt, *Bill Reid* (Seattle/London: University of Washington Press, 1986); George F. MacDonald, *Chiefs of the Sea and Sky* (University of British Columbia Press, 1989); Edward Malin, *Totem Poles of the Pacific Northwest* (Portland, Oregon: Timber Press, 1986); Vickie Jensen, *Where the People Gather* (Vancouver/Toronto: Douglas & McIntyre, 1992); Dee Brown, *Bury My Heart at Wounded Knee* (London, Book Club Associates, 1970); Joseph Epes Brown, ed., *The Sacred Pipe* (University of Oklahoma Press, 1953); William K. Powers, *Oglala Religion* (University of Nebraska Press, 1975, 1977); Rex Alan Smith, *Moon of Popping Trees* (University of

Nebraska Press, 1975); Mari Sandoz, *Crazy Horse: The Strange Man of the Ogala* (University of Nebraska Press, 1992); John G. Neihardt, *Black Elk Speaks* (Washington Square Press, 1972) and *The Twilight of the Sioux* (University of Nebraska, Bison Books, 1971); Geoffrey York and Loreen Pindera, *People of the Pines: The Warriors and the Legacy of Oka* (Little, Brown & Company, Canada, 1991); Ella Elizabeth Clark, *Indian Legends of Canada* (Toronto: McClelland & Stewart, 1960); Tony Angel, *Ravens, Crows, Magpies, and Jays* (Vancouver: Douglas & McIntyre, 1978); Frank Delaney, *The Celts* (London: Grafton, 1989); Proinsias MacCana, *Celtic Mythology* (Newnes Books, 1983); Alwyn Rees and Brinley Rees, *Celtic Heritage: Ancient Tradition in Ireland and Wales* (London: Thames and Hudson, 1961); Tim O'Brien, *Light Years Ago* (Dublin: The Black Cat Press, 1992); Eleanor C. Merry, *The Flaming Door* (East Grinstead: New Knowledge Books, 1962); Franz E. Winkler, *For Freedom Destined* (Garden City, N.Y.: Waldorf Press, 1974); Jakob Streit, *Sun and Cross* (Edinburgh: Floris Books, 1977); Georg Blattmann, *The Sun: The Ancient Mysteries and a New Physics* (Edinburgh: Floris Books, 1985); Arthur Zajonc, *Catching the Light* (New York: Bantam Books, 1993); *The Canadians at War 1939/1945* (Montreal: The Reader's Digest Association, Canada, Ltd., 1969, Vol. 1).

"The Two Trees," by W.B. Yeats, is published in *Collected Poems*, edited by Augustine Martin (London: Arena, 1990).

The lines from "Do not go gentle into that good night," by Dylan Thomas, are from *The Collected Poems of Dylan Thomas* (J.M. Dent & Sons, Ltd.). Used by permission of David Higham Associates. *In the U.S.A.:* from *The Poems of Dylan Thomas*, copyright © 1952 by Dylan Thomas. Reprinted by permission of New Directions Publishing Corp.

The lyrics sung by Roberta Flack in Part I, Chapter Ten, are from THE FIRST TIME EVER I SAW YOUR FACE by Ewan MacColl, © 1962 (renewed) by STORMKING MUSIC INC. All Rights Reserved. Used by Permission.

Caitlin's "sad song" in Part III, Act I, is her variant of SONNY'S DREAM. Composed by: Ron Hynes. Courtesy of TMP: The Music Publisher. © 1977 Wonderful Grand Music/ Sold for a Song/Universal Music Publishing Canada. Used by Permission.

I am especially indebted to the life and work of Rudolf Steiner, for bringing Waldorf education into the world and for enabling me to see more deeply into the human journey upon this earth. My wife, Marjorie, introduced me to Steiner's work and I thank her for that gift.

A number of people came to my aid during the evolution of *Raven's Eye*. Siegrun Price and Traudi Schneider gave me the lines in German for Part IV, 3. Robert Adams and David Zieroth did a thorough critique of the first full draft and made me aware of areas of the story I needed to strengthen, characters I needed to eliminate, and pitfalls I needed to avoid. My thanks to both of them. Readers who took on all or parts of the manuscript during my writing and rewriting of it were Lorna Williams, Steven Roboz, Monica Boyd, Dave and Jill Pearce, Renate Lundberg, Barry Scow, Gary Ward, Rita Costanzi, Jessica Huston, Les Tulloch, Bert Chase, Olaf Lampson, Ray McGrath, Charles Lawrie, Farley Wuth, Crystal Phillips, Cheryl Higgs, and Treasa O'Driscoll, who also refined some of the Irish words and nuances in Part IV. Members of the "Waldorf Poetry Group"—Linda and Michael Frosch, Monique and Herb Walsh, Josie and Randall Scott, Robert Adams, David Zieroth, Wendy and Steve Wilkins, and Reg Down—joined with me for a first reading of Part III. The members of the classes of 1996 and 1997 at the Vancouver Waldorf High School, along with my colleague, Eitel Timm, listened to my reading of Parts I, II, IV and V during the winter and spring terms of 1996, and did a second reading of Part III. Members of the class of 1999 listened to a reading of the story during their grade eleven year. I am grateful to all of the above for their comments and their support.

My thanks to Maureen Nicholson who worked as copy editor in preparing the manuscript for publication and whose suggestions helped shape the final form of the story.

Finally, I acknowledge my debt to Yataltanault (Carole Anne Newman), to whom, with Yah-Xath-anees (Ernie Willie), this book is dedicated. When she placed the copper engraved with Raven into the palm of my hand twenty-three years ago, *Raven's Eye* became a possibility. Though she will not read the story in this life, I can only hope Yataltanault would have approved of what I have done with her gift to me.

Philip Thatcher
North Vancouver, British Columbia
November 1999